From Ur to Us

Everything you need to know about
History

The Story So Far • History Notes • Country by Country • Appendices

Hugh Williams

St Edward's Press Ltd

Readers' Comments

Olly Figg - Author

From Ur to Us is stunning. It has the same effect on me that the Guinness Book of records did when I was a nipper; although a reference book, it's compulsively readable. One looks up one thing and then finds that an hour has somehow passed. Riveting stuff.

Michael Morley – History teacher

It is such an awesome production – far better than I had imagined because it is so compact. Its informative nature must have taken many years to collect. It is a marvellous and wonderful production.

Tim Rose Price - Scriptwriter

I am bowled over by the colossal achievement of this book. It is so much more than a collection of facts. Hugh is a natural educator and every page shines with his unique contagious enthusiasm for life

James Tuckett – Company Director

I think this is the perfect book for me to climb a few rungs on the history ladder.

Peter Deacon – Retired

A first rate book which every family with children should have. It would be a big help not only to the children but the whole family 11/10.

Lee-Ann Deacon – Administrator

I do now wish it had been completed when I was doing my GCSE in History as it would have come in very handy.

Harry Mount – Author and Journalist

I think the book is tremendously impressive - if only a tenth of all children knew a hundredth of it.

Jonathan Ruffer – Philanthropist and Chairman of Ruffer LLP

Utterly Brilliant!

Jacky Davies – Deputy Lieutenant

What a terrific book!!! The layout of the book is quite brilliant too.

Brian King – Inheritance Tax Consultant

This is the most user-friendly history book I have ever come across. Was there ever a history book so difficult to put down? Every school child ought to own a copy of this book: it should be mandatory.

From Ur to Us

Formal notes

From Ur to Us

First published in 2013 by
St Edward's Press Ltd
Court House
The Crescent
Crapstone
Yelverton
Devon
PL20 7PS

ISBN 978-0-95541-8853

Further copies of this book may be ordered using the order form at the back.

Designed and printed by Printbridge, Bodmin PL31 2DU

From Ur to Us

Contents

Dedication

From Ur to Us is dedicated to the memory of the late, and much missed, Geoff Stevens.

He died as long ago as 1984 but his friends still talk of him often, with both enormous gratitude for having known him and, at the same time, a persistent lump in their throats.

He was a wonderful man with a brilliant brain, the very best of friends and the one whose guidance and inspiration started the author on the long, but fascinating, road of discovery that has led, amongst other things, to the preparation of this book.

Why "From Ur to Us"?

"Ur" was where Abraham lived, and, from his time, we start to have reliable historical records, and "Us" is you and me.

About the author

Hugh Williams is 66 and has had an eventful life, enjoying a wide range of experiences. Educated at Eton he qualified as a chartered accountant in London but decided to set up his own practice in the unusual setting of a small farm on Dartmoor, where he also kept a small herd of Red Devon cattle and some Arab cross ponies.

He lived and worked there for nearly thirty years before moving the practice to Plympton where it has since won three national awards, principally for customer service.

His writing career began with a book on Company Law, which was published by the Institute of Chartered Accountants in England and Wales and was in print for nearly twenty years. There have since been many other publications to his name, all of which try to simplify the worlds of taxation, business administration and management.

In addition to running a business from this remote setting he and his wife, Alice, decided to teach their eldest children at home, which they did to GCSE level – Hugh even sitting a paper himself, the better to understand what his children would be facing; they also taught their other children to secondary school level. His job in the home school was to teach his children history, the notes of which now form the backbone of this book.

While Hugh Williams is the main author of this work he is indebted to Daniel Joyce, MA, Cantab., for his invaluable help in both correcting the original script and presenting the text in a more readable way.

Preface

Hugh Williams has invited me to write a few words about why I have been pleased to be associated with this book, as its main editor, and why I believe that its publication should make an important contribution towards filling the somewhat alarming gap that many people seem to have in their knowledge of history. Needless to say I am delighted to do so, for I cannot emphasise enough the timeliness of a work of this kind.

It is a well-known and quite accurate maxim that one must learn from the mistakes of the past in order not to repeat them in the future. It may equally be said that a profound knowledge of what is good and has worked in the past will equip one to ensure success in the future. This works as much at the level of the individual as it does at the highest tiers of government (where the consequences are far graver for a greater number).

Indeed, it is to an increasing ignorance of and refusal to engage with history that one may quite justly attribute many of the serious mistakes of recent times. Had Tony Blair a real knowledge of the several failed attempts to occupy Afghanistan, would he have sent so many troops to their deaths there? Did Margaret Thatcher know of the Peasants' Revolt in 1381, which was largely the consequence of the introduction of a poll tax, would she have introduced the Community Charge which resulted in similar riots? Or would an unprejudiced knowledge of the history and make-up of Palestine have seen so many Western leaders support the state of Israel, with the resulting terrorism (spawned by the displacement of Palestinians) and permanent turbulence in the Middle East?

At any level: the political, economic, military, cultural, social, personal; knowledge of history is vital, informs one's identity, gels society together, and enables greater subtlety in decision-making for the future. And when should this essential process of learning about the past take place? I would answer, "As early possible!" Imparting a sound knowledge of history belongs in the schoolroom and also the family home.

Today, the study of history may be fairly described as being in crisis. In 2002, HRH the Prince of Wales convened a conference on the state of history and literature in modern education at Dartington Hall, Devon, following which he concluded that, "education has become so shallow rooted that we now lack an understanding of our national heritage." This notion has been consistently shared by historians and academics in recent years, leading Dr David Starkey to denounce the "catastrophic" state of modern history teaching, opining that, "whole generations are emerging with no notion of the history of their own country" (*Daily Telegraph*, 2001). And this situation seems only to be getting worse. In 2010, UK schools minister, Nick Gibb, quoted a study of schoolchildren which showed that, "almost twice as many students thought Nelson rather than Wellington was in charge at the Battle of Waterloo and nearly 90 per cent couldn't name a single British prime minister of the 19th century." He added that these results showed "depressing evidence of the state of teaching knowledge in history."

In short, the teaching and knowledge of history appear to be at all-time lows. It really may be said that modern man seems to be interested only in the distractions of the present, with a naïve and ill-informed notion of the future, and cares not about the past, over which he draws a veil, choosing instead a vague notion of "human progress" (and thus deeming the past an irrelevance), or a merely sensual notion of "living for the moment." This book seeks to make a contribution to rectifying this dire situation. It also seeks to free the study of history from the shackles of political correctness and the undisguised bias of so much that has passed for history, especially in recent years, providing instead a straightforward and accurate presentation of history as it really happened. However, do not think this a heavy or turgid tome: its greatest asset is that it is light, succinctly written and easily digestible, with the extensive index making the fact for which you are looking readily accessible.

Whether you are a child at school, a student at university, a parent home-schooling or filling in the serious gaps in the schooling of your children, or whether you simply wish to rectify the holes in your own knowledge of history and have a handy reference book into which you may delve to swiftly reach the historical information you need, *From Ur to Us* is the book for you, and will soon cause you to wonder how you ever managed to live without it. Oh, and you will thoroughly enjoy reading it too!

Daniel Joyce, MA, *Cantab*.

How to use this book

This book has been designed for its ease of use:

- The first unique feature of this book is that the (very extensive) <u>Index</u> is at the front. This is so that, as you cross the threshold of this work, looking for a historical fact, you will find help at the gateway to the information herein, rather than at the back. It is far better to know where to find what you want as you arrive.

- The section entitled <u>World History: The Story So Far</u> is written in refero-descriptive format. This means it may be used primarily as a source of quick reference, but may also be read from start to finish – it wouldn't take long to do so.

- The <u>History Notes</u> section on British history (or topics pertaining to it) is arranged chronologically using bullet points, and will be of particular use to the student, providing greater detail of British history than in <u>World History: The Story So Far</u>, but still designed for quick reference and useful for revision.

- The <u>Country by Country</u> section provides a brief history of over one hundred countries, laid out for quick reference. This section would be ideal for the traveller, as well as for anyone seeking an introductory overview of the main points of a country's history. For instance, if you are heading off to (say) Austria and want a very quick introduction to Austrian history (so you can understand what the museum guide means when she refers to Rudolph of Habsburg) this section will be for you.

- The <u>Appendices</u>, containing much useful information (such as lists of Kings and Queens of England, Popes, US Presidents, etc.), speak for themselves.

Guarantee
Should this book not meet your estimation, simply send it back with proof of purchase, and you'll be sent a full, non-quibble refund.

Comments welcome and indeed rewarded on this book
It is inevitable that a book of this kind can never be complete. Indeed, history books, by their very nature, become dated as soon as they are published. In spite of every effort, there are bound to be omissions. So, if you think you have found an error or omission, please write to the publishers, informing them of what it is, and if you are first person to point out this particular error, they will:

- if the author agrees with you, make the necessary correction
- send you a free copy of the following edition of the work, if the correction has been incorporated.

It is hoped that this book will go a long way to increase your knowledge and awareness of history, as well as inspire you to look at events, often misunderstood or misrepresented, with an objective and more discerning eye.

St Edward's Press
2013

Further copies of this book can be ordered by using the order form at the back from:
St Edward's Press Ltd, Court House, The Crescent, Crapstone, Yelverton, Devon, PL20 7PS
Email Enquiries@stedwardspress.co.uk   www.stedwardspress.co.uk

Index

PLEASE NOTE that, where a date is given in this index it is often simply a means of reference to help you find what you are looking for. The actual date will be in the text.

Index

Index

Index

Index

Index

Index

Index

Index

Index

Index

Index

Index

Index

Index

Index

Index

Index

Index

Index

Index

Index

Index

Index

Index

Index

Index

Index

Index

Index

Index

Index

Index

Index

Index

Index

Index

Index

Index

Index

Index

Index

Index

Index

Index

Index

Index

Index

Index

Index

Index

Index

Index

Index

Index

Index

Index

Index

Index

Index

Index

Index

Index

Index

Index

Index

Index

Index

Index

Index

Index

Index

Index

Index

Index

Index

Part One

World History - The Story so Far

Contents

Part One
World History: The Story So Far

"Religion is the true key to history." The Most Reverend Alban Goodier, SJ.

Introduction

Where do we start?
I doubt if there are two historians who will agree on which should be the starting date for a work of this kind. We have to start somewhere, though, and I have chosen the most traditional one of all, the date for the creation of the world which can be deduced from the Bible.

This choice is not to imply that the reader must accept that this *was* the date of the creation of the world – most scientists claim that it was many millions, even billions, of years earlier, of course, though this is by no means proven, and is not presumed in, or in fact relevant to, the writing of this book. Rather, the reason for starting with 4000BC is that, from about this time, there begin to be written records, and thus it is from this time that we have an indication (not always reliable by any means) of what man has been doing, upon which the historian may draw. This written record supplements what has been deduced from fossil and other indirect evidence.

Before we get to the time of what, as the world now generally regards them, reliable records tell us, namely the time of Abraham, we need to give some background explanation about what happened before he appeared on the scene.

To do this we will start with a short preamble. This preamble may raise some eyebrows, because it draws from a source of historical record that is scarcely treated seriously today, namely the Bible. However, many peoples on earth do still use the Bible, and, in particular the Old Testament, because it contains a great deal of historical information. It seems to me therefore that, unless biblical information is replaced by something else, it remains an essential record from which to draw important details of the history of mankind, and no serious scholar may dismiss it outright. It is therefore appropriate and important to make use of it, at any rate to provide some background notes.

Preamble

4000BC The Biblical Date for the Creation of the World
As already mentioned, this is the approximate date for the creation of the world which has been calculated (by Professor Edward Hull, Archbishop Ussher and others) from what is said in the Bible. It also conveniently marks the date from which it is generally agreed that we can begin to rely on the records that we have, or the surmises we can make. For example, 4000BC marks the beginning of what archaeologists call the Stone Age, (from 4000BC to 2500BC). The names that are used to describe this age are Palaeolithic (the earliest), Mesolithic (the middle Stone Age) and Neolithic (the New Stone Age). Whilst these are archaeological and not accurate historical terms, we shall employ them as a useful means of navigation.

2500 BC The First Known Civilisations
The evidence for the first civilisations can be found at the end of, to use archaeological terms again, the Stone Age and the start of the Bronze Age (2500BC to 1500BC). From this point in time onwards, we discover the first two civilisations in the Middle East: the Sumerians and the Egyptians.

Noah's Flood

It is also worth noting that the biblical Noah's Ark and the Flood are traditionally dated at around 2500BC. For those who are surprised at the mention of Noah's Flood it is important to realise that there is a tradition held by <u>every</u> civilisation on Earth of there having been a huge world-wide flood at about this time (see Appendix 16). So far as this work is concerned, Arabs, Christians and Jews have traditionally believed that it happened and hold that only one family survived this cataclysm, that of Noah.

Apart from this widespread tradition, what more concrete evidence is there in support of a belief in Noah's Flood?

1. You may not believe it, but there are reports of the remains of a boat-like structure that is buried in a glacier high on Mount Ararat in Turkey (in the Bible it is stated that Noah's Ark came to rest on Mount Ararat). There are no photographs of this structure, but there are some sketches drawn by a number of different people who, on different occasions, claim to have seen it, and the sketches do all seem to be depicting the same thing.

2. Following a sighting by two Russian air force pilots, Tsar Nicholas II commissioned an expedition to Mount Ararat in 1916. This turned out to be fruitful, but the evidence (including photographs and detailed measurements) collected from it was suppressed as a result of the Bolshevik revolution. However, articles from Russian scientific journals and newspapers, reporting their findings, still exist, and confirm other sightings and sketches of explorers who claim to have seen the Ark there.

3. Researchers, John Whitcombe and Henry Morris, have written a detailed analysis of the geological and other evidence in support of a world-wide flood about 4,500 years ago.

4. In addition, tree-ring dating experts (dendrochronologists) and other scientists working quite independently in Egypt, Israel, Iceland, America and Indonesia, have found all the evidence in tree rings of a world-wide and significant climate change that took place at this time.

5. In an article in *New Scientist* in November 2005, it was reported that ice cores also show widespread and dramatic climate change in South America about this time. Indeed, in that same article, it was asserted that only very recently (a few thousand years ago) the Sahara Desert dried out very suddenly from a land of lakes to desert. Furthermore it maintained that plant life found in ice cores at about this date had been frozen suddenly.

6. Ötzi, the name given to the man whose body was found frozen in a European glacier in 1991, met his sudden end a few thousand years ago.

In addition, the discovery, in 2013, of the body of a perfectly preserved woolly mammoth (including liquid blood) on a Siberian island also indicates that it was frozen very suddenly and only a few thousand years ago.

7. In 2000AD, the discovery and dating of a submerged village in the Black Sea by Robert Ballard is said, both by him and by many others, to give further proof of there having been a massive flood at about 2500BC.

We can therefore be sure that sudden and extraordinary climate change took place a few thousand years ago, but whether it can be associated with Noah's Flood is the subject of much controversy.

What caused this change is anyone's guess, but some suspect that a comet either hitting Earth or passing by extremely closely may have been the trigger for this event.

The earliest evidence we have of people living in Britain at about this time (early Bronze Age) is the signs of occupation that have been discovered at Kent's Cavern in Torquay (which is not to say that the first human inhabitants of Britain were only to be found in the South West).

Stonehenge, the Pyramids and Egypt
It is generally recognised that Stonehenge was erected around 2,500 BC, by the Bronze Age inhabitants of Europe, who tend nowadays to be referred to as Beaker Folk. There were many other stone circles and similar structures erected at this time, and of particular note are:

- The great circle at Avebury in Wiltshire
- The ancient monuments at Land's End
- The stone circle at Callanish in the Hebrides
- The huge alignments in Brittany, particularly at Karnak
- The complexes at Kilmartin in Argyllshire in Scotland.

Many of the Pyramids were also built in the Bronze Age, near the then capital of Egypt, which was ruled by a dynasty of Pharaohs from their capital Memphis, a few miles South of Cairo.

The modern view, held by Gerald S. Hawkins, and many others, is that, with so many of these structures built on a celestial alignment, their purpose may have been for observing the heavens, but how they served this purpose has yet to be demonstrated.

(Curiously, having mentioned these monuments, at the same time that an earlier draft of this work was nearing completion in 2000, yet another Stonehenge-type structure was discovered, in the USA.)

The ancient Egyptians were one of the earliest civilisations we know that made glass (by heating sand) and cement (by heating limestone and seashells). They also used the 365 day and 12 month calendars, as well as a system of measurement and writing on papyrus, the forerunner of modern paper.

Seven Wonders of the World
We have already mentioned the Pyramids, but the Great Pyramid of Giza deserves special mention because it is the only one of the seven wonders of the ancient world to survive.
The Seven Wonders were:
- The Great Pyramid of Giza
- The Hanging Gardens of Babylon
- The Temple of Artemis at Ephesus
- The Statue of Zeus at Olympia
- The Mausoleum at Halicarnassus
- The Colossus of Rhodes
- The Pharos (Lighthouse at Alexandria).

Semitic Peoples
When reviewing Biblical tradition and the story of Noah's sons, there springs an apparent solution to why there are the three main types of humans.
- Sem, (or Shem) the eldest, was the father of the Semitic peoples – Jews and Arabs.
- Cham (or Ham) is the father of the Africans and Aborigines, including North American Indians. These Indians are called Red Indians because they wore red ochre, as a protection against evil. In fact Cham's fourth son, Canaan, is reckoned to be the real father of these people. He founded the Canaanites who lived in Canaan, a land flowing

with milk and honey, which, after the Exodus from Egypt, would be populated by the Twelve Tribes of Israel (See also Canaan, 1235BC and 1230BC). In due course this land was to become Palestine and now Israel. The word for "black" in Hebrew is Cham.

And

- Japheth is reckoned to be the father of the Europeans, Indians and Asians.

Was Noah our ancestor?

While this notion that we can all be traced back to Noah may seem fanciful and not in line with what one might read in textbooks today, it should be noted that, according to a BBC report in May 2000, the discovery of a gene common only to Jews and Arabs gives scientific support to the belief that both Jews and Arabs (the people we call "Semitic") are descended from just one man, namely Noah's eldest son, Sem; and in 2004 the BBC reported that a group of scientists had suggested that *all* humankind had sprung from one man a few thousand years ago (of course, Adam is believed to be the first man, but because it is also believed that Noah's family alone survived the flood, this would make them the new starting point of common origin). Indeed, in 2007, scientists at the Cambridge University Department of Biological Anthropology concluded that all modern humans are descended from a small group of humans within the last few thousand years. Thinking these claims to be worth some elementary mathematical analysis, you may care to look at Appendix 15, where you will see how it is possible to explain how the size of the present population of the world, if you start from scratch, might have been achieved within just under 1,700 years. So, may be looking back to Noah is not such an inconceivable explanation, after all, of where we all came from.

Languages and Continental Drift

In the Bible (Genesis, chapter 11) there is an explanation of how the world's different languages began, after the Tower of Babel collapsed; and there is even apparent reference, in the genealogy in chapter 10 of Genesis, to "continental drift" happening after the collapse of the tower. This may explain how the different strands of humanity began to drift apart on their continental rafts.

These two points (continental drift and Noah's sons with their descendants) taken together *could* be an explanation of why the Earth is populated by such different peoples speaking such widely different languages. But, for the present, we will concentrate on...

Semites and Hebrews

The Semitic peoples, the descendants of Sem (or Shem), are those we can follow by tracing the Biblical record until we reach the death of Jesus Christ.

One of Sem's descendants was Heber, from whom we get the name "Hebrews", and one of Heber's descendants was Abraham who was an inhabitant of the city of Ur.

(At this stage we find that the secular and other accepted records of human events begin to coincide with the Biblical story, and what most people now regard as reliable dates start to appear. Now is the time to end this preamble and for us to get going properly. You will see that, while the Bible remains the main source of information for the next few pages, it is not long before other known, but non-biblical, events begin to appear in these annals.)

From Ur to us

Chapter 1   From Ur (Abraham) to Jesus Christ

1996BC The Birth of Abraham

Two peoples lived in Mesopotamia; the Sumerians, north of the Euphrates, and the Chaldeans, south of that river. The Sumerian capital was Ur and a resident of that city, Abraham, was born in 1996 BC. The Bible teaches that Abraham was appointed by God (as is believed by Jews, Christians and Muslims) to be the father of the race that was to produce the Redeemer who would undo the effects of Original Sin. The strange, and often overlooked, fact is that Abraham himself was not a Jew. As we say below the name "Jew" is derived partly from Judah, the fourth son of Jacob (Abraham's grandson), partly from the Kingdom of Judah which consisted of the tribes of Judah, Benjamin and Levi.

Why does the Bible say that a Redeemer was needed?

Biblical teaching says that, as a result of the first sin being committed by Adam and Eve (Original Sin), not only did its effect weaken mankind and render all people susceptible to committing further sins, but, in addition, as a result of original sin, God closed the gates of Heaven to man. Indeed if man was thereafter ever going to be able to attain Heaven, it would only be after a Redeemer had been sent, to atone for man's sin. Christians believe this Redeemer to be Jesus Christ.

This explains why Abraham is regarded as the father of the Jews and his appointment (the fact that he was chosen or appointed to this post) explains why the Jews are known as "the chosen race."

1900BC Isaac, Jacob, the origin of Jews, Arabs and Islam

Abraham, by his wife Sarah, was the father of Isaac, who was the father of Jacob, who was also called Israel. Jacob had twelve sons, the fourth of whom was Judah.

Where the name "Jew" comes from

First of all, we get the name "Israelites" from Abraham's grandson, Jacob, who, as we have just seen, was also called Israel. After the time of Moses, the Israelites reverted to a name derived from the name Judah, namely, Jews, who, as you will see, fill a central role throughout the whole of history. Thus it is relevant that, during the second millennium BC, we spend some time following this family's history.

Where the term "Islam" comes from

Abraham had another son by his wife's maid Hagar. This son was called Ishmael and Ishmael's descendants would eventually become the Arabs embracing a faith called Islam, a name that some say is derived from Ishmael.

1500BC Joseph

In the Bible (Genesis 37) we learn that, in about 1725BC, Jacob's youngest son, Joseph, was sold by his brothers into Egypt. When his brethren followed him to Egypt they settled there and eventually their descendants became the slaves of the Egyptians in about 1500BC.

Iron Age

The Iron Age, following the Bronze Age, is estimated to have lasted from 1500BC to 300BC. However, please be aware that using this sort of modern dating convenience (using terms such as Iron Age) has no direct or identifiable link with lands described in the Old Testament.

Hindu Religion

There is no definite date when this (really a collection of different cults/philosophies, rather than a single, coherent religion) started, but the general view is that it is about this time. Its gods are Brahma, Vishnu and Siva. Hindus believe in reincarnation and in Karma, or fate. They also believe in cows being sacred. There are five main divisions or castes in the Hindu system of social stratification:

- Brahmins – priests
- Kshatriyas – warriors
- Vaishyas – merchants
- Shudras – serfs
- Untouchables or outcastes, who are considered apart from the other four and are usually barred from certain areas of life enjoyed by the rest of the Hindu community.

Mycenaean Civilisation

This was a powerful civilisation in Greece from about 1400 - 1100BC.

Minoan Civilisation

This was a powerful civilization in Crete during the Bronze Age (2500 - 1500BC.) However, following on from the remark just made, it is misleading to say that this civilisation flourished during the Bronze Age because the Minoans didn't only work in Bronze.

The Minoans built a Palace at Knossos on Crete, which was the only Minoan Palace to escape destruction in about 1500BC. The destruction was probably caused by a tsunami following the volcanic eruption on the Aegean island of Santorini (which is sometimes known by the name of its capital town, Thera) to the north (see below). The Minoan civilisation faded out as Greece and especially the Mycenae became more powerful.

Atlantis – did it exist?

Plato describes this island and utopian civilisation as being in the Aegean Sea. If it existed, it may have been on the island of Santorini (see also immediately above) which was destroyed by a volcanic eruption in about 1500BC. The island is a caldera - or remains of a violent volcanic eruption in the sea - and when this exploded the tidal wave it created may have been the one that devastated the Minoan civilisation on Crete to the south, and no doubt other areas. Tree rings laid down also give evidence of widespread climate change at this time.

While mentioning this explosion as being the potential cause of at least two natural disasters at this time, some historians even postulate that the tsunami may explain why the waters in the Red Sea suddenly withdrew and then rushed back together again, when Moses led the Israelites out of Egypt in 1275BC.

13th Century BC

Tutankhamen

He was King of Egypt from about 1352-1343BC. His fame comes not so much from the achievements of his short reign but from the discovery by Howard Carter and Lord Carnarvon of his mummified remains and fabulous treasure in Egypt in 1922AD.

The temples at Karnak and Abu Simbel were built around this time near the Egyptian capital, Thebes (not to be confused with Thebes which features in the Spartan Wars between Athens and Sparta). Luxor now occupies the southern part of ancient Thebes. (For information about the Egyptian dynasties see the page about Egypt in the Country by Country section.)

Trojan Wars

Although it is assumed by many to be Greek legend, there is evidence that these really happened in the Middle of the 13th Century BC, when there were indeed wars in this area.

The equivalent of the Christian Bible to the Greeks in pre-Christian times was Homer's two epics, the Iliad and the Odyssey. Their authenticity is denied by most "mainstream" scholars, but, even right up until recent times, it has been taken seriously enough for extensive archaeological research of the site of Troy near the Dardanelles to be made, most notably by German archaeologist Heinrich Schliemann in the 1870s.

As Homer tells the story in the Iliad, the Trojan Prince, Paris, abducted Helen (Helen of Troy), daughter of Zeus and wife of the Spartan King, Menelaus, and took her to Troy. Troy's King at the time was Priam, the father or Hector and Paris.

Menelaus sent an army under his brother Agamemnon to rescue Helen ("the face that launched a thousand ships," from Marlowe's Dr Faustus) and among his fighters was Achilles, the greatest warrior of the Iliad. After ten years and the Spartan deception with their wooden horse ("Greeks bearing gifts"), Troy was eventually captured.

The fall of Troy has been traditionally dated as either 1193BC or 1184BC.

After the fall, Priam's cousin, Aeneas, fled, but was shipwrecked at Carthage where he met and fell in love with Dido. But he abandoned her to continue his journey to Italy where he founded what was to become Rome.

Brutus – the first King of Britain

Geoffrey of Monmouth, as well as others, tells the story of the coming to Britain of Brutus, the grandson of Aeneas. At that stage, Britain was known as Albion, but Brutus changed its name to Britannicus. He is believed to have landed at Totnes, in Devon, but he founded and made his capital city London, which he called Trinovantum (New Troy). He divided the island between his sons Locrinus, Camber and Albanactus. Locrinus received (roughly) what we now call England, Camber was given Wales (hence Cambria, Cambrian Mountains, etc.) and Albanactus received the part that is now Scotland and which was then named after him and called Alba or Albany.

However, on the other hand, the word "Britain" may spring from "Pretannikai," or painted people, which is how the Gauls described the inhabitants of Britain to the Greek sailor Pytheas, because they wore woad (blue dye). These Gauls lived in Armorica, which is that part of northern France, now called Brittany.

While on the subject of the British, it has been said that the only people who are still entitled to call themselves British are, in fact, the Welsh. This is because they still speak the same language of 3,000 years ago. Whereas, after the coming of the Saxons, the original native language in the rest of Britain disappeared; for example, in due course, English replaced Gaelic (the original language spoken in Scotland). The Gaelic language is however currently enjoying a significant resurgence in parts of Scotland.

1275BC Moses

While there are doubts about the dating and chronology of ancient Egyptian civilization, it is now generally believed that, in 1275 BC, during the reign of Pharaoh Rameses II and on the night that the Israelites sprinkled the blood of the lamb on their door posts, so that the Angel of the Lord would spare them (the Passover), Moses led the Israelites out of Egypt (see also earlier note about Atlantis). The story is told in the biblical Book of Exodus, which goes on to narrate how the Israelites fled through the parted waters of the Red Sea into Sinai. On Mount Sinai, Moses received the Ten Commandments, the remains of which were kept in a moveable wooden coffer called the Ark of the Covenant (see also 1000 BC).

1269BC Hittite Empire overthrown
The Hittites had inhabited Anatolia (Turkey) and had been a great power between 1400BC and 1269BC. The modern view is that, while the Bible states that iron was being used soon after the Creation, the Hittites were probably the first people to use Iron instead of Bronze. They had been a violent, but great, people: their power collapsed suddenly when small groups of invaders, the Sea People, moved into Anatolia. The Sea People were a fearful confederation who invaded and settled in the eastern Mediterranean.

1235BC Joshua
After forty years of wandering in the Sinai desert, following the Exodus under the leadership of Moses in 1275, the Israelites, under their new leader, Joshua, entered Canaan. They at once took Jericho and other cities. The conquest of Canaan was finally completed in 1030BC.

1230BC Palestine
Soon after the Israelites had arrived in Canaan, the Philistines, a non-Semitic people who may have been one of the Sea Peoples (see 1269BC above), overthrew the Egyptians and then proceeded to occupy Canaan, which in time would be renamed Palestine, a name derived from the word Philistine.

1159BC Hekla erupts
This volcano in Iceland erupted causing severe seasonal changes in the Northern Hemisphere, particularly in Scotland and Ireland.

1043BC David & Goliath
We read in the first Book of Samuel that David killed the Philistine giant Goliath and, having won numerous battles and wars under King Saul, the first King of Israel, became a public hero fit to become King of the Israelites on Saul's death.

1030BC Jerusalem
By 1030BC, King David had removed all the Philistines, united the Kingdom of Israel and made his capital city Jerusalem, where he installed the Ark of the Covenant.

10th Century BC
Psalms
David also wrote the Psalms, which are a series of poems/songs which, as well as expressing the full range of the faith of Israel, prophesy the coming of the Redeemer.

1000BC King Solomon
As the second Book of Samuel relates, David's son, Solomon, became the next King and, while David had laid the foundations, Solomon completed the first temple in order to house the Ark of the Covenant (see also 1275 BC). Under his sovereignty Israel enjoyed at the peak of its prosperity, power, influence and general glory. Solomon reigned at first wisely but gradually became greedy and cruel. Solomon is also famous for his liaison with the Queen of Sheba (Saba), which is in Yemen. She bore him a son who became the first King of Ethiopia, then called Abyssinia.

922BC   Jewish Kingdom split
In 922BC, Solomon's son, Rehoboam became King of the United Monarchy of Israel, but, as a result of Solomon's misrule, the kingdom was so weakened that it split into a Southern Kingdom, based on Jerusalem and called Judah (over which Rehoboam was King), consisting of the Tribes

of Judah and Benjamin, and a Northern Kingdom of the rest of the Tribes of Israel, called Israel. Both kingdoms were weakened and most of David's conquered lands were lost.

The Lost Tribes of Israel
We now appear to lose sight of the tribes of the Northern Kingdom. It is these ten tribes that are known as the Lost Tribes of Israel. Some say that they eventually spread north into Europe and reappear as tribes such as the Saxons (which apparently means "Sons of Isaac"). On the other hand, others say that a number sailed west past Gibraltar, through the Pillars of Hercules, turned north and ended up in what was to become Cornwall. And then still more others say that they stayed more or less in the same place and never got lost at all, but gradually were absorbed into the other populations in that area. There is probably truth in all of these, and may be other assertions.

850BC   The Prophet Elias and the Pagan god Baal
In the Book of Judges we read that in the Northern Kingdom, King Ahab and his wife Jezebel (c.850BC) worshipped the Pagan God, Baal. The prophet Elias proved that *his* God was the one true God, when his water-drenched bullock was consumed by fire, leaving the dry bullock of the false priests of Baal unburned. Jezebel ordered Elias's arrest, but God appointed a new king and she was put to death.

776BC   First Olympic Games
These were held in Greece near Mount Olympus.

753BC   Foundation of Rome
This is the recognised date for the founding of Rome. According to traditional legend, Rome was founded not so much by Aeneas (see 13th Century BC) as by the twin sons of Mars, Romulus and Remus, who were suckled by a she-wolf on the banks of the River Tiber. The date is universally recognised because events in Roman history were described by the letters AUC (*Ab urbe condita* – foundation of the city) to denote the number of years after this date that the event took place.

735BC   The Prophet Isaias
In 735BC, the prophet Isaias (Isaiah) started to warn the Jews of the disasters that were about to fall upon them because of their bad conduct.

721BC   The Assyrians
The capital of the Assyrian kingdom was Nineveh, on the river Tigris opposite Mosel.

In 721BC, the Assyrians, who had adopted the Sumerian religion and who, since the collapse of the Tower of Babel, had occupied Mesopotamia (now known as Iraq), overran first the Northern Kingdom, and brought it to an end, and in 682BC they entered the Southern Kingdom. They absorbed ten of the twelve tribes of Israel and this Northern Kingdom, whose inhabitants were not Jews, which then became known as Samaria; named after its capital city. Its people, the Samaritans, were hated by the Southern Kingdom, which consisted of the last two tribes of Israel, the tribe of Judah and that of Benjamin.

One of the other ten tribes was that of Levi. Only priests and Levites (assistants to priests) could belong to this tribe. Levites lived in both Kingdoms.

The tribes of Judah, Benjamin and Levi, who were living in the Southern Kingdom, were to become the Sephardic Jews as we now know them. Sephardic Jews are descended from the Jews of the Diaspora. Ashkenazi Jews, the other main type, are Jews who have embraced the Jewish religion but who are not necessarily of the Tribe of Judah

In 612 BC, the Babylonians and Medes sacked Nineveh and thus ended the Assyrian Empire, which was absorbed into the Persian Empire.

626BC   Death of Ashurbanipal
He was the last King of the Assyrians of any importance and his reign is connected with the exploits of Gilgamesh, an ancient Mesopotamian hero.

6th Century BC   Croesus
Croesus, the last King of Lydia (the western part of Asia Minor) and famed for his fabulous wealth, began a system of coinage. Metal coins of a defined purity and weight were used as coins.

587BC   The Babylonian Exile
The Jews paid little attention to the prophetic warnings they had been given by Isaias and others, and, in 587BC, Jerusalem fell to the Babylonians under King Nebuchadnezzar. The temple was destroyed, the Ark disappeared, and in the book of the prophet Jeremias, and elsewhere in the Bible, we learn that the Jews were taken into exile (referred to today as "the captivity") in Babylon. Nebuchadnezzar turned Babylon into a fabulous city with magnificent public works and buildings.

C580BC Sappho dies
Sappho was born in about 612BC. She was a priestess who lived on the Greek island of Lesbos and was a major poet.

539BC   The Prophet David & Balthazar's Feast
In the Book of Daniel we read that Balthazar (or Belshazzar) held a great feast (Belshazzar's Feast) in Babylon at which, the Bible records, miraculous handwriting appeared on the wall ("the writing on the wall"). Daniel, the prophet, explained that this foretold the imminent collapse of Babylon. In proof of this, soon afterwards, Cyrus, King of Persia, invaded and, with his ally Darius, King of the Medes, took Babylon and became ruler of all known lands west of India.

Zoroastrianism
The Persians brought with them the ancient religion of Zoroastrianism. Although this religion had a lofty moral code, it was far from free from aberrations. For instance, to cut a tree was sinful and it was as grave an offence to refuse a dog its food as to allow a priest to die of starvation. Zoroastrianism is still practiced by the Parsee sect in India and in other scattered communities (such as in Iran). Its teachings are set out in the Avesta.

The religion got its name from Zoroaster (or Zarathustra) who lived in Iran from about 628BC to 551BC. (See also 722AD.)

Pythagoras (580-500BC)
Pythagoras was a Greek mathematician and philosopher, who carried out important work on the planetary system and formulated his famous theory about right-angled triangles.

538BC   Return of the Jews
The Jews were allowed by King Cyrus to return to Jerusalem in 538BC, where, shortly afterwards, they rebuilt the Temple (2nd Temple). This building, that was to last until its destruction by the Romans in 70AD, had extensive additions made to it by Herod the Great.

510BC   Etruscans
In 510BC, the Romans had defeated the Etruscans and occupied their land (Tuscany). The Etruscans had been a main threat to Rome.

509BC   Foundation of the Roman Republic

After the expulsion of the seventh and last King Tarquin from Rome and the abolition of the Roman monarchy, the Roman Republic was founded. It would last until 27BC when Octavian, a Roman general, who had been master of the Republic, took the title of Emperor.

History of Ancient Greece

490BC   Battle of Marathon

In 490BC, the Persians landed at Marathon, in Greece, but were defeated by a much smaller Athenian army under Miltiades. The news of the victory was carried the 26 miles to Athens by a runner, hence the modern marathon.

483BC   Death of Buddha

Buddha was an Indian prince, whose teachings form the basis of Buddhism. There are three types of Buddhism:

- Theravada (SE Asia) which emphasises begging and meditation;
- Mahayana (N Asia) which teaches the emptiness of all things;
- Zen (Japan) which teaches silence and self-realisation.

Another Buddha is expected in AD3000. Like Hindus, they believe in Karma or fate. They believe that we should strive to attain Nirvana (perfect peace of mind), but that this may only be truly achieved at death.

480BC   King Xerxes

The Persians tried again to conquer Greece in 480BC under King Xerxes, with an army of one million. This time the Athenians enlisted the help of the Spartans who, under Leonidas, laid in wait in the mountain pass of Thermopylae, north of Athens.

The Spartans were heavily outnumbered, but they heroically held up the Persians for just long enough, thereby allowing most of the Greek army to escape. The Persians pressed on to Athens, burned it to the ground, but, later in the same year, were defeated by the Greeks under the command of Themistocles in the sea battle of Salamis.

479BC   Death of Confucius

This Chinese philosopher taught piety, personal and societal morality and brotherly respect.

430BC   The Parthenon and Athens' greatest era

After defeating the Persians, the Greeks, ruled by Pericles, enjoyed great prosperity. This prosperity was enjoyed in spite of the two Peloponnesian Wars (457 and 431-404) between the Athenians and the Spartans under Alcibiades. The story of these wars is told by the historian Thucydides.

Achievements of the Greeks:

- The Parthenon (the Temple to the Greek gods) was built on the Acropolis, a hill in Athens in 430BC
- Aeschylus, Euripides and Sophocles wrote plays (the Athenians invented the theatre)
- Euclid developed geometry
- Hippocrates studied medicine
- It was the era of the great Greek sculptures
- Herodotus, the father of history, began writing a Greek, indeed a world, history – he refers to the British Isles as the Cassiterides, because they were the main source of tin.
- The Greek writer Aesop wrote his Fables in this century

- The Greeks also developed Democracy (the formal origin of which is attributed to them), and much else.

Socrates, Plato and Aristotle

Socrates, Plato and Aristotle developed philosophy (the use of reason and logic to study the great questions of life, death and the universe). Socrates was Plato's tutor, and Plato, in turn, tutored Aristotle. In due course Aristotle was to tutor Alexander the great.

Logic

The Greeks gave to the Romans the logic that is still used in Western Europe and America, and this is one of the reasons why the Western world has been more scientifically advanced than, for example, the Chinese, who have not been driven by logic. Christianity is also essentially a rational religion, as can be seen by the application of Plato and Aristotle to it.

371BC   Third Peloponnesian War

In this war, Boeotia, whose capital was Thebes, fought with Sparta against the Athenians.

338BC   Philip of Macedonia

When Athens was defeated by Sparta, Philip II of Macedonia became the leader of the Greeks in 338BC. His son Alexander succeeded him in 336BC and defeated Thebes.

325BC   Alexander the Great (356-323BC)

By 325BC, Alexander had conquered Egypt, Persia and most of India, thus uniting Europe with that part of Asia. This was a feat unheard of before or since. He founded many cities called Alexandria in his campaigns and this is why, at the time of Christ, the whole civilized world spoke the Greek language. This is why he is called Alexander the Great. After Alexander's death the Persian Empire was split into four. One of these was Egypt, which Ptolemy I seized.

323BC   Ptolemy I rules Egypt

He came from Macedonia and was one of Alexander's generals. He built the great library at Alexandria and established a dynasty of Egyptian kings that was to last 300 years.

308BC   Stoics

This was one of the schools of Greek philosophy. They held that virtue was the highest good and that passions and appetites should be rigidly subdued.

300BC   End of the Iron Age

This is the generally recognised date for the end of what is known as the Iron Age.

Epicureanism

This was a school of philosophy that developed in Athens about this time. It was founded by Epicurus who taught that the highest good was pleasure and the avoidance of pain. Some who practice this philosophy by pursuing pleasure are regarded as unashamed sensualists. True Epicureans seek serenity through detachment from worldly affairs.

278BC   Pyrrhic victory

Pyrrhus, King of Epirus (modern Albania) and ruler of Greece, attacked Italy in 280BC, and again in 278BC. He won the battles, but suffered such heavy losses as to make the victory worthless – hence the expression Pyrrhic victory.

275BC   Beginning of Roman Empire

In 275BC, Pyrrhus tried again to attack, but this time failed, and the Italians, who were based in Rome, gained control of all Italy, thus strengthening the Roman Republic which grew to become the Roman Empire.

270BC   Aristarchus

Aristarchus, from Greece, is recognised as being the first Astronomer. He was the first to suggest that the Earth moves around the Sun, but he had little influence with this theory, in which he anticipated the works of Copernicus and Jesuit astronomers by 1,700 years, because Aristotle demolished this notion.

264BC   The Punic Wars

The only Semitic race (i.e. Jewish and Arab peoples) to become seafarers was the Phoenician, which lived in modern day Lebanon. They had also established trading posts at Carthage in Tunisia and Gadez (Cadiz). One of their generals, Hamilcar, was also a trader, particularly in tin from Cornwall.

Rome saw Carthage as a rival and, in recognition of this, Cato the Elder, the Roman statesman and historian who died in 149BC, ended all his speeches with the famous words "*Delendo Carthago est*" (Carthage must be destroyed). These wars were known as the Punic Wars, from the Latin for Phoenicia.

The Romans won the first Punic War in 264BC and, as a result, captured Sicily, thereby becoming the dominant naval power in the western Mediterranean.

C250BC Decimal system of counting

The Indians (in Northern India) began to invent the system of counting, using nine digits and a zero, which we now use today. This was codified and better defined by the Arabs in Baghdad in 825AD.

226BC   Great Wall of China

This Great Wall dates from this time. It was built from the Yellow Sea, north of Beijing, nearly 1,500 miles inland as a defence against nomadic tribes.

218BC   Hannibal and the Second Punic War

In 218BC, Hannibal (the Carthaginian General) crossed to Spain, enlisted help from the Gauls and, with elephants, marched south across the Alps on Rome to confront the Roman General Quintus Fabius Maximus. Hannibal defeated two Roman armies before Scipio defeated him at the battle of Zarna in 202B.

212BC   Archimedes dies

He was the most celebrated Greek mathematician and inventor. He lived in Sicily and Egypt. His principle (that, when a body is immersed in water its loss of weight is equal to the weight of water displaced) is said to have been discovered by him when in Syracuse, a seaport in Italy. He was also responsible for inventing the screw, the screw pump and a devastating catapult-type war engine.

2nd Century BC   Essenes

This Jewish monastic sect was formed about this time. They lived a monastic life and did not offer animal sacrifices. Their lives and beliefs were much closer to those taught by Christ than those practised by the rest of the Jewish people.

149BC   Third Punic War

In 149BC, the third Punic War, a short affair, resulted in Carthage's destruction. After this victory, Rome was to increase its power by taking Athens, Greece, Crete, Syria, Armenia, Gaul and Jerusalem.

The Holy Maccabees
168BC   Seleucids

In 168BC, the Seleucids, from Greece, ruled Palestine and outlawed the Jewish religion. They eventually took control of the lands conquered by Alexander the Great.

166BC   Judas Maccabeus

From the Bible (the Books of Maccabees) we learn how, in 166BC, the sons of Mattathias, a priest, rose against the Seleucids (Syrians), under the eldest son, Judas, who was nicknamed "Maccabeus, the Hammer." Their action cleansed the Temple that the Seleucids had defiled and is commemorated to this day by the Jews as the feast of Hanukkah.

141BC   Jews again control Jerusalem

In 141BC, the Jews, led by Jonathan and Simon, the last of the sons of Judas Maccabeus, retook Jerusalem and were thus in control of their destiny for the first time since the Babylonian exile in 587BC. The Maccabee dynasty was a peaceful age for Jerusalem (a truly model society) which ended when that city was taken by the Romans under Pompey in 63BC.

1st Century BC   The establishment of the Silk Road

Silks came to Europe from China and the main route the traders took to Rome via Samarkand was known as the Silk Road.

Julius Caesar
73BC   Spartacus

Rome continued its corrupt regime after 149BC until 73BC when Spartacus led a slave rebellion (the third of the slave wars), which was crushed.

63BC   Romans occupy Palestine

In 63BC, the Romans occupied Palestine.

55BC   Invasion of Britain

Julius Caesar, who was only a general at the time, began to expand the Empire and visited Britain in 55 and 54BC. His main enemy was the Celts, who had occupied most of northern Europe, from the Baltic to the Mediterranean seas, including the British Isles. The Romans called them Gauls, but the Romans never totally subdued them, leaving them to occupy the outer fringes of North West Europe. The Romans did not successfully invade Britain until 43AD under the Emperor Claudius.

Celts

The Celts were the original inhabitants of Britain and the western fringes of Europe. In time, it was to be from their number that Christian missionaries such as St Patrick and St Columba would spread Christianity through Northern Europe.

Christian tradition holds that the Celts were the original inhabitants of Europe after the dispersal of peoples from Mesopotamia (in Iraq) following the collapse of the Tower of Babel (see the Preamble to this section). Indeed, even today, there is a remarkably distinctive DNA sequence to be found in the peoples who live in the lands occupied by the Celts, particularly in Cornwall, Wales, the Isle of Man, Galloway and the Hebrides.

Some even say that their language, Gaelic, was the language spoken in the Garden of Eden, which is believed to have been in Mesopotamia. This may be fanciful, but there are at least two indications that this may be true:

- Indian Sanskrit contains many words that are similar to Gaelic. In other words, the contention goes, might this not suggest that both have the same origin in Mesopotamia, which lies roughly halfway between where these two peoples now live?
- There is a tradition in the Basque Country (on the north coast of Spain) that they speak the same language as Noah and that it was brought to their land by Tubal, Noah's grandson.

The religion of the Celts at this time was usually Druidism.

50BC   Vercingetorix
Julius Caesar put down a rebellion in Gaul led by Vercingetorix in 50BC, and his campaigns against the Gauls (the Gallic Wars) lasted from 58-51BC.

Crossing the Rubicon
Pompey pressured the Senate to declare war on Julius Caesar if he should cross the River Rubicon on his march south towards gaining control of Rome. Julius Caesar did indeed cross the Rubicon and, as he advanced, Pompey fled. The result of this was the end of the Roman Republic (509 – 27BC) and ushering in of the Roman Empire (27BC – 476AD). ("Crossing the Rubicon" means taking a step after which there is no turning back.)

Cleopatra
Pompey fled to Greece, and then to Egypt where Julius Caesar defeated him; Julius Caesar then married the Princess Cleopatra, who would be the last of the Ptolemies.

46BC   Julian Calendar
On the advice of his own astronomer Sosigenes, Julius Caesar reformed the calendar and the Julian Calendar began. July is named after him.

44BC   Assassination of Julius Caesar and Death of Cicero
Julius Caesar returned to Rome and was appointed dictator for life. He was assassinated by Brutus and Cassius on 15th March 44BC, during the Ides of March. Cicero, the great orator, statesman, philosopher, man of letters and prose-stylist also died in this year. **Mark Anthony** then became Caesar, defeated Brutus and Cassius at the Battle of Philippi, in Greece. He deserted his wife, went to Egypt and married Cleopatra. However, both Anthony and Cleopatra committed suicide in 30BC.

31BC   Battle of Actium
Octavian challenged Mark Anthony and defeated him at the Battle of Actium in 31BC. In 27BC, not only did Octavian change his name to Caesar Augustus, but he proclaimed the end of the Roman Republic and the beginning of the Roman Empire which, as has been said, would last until 476AD. In 8BC, the month of August was named after him, and it was given an extra day (taking one from February) so that Augustus's month would not be shorter than Julius Caesar's!

Caesar Augustus and Tiberius
Caesar Augustus ruled from 31BC to 14AD and was succeeded by his stepson Tiberius who in turn was succeeded by Caligula. By now, the Romans controlled nearly all of Europe and the Mediterranean, providing a unified Empire in which Greek was almost everywhere spoken and in which Christianity might begin to grow.

During this period, the Roman lyric poets, Horace and Virgil wrote their best known works. Horace's most quoted saying is *"Carpe Diem"* ("seize the day," or "take every opportunity when it comes"). Virgil's most famous works are his *Georgics* and the *Aeneid*.

This was also the time of Plutarch, the great Greek biographer and essayist. He was a citizen of both Athens and Rome.

1 – 33AD   The Life of Christ
Jesus, an historically documented person
Jesus Christ, the long-awaited Redeemer (see 1996 BC), is an authenticated person. His life and death can be verified from records independent from the New Testament – especially the works of the Jewish historian, Josephus.

However, the Gospels themselves are an impressive record because they were written so close to the time of his life – much closer than most other ancient sources to the events they describe.

1AD (There was no year 0) Christ's Nativity in Bethlehem
There are those who question the date of the first Christmas, but reliable historians can prove that 25th December *was* the date of Christ's birth. Having said this, others hold that Christ was born in 4BC. However, with this possible error not having been discovered until some hundreds of years later, and with 1AD having the longest tradition behind it, it is now taken as the start of the Christian era.

The name Jesus, which Christians regard as a holy name, means "Saviour" – the name Christ means "Anointed."

1AD – 7AD   Flight into, and Exile in, Egypt
Shortly after Christ's birth, His mother, the Blessed Virgin Mary, and His foster father, St Joseph, fled with Christ to Egypt to escape Herod the Great's murderous intentions. In 7AD, they returned to their home town, Nazareth.

7AD – 30AD   The Hidden life of Christ
Christ lived in Nazareth, working as a carpenter with His foster father.

12AD   The Finding in the Temple
The incident recorded in the Bible of the finding of the child Jesus in the Temple occurs in 12AD.

Did Jesus visit England?
What follows is highly likely to be pure legend because the Catholic Church has no tradition whatever of it being true. Nonetheless there is increasing interest in this idea and it might be helpful to give the following explanation of the meaning of the Hymn *Jerusalem*.

The legend goes that between 12 and 30AD we have no record of Christ's doings nor of His whereabouts. After the death of St Joseph, Jesus *may* have become the ward of St Joseph of Arimathea, His uncle. This Joseph was an importer of tin and other minerals. He is reckoned to have visited West Cornwall, the centre of the world's tin production and that he *might* have taken his ward with him.

Local Cornish tradition states that they visited Ding Dong mine near Land's End and also stayed for some time near the lead mines in Somerset, near Glastonbury. This local tradition says that this supposed visit *may* explain why the Celtic Christian Church in West Cornwall was so strong and also why Glastonbury is considered by so many to be a deeply mystical place.

One reason why Jesus is thought to have chosen Glastonbury is because it was a strong centre of Druidism which, like Zoroastrianism, is a God-centred faith that looked for and depicted a Redeemer. Indeed there is evidence that St Joseph of Arimathea returned to Glastonbury within a few years of the Resurrection to look after the dwelling where he and Jesus had stayed, and to bring the Christian Faith to Glastonbury at a very early stage. There are some who maintain that he brought with him the Holy Grail, the Chalice that Christ used at the Last Supper and that this is the origin of the relic at Strata Florida, near Aberystwyth in Wales.

There is also a school of thought that, while in Britain, St Joseph of Arimathea built the very first Christian Church in the World. After all, neither Palestine nor Rome allowed Christians to worship Jesus, let alone build churches.

To further support this view, the British bishops were held in high esteem at Catholic Councils in the early centuries – the reason given was, as we have just seen, that they represented the country that could claim to have built the first Christian Churches. (While mentioning this, it is interesting to discover that, in Brittany, the French openly acknowledge that Christianity was brought to them from England.)

As is stressed, this tradition, that Christ visited England, can only be regarded as unsubstantiated legend but, if it is true, it would explain why Christianity was already strongly established in South West Britain when St Augustine arrived in Kent in 596AD. It would also explain why, if the French in Brittany acknowledge that it was the inhabitants of the South West of England who first brought Christianity to them, both areas share many places dedicated to Celtic Saints.

As already indicated, the contents of this box may explain the words in William Blake's poem and hymn *Jerusalem*.

30 – 33 The Public Life of Jesus Christ

These three years mark the public life of Jesus Christ, culminating, on 25th March 33AD (Good Friday), in His death on the cross, after a flagrantly unjust trial, at the end of which His judge, Pontius Pilate, the Roman Procurator at the time, declared Him innocent, but nevertheless sentenced Him to death by crucifixion, as demanded by the Jewish authorities of that time, at the age of 33. His Crucifixion and Death was attended by very few of His supporters: only His Mother, the Blessed Virgin Mary, St John, St Mary Magdalen, and a few others, had the courage to follow Him to the end.

His Crucifixion was, in part, due to His teaching, as well as His miracles, which created enmity against Him, amongst the leaders of the Jewish Temple. These leaders included:

- The High Priests, whose authority He appeared to undermine
- The Scribes, who interpreted Jewish law
- The Pharisees, a self-righteous sect of high-standing individuals who were obsessed with avoiding impurity
- The Sadducees, another sect, who didn't believe in angels or the resurrection of the dead: they adhered to the strict letter of the law and their members tended to form…
- The Sanhedrin, the Jewish council that tried Jesus.

33AD   Easter Day

Two days later (on the Third Day as the days were counted at this time), on Easter Sunday, Jesus Christ rose from the dead and, over the next few weeks, was seen at close quarters by hundreds of people before His Ascension. His tomb may still be visited at the church of the Holy Sepulchre in Jerusalem.

The Shroud of Turin

One piece of evidence from the first Easter Sunday, still existing today, now begins to thread its way through the years down to the present moment, namely the shroud in which Christ was laid after His death. (According to Jewish tradition, He was buried with the instruments of his Crucifixion.)

In spite of modern supposed dis-proofs, there are overwhelming aspects of this cloth that lead Christians, and others, to believe that it is no forgery. For example, it is an anatomically perfect image, made in negative form centuries before photography was invented and without a trace of paint or any form of ink.

Indeed further studies of this cloth and its journey are highly recommended, but for the moment we will leave it at this brief mention and pick it up again as we follow its path to its present home in Turin.

The Ascension

Forty days after the Resurrection, in the presence of His disciples (the Apostles whom He had instructed to spread His message to all nations), Christ ascended into Heaven from the top of the Mount of Olives, Jerusalem (AD33).

Descent of the Holy Ghost

Ten days after Christ's Ascension, and fifty days after His Resurrection the Holy Ghost descended upon the Apostles (Pentecost). Thus the Christian Church was formally commissioned under St Peter's leadership – St Peter became the first Pope ("Thou art Peter; and on this rock I will build my Church," Matthew, 16:18).

Chapter 2   From Pentecost to Islam

The Christian Era

37   St Stephen

In 37AD, when Jerusalem temporarily had no governor, the Christians were persecuted with great violence and Stephen became the first Christian Martyr, being stoned to death. One of the main persecutors was Saul, a Christian-hater, who had not just been present at, but considerably influenced the Jewish crowd to assist in the killing of St Stephen. However Saul was converted to Christianity on the road to Damascus, and thereafter became the Apostle to the Gentiles, taking the name Paul.

42   The Christian Church moves to Rome

By 42AD, St Peter had realised that Christians had to cut all ties with their persecutors, and he transferred the Christian Church and his See from Antioch (the first place where Christ's followers were called Christians) to Rome – it was important for the Church, if it was to grow, to be situated in the most important city in the known world, and known for most of its history as "The Eternal City".

The Holy Shroud's first move?
While this may be legend, the tradition is that Jude moved the Holy Shroud to Edessa, 350 miles north of Galilee, where it stayed until the 6th century.

46-57   St Paul's Missionary Journeys

Paul made three missionary journeys to the Middle East, Greece and Asia Minor, writing his various Epistles to the people he visited, alongside St Luke. These Epistles constitute what is known as the Pauline Tradition, and form an important part of the New Testament of the Bible.

67   Martyrdoms of St Peter and St Paul

St Peter was martyred in 67AD. This event is connected with the Christians being blamed for the Great Fire in Rome, which the Emperor Nero may even have started himself just so he could blame it on the Christians and renew his persecution. This, together with St Paul's execution in Rome on the same day, was part of the general persecution Christians were then suffering. One can still visit the underground prison (the Mammertine) in Rome where St Peter was held.

Another famous name from this time is that of Seneca. In fact there were two people of this name, Seneca the elder who was a Rhetorician and his son who was Nero's Tutor.

70   Jerusalem is destroyed, and the Diaspora

In 70AD, the Romans destroyed Jerusalem together with its Temple, thus fulfilling one of Christ's many prophecies. The only part of the Temple to survive is the Wailing Wall, (part of the Western Wall of the old Temple) where, to this day, Jews still go to pray.

In their hatred of Christ, the Romans had erected two huge statues, one to Jupiter, the other to Venus, over the site of Calvary and the Holy Sepulchre. In intending to cover all vestiges of these holy places, they were conveniently marking, indeed confirming, their locations and enabling future rediscovery.

Following this defeat, Jews who were still living in Palestine left their homeland and were once again without a country of their own (the Diaspora). This is something they were unable to rectify until 1948 when, amid great controversy, which continues to this day, and with British and American support, they re-established their homeland in Palestine, renamed it Israel and removed the Arabs who had been there for centuries.

79   Vesuvius erupts

Vesuvius erupted destroying the Roman cities of Pompeii and Herculaneum. The remains of these towns, both human and other remains, were preserved in ash and pumice and provide a record of some considerable socio-historical importance from nearly 2,000 years ago.

98   Persecution of Christians

From 98 to 161, the Roman Empire was ruled by three good Emperors (Trajan, Hadrian and Antoninus Pius), but the following hundred years or so to 283 saw the horrors of the earlier Roman Empire return with wide-scale persecution of Christians.

Catacombs

During this period, the Catholic Church was continuing to grow under a succession of popes. One of these, St Callisto, gave his name to one of the Catacombs in Rome. Catacombs are underground dwellings, places of worship and burial chambers. A number are still open to the public.

120   Tacitus dies

Tacitus was a Roman historian and politician.

122   Hadrian's Wall

In Britain, the Roman Governor and future Roman Emperor, Hadrian, built this wall from the Solway to the North Sea to restrain the Picts, who lived to the north of it.

168   Death of Ptolemy

Ptolemy was an Egyptian astronomer who, having studied the writings of Plato and Aristotle, developed their theory that the Earth is the centre of the Universe. This was not challenged until 1543 when Copernicus proposed his theory of Heliocentricity, that the Sun is the centre of the Solar System. Ptolemy was also an important geographer. He was born in 90AD.

180   Marcus Aurelius dies

He is known as the Philosopher Emperor and founded chairs in Athens for each of the four leading schools or sects of philosophy: Platonic, Stoic, Peripatetic and Epicurean. The Peripatetic was the only true system of philosophy, but Marcus Aurelius, himself, was a stoic. He was also a terrible persecutor of Christians.

3rd Century AD   Manichean Heresy

The Manichean heresy centred on the erroneous belief that matter is intrinsically evil. Its effect lasted for many years after it had been officially condemned. It was an extension of Gnosticism, a creed shrouded in mystery, which said that God was good and matter evil.

200   Galen of Pergamum

The ideas of Galen, a Greek physician, dominated medicine until the Renaissance. He wrote a textbook on human anatomy and deduced that the pulse is an indicator of health.

225   Death of Tertullian

Tertullian is regarded as being Africa's father of the Catholic Church.

254   Death of Origen

Origen is reckoned to be one of the greatest Christian philosophers and writers but, paradoxically, was also a heretic (his belief in *apocatastasis* – a belief in the restoration of the state of the world as it existed before the fall, as a result of Christ's sacrifice, with universalist consequences – being condemned at the Synod of Constantinople in 543).

284   The Roman Empire Splits

In 284 Diocletian came to power and divided the Empire into two halves, with the eastern half in Asia Minor.

304   Diocletian Persecutions

While Diocletian began as a good Emperor, his deputy, Galerius, (the son of a pagan priestess, Romula, who lived in Germany and influenced her son) urged him to persecute Christians terribly from 304 to 312.

305   St Alban Martyred

While it is by no means certain, this is recognised by St Bede as the date of the martyrdom of St Alban (the *Anglo-Saxon Chronicles* places it in 283). Alban was a convert from Paganism to Christianity in Roman Britain, and the first English Martyr.

Constantine

The man chosen to be the next Emperor of the Western half of the Roman Empire after Diocletian was Constantius, but Galerius would not allow his succession. When Constantius died in France in 305, the legions in Gaul proclaimed his son Constantine as Emperor. Meanwhile Maxentius, Constantine's rival, was in Rome with a bigger army. When Constantine was marching south on Rome to confront Maxentius, he saw a cross in the sky with the words "*Hoc Vinces*" ("In this sign shalt thou conquer") written underneath. Constantine promptly ordered a cross to be made and carried in procession ahead of him before he marched on.

312   Constantine becomes Emperor

Having beaten Maxentius at the Battle of Milvian Bridge, Constantine entered Rome as Emperor and reunited the two halves of the Empire.

Constantine dissolved the Praetorian Guard, the force of bodyguards that had been used by Roman Emperors since Julius Caesar. Before him, the term had usually been applied to the bodyguards of Roman generals since the time of Scipio (275BC). Constantine dissolved them because they had made up most of Maxentius' army.

313   Edict of Milan

In 313, under the Edict of Milan, Christians were allowed to worship freely. Constantine was baptised, Sundays became a festival day, in honour of the day of Christ's Resurrection – His overcoming of death – and gladiatorial fights and crucifixions were abolished.

Roman Empire becomes more Christian

Constantine changed the laws of the Empire to reflect Christian principles.

St Helena

Much of the credit for Constantine's good rule must go to his British born mother, St Helena. Some historians say that she was the daughter of King Cole of Colchester (Old King Cole). It was Helena who located the buried Cross of Christ and also either discovered or rediscovered many other holy relics when she visited Jerusalem. These relics were taken to Rome after the Muslims had captured Jerusalem in 638.

321   Arius and St Athanasius

In 321, a deacon, Arius, denied the divinity of Jesus and claimed that he was inferior to God – an idea that proved to be popular. Bishop Athanasius countered by saying that Jesus was God and had always existed and was heavily persecuted for it. Constantine asked the bishops to assemble in 325 at Nicaea to decide the issue.

Nicene Creed

The argument surrounding the Arian heresy centred on whether Jesus was "homo-ousion" (of the same substance with the father) or "homoi-ousion" (of like substance). The Council declared in favour of homo-ousion, as Athanasius had maintained. One of the results was the Nicene Creed in which we find the words, "being of one substance with the father," and, "very God of very God."

Although the heresy (a teaching contrary to what the Catholic Church teaches has been revealed to mankind by God) was quashed, Arius did not give up and even tried to destroy Athanasius by falsely accusing him of murder; a plot which utterly failed. St Athanasius, St Basil, his brother St Gregory of Nyssa and St Gregory Nazianzen were the great defenders of the Faith, against the Arian Heresy. So widespread was this Arian heresy that Athanasius said of its adherents: "They have the churches, but we have the Faith."

Another heresy at this time was that of the Donatists. Begun by Bishop Donatus Magnus, from Carthage, they believed that the validity of the sacraments depended on the personal holiness of the minister.

330   Constantinople

The Emperor Constantine set up a new capital city at Byzantium in 330, renaming it Constantinople. From this point, Constantinople became the secular headquarters of the Roman Empire, and Rome, under the direct control of the Papacy, became the spiritual headquarters. The name of this city would be changed again, in 1930, to Istanbul.

The Barbarians and The Church

400   The Barbarians

By 400AD, the corruption inside the Roman Empire had weakened the Romans' will to defend the Empire to such an extent that the Roman generals were forced to recruit soldiers from the neighbouring Barbarians.

Japan

This is when the recorded history of Japan begins.

404   Latin Bible (Vulgate)

The Latin version of the Bible, after exhaustive work by St Jerome, was compiled and approved by the Catholic Church. At this point it would make sense to mention the so-called *Apocrypha*. The books that the *Apocrypha* contains come from the Greek version of the Old Testament, but do not form part of the Hebrew version. Later Protestant Bibles usually omit the *Apocrypha*, whereas Catholic, Orthodox and Coptic Bibles include these books as part of the original Canon of Scripture.

406   Barbarian Invasion

The Barbarians (Vandals, Goths and Visigoths) started their eventually successful attacks on the Roman Empire. When the Rhine froze over in 406, they swarmed westward overrunning Gaul and Spain.

410   Rome falls

Italy was invaded by Visigoths under Alaric. Rome was captured and sacked. The Roman legions in Britain were withdrawn to help protect Rome.

420   Death of Pelagius

Pelagius, a British monk, launched the Pelagian heresy, which denied the belief in original sin and the need for sanctifying grace to save one's soul.

452   Attila the Hun

In 452, Attila the Hun, known as "the Scourge of God," swept through northern Italy with his forces, uniting Vandals, Ostrogoths, Franks and others under his banner and dominating much of the world from the frontiers of China to the frontiers of Gaul. When Attila arrived in Rome, he was persuaded to withdraw by the personal mediation of Pope Leo I. The following year the Huns all disbanded, following Attila's death.

The space in Asia abandoned by the Huns was filled by the Avars, who themselves spread west as far as the Balkans. However, they did not oust the Slavs, who had arrived there in the 2nd and 3rd Centuries BC, who themselves had also arrived from Central Asia.

The Avars were defeated by Charlemagne in 796AD.

The Huns introduced stirrups into the known world, dramatically adding to what could be done on horseback in both peace and war.

Bulgaria

At about this time, the Bulgars, living north of the Black Sea, moved west and formed Bulgaria.

476   The Fall of the Roman Empire

Eventually the Roman Empire collapsed in 476 and Barbarian and other tribes took over: Visigoths in Spain; Vandals in North Africa; Franks in France; Ostrogoths and Lombards in Italy; Angles and Saxons in England.

The Barbarians get their name from the Berbers, the oldest inhabitants of the north coast of Africa, the Barbary Coast.

It might be helpful to give some more information about these and other tribes from this time:

- Goths – from Gotland in Scandinavia, who had moved into the Ukraine in the 2nd century AD. They converted to Arian Christianity and their empire would be destroyed by the Huns, who divided them into
    - Ostrogoths, those who lived west of the River Dniester
    and
    - Visigoths, those who crossed south of the River Danube.
- Vandals from Germany. They were immensely destructive and gave their name to the term vandalism.
- Saxons – a Germanic people who, with Angles and Jutes, invaded Britain. Those who remained on the Continent were defeated by Charlemagne and converted to Christianity. Some maintain that the name Saxon is derived from "Sons of Isaac" and that they were one of the ten lost tribes of Israel.
- The Angles came from the Angeln district of Schleswig in Germany. They settled in Northern England but, in time, would form an Anglo-Saxon dynasty, ruling with a parliament or Witan (council of wise men).
- The Jutes, also from Germany, settled in Kent.
- Franks – a Germanic people who invaded Gaul (forming the nucleus of France) and converted to Christianity. Their conversion resulted from the Frankish King Clovis who converted in 496AD. He was of the Merovingian line of kings who had been greatly influenced by the conversion of his beautiful and pious wife, Clothilde. In time, the Frankish Church would be properly organised by monks from Ireland and England.
- Lombards – a Germanic people who invaded Italy, but would be defeated by Charlemagne.

The collapse of the Roman Empire did not prevent the Catholic Church from continuing to grow.

Byzantine Empire

The Eastern Roman (the Byzantine) Empire remained unaffected by the collapse in the West and the invasion of the Barbarians.

The "Dark Ages"

The so-called "Dark Ages" had begun – they lasted from 476-1050AD – though, as we will see, the term is a misnomer.

St Patrick and St Bridget

It was only in Ireland that peace and justice reigned, and this is was due to British-born St Patrick (400-493) and St Bridget (450-525). Ireland was converted to Christianity, without a single martyrdom, and for several centuries Ireland was the "University of Europe" because it was to Ireland that students went to study. Irish education was so highly regarded that, for example, Charlemagne persuaded Irish monks to migrate to France to set up a system of education there.

St Columba

St Columba left Ireland and began evangelising the rest of the British Isles. He may have started on the Island of Colonsay, but it was on the Isle of Iona, which was a centre of Druidism, that he made his base. By the time he died in 597, he had given Scotland its first Christian King in the person of Aidan. Shortly after this St Aidan founded the Lindisfarne Monastery on Holy Island, off the Coast of Northumberland.

The Talmud, The Torah and The Kabbalah

The Talmud is the most important collection of Jewish literature to be written after the death of Christ. It was written and edited about this time by Talmudists, who are the descendants of the High Priests of the old Jewish Temple. Thus it is that the Talmud is strongly anti-Christian, and, for many Jews, has supplanted the Old Testament in importance. Another famous Jewish book is the Torah. There are many definitions of the word "Torah" but the most common refers to the first five books of The Old Testament.

There is a third important Jewish book, the Kabbalah, but this was not written until the 13th century in Spain. It is a mystical book and in it is reckoned to be the seed-bed of many later beliefs such as:

- Protestantism
- The Occult
- Theosophy
- Rosicrucianism
- Communism

In part, the Kabbalah revives the heresies of the Gnostics, Manicheans and Albigensians.

6th Century   St Brendan

St Brendan, an Irish monk, sailed west and is now generally believed to have discovered America, 1000 years before Christopher Columbus. After him, in about 1000AD, Leif Eriksson, son of Eric the Red (both Norwegians), is understood to have visited the north eastern coast of America; Eric the Red having visited Greenland.

Counting the years

Dionysius Exiguous, a Scythian monk, who spent most of his life in Rome, introduced the use of the Christian era, assigning year 1 to the birth of Christ. The counting of years had originally begun 753 years earlier at the foundation of Rome. His system had been universally accepted throughout Christendom by the 10th century.

520   St Benedict

In 520, St Benedict, having begun his spiritual life in a cave at Subiaco, founded the first Christian Monastery at Montecassino (both near Rome), and it was through the monasteries that civilization was preserved throughout the (so-called) "Dark Ages." The monasteries practised prayer, simplicity, regularity, discipline, charity and self-control.

The Legend of King Arthur

This legend is set in the first half of the sixth century. King Arthur is said to have presented a unified force to defend Britain against Pagan invaders.

535   Krakatoa

We normally associate Krakatoa as having erupted in 1883AD. Geologists now believe that it exploded with considerably more force in 535, causing dark skies and dramatic climate change for a number of years. Whether caused by Krakatoa or not, information gleaned from tree rings laid down at that time gives first hand evidence of the climate change. Some archaeologists suspect that, rather than a volcano, it was caused by a comet hitting Earth.

596   Pope St Gregory the Great

In 596, Pope St Gregory the Great sent St Augustine (also known as St Austin) to support Catholic Queen Bertha of England who lived near Canterbury. This led to the establishment of Christianity, first of all at Canterbury and later throughout Britain. This start was consolidated after the Synod of Whitby in 664, which confirmed that the date on which Easter should be celebrated was the one decreed by Rome. St Gregory is also known as the Father of Christian Worship, because of his ordering of the liturgy of the Roman Rite, and the ancient Gregorian chant, for the singing of the Divine Office and Mass, is named after him.

622   The Rise of Islam
Mohammed

In 622, Mohamed fled to Medina from Mecca because of opposition to his teaching. He had claimed that, in a moment of divine disclosure, he had had a revelation communicated by God through an angel that God, or Allah, was one, that God would judge humanity and that God had commanded various religious observances.

Mohammed claimed that of the three people, Abraham, Jesus and himself, he was the greatest and he started to count the years from this date. He called the religion he started "Islam" or submission, and it appears that it found its origins in both Heathenism (Mohammed's tribe worshipped the moon god, *Al-ilah*) as well as Judaism. This is not that surprising when one considers that, while the Diaspora had indeed dispersed the Jews far and wide, there were still many Jews living in Arabia after the Diaspora.

The beginnings of Islam may have arisen as a result of the strife between Jews and Christians in Arabia. Indeed Mohammed's teaching seems to have been more influenced by the Jews. For one thing, until Mecca became the city towards which Muslims faced when they prayed, Mohammed originally chose to face Jerusalem.

In 625, Mohammed reputedly started to dictate the Koran (he himself was illiterate) which was to be the sacred book of his followers.

In 630, he was able to return to Mecca and this was followed in the next two decades by a huge succession of conquests in Arabia.

Mohammed died in 632 and his tomb is at Medina. (See also Fatimids - 638)

638   Jerusalem falls to Islam

When Mohammed died in 632, his successors (Caliphs) enforced the faith he left behind, Islam, with frightening cruelty. In 638, they took Jerusalem. Although the Crusaders were to retake Jerusalem in 1099, Saladin recaptured it in 1187 for the forces of Islam. From 1517, the Ottoman Turks were to control it until 1917.

Islam is divided into:

- **Sunni** Muslims, who believe that the first three Caliphs were all legitimate successors to Mohammed, and who follow the Koran, the book that Muslims believe contains the revelations given to Mohammed.
- **Shiite** Muslims, who follow Ali, the fourth Caliph, and who gave their spiritual leaders more authority. Shiites have a sub sect, the Ismaili, whose leader is the Aga Khan.

In due course, the Ismaili sect would have its own sub-sect, the Fatimids, who were a dynasty that ruled Egypt from 909 to 1171AD. They claimed their descent from Mohammed's daughter, Fatima.

Another branch of Fatima's descendants are the Hashemites. While they originate from the Hejaz region of Saudi Arabia (along the Red Sea coast) they are now better known for being the origin of the Hashemite kingdoms of Jordan, Iraq and Syria. They take their name from Hashim ibn Abd al-Manaf, the great-grandfather of Mohammed.

While mentioning Islam, it might be helpful to give an explanation of two officials in Islam whose titles are in everyday parlance:

- Mufti – this is the expert in Muslim law for a particular area.
- Mullah – this is someone learned in Muslim theology.

It was about this time that the process of strict Islamic law, or Sharia, was developed.

687   Death of St Cuthbert

This Englishman evangelised most of Northumberland, was Bishop on Lindisfarne (Holy Island) and was buried in Durham Cathedral.

722   Spain and the Moors

The Muslim Army then began to conquer the neighbouring territories and ended up controlling Persia, Afghanistan, Northern India, Africa, and parts of Spain as well. They controlled nearly all the Middle East by about 700.

They drove those practicing Zoroastrianism in Persia towards India where they have become known as Parsees, a name that derives from the word "Persia". Parsees don't bury their dead, but leave their bodies in high towers (Towers of Silence) in cities like Bombay to be scavenged by vultures and other birds.

In 722, the Spaniards, whose chief stronghold was in the Asturias, began to drive them back at the Battle of Covadonga. Moslems (in Spain they are called Moors) were particularly zealous because they believed that, if they died in battle for their faith, they entered Heaven instantly.

In 763, the Moslems built their capital city, Baghdad, which became the Islamic world's leading centre for literature, architecture and science, especially astronomy. In 794 they opened the first paper-making factory, an art they learned from a Chinese prisoner. They invented algebra and they probably built the first museum.

Coptic Church

In Egypt, those Christians who refused to accept both Islam and the Catholic Faith called themselves Copts. However, the Catholic Church regards them as heretics because they have adopted the Monophysite doctrine that Christ had only one nature.

Maronite Church

In Lebanon, the Maronite Church is an eastern rite part of the Catholic Church, and claims always to have been subject to the Holy See in Rome. It takes its name from St Maron, a fourth century hermit, or St John Maron, Patriarch of Antioch from 685-707. Despite this tradition, there is evidence that for a time the Maronites were Monothelite heretics (followers of Sergius, Patriarch of Constantinople, who taught that Christ had only a divine and no human will), who sought reunion with the Latin Patriarch of Antioch in 1182, being brought to full fruition in the 16th century, thanks to the efforts of the Jesuit John Eliano, whereupon Pope Gregory XIII founded the Maronite College in Rome in 1584.

731   St Bede the Venerable

In Britain he is more generally known as the Venerable Bede and was a renowned Saint, theologian and historian. In 731, he finished his great work, *The Ecclesiastical History of the English People*, which is still in print.

Catholic Church during the "Dark Ages"

As can be seen from the preceding pages, and rather than is commonly supposed, that the Catholic Church suppressed learning and knowledge, if it hadn't been for the work of Catholic monks during the "Dark Ages," the lights of learning, faith and good order would long ago have been extinguished.

Chapter 3   The Start of The Holy Roman Empire to the High Middle Ages

730   Iconoclasm
The Iconoclastic heresy, which was instituted by the Greek Church under the Byzantine Emperor Leo II, saw the veneration of icons in Asia Minor and elsewhere prohibited between 730 and 787. It happened again between 815 and 843.

732   Martel
In France, the forces of Islam were repelled at the Battle of Tours (732) by the Franks under Charles Martel.

754   The Papal States
Since the time of the Emperor Constantine, the Church had been accumulating territory and in 754 it began to strengthen its position and influence by anointing the Barbarian King Pepin as King of the Franks and official defender of papal territory. In return, Pepin gave the Church some land in Italy, thereby founding the Papal States.

793   St Alban's Abbey founded
Saint Alban had been martyred by the Romans in the 3rd century and a Benedictine Abbey was founded in his memory this year.

800   Charlemagne (the First Holy Roman Emperor)
King Pepin's son, Charles, ruled the Franks so peaceably and well from 768-813, that in 800 he was crowned Emperor of the lands in which Christians predominated. His coronation saw the end of the Merovingian line of kings, becoming the first Carolingian king. He was called Charles the Great (Charlemagne) and thus became the first Holy Roman Emperor and is now regarded as being the Father of Europe.

He zealously promoted education, agriculture, manufacturing and commerce. It is thanks to him that we can now read the famous Latin and Greek authors.

During his reign, upper and lower case letters were developed as well as spaces between words. One of his chief advisers was Alcuin of York.

The Holy Roman Empire, which, in effect, lasted for over 1100 years, was a unifying force in Europe and one of its principles was that kings and queens have an authority to which even they must submit, namely the Papacy.

One of Charlemagne's most significant accomplishments was at the battle of Roncesvalles in North East Spain, after which the Moslems began to retreat. This battle was to be the inspiration for countless works of literature, the greatest being La Chanson de Roland.

9th Century   Use of Arabic numerals begins to take over from Roman

843   The Treaty of Verdun
After Charlemagne's death, his three grandsons, Lothair, Louis II and Charles II fought over who should be Emperor. Lothair inherited the title of Emperor.

As a result of the Treaty of Verdun (843), they were each granted land, and these lands represented, roughly, the modern countries of France, Germany, Holland, Belgium and Northern Italy. This division marks the start of the French-German division, a division that was to be part of European history right up to the present day.

The Treaty of Verdun split and weakened the Empire, and, by the start of the 10th Century, it looked as if it was going to be overrun by Barbarians again.

The Vikings
866   Vikings occupy France
In 866, the Vikings, or Norsemen, from Scandinavia occupied most of France and laid siege to Paris. However, within 200 years, the Vikings would return home as Christians to their native Scandinavia.

Viking literature and art are noted for their dynamic vitality.

878   Alfred the Great
In the 9th century, Vikings raided the East of Britain and it was not until Alfred the Great defeated them at the Battle of Ethandune in 878 that they began to be repulsed.

Feudalism
In Europe generally, the inhabitants, who were for ever living in fear of the Vikings, developed a system of protection whereby they tended to work for one man who offered them safety in return. The men who provided protection were knights or barons; those who worked for them were serfs, and the system was called feudalism.

It should also be noted that, during this time, slavery in Europe was gradually abolished. Slavery gave way to the benign system of serfdom and was abolished altogether by the 14th century.

Rekindling of the Holy Roman Empire

936   King Otto the Great
In 936, the Saxons (from Saxony in Germany) appointed Otto as their King. The Saxons had not been invaded by the Vikings and from this undisturbed base, Otto would rekindle the Holy Roman Empire, once he had defeated the Magyars in 955. After Otto's coronation in 962, the Holy Roman Empire became based in Germany rather than in France.

The Magyars
In about 1000, Magyars, from Hungary, joined the Holy Roman Empire.

Cluny and Monasticism
This monastery had been founded in 909 at Cluny in Burgundy in France. It was to become a seat of great scholarship and the centre for the development and expansion of Christian monasticism. Particularly important were the evangelical works of Saints Cyril and Methodius in Eastern Europe. Indeed the Cyrillic alphabet, the one used for Russian and other related languages, and which was developed from the Greek alphabet, is named after St Cyril. It is interesting to note that many civilisations only developed a written language after they had developed a zeal for reading that had been inspired by Christian missionaries.

943   Holy Shroud moves to Constantinople
In 943, the Holy Shroud was rescued from Muslim Edessa and taken to Christian Constantinople.

Beowulf
This epic Anglo-Saxon historical poem was written about this time.

1014   King Brian
Ireland was divided into four provinces, Ulster, Munster, Leinster and Connaught, which were united under a High King, the most famous of which was Brian who defeated the Vikings in 1014.

11th Century
The High Middle Ages

The High Middle Ages lasted from about 1050 to 1450 and during these years the Catholic Church dominated Europe. The Middle Ages themselves are generally reckoned to have lasted from 476AD (the Fall of Rome) to 1492AD, the discovery of America. The word "Catholic" means "universal" from the Greek words "cath", throughout, and "holos", the whole. The word "mediaeval" is from the Latin for Middle Ages.

Achievements of the Catholic Church in the Middle Ages

- Under the Church a strong system of trading, commerce, markets, fairs and business centres developed.
- While some regard the first university as having been founded by St Patrick in Armagh, and that Oxford University was founded by Alfred the Great, universities, as we know them today, began to develop during this period, mainly as a result of the influence of St Dominic. The earliest university is generally recognised as having been at Bologna (founded in 1088), followed by Paris (the College of the Sorbonne being founded in 1257, but earlier colleges pre-date it by a century), and (possibly earlier still) Oxford (where there is evidence of teaching as far back as 1096).
- Amongst the finest achievements of the period, during which nearly everyone in continental Europe was not only Catholic, but also a member of the Holy Roman Empire, were the Cathedral at Chartres, the *Summa Theologica* of St Thomas Aquinas and the life of St Francis of Assisi. The writings of St Thomas, who is sometimes known as the Dumb Ox, are recognised as being the pinnacle of Scholasticism, the enormously significant chapter of Western intellectual history.
- The Catholic Church encouraged scientific enquiry through the teaching of the *Quadrivium* (arithmetic, geometry, music and astronomy). Once students had mastered that, they were taught to relate their discoveries through the subjects of the *Trivium* (grammar, rhetoric and logic).
- Two of England's most enduring buildings were erected about this time: Westminster Abbey and Westminster Hall. The first was rebuilt by its holiest King, St Edward the Confessor, 1003-1066, and the latter by William II and Richard II.
- It is seldom realised that the great mediaeval cathedrals were also designed to be used as solar observatories, with particular regard to predicting the correct date for Easter.
- The Catholic Church started a system of inns for travellers, where accommodation was free.
- They developed a system of warning ships about dangerous rocks at sea.
- A monk, Eilmer, even built a glider which flew 600 feet in the eleventh century.
- They not only developed improved agricultural practices, with improved breeds of cattle, they also established fisheries, particularly salmon fisheries. They developed the use of phosphates for fertilizer. This product came from iron production which resulted in high grade iron products.
- They were highly skilled in forestry.
- They also provided agricultural land at low rent to farmers on very long leases. After the Reformation such tenants were driven from their land and made destitute.
- The Catholic Church, through its monks and nuns, developed a universal health service through a system of building hospitals, one of which would be attached to every large church or religious house.
- The Church developed a universal system of comprehensive education.
- They also set up model factories and systems of social security and human rights.
- They established vineyards with Dom Perignon discovering how to make champagne.
- They created systems for both national and international law and also of sound economics.

- They developed the use of water for power, which was used particularly in the production of cloth and leather goods.
- They developed systems for waste disposal.
- Their works of art and architecture were without equal, and indeed still are.
- They developed a whole concept of charitable giving that would be destroyed by Henry VIII at the time of the Reformation.

In short, as you can see, the Catholic Church was the father of European civilisation. It civilized what had been a barbarous and chaotic continent.

1048   Omar Khayyam
While we are not absolutely certain, the Arab scholar, astronomer, mathematician and poet, Omar Khayyam, is reckoned to have been born in 1048.

1054   Orthodox Church
In 1054, the Church in the East split away from Rome and became the Orthodox Church. This resulted, essentially from a dispute over papal authority, and the insertion of the *Filioque* clause into the Creed (which stated that the Holy Ghost proceeded from the Father and the Son, not the Father alone). The reality of this schism was confirmed at the time of the Fourth Crusade in 1204. In due course, about sixteen variations of the Orthodox religion would develop, of which the Russian, Greek, Romanian, Serbian and Bulgarian are the best known, but all are in full communion with each other.

Papal Elections
Shortly after this, in 1059, popes began to be elected by the College of Cardinals.

1065   El Cid
By 1053, about a quarter of Spain had been recaptured by the Christians. The reconquest was further advanced under the legendary leadership of El Cid between 1065 and 1095.

1066   Norman Conquest of England
In 1066, the Normans, who were originally Norseman (i.e. Vikings), under their Duke William, conquered England at the Battle of Hastings. In order to establish and protect their supremacy, they built numerous castles (Norman castles) in England, including the Tower of London, begun in 1078.

1076   Synod of Worms
In 1076, Holy Roman Emperor Henry IV held a meeting of bishops at Worms (the Synod of Worms) which accused Pope Gregory VII of ridiculous charges and declared him to be deposed. Pope Gregory replied by excommunicating Henry. In due course Henry craved forgiveness and the political chaos which the Synod had caused was thus abated.

1079   Peter Abelard
Peter Abelard the brilliant but controversial scholar was born in 1079 and helped foster the development of universities. He was destroyed by his famous affair with Eloise.

1095   The First Crusade
In 1095, Pope Urban convoked the Council of Clermont which summoned the first Crusade to open up the Holy Land again to pilgrims. In fact, Christians had been making pilgrimages to the Holy Land since the time of Christ, but the Seljuk Turks (Mohammedans) had taken control of the Holy Land in 1070 and had barred Christians from entering Jerusalem. The Crusaders called their opponents Saracens, a name originally given to nomadic tribes of the desert.

1099   Knights of St John

In 1099, Jerusalem was taken by the Crusaders, who brought the First Crusade to an end. In 1100, Jerusalem was established as a feudal kingdom with Godfrey de Bouillon, a Crusader leader from France, as the first King. The order of the Knights of St John of Jerusalem was founded principally to protect the holy sites.

The order of the Hospital of St John (Hospitallers) ran the hospital in Jerusalem for pilgrims, Jews and Muslims. After the fall of Jerusalem in 1187, the Hospitallers established their order in Cyprus, Rhodes and Malta. In due course some would be called the Knights of Malta.

1101   St Bruno dies

St Bruno founded the Carthusian order of monks. They are the strictest of the contemplatives and take their name from the monastery at La Grande Chartreuse near Grenoble.

1113   St Bernard

St Bernard of Clairvaux, joined other monks who had founded a monastery at Citeaux (originally founded in 1098), wanting a more faithful observance of the Rule of St Benedict, giving birth to the Cistercian Order of monasteries, which followed this strict observance. He was one of the most important influences throughout Europe, in terms of his enormous contribution towards the way the Catholic Church operated. The influence of the Cistercian monasteries on land-management and farming is also prolific.

1119   Knights Templar

This was a Christian military order founded in Jerusalem in 1119 and in rivalry to the Hospitallers. It was devoted to the recovery of all of Palestine from the Muslims and became a powerful military and financial organisation. The order was suppressed in 1308, accused of heresy, gross immorality and sacrilege, and a number of the knights were executed. Those who escaped this persecution met later in obscurity, and presented and communicated their ideas symbolically to the outside world, a method which, in time, would be copied by Freemasonry.

1120   The Premonstratensian Order of Canons was founded

This Order, founded by St Norbert, gets its name from the French town of Premontre and was nearly wiped out in the French Revolution.

1145   The Second Crusade

In 1145, Pope Eugenius III called for the Second Crusade to defend Jerusalem and Antioch against the Turks, who had captured the Crusader's outpost at Edessa, in South Eastern Turkey. At the Pope's request, St Bernard preached widely in support of the Crusade and was the most important intellectual figure demonstrating its justification. However, the leaders of this Crusade were disunited and it failed.

1150   Samurai

These were members of the feudal military caste in Japan and were armed retainers who defended landowners and their interests. About 8% of the population belonged to Samurai families. The system was abolished in 1869.

1154   An English Pope

Nicholas Breakspear became the only English Pope, taking the name Hadrian IV (or Adrian IV). He died in 1159.

Leaning Tower of Pisa was built

1170   St Thomas Beckett

On 29 December 1170, Thomas Beckett, Archbishop of Canterbury was murdered in his cathedral by King Henry II's knights who thought they were acting on his orders. Beckett had incurred Henry's displeasure by reorganising the English Church. Henry responded by drawing up the Constitutions of Clarendon which Beckett refused to accept and fled to Rome where he received full backing from the Pope as well as other lesser authorities. Beckett, reassured by both this backing as well as having been reconciled with Henry a few months earlier, returned to Canterbury but only to his martyrdom.

Canterbury thereafter became a place of pilgrimage of great significance; hence Chaucer's Canterbury Tales. His shrine, the focus of pilgrimage, was destroyed and any sign of it removed on the orders of Henry VIII at the Reformation.

King Baldwin and Saladin

During the 1170s and 1180s, Baldwin, the Christian King of Jerusalem successfully defended the Holy Land against the Turks led by Saladin. Saladin led the Turkish force that defeated the Fatimid Dynasty in Egypt in 1171. It was Saladin and his forces that recaptured Jerusalem in 1187.

11th to 14th Centuries   The Cinque Ports

During this period five coastal towns in Kent and Sussex provided a Navy for the defence of Britain. These were Hastings, New Romney, Hythe, Dover and Sandwich. Winchelsea and Rye were added later.

12th Century   The Albigensian Crusade

These French heretics from Toulouse, known as Cathars in Florence, regarded the physical world as fundamentally evil and said there were two Christs. They condemned marriage, food and procreation and were themselves condemned by Rome and defeated by the Crusade against them.

The Cathars had derived some of their beliefs from the Gnostics; heretics in the early Christian era. Gnostics claimed they had "higher knowledge" and this belief is now reckoned to be another tenet that was, in due course, adopted by Freemasonry. Some writers have compared their creed to Russian Communism and cited its origins in the Manichean heresy.

1189   Richard I and the Third Crusade

In 1189, King Richard I of England, known to his contemporaries and to history as Coeur de Lion ("the Lionheart") joined the Third Crusade which succeeded in reopening Jerusalem to pilgrims for a limited period. It was also during this Crusade that England took the Island of Cyprus.

Prester John and Tancred

Prester John was a twelfth-century legendary priest-king, about whom many crusading stories were written. He may have come from China or Ethiopia. Another famous crusader from this period is Tancred, a Norman crusader chief, who was prominent at the sieges of Antioch and Jerusalem.

1190   Teutonic Knights

It was at Antioch that, during this Crusade, the Germans founded an order of knights called the Knights of the Cross. They were later known as the Knights of the Teutonic Order (Teutonic Knights) taking their name from a German tribe from Schleswig-Holstein. On their return home, they occupied Prussia and were instrumental in converting it to Christianity from Paganism. In due course this part of Germany (Brandenburg-Prussia) was to be controlled by the Hohenzollern dynasty which in turn was to give us Frederick the Great and Kaiser Wilhelm II of Prussia (Kaiser Bill). In time, Prussia would accept Protestantism (in the early days of the

Reformation). The land of Schleswig-Holstein has been claimed by both Denmark and Germany, but the Germans have always dominated it.

1202   Liber Abacci
Leonardo Fibonacci, of Pisa in Italy, wrote this book which introduced to the West to the Hindu/Arab decimal system of numbering.

1204   The Fourth Crusade
In 1204, the Fourth Crusade was begun, but once the main force had left Venice, it inexplicably diverted to Constantinople. There, led by the Venetian Doge, Enrico Dandolo, aged 96, it looted and burned the city, and never reached the Holy Land. The Holy Shroud was removed and the aggressive behaviour of the Crusaders damaged the chances of a reunion of the Orthodox Church with Rome. Venice secured a substantial part of the conquered Greek territories and became a recipient of much Byzantine art and influence.

1207   St Elizabeth born
St Elizabeth, Queen of Hungary, wife of Louis IV, was renowned for her pious humility and charitable work. She died in 1231.

1212   Children's Crusade
The Children's Crusade began in Germany, but the Lombards in Genoa refused them ships for their journey and so it never left port.

1213   Genghis Khan
Genghis Khan (the Great Khan) began the Mongol conquest of North China and India and advanced as far as the Crimea. When he died he probably controlled a larger area than any man in history. The empire broke up early in the 15th Century, but in India his Muslim descendants, known as Moguls, ruled until the 18th Century when Hindus began to take over and European commercialisation squeezed them out.

1215   Magna Carta
In 1215, Richard's brother, King John, who had behaved very high-handedly with his subjects, was forced to sign the Magna Carta at Runnymede in Surrey, England, giving rights to his people. Many regard this moment as the beginning of modern democracy in Europe.

1220   Westminster Abbey
The Abbey was completed, with the exception of the two west towers which were not added until the 18th century.

1227   The Holy Bible is divided into chapters
In 1551 it was divided into verses.

1230   St Dominic
St Dominic began his order of friars in about 1230, sending out preachers, teachers and nuns to establish religious houses and schools in many major cities, and eventually to establish missionaries in the New World, although the Jesuits superseded them in this last activity during the "Counter-Reformation." St Dominic was influential in counteracting the Albigensian Heresy, which teaches that there are two Gods and two Christs.

Tradition holds that it was to St Dominic that the Blessed Virgin Mary appeared, and revealed the 15 Mysteries of the Rosary to him, to propagate. The Order supplied leading officials for the Holy Inquisitions, notably the Spanish Inquisition. They are also known as "Blackfriars" from the colour of the outer cloak of their habit.

St Dominic was driven by his belief that, to civilize Europe (the world as it was the known) in a Christian way, everyone must be taught the same things and that this teaching must be spread to every corner of the globe. As we have already seen, it was this drive that was to lead to the strength and depth of learning in universities like Paris, Bologna and Oxford.

St Francis of Assisi

In Italy, St Francis and St Clare of Assisi began their orders at this time. These friars are called "Greyfriars" also after the colour of their habits.

Monks and Friars

Friars are members of mendicant (begging) religious orders, some of whose members travel the countryside doing pastoral work, preaching, etc., and often become missionaries abroad, whereas a monk remains principally within his monastery.

Monastic Houses include:

Benedictines, Cistercians (who also follow the Rule of St Benedict – see also Trappists, 1664AD), and Carthusians (though technically these are hermits with elements of common life).

Orders of Friars include:

Franciscans (Greyfriars), Dominicans (Blackfriars), and Carmelites (Whitefriars – from the outer cloak of their habit), founded on Mount Carmel in Palestine by St Berthold in 1154, though claiming a lineage back to Elias. Carmelites are the most contemplative of the friars.

Contemplative Orders for women include:

Poor Clares (an order of Franciscan nuns founded by St Clare of Assisi) and Carmelites (the female order is enclosed and contemplative). St Theresa of Avila and St John of the Cross reformed the Carmelites (both female and male) to become discalced, or barefoot (in fact they wear sandals), though the primitive order of Carmelites also continued to exist as a separate Order.

Chapter 4   The Thirteenth Century to the Reformation

Mafia
This is the century when the Camorra and the Mafia began to control Sicilian society with crimes and extortion. Somewhat like the Freemasons, both groups are secret societies with initiations involving daggers and symbolic blood-letting. In 1861, they were suppressed, and some members fled to New Orleans and Chicago, where they have flourished as Cosa Nostra ("Our Affair"). In due course the Mafia emerged again in Italy, in spite of a number of nearly successful attempts to suppress them again by the Fascists in the mid-twentieth century.

1234   St Louis
King St Louis IX of France, 1234-1270, who is considered to be one of the greatest and most devout Catholic kings of all time, died on the unsuccessful Fifth Crusade.

Chartres and Salisbury Cathedrals
Between 1194 and 1240, the great Cathedral of Chartres was built and the work was entirely carried out by guild workers. Chartres was one of the main centres of European learning in the 12th Century. Salisbury Cathedral was also built during this period.

1242   Alexander Nevsky
The Russians under Alexander Nevsky defeated the Teutonic Knights. He is venerated as a saint in the Russian Church.

1250   Mamelukes rule Egypt
The Mamelukes were originally freed Turkish slaves, but in 1250 one of their own number ascended the Egyptian throne, whence they ruled Egypt until the Turkish conquest of 1517.

1271   Marco Polo
Marco Polo began his marathon journey from Venice to China where he served the Emperor Kublai Khan. He did not return to Venice until 1296.

1274   St Thomas Aquinas
St Thomas Aquinas, 1226-1274, is recognised by the Catholic Church as its greatest philosopher and theologian. His book, *Summa Theologica*, summarises all Christian thinking. He was also known as the Dumb Ox.

1277   Roger Bacon
Roger Bacon, an Oxford philosopher and mathematician, saw the need to reform the calendar, but was condemned for his novel ideas. He is credited with inventing the magnifying glass and gunpowder, and even foreseeing aeroplanes. He was also attracted to alchemy, the forerunner of chemistry, whose adherents sought to discover the supreme object of their cause, the philosopher's stone, a unique substance from which it was believed one could turn metals into gold. The mystical aspects of alchemy survive in esoteric movements such as Rosicrucianism.

1278   Habsburg Dynasty
The Habsburg family from Switzerland began an almost unbroken 650 year period of providing Holy Roman Emperors, the first being Rudolph I (1218-1291). In Germany they had replaced the supremacy of the Hohenstafen family in 1254. Maximillian I and Franz Josef are perhaps the most famous emperors. In the 16th century, they controlled Bohemia, which was to become part of Czechoslovakia in 1918.

1282   Sicilian Vespers Massacre

In Palermo in Sicily, 2,000 French residents (Angevins) were massacred by Spanish Aragons, who deeply resented the French regime. Order was not restored until 1302 when, with Papal backing, the Spanish took control of the island.

1284   Cambridge University

The first college at this university, Peterhouse, opened its door to students, though the University itself dates to 1209.

1290   Reading glasses invented

The first reading glasses were made in Venice.

Jews expelled from England

In 1290, the Jews were expelled from England by King Edward I, although it is now reckoned that a number of Jews remained in England, in spite of the expulsion order.

1291   Holy Shroud

In 1291, the Holy Shroud was probably moved to Cyprus from Acre.

1305   William Wallace executed

Sir William Wallace, a Scottish patriot, led a revolt against the English and defeated them at Stirling in 1297, assuming the title of Governor of Scotland. However the English King, Edward I, defeated him at Falkirk in 1298 after which Wallace was captured and executed in London.

1306   Jews expelled from France

Following their expulsion from England in 1290, in 1306 Jews were also expelled from France. Indeed the Jews were expelled from numerous countries over the centuries:

Hungary	1360
Belgium	1370
Prague	1380
Austria	1420
Utrecht	1444
Spain	1492
Lithuania	1495
Portugal	1498
Parts of Italy	1540
Bavaria	1551.

They were also expelled from Scandinavia, Arabia, North Africa and Yemen. The only place from which they were never expelled was Rome.

The reason for these expulsions was their reluctance to be assimilated into their host country and embrace the Catholic Faith.

1307   Holy Shroud

In 1307, the Holy Shroud was moved to Paris and then to Livey, which is also in France.

1308   Duns Scotus dies

Duns Scotus, whose extraordinary erudition and intellectual skill earned him the title *Doctor Subtilis* ("Subtle Doctor"), was a great Scottish Franciscan philosopher.

Other Achievements of the Middle Ages (the 11th to 15th Centuries)

- Chivalry (valour, courtesy and generosity) became the way of life.
- There were improved conditions for labourers, as Serfdom replaced Slavery. By the 14th century Serfdom was scarcely more onerous than a modern farm tenancy.

- First mechanical clock (1300s). One can see what claims to be the oldest, still working, in Salisbury Cathedral.
- The Compass which had been used as an aid to navigation in the second century BC began to be used in earnest in the 13th century.
- Dante's Divine Comedy.
- Rules of warfare were introduced such as no fighting in Lent or on Sundays. Battles were organised on selected fields with the local peasants often continuing to work undisturbed next door.

Problems in the Church in the High Middle Ages

In spite of its position of huge influence, Rome fell into anarchy in 1303 and the Papal Court was moved to Avignon in 1305, until, after the Great Schism, St Bridget of Sweden and St Catherine of Siena helped resolve the schism and influenced the return of the Papacy to Rome in 1417.

Avignon and the Great Schism

At this time, some in the Church preferred that it be based in Avignon and elected another pope there (an anti-pope) with the result that this "Great Schism" did not end until the Council of Constance in 1414-1418. The Church was to suffer badly for this disunity; it was arguably a contributory cause of the Reformation.

1321   Dante

Dante, the Italian poet, finished his Divine Comedy.

1332   Playing Cards were invented.

1337   The Hundred Years War

The Hundred Years War began in 1337 when England, which claimed half of France, also claimed the French throne. The French won in the end (by 1453) even though the English won notable battles at Crecy (1346), Poitiers (1356) and Agincourt (1415).

St Joan of Arc

The French cause was given immense help by the extraordinary courage and visions of St Joan of Arc who, in 1429, led their forces to victory at Orleans and Patay. The English later captured her and, after a trial devoid of any legality, burned her as a witch in 1431. She was posthumously rehabilitated by a French court in 1456. She is now a canonised saint and is patron of France.

Giotto dies

Giotto, the painter and Architect, who was born in 1267, painted frescos in Assisi, Florence and Padua.

1348   The Black Death

In 1348, Europe was devastated by the Black Death or Bubonic Plague. It is estimated that 75 million Europeans perished.

The Order of the Garter

This is the oldest order of knighthood and was founded at about this time by King Edward III.

1350   Hanseatic League

Although founded in the 13th Century, it was between 1350 and 1450 that Hansa and the other towns of northern Germany agreed to join an economic grouping that what was in effect a small precursor of the Common Market, which has now become the European Union. It was an association for mutual trading, but it dissolved in 1669, due to disagreement amongst its members.

1356   Holy Shroud exposed
In 1356, the Holy Shroud began to be exhibited again in public, in Livey, France.

1382   Winchester College founded
William of Wykham founded this, the oldest public school in England.

1400   Air guns and Muskets
It was about this time that the existence of explosives led to the invention of the first firearms.

1402   Tamerlane
Timur the Lame, a Mongol, who was a descendant of Genghis Khan, subdued Persia, Georgia, parts of India and Syria. He finally defeated the Turks at Ankara in 1402, taking the Sultan prisoner and amassing a truly fabulous booty. His capital city was Samarkand where his beautiful tomb can still be seen.

1415   Jan Hus
Jan Hus, a resident of Prague, was burned at the stake for refusing to recant his heretical teachings. He was deeply influenced by the writings of John Wycliffe (1330-1384) and these two were, in effect, the first religious reformers (Protestants). Wycliffe's followers were called Lollards, thought to be due to the nonsense they spoke ("Lollardy" – mumbling in an uneducated manner).

1440   Eton College founded
Henry VI founded Eton College and King's College, Cambridge.

1453   The Advance of the Turks
In 1291, the Crusaders were forced out of Palestine by the Muslim Turks. About 10 years later the Turkish Sultan, Osman I, replacing the Seljuk Empire, which had ruled Anatolia and Syria since 1055, founded the Ottoman Empire which was to last until 1918, occupying most of the eastern end of the Mediterranean, known as the Levant. During its life it also controlled most of South Eastern Europe.

In Armenia, North East Turkey, the people strongly resisted the Muslim religion and formed their own Armenian Catholic Church.

In 1453, the Ottoman Turks took Constantinople, thus ending the Roman Empire in the East. They sacked the city and made it their capital.

The Ottoman Empire was to control most of South East Europe, until that control was brought to an end during the First World War in 1918.

The Holy Shroud moves to Chambery in France

1455   Gutenberg Bible printed
Johann Gutenberg invented printing in the West and printed the first Bible, the first book to be printed in Europe using movable print (a copy is on display at the British Library in London).

1456   Defeat for the Turks
The Turks then advanced on Belgrade in 1456, but were utterly defeated.

1470   The Printing Press and Calendars
The Printing Press having been invented some time earlier, the resulting mass production of calendars began to standardise time, days of the week, etc. The calendar had drifted away from

the true position of the sun relative to the earth by a number of days – since Julius Caesar's system began – and this was not to be rectified until 1582.

1471 Death of Sir Thomas Malory
Malory, the first acclaimed writer of English prose, had written *Morte d'Arthur*, the romantic tales of King Arthur and his Knights of the Round Table.

1480 The Knights of St John
The Turks attacked the Crusader outpost in Rhodes in 1480, but were defeated. It was after this battle that the Knights of St John (see 1099) adopted a white cross as their emblem.

Inquisition authorised
Pope Sixtus IV authorised the Inquisition against heresy in Spain. In 1492, this resulted in about 175,000 Jews being expelled. Any who converted to Christianity were allowed to stay – they were given three months in which to convert or leave.

1492 Spain finally ejects the Moors

Santiago de Compostella
The only part of Spain not conquered by the Moslems was the mountains of the Asturias in North Western Spain. In 825, the bones of St James the Greater (Sant Iago) were found in Compostella. He became the Patron Saint of the reconquest of Spain, and Santiago de Compostella is still one of the main places of pilgrimage in Europe.

Ferdinand and Isabella
From 1454, Spain was ruled by two Christian monarchs, Ferdinand and Isabella of Castile, who finally drove the Muslims out in 1492. In 1479, Aragon and Castille were united under them, which effectively laid the foundation of modern Spain

Exploring the New World
Prince Henry the Navigator
In the early 15th Century, Prince Henry of Portugal (the Navigator) organised the discovery of the sea route to India by sending Bartholomew Diaz and Vasco da Gama around the Cape of Good Hope.

Christopher Columbus and the settlement of America
Queen Isabella of Spain sent Christopher Columbus west across the Atlantic in 1492, to reach India, whereupon he "discovered" America. However, as we have seen, it is now generally believed that St Brendan had in fact got there first (see 6th Century). On his journey, Columbus first landed in the West Indies, but he also visited Panama and saw its strategic importance, linking the two great oceans. The Florentine explorer, Amerigo Vespucci, after whom the two American continents are generally believed to be named, certainly did not discover them. Vespucci explored Venezuela in 1499, but it is only by accident that his name was given to the continents. (However, having said this, the City of Bristol in England claims that the continents were named after their port's Customs official, Mr Americk, who served John Cabot before his exploration to Newfoundland in 1497.)

In 1521, the Spanish, under Cortez, ended the despotic Aztec Civilisation (under Montezuma) in Mexico. The Aztecs had effectively taken Mexico over from the earlier Mayan civilization.
In 1523, the Spanish, this time under Pizzaro, subdued the despotic Incas, who controlled much of the western shores of South America from their Capital, Cuzco, high in the Andes.
The Spanish Conquistadors (conquerors) made grave errors as they began to advance into the Americas, as no-one will deny. To begin with they were guilty of cruelty and injustice and it was

not until the 16th century that Catholic missionary priests criticized the injustices to such an extent that not only did the treatment of the natives improve, but this led to the natives willingly adopting the Catholic Faith. Indeed these two developments (the arrival of a system of justice and Catholicism) resulted in the first development of international law. By these means, in the countries in which they settled, the Spanish were to bring civilization to what had been a barbaric and excessively cruel people.

In general, between 1492 and 1644 there was gradual settlement by the British and Dutch of most of that part of North America which is occupied by the USA. In 1608, the French founded Quebec.

Caucasian
On the subject of the arrival of European immigrants in the USA, it would be as well to explain the term "Caucasian," which is used to describe white inhabitants of the USA. It stems inappropriately from the myth that US immigrants generally came from the region of the Caucasus Mountains in central Europe. Only a relatively few immigrants come from this region.

Magellan
In 1522, Ferdinand Magellan, the Portuguese navigator was the first to circumnavigate the globe. In 1577, Portugal acquired Macao (on the south coast of China) as a base for Catholic missionaries – this was returned to China with Hong Kong in 1997.

The results of European Exploration
Any impartial observer of how Europeans have explored and advanced into the rest of the world (the Americas, Africa, Asia and Australasia) cannot fail to notice how advanced and civilized the Europeans were in comparison to the peoples they were meeting. If such an observer should wonder why the Europeans were more civilized and cultured than say the Aztecs, Incas and Aborigines, the answer lies in the cultural and spiritual values absorbed by the European explorers from the Catholic Church. It was this civilisation that they imparted to these conquered lands.

1498   Savonarola executed
The controversial Dominican friar and his followers, "the weepers," had condemned extravagances in the Church and society. He totally disregarded the authority of the Pope and after years of disobedience was tried for sedition and condemned to death. He is regarded by some as an early Protestant martyr – a forerunner of the Reformation.

1500   Gypsies arrive in Britain
For Gypsy (an English corruption of the word Egyptian) one should say Romany. They are nomadic people whose language is called Romany and who originated in North Western India.

The Sikh Religion
This religion was founded in the 15th century. Their holy temple is the Golden Temple at Amritsar. They believe in God but not in the Incarnation. They reject the Hindu Caste system. Sikh men take the name Singh and their leaders are called Gurus.

1502   The Inquisition and Torquemada
Once the Moors had gone, it was necessary for Isabella and Ferdinand to unite and protect Spain by making sure that those left behind were truly Christian. (The term they used for such Christians was Hidalgo.)

Accordingly, they set up the Inquisition to check the Christian beliefs of all the Spanish, particularly Jews (1480) and Muslims (1502).

The Pope put Torquemada, a Dominican priest, in charge of the Inquisition and ordered that no torture be used. Many governments used torture routinely at that time and some criminals chose to be tried by the Inquisition, because of its relative leniency. The procedure used was the *Auto da Fe* ("Act of faith") at which the accused were asked to proclaim their belief in Christianity. Those who refused were punished, with some being sent into exile and some executed. Those who were executed were put to death for their heresy as well as their unrepented treason. Heresy was then regarded as a more serious crime than treason, and treason was (and still is) a capital offence in many countries. Those who did repent were given minor penances for their previous offences (hence the desire of criminals to be tried by the Inquisition).

The Jews who converted to Christianity were called Marranos, the Muslims who did so, Moriscos.

The Inquisition has attracted a great deal of criticism, but this needs to be examined in connection with the good effects that it brought to Spain. Unlike many other European countries that did not institute an inquisition, Spain suffered no civil wars or wars of religion in the centuries during which the Inquisition was set up. The bad reputation of the Spanish Inquisition would appear to come from sources in whose interest it was to misrepresent the facts. For example, the cases of the 400 Protestants who were executed by the Spanish Inquisition have been cited as part of this propaganda; yet execution for heresy was widely accepted as a just practice, and advocated by Protestants during and after the Reformation; and it is overlooked that it was not Catholic Spain, but Protestant countries that used torture routinely (one thinks of instances such as the use of rack in torturing Catholics in the Tower of London). Indeed, as has been mentioned, prisoners preferred to be tried by the Inquisition, as it was deemed a more just and gentle institution than the secular courts.

1509   The watch was invented in Germany
The pocket watch, a fairly bulky chronometer, but just small enough to be carried, was invented by Peter Henlein in Nuremburg.

16th Century Renaissance/Reformation

Renaissance means the rebirth of the culture of the Roman and Greek Empires, and some say it was the fulfilment of the Middle Ages. It was centred principally at Florence in Tuscany, where it was financed by wealthy families, particularly the Medici family.

While many of the works of art were religious, others were unquestionably immoral. Partly as result of their lewd nature, the renaissance led to a diminution of Christianity, which some thought to be less important than classical beliefs. As a result, Humanism and Liberalism began to spread.

The startling development in painting was the use of perspective. Modern research indicates that this may have been perfected by the use of the *Camera Obscura*.

The principle artists were:

	in:
The Bellini Brothers	Venice
Leonardo da Vinci	Florence and Milan
Raphael	Perugia and Florence
Michaelangelo	Florence and Rome
Titian	Venice
Tintoretto	Venice
Durer	Germany

The Borgias

The Borgias, a family from Spain, have an unfairly tarnished reputation for disgraceful conduct, including incest, fratricide, nepotism and other abominations.

The three most famous Borgias are:

- Rodrigo Borgia, who was elected Pope Alexander VI in 1492. He is said to be the father (in fact he was the uncle) of
- Cesare, whom Machiavelli regarded as the saviour of Italy, and
- Lucrezia, a virtuous lady who even some modern encyclopaedias now admit does not deserve her notorious reputation.

As for Alexander VI, in spite of popular tales to the contrary, there are no contemporary documents of *any* known sinful behaviour. On the contrary, there is every cause to believe he was a great and holy Pope, who was very popular (his election was unanimous), pious and highly respected by his fellow clergy. He instituted the saying of the Angelus and united all Europe against the Turks. His only "crime" was to root out tyranny amongst the European kings and princes (notably Italian) of his time, and, as we can see still happening today (one thinks of the treatment of whistleblowers, like Marta Andreasen, who tried to stop corruption in the EU), when anyone dares to tackle tyranny, the tyrants' invariable defence is to fight back by blackening the name of their accusers. In the same way, it is the deliberate falsification of the records written by those tyrants that Rodrigo Borgia sought to expose, who have blackened his name. Vatican archives prove that he was an extremely virtuous man.

Cricket

The first game of cricket appears to have been played in the 16th century, although there are reports of Cistercian Monks in Guildford having invented the game in the 13th century. They developed the game to illustrate the doctrine of the Holy Trinity, the bowler representing Satan.

Swiss Guard

Since this time, the fearless Swiss pikemen have been the personal bodyguard of the Pope in the Vatican.

1517   Martin Luther

In Germany, in 1517, Martin Luther began to preach that man is saved by faith alone – that sins have no bearing on salvation. When Pope Leo X sent St Cajetan to meet with Luther in 1518 to correct him, Luther refused to discuss the issue. This development was to be of huge religious, as well as political, consequence.

1521   Diet of Worms

In 1521, the Habsburg Emperor Charles called a meeting at Worms with Luther, (the Diet of Worms), after which Charles declared that Luther should receive no support whatsoever (the Edict of Worms).

Henry VIII
Defender of the Faith

In 1521, Henry VIII was awarded the title "Defender of the Faith" by the Pope, for (please note) his *defence* of Catholicism against Luther, in his pamphlet, *In Defence of the Seven Sacraments*. This work not only included a defence of the validity of Papal Supremacy, but it also defended the illegitimacy of divorce. These two points are particularly relevant, and indeed ironic, when one considers why Henry decided to break with Rome about ten years later. Indeed, it may be said to be highly misleading that successive monarchs have continued to proclaim the use of this title, but in defence of *Protestantism*. (This continuing use may be observed on current British coins, represented by the letters, "F. D.")

The Potato
The potato was introduced to Europe from the Andes in South America. It wasn't introduced into England until about 1580.

1527   The Sack of Rome
By this time Protestantism was spreading fast and the Muslims, taking full advantage of the chaos, advanced into Hungary. The Protestant and Muslim soldiers in Rome rioted in 1527 (the Sack of Rome), destroyed countless spiritual and artistic treasures, and temporarily imprisoned Pope Clement VII. The soldiers were somewhat surprisingly under the command of the Spanish Emperor, Charles V, but they were not acting under his orders

Death of Machiavelli
Niccolo Machiavelli, a Florentine statesman and historian, was born in 1469. He is best known for his book *The Prince* which the Church condemned because it declared that any means could be used to maintain authority. His name is now synonymous with treachery, intrigue, subterfuge and even treason. Indeed Satan's nickname "Old Nick" is reckoned to be derived from him.

Cardinal Wolsey and Anne Boleyn
In 1529, Pope Clement VII ruled against Henry VIII getting an annulment of his marriage with Catherine of Aragon, Emperor Charles V's aunt, and daughter of Ferdinand and Isabella. Henry wanted to divorce Catherine and to marry Anne Boleyn (whom some, including Anne's mother, declared to be Henry's own illegitimate daughter). Henry promptly dismissed Cardinal Wolsey, his Chancellor, whom he saw as being responsible for his failure to procure an annulment. In 1533, Henry married Anne.

1531   Death of Zwingli
Ulrich Zwingli was a famous Swiss Protestant reformer, who, amongst other things, called for the removal of saints and icons from churches, and had a strong influence on the wider Reformation (including in England).

1532   Turin Shroud damaged by fire
The damage caused by the fire is still clearly evident and it is this aspect, amongst others, that may have given incorrect radio carbon date readings when the shroud was tested in 1988.

1534   Act of Supremacy
In 1534, Parliament was forced by Henry, who threatened violence on members who did not co-operate, into passing the Act of Supremacy. This Act made Henry, who was neither priest nor in any respect trained as one, head of the Church in England. As such he was given the right to exercise even greater spiritual power than had belonged to popes, apart from the powers of confecting and administering the sacraments.

End of the Middle Ages
1534 is often recognised as being the year that marked the end of the Middle Ages and the start of the modern world (early modern era). It marked the end of papal supremacy in Great Britain.

Chapter 5   Europe and The Reformation

1535   Saints Thomas More and John Fisher martyred.

In 1535, Thomas More and Archbishop John Fisher were beheaded in London for refusing to accept the Act of Supremacy.

Dissolution of the Monasteries

That same year the suppression (destruction) of the monasteries began. Their vast assets, in virtually every case belonging to them as a result of freely given donations, were, in part, taken by Henry for himself and, also in part, given to Henry's favourites. And against this, the social and moral good they did through their hospitals, schools, road building and maintenance, hospitality for travellers and help for the poor, suddenly ceased, instigating an era of major poverty and hardship.

1536   Calvin

In France in 1536, John Calvin proposed a detailed scheme for the new religion that had emerged in Europe following Luther's reforms, from which he departed into an even more extreme form of Protestantism (Calvinism) which John Knox embraced and was very effective at preaching in Scotland. His religion (which taught that God created most people in order to send them to Hell) formed the basis of the doctrines of those reformed religions that are not Lutheran. It stresses man's total depravity, that the church should control the state and that "the elect" (later identified as those who were materially successful) are predestined for salvation with everyone else predestined for damnation. Of all the Protestant forms of belief it was to be the most influential.

The Protestant religion

The new Protestant religion (which was called Protestant because it <u>protested</u> against papal authority) called for war against the Catholic Church throughout Europe, with the demand that all who refused to give up their faith should be put to the sword. In view of this threat, the Catholic Church decided to defend itself vigorously and this led to the "Counter-Reformation" – see 1562.

The long-term effect of the Reformation was the introduction of Protestant thinking. This was to divide the world into two separate political systems. Whereas before the Reformation, authority came from God and the Catholic Church, afterwards it came either from the state (eventually Socialism and Communism) or from one's personal beliefs, whatever they might be; and this adoption of personal authority has led to the development of both Capitalism and Rationalism. Since the Reformation there has been no single institution in Europe unifying it and supplying the people with ethical guidance, which it then enforces.

Book burning

One of the greatest tragedies (and there were many great tragedies) of the Reformation, was the systematic destruction by fire of the books of the old religion. The spiritual masterpieces, as well as the books of mediaeval history were piled high and set alight. The monastic libraries were obliterated and their other possessions either destroyed or given away to Henry VIII's favourites.

Stifling of the circulation of knowledge

Before the Reformation, abbots in England would meet every year to disseminate knowledge of scientific advances. It is generally reckoned that the Reformation delayed the Industrial Revolution by two and a half centuries. Indeed, in 1550, no degree of any kind was taken at Oxford University.

Enclosures

In the mid-16th century, the enclosure of common land (enclosing what had hitherto been enjoyed by the community, and denying access by the community to it) curtailed common grazing rights and caused wide-spread hardship.

Originally, enclosing land had begun in the 12th century and had resulted in more efficient farming methods because it led to discrete farming areas being farmed systematically, mainly under monastic supervision. After the Reformation, when so much land was handed to the favourites of Henry VIII, the new owners saw how much more productive and therefore profitable the enclosed lands were and tended to keep the poor and their animals from using such areas.

By the early 18th century, almost all common land had been enclosed but the General Enclosure Acts of that time established procedures to safeguard tenant rights.

Anne Boleyn beheaded

In 1536, Henry divorced Anne Boleyn and then had her executed. He declared her daughter Elizabeth illegitimate and had her barred from succeeding to the throne. He married Jane Seymour (followed by three subsequent wives). Henry himself died in 1547.

Death of Erasmus

Born in Rotterdam, Desiderius Erasmus was a Dutch scholar, the most influential of Renaissance thinkers and a leading humanist (Humanism attaches prime importance to human rather than divine matters). He visited England and became a close friend of St Thomas More.

Khair-ed-din Barbarossa

A fleet under the command of this Turkish pirate defeated the Spanish Navy and gave Turkey control of the Mediterranean until 1571.

1540   The Plus Sign

This is the first time that the plus (+) and minus (-) sign is used. They were introduced by Jesuits who had invented them. The equals (=) sign first appeared in 1557.

1545   Mary Rose (Henry VIII's Flagship) sank. (It was raised in 1982.)

1553   Queen Mary

In 1553, Mary reigned in England until her death five years later (succeeding her half-brother, Edward, who reigned from age 9-15 and was a Protestant, under the control of Protestant advisers). When she ascended the throne, Parliament and the people immediately, voluntarily and enthusiastically, re-embraced the Catholic faith. Indeed, her accession to the throne and procession through London to claim it, was probably the most popularly endorsed, seeing, proportionately, the largest crowds, in England's entire history.

She is unfairly called "Bloody Mary" as a reflection of the 287 Protestants who were executed during her reign, all of who were executed for undoubted crimes, and which figure must be viewed in its proper historical context. All countries punished unrepented heresy by execution (usually burning), and some of its most enthusiastic proponents were Protestants, like Hugh Latimer. What is also often overlooked is that in her sister Elizabeth's reign, there were many more executions, particularly of priests and other Catholics, and Mary herself was not directly responsible for these death sentences (rather, any zeal that did exist may be attached to local judges and magistrates, but even then the number is comparatively low, compared with the number of Catholics killed under Elizabeth I, for instance – priests were executed under Elizabeth on the pretext that merely *being* a Catholic priest was a capital offence).

Mary's chief religious adviser was (the in fact rather progressive) Cardinal Pole, who was the last Catholic Archbishop of Canterbury and who, with Mary's husband, Philip II of Spain, was against capital punishment for heresy, and who implemented the policies of the "Counter-Reformation" with great success, in such a short time, in England.

1555   Peace of Augsburg
By the Peace of Augsburg, 1555, Protestants were allowed to practice their religion in the Holy Roman Empire if their nobleman was a Protestant. Emperor Charles died in 1556, having fought tirelessly against the advance of Protestantism, but after his death, a German principality, the Palatinate, became the main base for Calvinism.

1558   Queen Elizabeth I
Anne Boleyn's daughter, Elizabeth I, reigned from 1558 to 1603, in spite of having been barred from the throne by her father, King Henry VIII. While she had acceded to the throne as a Catholic, almost immediately after her accession, the Protestants, who surrounded her, arranged for their faith to be restored on a nationwide basis; and this in spite of the fact that the majority of the country wished to remain Catholic. Elizabeth was persuaded by her advisers to revert to the Protestant faith and thereafter she persecuted those who practised her deceased half-sister's faith. Accordingly, during her reign, there was a fierce campaign against Catholics. For example the priest holes that are sometimes found in sixteenth-century houses, used for hiding priests and vestments, etc., were constructed around this time.

Mary Queen of Scots
Elizabeth imprisoned her cousin Mary Queen of Scots for 18 years. This was because of the threat from Mary's rightful claim to the English throne. However, rather than representing such a threat to Elizabeth, Mary had fled to England seeking both a refuge as well as safety from the hostility of the Protestant Scots.

1559   Philip II and El Escorial
In 1559, Philip II, King of Spain, began to build El Escorial, a monastery and palace, in thanksgiving for his victory at the Battle of San Quentin over the French.

Philip ruled for most of the turbulent years of the sixteenth century and among his many interesting and notable involvements in it included:
- His marriage to Mary Tudor, Queen of England.
- His sending the Spanish Armada to invade England in 1588.
- His establishment and management of a vast Spanish Empire.
- His somewhat deformed son Don Carlos about whom Verdi wrote an opera.
- His half-brother, John of Austria (Don Juan) who was famous for leading the Spanish, Papal and Venetian fleets to victory against the Turks at Lepanto.

1560   Huguenots
In the 1560s, Calvinism became a powerful factor in France, with many nobles adopting it as their faith. The nobles saw it as a means of increasing their power at the expense of the King's authority, even though the great majority of ordinary French people remained Catholic. The French followers of this new religion were called Huguenots, a name attached to them by Catholics, in the same way that Catholics were called "Papists" by Protestants. The name "Huguenot" comes from the French town of Hugue, where they had met.

Puritans and Anabaptists
In Britain, some believed the Church of England still held on to too many Catholic trappings and this led to the development of the Puritan movement, which would last until it ultimately collapsed in 1660 after Cromwell's tenure. A related faith, Anabaptism, a rigorous version of Protestantism and which fostered the practice of adult baptism, had begun in 1521. Anabaptism

developed in Switzerland and Germany, especially Münster, and its members proved to be the forerunners of the Jacobins in France, some 200 years later where they instituted the Reign of Terror.

1562   The Counter-Reformation

St Ignatius of Loyola and the Jesuits

In 1522, St Ignatius of Loyola, in Spain, began his life's work as a Catholic, wrote his *Spiritual Exercises* and founded the Jesuit Order in 1534. His most important disciple and a very great friend was St Francis Xavier. St Ignatius sent missionaries to England, Brazil, India and Japan. The missions in the last two being founded by St Francis Xavier.

The Jesuits brought more with them to the Far East than the Catholic Faith; they were teachers, particularly of scientific method. Indeed, had not the work of St Francis Xavier and his followers been crushed at the instigation of Protestant traders from Holland and England, Japan and other nations in that area would now be Christian and what a different place the world would have been.

The main body of scientists within the Catholic Church were Jesuits.

The Council of Trent

In 1562 and 1563, a Catholic Council at Trent defined many dogmas of the Church in order to defend Catholic Truth against the perversions and errors so successfully promulgated by the Protestant movements. In addition, the Council addressed some abuses that had crept into its houses, introducing measures to counter them.

Amongst those who made sure the Church put its own house in order at this time, and their main areas of influence, were:

Pope St Pius V	Rome
St Charles Borromeo	Milan
St Teresa of Avila	Spain
St John of the Cross	Spain
St Philip Neri	Rome
St Peter Canisius	S Germany & Poland
St Francis de Sales	France
St Jane Frances de Chantal	France
St Francis Xavier	India, China and Japan
St Alphonsus Liguori	Both great spiritual writers
St Robert Bellarmine	in Italy who encouraged resistance to the Reformation.

However, in spite of the works of these saints, as we have seen, the Catholic Church found it constantly had to defend itself against the various assaults of Protestantism. This very defence led others to accuse the Catholic Church of being reactionary.

Baroque

The Baroque style of art and architecture complemented the "Counter-Reformation" (see St Peter's in Rome). Baroque is an Italian style of architecture, bold and confident in its depiction and representation of the Catholic Faith, and is a name which is also given to the music of various composers of the time, including Protestant Handel, who, as we see later, died in 1759.

1565   Siege of Malta
Seeing this religious upheaval, the Turks under Suleiman the Magnificent now threatened to invade Europe from the South. They tried to crush Malta under La Vallette, but the Christians in Malta, with Spanish help, heroically drove them away in 1565.

Spanish Netherlands
Spain controlled the Netherlands and this led to the Dutch Protestants wanting independence – the situation was made worse by the fact that Philip's son Carlos wanted to join the Protestants.

1566   Death of Nostradamus
Michel de Nostradamus was a French Jewish astrologer with extraordinary powers of prediction, that even today are the subject of much controversy. He was born in 1503.

Notzie Scritte
In 1566, the Vatican issued its first official newspaper.

1571   Battle of Lepanto
In 1571, Philip's half-brother, Don Juan, led the Christian forces against the Turkish fleet at Lepanto, near Greece, and won a decisive victory. The Turks had become a threat to the whole of Christendom in Europe and this victory finally ended their pretensions.

1572   St Bartholomew's Day Massacre
Prior to this massacre and for a number of years, there had been a great deal of unrest in France between Catholics and Huguenots. In 1572, and in an attempt to protect the Catholic Faith in France, Catherine de Medici provoked her son King Charles IX into ordering the killing of Huguenots in Paris, beginning on 23rd August, the eve of the Feast of St Bartholomew. It is estimated that Charles' soldiers killed nearly 5,000 Huguenots.

1578   The Holy Shroud moves to Turin
In 1578, Turin became the present home of the Holy Shroud.

1580   Palladio
Andrea Palladio (who died this year), an Italian renaissance architect, was born in 1508. He formed his ideas from the architecture of ancient Rome. One of his most famous buildings is San Giorgio Maggiore in Venice. His ideas were much in fashion in England in the early 17th century, where he influenced Inigo Jones and Sir Christopher Wren.

1581   Ivan the Terrible
In 1581, Ivan, the first Russian Tsar, having attacked his nobles, the Boyars, whom he saw as traitors, murdered his son and heir with his own hands.

1583   Galileo
Galileo Galilei founded the modern science of dynamics. He observed a lamp in the cathedral in Pisa and noted the way it swung. While he didn't invent the pendulum, within thirty years, and as a result of work by Jesuit researchers, it would be introduced into clocks. Galileo was criticised by the Catholic Church, not for his theories about heliocentricity, but because he insisted he was right before his theory had been proven. The Church is, and always has been, supportive of scientific endeavour, but it is equally and sensibly cautious about allowing unproved theories to be treated as fact until they have been proved.

1585   Belgium splits from Holland
By 1585, the Protestant Dutch, with British help, had been rebelling against the Catholic Habsburgs. The Netherlands were then divided – Holland became Protestant and Belgium remained Catholic. In due course (1830 – Belgian Revolution), Belgium would itself be split into a

Flemish North (Protestant and pro-Dutch) and a Walloon South (Catholic and pro-French), which is how things are today.

1586   Babington Plot
The circumstances surrounding this failed plot to rescue Mary Queen of Scots are disputed. Some say that it was incompetently organised, others that it never existed, but was fabricated by Elizabeth I's Secretary of State, Sir Francis Walsingham, and other enemies of Mary, to facilitate her execution the following year.

1587   Execution of Mary Queen of Scots
In February, 1587, after 18 years of being held prisoner by Queen Elizabeth I, Mary Queen of Scots was unjustly executed (some say "judicially murdered") at Fotheringhay Castle on a trumped up charge of treason against her cousin Queen Elizabeth.

1588   Spanish Armada
Outraged by the news of Mary's execution, as well as the unprovoked attack by the English seafarer Sir Francis Drake on Spanish lands and shipping, in the summer of 1588, Philip sent the Spanish Armada to the Netherlands to pick up troops for an invasion of England and to restore Catholicism to Britain. This ended in disaster and great suffering for the Spanish, mainly inflicted by the English fleet under Drake who had gained his maritime skills as a pirate or privateer in the West Indies, attacking Spanish treasure ships. (In the following century, such quasi-legal pirates were known as buccaneers.)

1589   Henry Bourbon
In 1574, Charles IX of France died and three rivals (all named Henri) claimed the throne: Henri III of Valois, who had no heir (and was thus the last Valois King of France – the first having been Phillip VI in 1328), Henri Bourbon of Navarre, a Protestant, and Henri Guise, a Catholic. Henri III assassinated Henri Guise in 1588, and he in turn was killed in 1589. Henri Bourbon, with English money, therefore took control of France, but was received back into the Catholic Church before he died. He started the Bourbon Dynasty which was to last from 1589 to the execution of Louis XVI in 1793. The French Bourbons were to be great rivals of the Spanish Habsburgs until 1683, when Philip V became the first Spanish Bourbon king.

1591   Nine Years War
The struggles in Ireland and Europe between 1591 and 1600 are called the Nine Years War. There is another "nine years war," also known as the War of the League of Augsburg, which took place one hundred years later.

.

Ireland defeats the English
In Ireland, the Catholics under the O'Neills and the O'Donnells defeated the English by 1600, and controlled the island again. At that time, Ulster was particularly anti-English.

Early in the seventeenth century, James I, who had given the Irish the right to practice their religion, attacked Ireland again and began to colonise Ulster with Protestants, mainly from Scotland (the Plantation of Ulster). This was to sow the seed for the troubles that would persist in later centuries and particularly throughout the twentieth century.

1595   Pocahontas
Pocahontas, a Native American princess, was born in 1595. She came to fame through her action in saving the life of one of the early colonists at the hands of her native Indian tribe. She travelled to England, was entertained as a princess at the English Court and married another colonist. She died in 1617, leaving a son.

1598   The Philippines

Before Philip II died in 1598, he had sent missionaries to the New World and particularly to the Philippines which are named after him. Philip is buried in El Escorial.

The Poor Laws

With no monasteries to provide for the relief of misery and destitution, the English Parliament realised that something had to be done for the poor (see also Charities Act 1601). We thus see the start of the Welfare State.

The Edict of Nantes

Henry IV (of Bourbon) issued the Edict of Nantes in 1598, which allowed Protestants freedom to worship in France. He was assassinated in 1610. Unlike Spain, France had no Inquisition and this lack of control left others free to worship as they chose; such freedom was formalised by this edict.

Cardinal Richelieu

Henry IV of France was succeeded by Louis XIII, who left the running of France to his chief minister, Cardinal Richelieu. The Cardinal's main aim was to suppress Protestantism, build up the power of the French crown, and put France into the most powerful position in Europe.

William Cecil dies

Cecil, the first Lord Burghley, was Queen Elizabeth's closest adviser and had been very strongly antagonistic towards the Catholic Church.

Chapter 6   The Gregorian Calendar to Seven Years War

The Scientific Revolution and the Gregorian Calendar is generally accepted

The following are considered to be the most important scientists of the 16th and 17th centuries:

Aloysius Lilius, Antonio Lilius, Christopher Clavius and Pope Gregory XIII	They formalised the calendar in 1582, the last year of Julius Caesar's calendar, the Julian Calendar. On October 4th, 1582, the calendar jumped ten days to October 14th and became the Gregorian calendar used the world over today.
Fr Kircher	Who debunked alchemy and founded the study of Egyptology
Isaac Newton	For his work on motion and gravity. His book *Principia* was published in 1684 with the help of Edmund Halley. While he is regarded as one of the greatest scientists of all time, some of his contemporaries could not understand his mathematics.
William Harvey	Who described the circulation of the blood, although this had been achieved independently by Jesuit researchers.
Johannes Kepler	Who, with invaluable assistance from Jesuit researchers, developed the theory that the planets had elliptical orbits
Nicolaus Copernicus	Promoted the idea of heliocentricity (a sun-centred solar system). He was a Polish astronomer

Metaphysical Poetry
The seventeenth century saw the birth of metaphysical poetry which involves concise verse that uses striking imagery. The foremost metaphysical poet is usually considered to be the Anglican clergyman, John Donne.

Political Parties
This century also saw the launching in England of the first two political parties: Whigs (Liberals) and Tories (Conservatives). However, party politics only became the established norm later in this century during the heated exchanges over whether James II, a Catholic, should be allowed to inherit the crown. Those who supported the Catholic succession were called Tories, a name given to Irish outlaws who plundered English settlers in Ireland (the Tories adopted the name "Conservative" in the 1830s). The term Whig was an abbreviation for Whiggamore, the name given to anti-royalists who had marched on Edinburgh in 1648.

The Stuarts
1601   James I & VI
In 1601, Mary Queen of Scots' son, James VI of Scotland, also became James I of England. His Catholic mother may not have been acceptable as Queen, but he, as a Protestant, was as King. It is interesting to note that Elizabeth I died childless whereas Mary Queen of Scots, through her son James, is the ancestor of all subsequent British monarchs. It was under James I & VI that the crowns of England and Scotland were united

Charities Act
The legal definition of a charity dates back to this Statute of Elizabeth I, of 1601. Prior to this date there were few, if any, charities in existence because, as we have seen, everybody's needs,

including those of the sick and poor, were looked after in Catholic England by the extensive network of monasteries. There was a legal requirement that 1/3 of a monastery's income belonged to the poor and needy and, with a monastery or priory of some religious order approximately every three miles in England, this law ensured that everybody's needs were attended to from the cradle to the grave.

The situation has been described very succinctly by Professor Thomas E. Woods who stated, "The Catholic Church invented charity as we know it in the West." After the Reformation, however, which involved the sudden destruction of the monasteries and the gradual disappearance of the guilds, which also operated under the same Catholic umbrella, the assets, which had been used to alleviate the needs of the poor, etc., including a vast acreage of land and extremely valuable treasures, were taken by Henry VIII who shared his plunder with his equally unscrupulous and greedy supporters. As a result, with no-one looking after the poor and needy, the nation's poverty and misery increased alarmingly. To begin with, the situation was made even worse by the passing of laws against vagrants and begging, but, within a few years, the situation became so desperate that even the rapacious rulers could no longer ignore it. As a result, during the second half of the sixteenth century, a publicly funded system developed whereby taxes paid by the developing middle classes began to alleviate the nation's suffering masses. As we have already mentioned under 1598, we now call this system the Welfare State.

Where the State failed to meet a particular need, well-meaning individuals began to set up their own benevolent institutions to fill the gaps. These institutions needed a legal framework within which to operate and thus we get the Charities Act of 1601.

1605   Gunpowder Plot
In 1605, the Gunpowder Plot resulted in further persecution of Catholics, although there is evidence to show that the plot was, at least in part, fabricated by Protestants with the aim that, through its inevitable and intended discovery, the Catholic Church would be denigrated.

Borghese Family
Paul V, a member of the influential Borghese family, became Pope. The Borghese Palace contains one of the finest collections of paintings in Rome.

1609   The Microscope was invented
The microscope was invented by a Dutch spectacle maker, Zacharias Janssen. It wasn't used in medicine until the eighteenth century.

1610   Tea and Coffee
This was the year tea was introduced into Europe by the Dutch.

Coffee drinking had begun in Arab countries in the fourteenth century, and coffee houses were opened throughout Europe in the 17th century.

1615   Harrow School
Harrow took its first pupils in 1615.

1616   Shakespeare dies.
William Shakespeare, England's greatest dramatist and poet, was born in 1564. Having said that he died in 1616, this generally accepted fact introduces just one of the mysteries about him. Some claim that many of his plays were written years after this date. Other mysteries include the apparent code on his monument in Westminster Abbey and the exact nature of his relationship with Francis Bacon? There is also very convincing evidence to suggest that he was a Catholic (and that this is discernible in his plays as well).

1618   Defenestration of Prague

In 1618, in an attempt to safeguard Catholicism in Bohemia, the Archbishop of Prague transferred local administrative power to ten governors, seven of whom were Catholic. On 23rd May, the Protestants in Prague seized two Catholic governors and threw them out of a window (the Defenestration of Prague), although they escaped with their lives. These events severely weakened the standing of the Catholic Church in Bohemia and, in 1619, following the death of Emperor Mathias, the Elector of Palatine, Protestant Frederick V, was elected Emperor instead of the devout Catholic Ferdinand, King of Bohemia.

The Thirty Years War (Following on from the Defenestration of Prague)

However, at another election a few days later, Ferdinand was indeed elected Emperor. Nevertheless, Catholicism was not saved by his election. The dispute led to The Thirty Years War between Germany and Denmark, with British and Dutch help on one side, and Catholic Austria and France on the other. The war lasted until 1648 and the signing of the Treaty of Westphalia. One result of the war was that Christendom was permanently split and Habsburg influence was severely weakened. In addition, with the Germans having been defeated, the Protestant population in the North was rescued and protected by Gustavus Adolphus of Sweden. With Germany thus divided, France under Richelieu was left in a very powerful position.

Execution of Sir Walter Raleigh

Raleigh, a highly favoured and renowned English courtier, had been rewarded with gifts of huge lands in Ireland, by Queen Elizabeth I. He was an adventurer and had made exploratory voyages to North and South America. He brought back tobacco and is popularly held to be the first European to smoke a pipe and to have introduced the potato into Britain. He was an author and historian, but his aggression against Spain brought him disfavour with James I, and hence his execution in 1618.

1620   Pilgrim Fathers

In 1620, a group of English men and women who wished for a simpler, more radical Protestant religion, and did not want to attend the official Protestant services in England, sailed from Plymouth in the Mayflower for America. They were non-conformists and separatists from the Church of England (largely English Congregationalists), but some two hundred years later became known as the Pilgrim Fathers.

1621   Newspapers in Britain

The first titled newspaper, *Corante,* appeared in Britain.

1629   Ship Money

In 1629, Charles I began to rule without Parliament for 11 years, raising taxes by the unpopular tax known as Ship Money.

The Covenanters.

Charles I, who had Catholic leanings, introduced a High Church prayer book (known as "Laud's Book," after Archbishop Laud) for Scotland in 1637, which the majority of Scots rejected in favour of Calvinism. To show their opposition to High Church thinking, the Scots signed a Covenant in Greyfriars church in Edinburgh, and became known as Covenanters.

1636   Harvard University

The first American University was founded at Cambridge, Massachusetts, in 1639, largely for the training of Congregationalist ministers, and was named Harvard (after John Harvard, its first benefactor).

1638   The Sun King and Versailles

When Louis XIV became King of France (1638) he took a strong hold on government, and built the enormous Palace of Versailles. He is known as the Sun King for the splendour of his reign and for extending prestigious patronage of the arts. The style that he influenced is known to this day as "Louis Quartorze." He reigned for 72 years and is the longest reigning French monarch.

1640   The Short and the Long Parliaments

Charles I waged two unsuccessful wars against Scotland in 1640. He dissolved Parliament within a month of elections (the Short Parliament, which lasted for only April and May of that year). He did so because the Puritan majority refused to vote for money for the crown and strongly criticised Charles I's ecclesiastical policy. He had conducted personal rule without Parliament for the previous eleven years. The Parliament which met later that year lasted for 13 years and is known as the Long Parliament.

1641   The Grand Remonstrance

In November 1641, Parliament passed the Grand Remonstrance, which was a list of supposed acts of misrule by Charles I and which condemned the King's ecclesiastical policies. The leader of the House, John Pym, stirred up fervent anti-Catholicism.

The First Calculator

Blaise Pascal, a mathematician, scientist and theological controversialist (he supported Jansenism, a rigorist movement which sought to radically limit the number of the Elect), in France, built the first calculator. He also worked with the Jesuit mathematician, Fermat, whose famous last theorem was solved in 1993.

Descartes

Descartes, who wrote *Meditation on the First Philosophy*, was a leading developer of the ideas of Metaphysics, the subject that is concerned with the nature and origin of existence. His most famous statement is *"Cogito Ergo Sum"* ("I think, therefore I am").

The English Civil War

Charles began to organise his supporters (Cavaliers) for war, and Parliament replied by putting Oliver Cromwell in charge of their army (Roundheads). The chief battles in the first civil war were:

Edgehill	1642
Marston Moor	1644
Naseby	1645

(N.B. There is much more detail on this topic – the English Civil War – as well as others in the History Notes section.)

1644   New York

In this year, the Dutch, under the authority of Director-General Peter Stuyvesant, surrendered what, in 1622, they had called New Amsterdam to the British. The British later renamed it New York, after James Duke of York who, with his elder brother Charles, were the sons of King Charles I. Charles was to become King Charles II and James, King James II.

1648   Pride's Purge

Colonel Sir Thomas Pride expelled those Royalist members of Parliament who tried to negotiate a settlement with the defeated Charles I. The minority of members who were left constituted the Rump Parliament.

Freemasons

At this time, Freemasons were usually Royalists who supported the restoration of the Catholic Faith in Britain and even Jesuits sought admittance to work with Freemasons. However, after its merger with Illuminism, Freemasonry became staunchly anti-Catholic (See also 1717AD and 1776AD). There are various degrees of Freemasonry into which members are initiated by a set of curious rituals. As they advance in this society, members are privileged to learn certain secrets that they are forbidden to reveal to others, under chilling oaths.

The main tenets of Freemasonry are now:
- Liberalism in matters of religion
- Internationalism and not patriotism
- That it is a society of mutual help and fellowship.

1649   Charles I executed
Cromwell, with his New Model Army also won the brief second civil war in 1648 at the Battle of Preston. Charles was beheaded in January 1649, after a trial for which there was neither precedent in history nor any legal basis, as a "tyrant and public enemy," etc. Cromwell called it a "cruel necessity."

Levellers
Later that year, the Levellers, a political group founded by John Lilburne, called for the "levelling of all differences of position or rank amongst men," and also for the abolition of the House of Lords, as well as the Monarchy.

Cromwell as Lord Protector
Cromwell dismissed what was left of the Long Parliament (which, as we have just seen, became known as the Rump) in 1649, abolished the Monarchy, suppressed the celebration of Christmas and, calling himself Lord Protector, ruled as a dictator. He declared England to be a Commonwealth or Free State. In 1656, and without repealing the 1290 Act of Parliament, he allowed the Jews to return to England during his Protectorate.

Cromwell attacks Ireland
Ireland rose in support of Charles II (Charles I's son) and Cromwell retaliated by laying siege to Drogheda and Wexford, killing many thousands and subduing the whole island. His troops massacred the entire Catholic garrisons of those towns for their refusal to surrender to the Parliamentary forces.

Charles II hides in an oak tree
In June, 1649, Charles II, hoping to regain his crown, landed in Scotland, was defeated in battles at Dunbar and Worcester, and fled to France. On his flight he had to hide in the Royal Oak of Boscobel.

1651   Thomas Hobbes published The Leviathan
Hobbes was considered to be the first English Protestant philosopher and he favoured absolutist government. His book caused a sensation because it upset both Parliamentarians as well as Royalists.

1653   Barebones Parliament
This was a short-lived Parliament named after one of its leading figures "Praise God" Barebones, which resigned its powers to Cromwell and was dissolved. It is also sometimes referred to as the "Parliament of saints."

1656   St Peter's in Rome completed

1658   Tumbledown Dick

Cromwell died in 1658 and his son Richard assumed the title of Lord Protector. However, the people, who resented the way that Puritanism was being established by force, were ready to welcome Charles II as King. Richard Cromwell, known as Tumbledown Dick, resigned in 1659.

1660   Restoration of the Monarchy

Charles II was formally invited to return by a group of men led by General Monk. Monk, later 1st Duke of Albemarle, had originally been a Royalist, but swore allegiance to the Parliamentary cause to fight the Irish under Cromwell. Charles was a Protestant and signed the Clarendon Code in 1661 which asserted the supremacy of the Church of England over the Catholic cause.

Charles's main political advisers were **C**lifford, **A**shley Cooper, **B**uckingham, **A**rlington and **L**auderdale – from which we get the term "Cabal."

Royal Society founded

This is the premier scientific society in Great Britain, and numbers Isaac Newton amongst its members. In 1857 it moved to Burlington House, just off Piccadilly, in London.

Transatlantic Trade and Limited Companies

Records show that by this time great wealth was arriving in Europe from the colonies across the Atlantic, mainly thanks to the institution of slavery. This trade led to the first limited companies being formed. Lloyds Insurance also began in Mr Lloyd's coffee house in 1687 with the "Lloyd's List" beginning in 1696.

1661   First bank notes

A bank in Stockholm introduced the first paper money to be circulated in Europe.

1664   Trappist Monks

Armand de Rance founded a reformed version of the Catholic Cistercian order (see 1230) at La Trappe in Normandy. This version is characterised by strict silence, labour and abstinence from fleshmeat (which had fallen out of observance in monasteries following the Rule of St Benedict). With a few exceptions, the monks communicated in sign language.

1666   The Great Fire of London

1669   Rembrandt dies

This prolific Dutch painter had been born in 1606.

1670   Spinoza

Spinoza published a *Treatise on Religious and Political Philosophy*. He was a free-thinking Dutch Jew who rejected the concept of Free Will. He was excommunicated by the Sephardic Jews from the Amsterdam synagogue for his heresy. He promoted Pantheism, which regards the natural world as being divine.

1673   Molière dies

Born as Jean-Baptiste Poquelin in 1622, he became the father of modern French comedy.

1678   Titus Oates and the Popish Plot

In England, in 1678, after the Test Act (1672) which required every official to be Protestant, Titus Oates fabricated the Popish Plot by spreading the rumour that the Pope had ordered Jesuits to overthrow Protestant Charles II, which, of course, would have been treason. This rumour created anti-Catholic panic and hatred in London, with the Irish priest Bl. Oliver Plunkett being executed on a trumped up charge of high treason. This whole episode was aimed at getting James, Duke of York, who was a convert to Catholicism, excluded from the throne.

1681   William Penn
William Penn was a leading Puritan and writer, who became a Quaker as Puritanism collapsed. In this year he was granted land in North America by Charles II, called Pennsylvania after his father who had the original claim to it.

1685   Charles II converts to Catholicism on his deathbed
In 1685, Charles was received into the Catholic Church the day before he died.

Revocation of Edict of Nantes
Louis, in response to the threat that the Huguenots were posing to France's official religion (Catholicism), revoked the Edict of Nantes, and forced these Protestants to flee from France and settle in countries like England, Holland and Switzerland. In Southern France this sparked a rebellion by Protestants known as Camisards.

Bloody Assizes
In 1685, the Duke of Monmouth led a Protestant invasion force to remove the last English Catholic monarch, James II. The force was defeated at the Battle of Sedgemoor after which Judge Jeffries presided over a series of trials in which those who had sided with Monmouth were brutally punished (the Bloody Assizes).

1688   James II and the (so called) Glorious Revolution
James II's next move was to relax the anti-Catholic laws. As a result of this, the Protestants invited William of Orange and Mary (daughter of James II) to invade in 1688. When William landed in Torbay, James II fled to a life of exile in Paris and this removal of a valid British monarch by an invading foreigner (who was his son-in-law, but had no blood claim to the English throne) is paradoxically known as the Glorious Revolution. While King James II is excoriated by history, he has left us a significant legacy that is hard to dismiss. First of all, as we have seen, New York is named after him. Secondly, before he became King, as Duke of York, he was commander-in-chief of the army and at other times in charge of a joint armed force with both France and Spain. He was also admiral in charge in two of our greatest sea battles fought before Nelson's time; as a result of this he can claim to be the real founder of the modern British Navy.

1688-97   War of the League of Augsburg
This war was fought against France's territorial expansion. France lost and was forced to give Lorraine its independence. This war is also known as the Nine Years War, but it should not be confused with the war of that name that took place one hundred years earlier.

1689   Battle of The Boyne
In 1689, James II landed in Ireland to rally support for his claim to regain the English throne. William of Orange (who, as we have seen, was James's own son-in-law) defeated James's forces at the Battle of the Boyne, on July 12th. The legacy of this battle's victory over Catholicism forms part of the long-running turmoil in Ireland in the centuries that have followed.

1689   Battle of Beachy Head
The French, sailing in support of the exiled James II, inflicted a disastrous defeat on a joint British-Dutch fleet.

1692   Battle of Cap de La Hogue
The British defeated the French navy in this naval battle.

1693   Battle of Cape St Vincent
The French were again victorious over a British fleet at the first battle of Cape St Vincent.

1694   Bank of England founded

The Bank of England was founded as a private company by William of Orange's backers to finance the nation's affairs following the Glorious Revolution. It would later be used to finance the wars that England waged against France and thus the National Debt effectively began at this time and for this purpose. Nowadays, the National Debt is the sum the Government has to borrow to finance all its activities that are not paid for by tax revenue.

While the Bank of England remained privately owned until its subordination to the Treasury in 1931, and nationalisation in 1946, its tiers of ownership are somewhat convoluted and it is still, essentially, like the US Federal Reserve, a private business run by bankers. The reason for this, we are told, is that, logically, a government cannot lend money to itself.

Gentleman in Black Velvet

William of Orange (William III) died when his horse stumbled on a molehill – resulting in English Jacobites (supporters of James II and his heirs) toasting the "gentleman in black velvet."

1695   Window Tax

This was a tax levied on the number of windows in a house, which led to the bricking up of windows in old houses. It was abolished in 1851.

1700   France expands into North America

Louis XIV supported the French exploration of and settlement in North America. By 1700, the new French territory stretched from the Gulf of Mexico to Quebec.

St Vincent de Paul

In Paris, St Vincent de Paul, by means of the order which he founded, the Sisters of Charity, encouraged wealthy ladies to help the poor and destitute, while St Margaret Mary Alacoque encouraged devotion to the Sacred Heart of Jesus, following a vision.

18th Century   Liberals and Despots, Freemasons and Liberalism

In the eighteenth century, Freemasons such as Diderot, Voltaire, Rousseau and Mesmer, began preaching their liberal ideas which attacked all authority, especially that of the Catholic Church. The spirit of Liberalism therefore began to spread over the continent of Europe. The spread of Liberalism resulted, it appeared to begin with, in a more tolerant attitude being shown towards Catholics, which was not what the promoters of Liberalism intended in the longer-term and is certainly not what finally resulted.

Rococo

This movement in arts tending towards light, elegance and more florid delicacy became widespread in France, South Germany and Austria, and grew from the Baroque. It was developed by Oppenord. Its literal meaning is "rockwork" and its influence was to lead to the Neo-Classical style.

Jansenism

This heresy, characterised by excessive rigorism in its moral code and most aspects of the spiritual life, was condemned by the Church in 1713. A Jansenist crucifix portrays the arms of Christ hanging very nearly vertically, exaggerating the narrowness of the path to salvation and fewness of the saved.

1701   War of the Spanish Succession

The War of the Spanish Succession was triggered by the French King Louis XIV's wish to carry out the dying wishes of Charles II, the last Habsburg King of Spain, and place his own grandson, Philip of Anjou, on the Spanish throne. England, the Dutch republic and the Holy Roman Empire formed an alliance in opposition to the economic threat posed by this union of France with Spain. This led to a war against France that began in 1701 and lasted until the Treaty of Utrecht in 1712. The result of the war was that, while it brought an end to French expansionism under Louis XIV, it was the French Bourbon claimant that was preferred to the Austrian Habsburg Leopold I. The English general, the Duke of Marlborough, won the battles of Blenheim, Ramilles, Oudinarde and Malplaquet – all against the French. Marlborough was granted Blenheim Palace in Oxfordshire as a reward.

The Act of Settlement
In England, an Act was passed preventing any Catholic from becoming monarch or marrying a monarch. The Act stipulated that the monarch must be a Protestant.

Yale University
This university was founded at New Haven, Connecticut.

The status of Kingdom was conferred upon the Dukedom of Prussia.
Under Frederick II, Prussia expanded to take in Silesia and was eventually to emerge as the most powerful German State.

1703   Buckingham Palace built
This was originally built for the Duke of Buckingham but was bought by George III in 1762 and reconstructed by John Nash. A new front was added in 1913.

1705   Halley's Comet
This was the year Sir Edmund Halley identified a number of comets, including the one which returns every 76 years and is named after him. It was next to return in 1758. He also rediscovered how to predict eclipses, a skill that had been developed by the Greeks two thousand years before, but was lost.

1707   Act of Union between England and Scotland
Under this Act, England and Wales united with Scotland to form Great Britain.

1713   The Treaty of Utrecht and Gibraltar
Under the Treaty of Utrecht, Gibraltar was ceded to Britain, but to this day Spain continues to claim sovereignty in spite of fierce loyalty to Britain amongst the Gibraltarians.

Pragmatic Sanction
While this edict had been in existence for many centuries, the term "Pragmatic Sanction" is usually applied to this particular Habsburg-family law in 1713, which decreed who was to inherit the Habsburg lands, and that they should not be divided. It was devised by Charles VI.

1715   The '15 Rebellion
In 1715, James, son of James II, landed in Britain to promote what Rome and a number of European countries regarded as his legitimate claim to the British throne. He lost the Battle of Sherriffmuir and retreated. His forces were called Jacobites and were led by the Earl of Mar, known as Bobbing John. After the rebellion, General Wade built a system of military roads with which to control Scotland.

This James is known by his enemies as "The Old Pretender." He had two sons, Charles (Bonnie Prince Charlie - by contrast, "The Young Pretender") and Henry who was a cardinal. After Charles' death, and for those who recognised the Jacobite cause, Henry became the only cardinal-king in history. Henry, whose grandfather, James II, had fled from England with the crown jewels, returned them.

1717   Freemasonry established in London

Freemasonry, the secret society which by this time had developed a strong anti-Catholic stance, set up its first lodge in London in 1717. This lodge is considered to be the "Mother Grand Lodge," or the most senior in the world.

1721   Sir Robert Walpole

He was effectively the first British Prime Minister. Until the reign of George I, who spoke no English, the monarch chaired cabinet meetings. (It was not until 1905 that the term "prime minister" was formally acknowledged.) Sir Robert lived at No. 10 Downing Street, his official residence.

His brother-in-law, Charles Townshend, better known as Turnip Townshend, is renowned for his encouragement of improved farming methods.

1723   Après moi le deluge

King Louis XV was a weak king whose reign discredited the French crown and led eventually to the French Revolution. He was dominated by his powerful mistress, Madame Pompadour. He cared little for his responsibilities, declaring: "Après moi le deluge."

Peter the Great

In Russia, Peter the Great, of the Romanov family, began to westernise the country in the 18th century, and moved his capital from Moscow to St Petersburg.

The Old Catholic Church

A group of Catholics in Utrecht, Holland, founded what would be called the "Old Catholic Church" which, like other "reformed" religions, would reject certain Catholic dogmas. In due course and after the First Vatican Council, they would reject the dogma of papal infallibility. The Old Catholic Church today is now heavily fragmented into different sects and is in full communion with the Church of England.

Catherine the Great

When Peter the Great died, his nephew, Peter, became Tsar in 1725. When Peter died, his German widow Catherine ruled Russia and made it very powerful. She is known as Catherine the Great.

1727   Rob Roy

In 1727, Rob Roy (Robert Macgregor), a famous Scottish outlaw and champion of oppressed Scots, was pardoned for his behaviour as a brigand. He is believed to have become a Catholic before he died.

1737   Death of Antonio Stradivari

This most famous violin maker worked in Cremona and his instruments are known by the Latin version of his name, Stradivarius. One may be seen on public display at the Ashmolean Museum in Oxford. His violins, violas and cellos are still reckoned to be the finest.

1738   John Wesley/Methodism

In 1738, Wesley, who was an Anglican, founded Methodism, which was an attempt at evangelical renewal/revival in the Church of England. The Anglicans forced them out of their churches to preach in the open air, and from this a separate church was born.

Value Pricing

This was also the year in which a paper by Bernoult, a Swiss mathematician, was presented to the Imperial Academy of Sciences at St Petersburg. It developed the notion that the value of an item should not be based on its cost (time spent to make it, materials, processing, etc.), but rather on the utility that it yields. The former is one of the tenets of Communism (see Marx 1848), whereas the latter is a tenet of Capitalism. In effect, Bernoult launched the notion of the free market economy which can be traced back to a 13th Century Franciscan friar called Pierre de Jean Olivi and even, it could be argued, to St Augustine of Hippo, though the Catholic Church advocates neither Capitalism nor Communism, citing grave, materialist errors in both.

1741   Frederick the Great and the War of the Austrian Succession
In Austria, the Habsburg Maria Theresa became Holy Roman Empress in 1740. In spite of signing the Pragmatic Sanction which offered support and security to her, her Protestant neighbours in Prussia, under Frederick the Great, annexed the Austrian province of Silesia. In the ensuing war, France and Spain sided with Prussia, and Britain supported Maria Theresa. Austria won the Battle of Dettingen against the French and Prussians in 1743, at which the combined British and Austrian forces were commanded by King George II – the last occasion when a British Monarch led his nation's forces into battle. In 1746, however, when the British went to her aid again, they were defeated by the French under Marshall Saxe at Fontenoy. The war lasted for seven years and, although Silesia was granted to Prussia at the Treaty of Aix la Chapelle, as a result of her ultimate victory, Maria made Austria a very powerful force in Europe.

Dettingen was also the last battle in which the Yeomen of the Guard (Beefeaters) fought. These now ceremonial guards were established by Henry VII in 1485 as the bodyguard of the British sovereign. They are not the same body as the Yeoman Warders who guard the Tower of London.

1745   Bonnie Prince Charlie and the 1745 Rising
Thirty years after his father's attempt to regain the crown for the Stuarts, Bonnie Prince Charlie, "The Young Pretender," decided to try again.

He landed at Glenfinnan (west coast of Scotland) and within a month had reached Edinburgh where he defeated the English at Prestonpans. After reaching Derby, by which time the Hanoverian King George II had packed his possessions and was ready to flee, Bonnie Prince Charlie, with victory in his grasp, was betrayed by General Murray, who persuaded the Highland chiefs that they should retreat.

1746   Battle of Culloden
The English, under the Duke of Cumberland (son of George II), chased the retreating Bonnie Prince Charlie and defeated him at Culloden on 17th April 1746. The defeated Scots were treated with great cruelty and many were killed by "Butcher" Cumberland, but after an exciting pursuit, Bonnie Prince Charlie escaped to France.

This rising ended all Jacobite hopes of both unseating the Protestant Hanoverian kings, as well as successfully pursuing their claim to the British throne – a claim widely recognised in Europe.

"God Save Our Gracious Queen (King)"
The Jacobite rising also resulted in the National Anthem being written and sung, to a tune by Thomas Arne, to encourage a show of patriotism in defiance of future attacks of this nature.

1748   Trooping the Colour
This annual parade began this year, to celebrate the monarch's official birthday.

1750   Johann Sebastian Bach dies
This prolific German composer, who had been born in 1685, was one of the supremely great composers and one of the founders of what is now called classical music.

1751   Gin Act

Gin was being drunk in London to such an extent that the city was said to be addicted to it; indeed Hogarth's prints are now famous for depicting the horrors that ensued from excessive gin consumption. This Act imposed a heavy duty on the drink and decreed that only licensed dealers could sell it.

1752   Britain finally adopts the Gregorian Reformed New Style Calendar

In Britain, eleven days were removed from the calendar with September 2nd being followed by September 14th. This move was very unpopular with the public. Rioters in London shouted, "Give us back our eleven days." In addition to this change, and henceforth, the year in Britain began on 1st January, and not 25th March.

The UK tax year however continues to begin, not on 25th March, but twelve days later on 6th April. This is not only because the Treasury thought they might lose eleven days of income as a result of the change and extended the end of income tax year to compensate, but they exacerbated the confusion by wrongly believing that the year 1800 was a leap year, and thus added an extra day to the eleven. This is why the income tax year ends on 5th April, despite calls to change it to a more convenient date.

1753   British Museum was founded

1755   Lisbon Earthquake

Until the Asian tsunami in 2004, this was probably the most catastrophic earthquake and tsunami in human history. It destroyed the city of Lisbon and killed over 30,000 people.

1756   The Seven Years War

Britain, Prussia and Hanover fought against France, Austria, Russia and Spain for overseas supremacy in the Seven Years War (1756-1763). The war was precipitated by Austria's desire to regain Silesia from Prussia.

During the war, in 1759, the French attempted an invasion of Britain, but were routed at Quiberon Bay, off Brittany.

In due course Russia defected to support Prussia, a move which would leave Prussia the dominant power in Europe. Elsewhere the British won a series of spectacular victories in India (under Clive) and in Canada (under Wolfe) and, by the Treaty of Paris, Britain was confirmed as the supreme world power. Thereafter, Britain began to develop the British Empire with possessions in America, India and the Antipodes. It would eventually cover ¼ of the globe and become the biggest empire the world had ever seen.

Black Hole of Calcutta

The Nawab of Bengal confined 146 British prisoners in one small room on 20th June – only 25 survived.

1759   Handel dies

George Frederick Handel, the famous musician and composer, who was born in Germany in 1685, became a British subject in 1726. He is strongly associated with the Baroque movement in music.

Chapter 7   American War of Independence to First Vatican Council

1768   Encyclopaedia Britannica
This was the date of its first publication in Scotland. Since 1929 it has been published in the USA.

Canaletto dies
This Italian painter from Venice, whose real name was Antonio Canal, is famous for his oil paintings of his home city, as well as of England. He was born in 1697.

1769   Mason Dixon Line
Two British surveyors, Charles Dixon and Jeremiah Mason, settled the line of the border between Pennsylvania and Maryland – a border that was to become world famous as the dividing line between the "slave states" and the "free states" in the American Civil War.

1772   Advances in astronomy and map-making
The surveyor and Astronomer Royal, Nevill Maskelyne, together with the mathematician, Charles Hutton, estimated the mass of the Earth, Sun, Moon and planets by measuring the mass of the Scottish Tayside mountain Schiehallion. Hutton also invented contour lines on maps

1773   Jesuits suppressed
Due to pressure from European rulers, who cited alleged abuses in the order, Pope Clement XIV suppressed the Society of Jesus (Jesuits). It was reinstated in 1814.

1775   American War of Independence
While the British claimed that, under their rule, the Americans were the freest people on earth, the Americans declared that they found the English arrogant and hostile towards them, and revolted. Indeed, there was massive propaganda by the Americans to get the conservatively-minded inhabitants to join the revolt, with many being terrorised into doing so. The Americans won their independence in the American War of Independence (1775 – 1783).

In 1770, the Boston Massacre, 5 Americans were killed by British Troops. In 1773, anger against the English was particularly violent at the Boston Tea Party, when 342 chests of tea were wantonly destroyed by the Americans, one of whom was Paul Revere. Revere is more famous for his action in 1775 when he rode from Concord to Lexington rousing the troops (called "minutemen" because they could be ready within a minute) to take up arms. The British were defeated at the battles of Concorde, Ticonderoga and Saratoga. In due course, one of the American Generals, George Washington, became the first US President, 1789-1797.
What is usually overlooked is that, after the revolution, Americans were less free and taxed more heavily.

Frederick the Great and Prussia
In Prussia, the Protestant part of Northern Germany, the leader, Frederick I (Frederick the Great, from the Hohenzollern family), had expanded his kingdom, thus making it the most powerful German State by about 1750. In 1775, Frederick finally suppressed the calendar used by Protestants, namely the Julian calendar, and adopted the Catholic Gregorian one.

1776   The American Declaration of Independence was signed in 1776.
The Declaration was adopted by the 13 colonies of North America that announced their independence from Britain. The Declaration, written by Thomas Jefferson, is one of the most influential proclamations in Western political tradition.

Death of John Harrison
He was the English inventor of the chronometer, a time-keeping apparatus with compensating mechanisms that could work at sea, or in any climate. This made time-keeping at sea, and

therefore measurement of longitude, much more accurate. His contribution towards safety at sea is greatly under-appreciated and at the time the Admiralty made it very difficult for him to be recognised and rewarded for his achievement.

Adam Weishaupt

In 1776, Weishaupt founded the Order of the Illuminati, a highly secretive organisation that determined on the overthrow of the Catholic Church and the initiation of a New World Order founded on the principles that we now call Communism. His five openly declared aims were:

- Abolition of monarchies
- Abolition of private property and inheritances
- Abolition of patriotism and nationalism
- Abolition of marriage and family life and the establishment of communal upbringing of children
- Abolition of all religions.

By 1782, Illuminism had been suppressed in Bavaria and it merged with European Freemasonry. While the existence of this sort of fearful organisation, which is hidden from and apparently never impinges on ordinary people in their everyday life, may appear fanciful, one member, Professor John Robison from the University of Edinburgh, who did not like what he saw, published a book called "Proofs of a Conspiracy" in which he wrote "[This is] an association [that] has been formed for the express purposes of rooting out all religious establishments and overturning all existing governments...the leaders would rule the World with uncontrollable power, while the rest would be employed as tools of the ambition of their unknown superiors." Indeed, in 1880, Freemasonry would openly declare "Catholicism is our enemy."

Adam Smith's Wealth of Nations

This was also the year in which this Scotsman published his famous book which described an economic theory that was to provide the ideological foundation to the Industrial Revolution.

1779   Murder of Captain Cook in Hawaii

James Cook, a navigator and cartographer from Whitby in Yorkshire, made three journeys around the World. On the first (1769-71) in the Endeavour he visited Tahiti, New Zealand and Australia, and saw the Transit of Venus (when Venus can be seen crossing the disc of the Sun); on the second (1772-75) he visited the South Pacific and on the third (1776-79) he visited the North Pacific, but was murdered after a quarrel in Hawaii.

1780   The Derby

This foremost flat race for horses was first run. It is named after the 12th Earl of Derby, one of the promoters.

1783   First human flight

Whilst there are earlier claims involving all sorts of early gliders, dating back centuries before, the first substantial human flight is generally attributed to the Montgolfier brothers using a hot air balloon, which took place in Paris.

Larousse Grand Dictionary

This was first published in 1783.

Poland disappears

During the late 18th century, after a civil war in Poland, Prussia, Russia and Austria annexed parts of Poland and the name Poland disappeared from the map until the Congress of Vienna in 1815.

Death of Capability Brown

This famous British Landscape designer had been born in 1716.

1787   Mutiny on the Bounty

This took place at Tahiti. The crew of HMS Bounty mutinied, leaving Captain Bligh and 18 officers aboard a small boat without maps. However, Bligh sailed over 3,500 miles to safety and, at a later court martial, was exonerated of any mistreatment of his crew, which might have led to the mutiny.

Lord's Cricket ground

Thomas Lord opened his cricket ground at Dorset Square in London as the home of the Marylebone Cricket Club. It was moved in 1814 to its present site in St John's Wood. Since 1884, every cricket test series has seen one match played there. The Oval became a cricket ground in 1845.

Romanticism

This was a fundamental and some would say degenerate development in Western art, music and literature. It flourished at the end of the eighteenth century and throughout much of the nineteenth. It embraced a concern for the relationship between man and his environment, particularly exploring the emotions.

Romantic poets included: Keats, Byron and Shelley.
Authors: Walter Scott, Jane Austen, Goethe, Schiller and Victor Hugo.
Painters: Turner, Constable, De la Croix and David Roberts
Composers: Beethoven, Paganini and Schubert.

The French Revolution
1789   Louis XVI and Marie Antoinette

Louis XVI and Marie Antoinette (daughter of Marie Therese of Austria) were more victims than the causes of the Revolution. Louis pursued a course of government that reduced the price of food and helped the oppressed.

The Neoclassical French style of furnishing known as "Louis Seize" came into fashion during this reign and was to remain in vogue for some time after his execution.

The National Assembly

The revolutionaries, who had been inspired by the merged societies of Illuminati and Freemasonry, who sponsored the Jacobins, were determined to destroy the Catholic Church, the Monarchy and, with it, the French aristocracy. These last three were referred to as the *Ancien Regime*.

All of Louis' plans for helping the populace were thwarted by the National Assembly, which drew up the Declaration of the Rights of Man, and its plan to end privilege in France.

Storming the Bastille

The Liberals stirred up the people of Paris to riot in 1789, and, on 14th July, the nearly empty Bastille was stormed and a mere handful of prisoners set free (a strange event to commemorate as a national holiday). The reason this prison was chosen was because it was where the French King could imprison his enemies without trial on the basis of secret warrants known as *Lettres de Cachet*. The Bastille symbolised what the rebels regarded as an unjust regime.

Left and Right Wing Politics

In the French National Assembly, the Conservatives sat on the right, the Liberals on the left, and this is the origin of right-wing and left-wing politics.

Versailles stormed

The mob stormed Versailles and forced the King and Queen to go to Paris and live in the Tuileries. It was a simple matter for Versailles to be stormed because the King had always kept the gates open, allowing free access to his people (when the guards tried to close the gates against the on-rushing mob, they found the hinges had rusted, thus preventing their closure).

The Assembly then seized all Church land and, in the following year, 1790, the religious orders were suppressed.

Talleyrand and Fouché

Bishop Charles Maurice de Talleyrand-Périgord was surprisingly both a freemason and one of the chief authors of these anti-Catholic changes. He lived for some of his life after the revolution in England, but returned to serve France in a ministerial capacity, representing her at the Congress of Vienna in 1815. He even consecrated French bishops (from which most of the French hierarchy would trace its orders), despite his irreligiosity.

Joseph Fouché, Duc d'Otrante, a priest, was politically very active in the Revolution. He voted for the guillotining of Louis XVI and was Minister of Police.

Robespierre and Danton

The other revolutionary leaders were:
- Louis Philippe, the Duke of Orleans – known as Philippe Egalité
- Robespierre, the Mayor of Paris and leader of the extreme left wing Jacobin party, whose deputies in Parliament (the Convention) were called "the Mountain" because they sat on the highest seats in the chamber. The Jacobins were violently anti-Catholic.
- Georges Jacques Danton
- Jean Paul Marat
- Emmanuel Joseph Sieyès.

The first three were all guillotined and the first four all freemasons.

1790   Flight to Varennes

In June 1790, the Royal Family tried to escape, but were arrested at Varennes, and returned to Paris.

The Storming of The Tuileries

The Revolutionaries summoned a mob from Marseilles who not only brought with them what is now the French National Anthem (Marseillaise), but also stormed the Tuileries and killed everyone except the Royal Family, who were thereafter imprisoned.

Death of Benjamin Franklin

He was a famous and very talented US diplomat, author, scientist and inventor.

1791   Mozart dies

Wolfgang Amadeus Mozart, from Austria, and one of the very greatest composers of all time, was born in 1756.

Uranus

British Astronomer, William Herschel, who had built the largest telescope then known, discovered the planet Uranus.

1792   The September Massacres

In September 1792, hired assassins murdered 1,400 innocent French civilians (known as the September Massacres) in Paris within 3 days, as part of the wider revolutionary mob violence, particularly directed at the Catholic Church.

Death of Robert Adam

He was born in 1728 and, with John Nash, was the most influential British Architect of this period. Charlotte Square in Edinburgh is probably his most impressive creation, but he was also strongly influential in the design of the beautiful Georgian buildings in Bath.

1793   Marat is murdered

In 1793, Marat was killed in his bath by Charlotte Corday. This event triggered the start of the two year Reign of Terror in which many thousands of nobles and priests throughout France were put to death by the revolutionary government. The opponents of this reign were called Girondins and many of these were also killed.

It was also in this year that the French Republic declared war on a number of countries, including Britain, thereby starting the two decades of warfare which were to become known as the Napoleonic Wars. The Republic also annexed modern Belgium and the Austrian Netherlands.

The King and Queen guillotined

Louis XVI was guillotined in January 1793 and Marie Antoinette in October of the same year. The atrocities continued until July 1794.

1794   Battle of the Glorious 1st of June

The British, under Richard, 1st Earl of Howe, defeated the French near Ushant at this first naval encounter of the Napoleonic Wars.

1795   Orange Order

This organisation began in Northern Ireland as a secret society based on Freemasonry. Its aim was to act as the backbone of Ulster's resistance to the Irish Home Rule movement, as well as to counteract Catholic influence in the province. To this day it articulates hardline Protestant Unionism.

1796   Napoleon Bonaparte

In 1796, Napoleon Bonaparte, from Corsica and only in his mid-twenties, was placed in charge of a French army that successfully subdued Northern Italy.

Robert Burns dies

This famous Scottish poet had been born in 1759.

1797   Kubla Khan

This was the year Samuel Taylor Coleridge wrote his famous poem, *Kubla Khan*. Kublai Khan was the grandson of Genghis Khan.

Naval Mutinies

It was also the year of the Spithead and Portsmouth Mutinies.

Edmund Burke dies

He was a great and influential British conservative political philosopher.

1798   Pope Pius VI imprisoned

Napoleon forced Pope Pius VI to leave Rome and imprisoned him in Valence in France. Rome was looted by his troops in the same year.

Napoleon moves on Egypt

Napoleon then subdued Holland and Switzerland and decided to occupy Egypt in order to cut off Britain's trade route with India.

1799   Battle of the Nile

In 1799, Admiral Nelson destroyed the French Fleet at the Battle of the Nile, forcing Napoleon to return to France.

Income Tax first levied

In 1799, Income Tax was levied in England to pay for the war against Napoleon.

Beaumarchais dies

Pierre-Augustin Caron de Beaumarchais, the most successful French comic playwright and dramatist, was born in 1732. Rossini's opera *The Barber of Seville* and Mozart's *The Marriage of Figaro* were both adapted from his plays.

The Age of Napoleon

1800   Battle of Marengo

In June 1800, Napoleon defeated the Austrians at Marengo in Northern Italy, thus strengthening his control of that area – by 1809 he controlled all of Italy, including the Papal States.

Britain and Ireland united

The Act of Union between these countries was passed in 1800. As part of this process, William Pitt the Younger, the British Prime Minister, used bribery to persuade the Irish Parliament to vote itself out of existence. The Union lasted until 1921.

1801   Thomas Paine dies

Paine, who was born British, but became an American political writer, encouraged both the American and French Revolutions. He wrote *The Rights of Man* and *The Age of Reason*.

Treaty of Amiens

Also during this year, this treaty brought hostilities between Britain and France to a halt for just over a year.

1802   First British Elections

This was the year in which the first parliamentary elections to the House of Commons of the new united Parliament of Great Britain and Ireland were held, although voting was severely restricted. It would not be until 1929 that universal suffrage was granted to all men and women over the age of 21.

Louisiana Purchase

Napoleon, with little interest in the New World and needing money for waging war, sold Louisiana to the United States for $27,267,622 – the Louisiana Purchase. The purchase of this vast tract of land, much larger than the present Louisiana, doubled the size of the USA and established US dominance in North America.

1804   First Empire

Napoleon established his First Empire, appointing himself Emperor. Without children of his own, he appointed his wife Josephine's grandson, Louis, as his heir – the latter was to become Louis Napoleon. Napoleon divorced Josephine in 1810.

1802   Rothschild

Meyer Amschel Rothschild, a money-lender who took his name from the Red Shield signboard on his father's house, set up a number of Rothschild Houses in London, Naples, Paris and other places. He initiated international money-lending by the British and other governments.

Death of Kant

This German philosopher, born in 1724, developed a philosophy called Transcendental Idealism and was to be a major influence on subsequent philosophers.

1805   Battle of Trafalgar

In 1805, the French, being unable to launch an invasion of England, left the Northern French ports for the Mediterranean. Admiral Horatio Nelson caught up with them on 21st October, off Cape Trafalgar, South-West Spain, and comprehensively beat them, thus ending French sea power. Nelson died in the battle but his flagship, HMS Victory, can still be visited in Portsmouth.

Battle of Austerlitz

Napoleon now concentrated his expansion on land movement. He beat the Austrians and Russians at Austerlitz in 1805 and the Prussians, under Blucher, at Jena in 1806.

Martello Towers

These round towers (74 of them) were built on the south coast of Britain from Beachy Head to Folkestone as part of the defences against the threat from Napoleon. The name comes from Martello in Corsica where the French had built something very similar which had been very effective against British Bombardment.

Roll up that Map

By 1805, Napoleon controlled so much of Europe after Austerlitz, and his power was so firmly entrenched, that the British Prime Minister, William Pitt the Younger, said "Roll up that map (of Europe) – we will not need it for the next ten years."

1806   The Berlin Decrees

Napoleon now issued the Berlin Decrees of 1806, forbidding any country that he had subdued from trading with Britain. This continental blockade was not only ineffective but resulted in Britain successfully being able to blockade all of France's territories.

1807   Slavery

The transport of slaves was abolished in the British West Indies, principally as a result of the efforts of William Wilberforce MP. The ownership of slaves was not to become illegal in the British Empire until 1833.

1808   Napoleon conquers Spain

In the spring of 1808, Napoleon marched into Spain – the only country in continental Europe he had not yet conquered – and made his brother King of Spain. He killed many civilians in Madrid, but could only subdue Zaragoza after a year of siege. The Spanish rose in revolt which led to the Spanish War of Independence – more commonly known as the Peninsular War, which was to continue until 1814.

The expression "guerrilla warfare" comes from the Spanish word for war and the untrained but heroic Spanish army that stood up to Napoleon. After capturing Madrid, he turned on the British forces under Sir John Moore, who were forced to retreat to Corunna in Galicia, North-West Spain. In the ensuing battle, the French were defeated, but Moore was killed – as recorded in Wolfe's famous poem. With Moor dead, Sir Arthur Wellesley, later to become Duke of Wellington, took command of the British forces.

1809 Haydn dies
This prolific Austrian composer who formalised the structure of the symphony and the string quartet, and who was born in 1732, taught both Mozart and Beethoven.

Battle of Wagram
Napoleon defeated the Austrians at Wagram and forced them to seek an armistice.

1810 The Peninsular War
The British forces, now under Sir Arthur Wellesley, wanted to lessen Napoleon's influence; they took Oporto in Portugal and Talavera in Spain. The French counterattacked, and Wellesley retreated to Lisbon in 1810 and dug impregnable fortifications (the Lines of Torres Vedras), which the French never broke through.

When the French withdrew, principally to provide Napoleon with an army to march on Russia, Wellington pursued their retreating army, defeating them in many battles, but most notably at Albuera in 1811, Salamanca in 1812 and Vittoria in 1813, thus returning Spain to the Spanish.

Spanish American Wars of Independence
These lasted from 1810-1826 and resulted in independence from Spain for Venezuela, Colombia, Ecuador, Peru, Bolivia, Argentina and Chile. The leading South American revolutionary was Simon Bolivar.

Highland Clearances
When owners of land in Scotland decided to try to improve it by introducing sheep, they cruelly evicted those who had previously been farming the land. This barbaric process led to mass emigration to Australia and North America, but with no improvement to the land. The clearances were also heavily directed at the Catholic population.

1811 Luddites
Named after Ned Ludd, who smashed a textile machine in Leicestershire because it threatened his livelihood, these rioters were active between 1811 and 1816 and put the handloom operators out of work.

The dominance of the famous Lancashire Textile Mills, which flourished during this century, ended after World War I when British-financed mills were built in India.

1812 Napoleon's retreat from Moscow
Napoleon's march on Moscow in 1812 was a disaster. Although the French took Moscow and won the Battle of Borodino, they had to withdraw in bitter winter weather and the remains of the army were utterly defeated at Leipzig. In 1814 Napoleon was sent to exile in Elba.

Gerrymandering
In his role as Governor of Massachusetts, Eldridge Gerry reluctantly signed the order whereby the electoral boundaries of his state were redrawn so as to benefit his party. The new shape happened to look like a Salamander – hence the political term "to Gerrymander."

1815 Congress of Vienna
The French Empire was re-distributed at the Congress of Vienna (at which all the powers formed a "Holy Alliance" which even France was eventually to join). However, in February 1815, Napoleon escaped from Elba.

The Hundred Days
Napoleon entered Paris amidst wild acclaim and thus began his hundred days.

Battle of Waterloo

Wellington and Blucher who, at the age of 73, still commanded the Prussian forces, were near the French in Brussels, but separated by 14 miles. Napoleon held Blucher at Ligny and the rest of the French army then faced the British forces under Wellington at Waterloo on 17th June. Napoleon was aided by his loyal colleague from his previous campaigns, Marshal Michel Ney, whom Napoleon called "the Bravest of the Brave." (Ney had been sent to arrest Napoleon but decided to join him instead.)

Wellington defeated Napoleon in a very closely fought battle at Waterloo, but if General Blucher had not appeared when Napoleon had all but won, it is generally regarded that the outcome might have been different.

Wellington not only never lost a battle; he never lost a single gun.

Napoleon was sent into exile on the Atlantic island of St Helena where he died in 1821.

1816   Elgin Marbles arrive in England

This collection of ancient Greek sculptures, taken from the Parthenon in Athens, was saved from destruction at the hands of the occupying Turks by the Earl of Elgin. While the Greeks continually call for their return, until and unless they are returned to Greece, they can be seen on display in the British Museum in London.

Metternich

With Napoleon in exile on St Helena (where, as we have just seen, he died in 1821) French territory was governed for 30 years by Metternich, the Prime Minister of the Habsburg Empire.

With the French Monarchy restored to the throne of France, Louis XVIII reigned from 1814 to 1824.

Ghurkhas

Since 1815, Nepalese soldiers, called Ghurkhas, have been recruited to the British Army

1820   Rosetta Stone decoded

This slab of black basalt, found by Napoleon's army in 1799 in Egypt, was surrendered to the British and presented to the British Museum in 1802. It contains hieroglyphs in both Egyptian and Greek which, once decoded, enabled archaeologists to translate many other hieroglyphic writings.

1820s   Raffles

Sir Thomas Stamford Raffles established a trading port in Singapore. He founded the Zoological Society of London (London Zoo).

1824   National Gallery in London founded

This institution moved to its present building in Trafalgar Square in 1838.

1825   First Steam Train

George Stephenson built his steam train, the Rocket, which travelled the 15 miles between Stockton and Darlington in Northern England.

1826   First photograph

The first elementary photograph was taken by Joseph Niepse in France. However it was not until 1851 that the foundations of modern photography were properly established by Daguerre (Daguerreotypes) and William Fox Talbot who successfully exposed a negative in 1835.

1827   Beethoven dies

Ludwig van Beethoven, arguably one of the greatest composers of all, was born in 1770 and died stone deaf.

1829   Catholic Emancipation Act

The British government reluctantly began to grant concessions to British and Irish Catholics who were thereafter able to become Members of Parliament and achieve high office in Ireland. Shortly afterwards (1833), the Oxford Movement began, under John Keble, John Henry Newman and Edward Bouverie Pusey. This movement began to emphasise the Catholic principles on which they claimed the Church of England rested. However, in 1845, Newman converted to the Catholic Church and in 1879 he was made Cardinal.

The Boat Race

The Oxford and Cambridge Boat Race was first rowed on the River Thames at Henley in 1829, but was moved to its present course in London in 1836.

First Horse-drawn Bus service

London started its first horse-drawn bus service between Paddington and Bank.

1830   Louis Napoleon

When Louis XVIII died, he was followed by Charles X, France's last proper king. Charles ruled as an absolute monarch and so revolution again broke out in 1830. When this ended, the son of the Duke of Orleans, Louis Philippe, came to the throne. Louis Philippe was followed in 1851 by Napoleon's appointed heir Louis Napoleon (Napoleon III) who declared the French Empire re-established. This was to last until 1870.

Anti-Masonic Party

This party was formed in 1830 in the USA by Americans determined to drive Freemasonry out of public life, following the highly publicised disappearance in 1826 of the author of a book revealing Masonic secrets.

St Catherine Laboure

In 1830, Catherine Laboure had a series of visions of the Blessed Virgin Mary which resulted in the Miraculous Medal, which was revealed to her to be worn as a sacramental (a blessed aid in the Christian life, which helps sanctify the soul).

1831   French Foreign Legion

This tough fighting force was formed by France for non-French citizens wishing to fight for France in her overseas campaigns.

1832   Death of Sir Walter Scott

Scott was a famous Romantic Scottish author – Ivanhoe being one of his best known stories, dealing with the Age of Chivalry. He is also famous for his Waverley Novels.

Death of Goethe

Johann Wolfgang von Goethe, the famous German poet, scholar and statesman died in 1832. His greatest work is *Faust* which was written in 1808.

1833   The Industrial Revolution

This was the century of the Industrial Revolution, whereby a simple slow-moving way of life was transformed into a materialistic and complicated one.

Inventions included:
- James Watt's steam engine in 1769
- Kay's Flying Shuttle
- Hargreaves' Spinning Jenny
- Cartwright's Power Loom
- James Bindley's Canals, John Macadam's Tarmac
- Stephenson's Rocket in 1825.

Other famous engineers of this time were Richard Trevithick, whose work started the widespread use of steam engines, and Isambard Kingdom Brunel, who built bridges, ships and railway tracks, many of which still survive, in use, today.

The Factories Act
Working conditions were so bad that, with the inspiration and efforts of the Earl of Shaftesbury, the Factories Act of 1833 was passed to protect workers of all ages. For example, it forbade the employment of 8-year-olds and reduced the working week for 9-13 year-olds to 48 hours.

1834   Absolute Monarchy ends in Spain
The transition of Spain from an Absolute Monarchy to a Liberal State began. There were three Carlist Wars fought by Don Carlos, claimant to the Spanish throne, but the armies he commanded failed to keep Spain a Monarchy.

Tolpuddle Martyrs
Six farm workers from Tolpuddle in Dorset, England, were transported to Tasmania for administering illegal oaths and for forming a trade union. Their sentence was eventually remitted, but, in time, this event led to the development of the Chartist Movement in 1838, which called for political reform and ultimately led indirectly to the formation of the British Labour Party in 1900.

Tamworth Manifesto
Sir Robert Peel, in a speech to a gathering of the Tory party in the town of Tamworth in 1834, issued his manifesto in which he set forth his vision of a new liberal conservatism, resulting in the Tory party changing its name to the Conservative party.

Palace of Westminster burned down
This building, also known as the Houses of Parliament, was rebuilt in its present Gothic Revival design under the architectural supervision of Charles Barry and Augustus Pugin.

1835   First Computer
The first computer was conceived by Charles Babbage, who lived in Totnes, Devon. His "analytical engine" was finally built in 1991.

Death of John Nash
This famous British architect, who was born in 1752, created many famous buildings, including Buckingham Palace and Regent's Park in London, as well as the Royal Pavilion in Brighton.

The Great Trek
The Boer (Dutch) settlers in South Africa began to move to the north and east of the River Orange to escape British rule.

1836   Battle of the Alamo
During the Texan Revolution, whereby Texas wanted independence from Mexico, some 180 Texans, including the legendary Davy Crockett, defended the Alamo Fort for 12 days until they

were totally overwhelmed by the Mexicans – there were no survivors. In 1845, Texas joined the Union.

1837   John Constable dies
This English landscape painter from Suffolk had been born in 1776.

1838   First Afghan War
There were three Afghan Wars (1838-42, 1878-80 and 1919), fought by Britain against Russia, partly to prevent Russia advancing into India and partly to try to subdue the rebellious Ghilzai.

Grand National
This race was first run at Aintree, Liverpool. The most famous Grand National Horse was Red Rum which won in 1973, 1974 and 1977, coming second in 1975 and 1976.

Grace Darling
This lady, aged 23, and daughter of a lighthouse keeper, is famed for rescuing five people from their wrecked ship on the Farne Islands off the coast of Northumberland in her rowing boat.

1839   Henley Royal Regatta
This was held for the first time this year.

Opium Wars
The first of these lasted from 1839 to 1842. It was between Britain and China and it started when the Chinese government confiscated the British Opium stores in Canton in an attempt to end the British monopoly of the trade in this drug in parts of China. This event was followed by British sailors murdering a Chinese official. The Chinese army was severely weakened by opium addiction and the British soon won the war. The ending was formalised by the Treaty of Nanking, in which the British were granted rights to expand the opium monopoly to several designated offshore islands.

When the British demanded the right to sell opium throughout mainland China, the Chinese resisted, whereupon the British attacked, thus starting the second Opium War, which lasted from 1856 until 1860. It was fought between Britain and France on the one side and China on the other. The consequence of these wars was that the British were indeed granted the right to the monopoly in the mainland and thus opium was legalised throughout China.

David Sassoon was the man who administered the British monopoly.

Ships that had taken opium from Afghanistan to China would return to Britain laden with tea.

Bicycle invented
Kirkpatrick Macmillan, from Dumfries in Scotland, invented the modern bicycle with pedals and brakes.

1840   Entente Cordiale
During the nineteenth century, colonial expansion by both France and Britain caused tension between the two nations. To counteract this, diplomats established the "Entente Cordiale," an expression that can be traced back to this date. It was an informal term used to describe the close relationship and co-operation that then began to develop between Britain and France.

Irish Potato Famine
Catholic Ireland longed for independence from Protestant Britain, and this longing was increased by the terrible suffering of the Potato Famine in the 1840s. Almost 1 million people died and a further million emigrated.

First Postage Stamp
This was the year in which the first postage stamp was sold.

1842   Penal Settlements in Australia
These were set up after 1842 for British convicts sentenced to transportation to Australia. Life in them was particularly harsh.

Doppler Effect
This was the year that the Austrian, Christian Doppler, explained the Doppler Effect. This effect can be noticed when one hears the drop in intensity of sound when, for example, nowadays, a police car with its siren sounding, approaches, passes and then speeds away.

1843   Telegraph
The first Telegraph service began between Paddington and Slough. This was followed by the US invention in the following year (1844) of the Morse Code, by Samuel Morse.

1846   Repeal of the Corn Laws
The repeal of the Corn Laws ushered in world-wide free trade, the effect of which was to impoverish Britain and Ireland through cheap imports. The only part of the British Isles to benefit from this was the City of London, which became the financial capital of the world.

Two further developments of this world trade:
1) The British Empire became arguably the greatest empire the world has ever seen.
2) The financial institutions in the City of London needed to know what was going on around the world, so they could influence events, and this led to them starting their own intelligence service which, in due course, would become the nation's secret services in 1909.

Apparition of the Blessed Virgin at La Sallette in France
In 1846, the Blessed Virgin Mary appeared to two French children and foretold of great disasters that would happen to the Catholic Church. It may be clearly seen that these disasters have indeed subsequently taken place.

1848   Marx & Engels
Marx and Engels published their famous book, *The Communist Manifesto*, in 1848 – the last words of this book being: "Workers of the world unite." Their main tenet was that the value of an article or service is based on the time taken to supply it, which was directly contrary to the theory of Value Pricing (see 1738). Employed by a secret society (translated as the "League of Just men"), Marx and Engels devised policies for the overthrow of both society's representative government, as well as the Church, through plunder, violence and deceit; in time these policies were to lead to the mass murder of millions of workers in Russia (Soviet Union), but did nothing to improve their lot.

In 1867, Marx wrote *Das Kapital*.

The Year of Revolutions
There was a revolution in France which forced King Louis-Philippe to resign whereupon the Second Republic was proclaimed.

There was a five day revolution in Milan, another in Prague and even one in Switzerland.

In Austria, revolution broke out against the Habsburgs in 1848 and Metternich was forced to resign. Franz Joseph restored order and became emperor for 68 years. Franz Joseph was probably the last great Christian European leader.

Austria then restored order to Hungary and, in 1849, General Radetsky subdued the Italians. However, in 1859, Austria lost its control of Northern Italy at the Battle of Solferino where the victorious Italian side were led by Count Cavour.

In 1861, however, Savoy, an area of France between the Alps and the Rhone, was ceded to France by Victor Emmanuele. It was a mediaeval duchy which, in 1720, had become a province of the Italian island of Sardinia. Savoy was ceded to France as a reward for helping the Italians drive the Austrians out of their country.

1850   The Height of the Pre-Raphaelite Painting Brotherhood
These British painters wanted to shun the influence of all artists after Raphael and to try to emulate Italian painters before him. Their most famous members were Rosetti, Millais, Holman Hunt and William Morris. Closely associated with them was the art critic John Ruskin. In part they had drawn their inspiration from the Nazarenes, a group of Dutch and German painters who worked in Italy at the beginning of the 19th century.

William Wordsworth
This English poet started life with strong republican beliefs, but later developed both a conservative outlook as well as feelings of mystical union with the countryside. He died on St George's Day, 1850. He was born in 1770.

Balzac
Honore de Balzac was a famous French novelist and playwright, who died in 1850. He was born in 1799.

Disraeli exposes a world-wide conspiracy
In a speech to the House of Commons, Benjamin Disraeli, a future prime minister, said, "It is useless to deny, because it is impossible to conceal, that a great part of Europe is covered with a network of secret societies to change the tenure of land, to drive out the present owners and to put an end to ecclesiastical establishment."

1851   Turner dies
Joseph William Mallord Turner, the great English landscape painter was born in 1775.

Foucault's pendulum
Jean Foucault designed a 67 metre long pendulum with a heavy bob that slowly rotates through 360 degrees in 24 hours.

1852   Second Empire
This was the government set up in France by Louis Napoleon (Napoleon III) which continued until he fell from power and fled to England in 1870.

First Airship
The first steam-powered airship flew over Paris in 1852.

1853   First true aeroplane flight by Sir George Cayley.
This was a flight in a glider.

1854   Doctrine of Immaculate Conception
In 1854 (on December 8th), Pope Pius IX proclaimed the doctrine of the Immaculate Conception of the Blessed Virgin Mary (her conception free from original sin). This had been a disputed question for some time.

The Crimean War

In 1854, the Russians wanted to overrun the Islamic state of Turkey. They were resisted in the Crimean Peninsula by the British and French. Florence Nightingale is famed for her nursing in the war, but contemporary records show that the Catholic Sisters of Mercy were the real nursing heroines of the war.

Chechnya

It was during the late 1850s that Russia conquered the Islamic state of Chechnya.

1856   Victoria Cross

This is the highest award for military heroism and it was instituted this year. The medals are struck from Canons used in the Crimean War.

1857   Indian Mutiny

Indian soldiers (Sepoys), who formed more than 95% of the British army in India, revolted against the British, seized Delhi (only to lose it again) and unsuccessfully besieged Lucknow. Part of the Indian fury was against the British use of animal fat to grease their cartridges. The use of pork fat upset the Muslims and the use of beef fat the Hindus. In part the mutiny was caused by the sub-rulers, who resented British authority, stirring up the soldiers. Sometime after the mutiny ended, the British East India Company released control of India to the British Crown.

In 1947, India was partitioned into the two independent Dominions of India (mainly Hindu) and Pakistan (Muslim) with massive loss of life due to the associated fighting.

1858   Apparition of Blessed Virgin Mary to St Bernadette at Lourdes

The Blessed Virgin Mary appeared to a young French girl, Bernadette Soubirous, and confirmed that she was indeed the Immaculate Conception. Lourdes became a place of pilgrimage and healing, and remains so to this day.

1859   The Origin of Species

This work, *On the Origin of Species by Means of Natural Selection*, written by Charles Darwin, was published and launched the theory of Evolution. Its publication aroused bitter controversy because his view that species evolve as a result of mutations was seen to conflict with both biblical creation as well as the conclusions of the Austrian friar and founder of the science of genetics, Gregor Mendel. Alfred Russell, a contemporary of Darwin's, said that Mendel's discoveries, which were supported by laboriously collected scientific evidence, were a serious threat to Darwin's theory because Darwin's views were merely a series of assumptions that had not been proved by observation.

Big Ben

This famous bell, which was recast from its short-lived predecessor (which cracked within two years of being cast), was hung in its present home, St Stephen's Tower, at the north end of the Houses of Parliament.

Death of De Tocqueville

He was a famous French political scientist and writer.

1860   The Open (the first British Open Golf Championship)

The first Open Golf Championship was held at Prestwick in Scotland. The game of golf originated in Britain.

Burke and Wills

These two explorers completed the first south-north crossing of the Australian continent.

1861-65   American Civil War

In part, this war was caused because the Northern States (the Union), under Lincoln, wanted slavery abolished – the Southern Confederate States, where slavery was practised, were against abolition. However, the driving cause of the war was that the Southern States deeply resented being controlled by the Federal government, particularly with regard to trade tariffs. When Lincoln called up 75,000 volunteers to invade the Southern States and suppress Southern independence, Tennessee, Virginia, North Carolina and Arkansas seceded from the Union. Indeed, so incensed were five tribes of Indians at the heavy-handed attitude of the Northern States under Lincoln that they openly declared their support for the South.

The Southerners called the Northern, Union inhabitants "Yankees," being a corruption of Jan Kees, the nickname given to the Dutch settlers in the New York area.

One famous character from this period is John Brown, about whom the song, *John Brown's body lies amoulding in the grave*, was written. Espousing the cause of freeing slaves, Brown attacked five families, butchering the men in front of their wives and children (none of whom actually owned any slaves) and escaped. When he attacked the arsenal at Harper's Ferry, to steal weapons to ferment a slave insurrection, he was caught and hanged. Many regarded him as a quasi-saint, but Nathaniel Hawthorne, the US novelist and key figure in the development of 19th century American literature said, "Nobody was ever more justly hanged."

The war started when the Confederates attacked the Union stronghold of Fort Sumter and forced it to surrender.

The turning point of the war was the Union victory at the Battle of Gettysburg in 1863. This was followed by Lincoln's Gettysburg address, which lasted for less than three minutes and contained his famous quotation that "government by the people, of the people, for the people" cannot fail.

The end of the war, one of the most terrible wars in history, (600,000 men lost their lives) came when the Confederate General Robert E. Lee surrendered to Ulysses S. Grant.

1861   Victor Emmanuel

In 1861, Victor Emmanuel was proclaimed King of Italy.

Bismarck

When Bismarck became Chancellor of Prussia in 1861, he wanted to increase Prussian dominance, and bullied Austria on to his side. Bismarck, a freemason, was anti-Catholic, putting over 11,000 priests in prison. He was enormously influential in the creation of modern Germany. It was said of him that, "he did bestride this narrow world like a Colossus" (Cassius in Shakespeare's Julius Caesar).

1863   Baha'i Faith founded

Baha'is advocate a universal, syncretistic faith, an international language, equality of men and women, world peace and the abolition of all prejudices. Their headquarters are in Israel.

1864   Syllabus of Errors

In 1864, Pope Pius IX issued the syllabus of errors which condemned Liberalism, and in 1869 he called the First Vatican Council, which settled a number of issues, the most important of which being that of Papal Infallibility.

Chapter 8   Lincoln Assassinated to the Sinking of the Titanic

1865   President Lincoln assassinated

Lincoln was shot by John Wilkes Booth. There were a number of fascinating connections between Lincoln's and Kennedy's assassination 100 years later – see note after Kennedy's assassination in 1963.

1867   USA purchases Alaska

This State had been under the control of the Russian American company. It became the 49th State of the Union in 1959.

Confederation of Canada

Lower Canada (now Quebec) Upper Canada (Ontario) Nova Scotia and New Brunswick formed the confederation of Canada. Other provinces would join later: Manitoba in 1870, British Columbia in 1871, Alberta and Saskatchewan in 1901.

Walter Bageot

Bageot, editor of *The Economist*, finished writing *The British Constitution*.

Japan restores imperial control over its affairs, and the end of the Shogunate

The Japanese system of having Shoguns (military dictators) finished. Two years later the Samurai, armed retainers of a landlord, were disbanded. This Japanese feudal system had been the bedrock of Japanese society since the 12th Century.

1869   Suez Canal Completed

Ferdinand de Lesseps was the engineer in charge of its construction. He also began to build the Panama Canal in 1879, but failed to complete it. The United States completed it in 1914.

1870   Garibaldi

In 1870, the Italian liberal leader Garibaldi, who was a Freemason and anti-Catholic, declared himself dictator, took over Rome and made it the capital of Italy. This completed the unification of Italy, called the Risorgimento.

Death of Charles Dickens

(See History Notes, 204.)

Franco-Prussian War

William I (Wilhelm I), King of Prussia, sent a telegram (known as the Ems telegram) to his Chancellor, Otto von Bismarck, in which the King described a disagreement he had had with the French ambassador over whether a relation of William should be crowned King of Spain. Bismarck changed the wording of the published version of the telegram to make it read as if both parties had insulted each other. The result of this was that France declared war on Prussia. In the ensuing Franco-Prussian War, Prussia beat France and occupied Paris. After the war, France ceded Alsace and Lorraine to Germany.

Following the unification of Germany and Prussia by Bismark in 1871, William became the first German Kaiser and would reign until 1888 when he was succeeded by his son, Wilhelm II (Kaiser Bill).

The term Kaiser is derived from "Caesar," and had been adopted by the German kings who had been Holy Roman Emperors (the Russian title, Tsar, is also derived from "Caesar").

The End of the French Monarchy
In France, Napoleon III was overthrown following the Battle of Sedan in 1870, and, after bloody and violent scenes, the Tricolour became the flag of France. The Third Republic was thus established and the French Monarchy finally ended.

FA Cup first held and RFU formed
It was in this year that the Rugby Football Union was formed. In 1890, Rugby school claimed that this game had been invented there when, in 1823, William Webb Ellis picked up the ball in a game of what is now called football (or soccer).

In 1883, England, Scotland, Wales and Ireland began the "Home Nations" Rugby Championships. France joined in 1910 ("Five Nations") and Italy in 1997 ("Six Nations").

In 1895, the world of Rugby was split when the Northern clubs formed what became known in 1922 as the Rugby League. In 1906, the League game reduced the numbers of players from 15 to 13.

1870   Impressionist Painters
The Impressionist movement in painting aimed to capture the fleeting effects of light and weather in paint with dabs of bright colour and a minimum of drawing. They dominated painting in Europe and North America in the late nineteenth century. The most famous painters were Renoir, Degas, Monet, Manet, Cezanne and Sisley. The name of this movement sprung from Monet's 1972 painting entitled *Impression: Sunrise*.

1873   Death of John Stuart Mill
Mill was a British philosopher, political theorist and sometime MP, who advocated Utilitarianism and women's suffrage. His most famous work was *On Liberty*.

Death of Manzoni
This Italian novelist and poet, whose most famous work was *The Betrothed*, was born in 1785.

1874   First Typewriter
The first typewriter was made by Remington.

1875   Garcia Moreno
Gabriel Garcia Moreno, head of state in Ecuador, and one of the world's greatest Christian political leaders of all time, was assassinated.

1876   Telephone
The telephone, which had been invented by Scottish-born US scientist Alexander Graham Bell in 1872, was granted its first patent in 1876. Bell also invented the gramophone in 1887.

Custer's last stand
General George Custer, of the US Cavalry, commanded the 7th Cavalry during the campaigns against the Indians. When trying to round up the Cheyenne and Sioux forces under Chief Sitting Bull, his own forces were massacred at the Battle of Little Big Horn.

1877   Austria was handed the government of Bosnia-Herzegovina
In 1877, Russia allowed Austria to govern Bosnia-Herzegovina, but Serbia, which was on Russia's side and Russian Orthodox, felt threatened by this development because Catholic Austria already controlled what is now neighbouring Croatia.

Wimbledon and Test Cricket
The first men's singles tennis championship was held this year. It was also the year of the first cricket test match between England and Australia in Melbourne.

1878   Congress of Berlin
After Russia had defeated Turkey in 1878, the Ottoman Empire was carved up at the Congress of Berlin. By this congress, Serbia, Romania and Bulgaria were granted independence from Turkey and under the same terms Britain occupied Cyprus, and Austria was allowed to continue to occupy Bosnia-Herzegovina.

Leo XIII
Pius IX was succeeded by Pope Leo XIII who was an exceptional international and spiritual leader. Apart from being one of the greatest popes, he also set out ideals for the right economic path between Capitalism and Socialism.

1879   Zulu War
This South African war ended in defeat for the Zulus by the British, with Zululand being incorporated into the Natal. With the Zulus defeated, the Boers were then encouraged to throw off British occupation of the Transvaal (a province in Northern South Africa which the British had annexed in 1877). This resistance led to the Boer War, 1899-1902 (see later). There were three important battles in the Zulu War:

- The siege of Rorke's Drift, when 140 British soldiers held off more than 4,000 Zulu warriors.
- Isandhlwana, a few miles from Rorke's Drift and fought earlier on the same day – a Zulu victory
- Ulundi, which gave the British victory.

Thomas Edison
This US inventor introduced his most important invention, the electric incandescent light bulb.

Moving images on film
In France, a projector was developed for showing moving images on a screen.

1881   Savoy Theatre
This was the first public building in Britain to be lit by electricity, with electric street lighting following shortly afterwards.

Assassination of Tsar Alexander II
After the assassination of the Russian Tsar Alexander II, he was succeeded by his son Alexander III, who made the Jews the scapegoats for his father's death. This resulted in a series of pogroms against Russian Jews which caused millions of Russian Jews to emigrate.

1883   Krakatoa
In the biggest volcanic eruption in recorded history, this Indonesian volcanic island blew up, killing 36,000 people.

Primrose league founded
The purpose of this organisation was to promote British Prime Minister Benjamin Disraeli's ideals.

1884   Gordon of Khartoum
General Gordon was sent to the Sudan to rescue the British who had been attacked by the Mahdi. The Mahdi (the leader of the Mohammedans, who believe in a soon-to-come messiah)

attacked Khartoum. Gordon successfully defended the city but was killed before he could be rescued.

Madame Tussauds
This opened in its present site in Marylebone Rd in London. The neighbouring Planetarium opened in 1958, but has since closed.

Brompton Oratory
This massive Baroque Catholic church, inspired by Father Faber, was the largest place of Catholic worship in London, until Westminster Cathedral was completed in 1903.

Greenwich Meridian
This was accepted as the Prime Meridian or 0 degrees longitude from which the standard times of different areas of the world were calculated. In 1986, this was succeeded by Co-ordinated Universal Time.

1886   Geronimo
Geronimo, one of the most feared Apache chiefs, surrendered. He was a convert to Catholicism and, in time, became a respected public figure in the USA. He died in 1909.

Joe Chamberlain
He was a prominent liberal who broke away to start his own party, the Unionist Association, because he favoured Ireland being united to Britain. This association then merged with the Conservative party. Chamberlain was against Home Rule for Ireland. He had two sons, Austen and Neville, the latter being famous for signing the Munich agreement.

1887   Michelson Morley Experiment
The purpose of this experiment was to disprove the existence of the ether, the invisible substance that had been thought to permeate the whole of space, but the experiment failed to do so. This was not very convenient for science, which denies the existence of the ether – indeed the theory of Relativity relies on its non-existence – and the result of the experiment led Einstein simply to ignore it when promoting his theory.

1888   Kaiser Wilhelm II
In 1888, Queen Victoria's grandson, Kaiser Wilhelm II, came to the German throne and two years later made Bismarck resign. He became known to the English as Kaiser Bill and he remained in power until the end of the First World War (1918).

James Keir Hardie
He formed the Scottish Labour Party, which eventually developed into the (British) Labour Party in 1920.

1889   Mayerling
This sporting estate near Vienna was the scene of the violent death of Crown Prince Archduke Rudolph of Austria-Hungary, the son and heir of the Austrian Emperor, Franz Joseph, together with Rudolph's mistress. It is assumed that he shot her before killing himself.

1890   Forth Railway Bridge completed

Battle of Wounded Knee
This massacre of Indians was the last battle between native North American Indians and US troops.

1891   Baccarat Scandal
The Prince of Wales, the future Edward VII, had been present at a game of Baccarat at Tranby Croft, near Hull, at which one of the players had been accused of cheating. The Prince appeared as a witness in the ensuing libel case.

Death of Joseph Bazalgette
This Englishman rebuilt the London sewers, which resulted in greatly improved air quality in the city. The surface buildings associated with his work still stand and have a character all of their own.

1895   Promenade Concerts (The Proms)
Sir Henry Wood organised the first of these now world-famous annual concert seasons in the Royal Albert Hall, London.

1896   Cecil Rhodes resigns
Rhodes was Premier of Cape Colony in South Africa. Rhodesia, now called Zimbabwe, was named after him. His will provided scholarships at Oxford for Americans, Germans and Colonials (Rhodes Scholars).

Henry Ford
He built his first Model T Ford in 1896 and in 1913 introduced assembly-line manufacturing.

1897   First Zionist Congress
Theodore Herzl convened this congress in Basel, Switzerland, establishing the Zionist Organisation (to become the World Zionist Organisation in 1960) with its aim of establishing a home for the Jews in Palestine. The reason given for doing so was to give Jewish people a refuge, a place to live, free from European anti-Semitism.

Mount Zion is a hill in Jerusalem and nearby is Temple Mount on which the Jewish Temple had been built and where the Western (or Wailing) Wall, the only part of the original temple to survive, can still be seen. Temple Mount currently has the Arab (Muslim) Dome of the Rock crowning it, which is at odds with the Jewish plan for rebuilding the Temple on that very site.

1897   Battle of Omdurman
Anglo-Egyptian forces under General Horatio Kitchener, with modern weapons, effectively defeated the forces of Caliph Abd Allah. He was the Sudanese leader and the successor of the Mahdi and his army was known as the Caliphate. Kitchener conquered the Sudan and recaptured Khartoum.

Joshua Slocomb
This Canadian completed the first solo circumnavigation of the world.

Spanish-American War
In this war, Spain lost the remains of her colonies, Cuba, Puerto Rica and the Philippines, to the USA.

1899 – 1902   Boer War
This war began when the British wanted to bring the Dutch gold mines in South Africa under British control. The result of the war was that the Boers won the peace on their terms and remained friendly towards the British. A lasting legacy of this war was the British use of Concentration Camps, in which 25,000 Dutch (mostly women and children) died. A few years later the Germans were to use a similar system in German South West Africa, and then later, of course, in Germany itself.

1900   Radio broadcasting invented

In 1901, Marconi transmitted the first transatlantic radio signal from the Lizard Peninsular in Cornwall to the USA. This peninsular was used again in 1962 when the Post Office built its radio dishes at nearby Goonhilly Down for receiving signals from space satellites.

Max Planck unveils his Quantum Theory

British Labour Party

This political party, whose roots go back to the Tolpuddle Martyrs, was formed as the Labour Representation Committee this year. It changed its name to the Labour Party in 1906.

Death of Nietzsche

Friedrich Nietzsche, a German philosopher, rejected Christianity and proposed a confused philosophy that God is dead and man is free and powerful. This was an idea that influenced the Nazis thirty years later.

1901   Giuseppe Verdi dies

This prolific Italian composer of opera was born in 1813. His most famous operas are *La Traviata*, *Il Trovatore*, *Rigoletto*, *Nabucco* and *Aida*.

Death of Queen Victoria

Queen Victoria was born in 1819 and ascended the throne in 1837. At the time of writing this book, she is the longest reigning British monarch, to date. Her sense of duty and strict moral code came to symbolise the ethos of the 19th century.

She married her cousin, Prince Albert of Saxe-Coburg-Gotha, who died in 1861. Her close friendship with the conservative Prime Minister, Benjamin Disraeli, who created her Empress of India in 1876, contrasted with the tension that existed between her and Disraeli's Liberal rival, William Gladstone.

Commonwealth of Australia

In this year, the six colonies of Australia, (New South Wales, Victoria, Queensland, Northern Territory, Western Australia and Tasmania) were federated to form the Commonwealth of Australia, thus becoming an independent dominion of the British Empire.

The first film was made in France

First running of the Tour de France bicycle race

1905   Geneva Convention ratified

This had been drawn up in 1864 to cover national conduct in war and particularly the safety of the Red Cross, which had been founded in that year.

Sir Henry Campbell Bannerman

He became Liberal prime minister of Britain and helped heal the divisions within his party, especially between the imperialists and the pro-Boer factions.

1906   Colour film was patented

1907   Kelvin's Death

The Kelvin unit of temperature is named after this famous physicist, William Thomson Kelvin, who was born in 1824.

1908   Tunguska Explosion
6,500 square miles of forest in Siberia was laid flat by a mysterious explosion – an exploding meteor is suspected, but in 2002 researchers now think it may have been caused by an explosion of escaping natural gas.

1909   North Pole reached
US Polar explorer Robert Peary was the first to reach the North Pole. He beat the Norwegian Roald Amundsen who, in 1903/06 was the first to discover the North West Passage. In 1910, Amundsen was the first to reach the South Pole, a few days ahead of British Captain Scott.

1910   If
Rudyard Kipling wrote this famous poem.

1912   Titanic sank

Sliced Bread
This was the year in which a machine for slicing bread was invented, which might be of interest, bearing in mind the often used expression, "[X] is the best thing since sliced bread."

1912 – 1913   Balkan Wars
These were two military confrontations that preceded World War I. In the first, Bulgaria, Serbia, Greece and Montenegro (the Balkan League) defeated Turkey. In the second, the Balkan League fought amongst themselves over who should control Macedonia. In the ensuing peace, Bulgaria was denied control of the country.

Death of Mark Twain, famous US novelist

Harrods Department Store opened

1913   Crossword puzzle
This was the year that saw the first publication of a crossword puzzle, by Englishman Arthur Wynne, in US newspaper, *The New York World*. Britain was to follow in 1924.

Chapter 9   World War I

1914   Background
In the 19th Century (the Victorian era), **Britain** had extended its influence over India, Africa and Australia, thus enlarging the British Empire into an area on which the sun never set.

Britain had also made a pact to defend France; a pact that was so secret that the British Cabinet did not know about it. Indeed, after the war, senior politicians said that, if this pact had been known, World War I could have been avoided.

In recent years, Britain had built up an enormous navy and started to make belligerent noises against Germany, even though it had no apparent reason to attack Germany.

Austria was vulnerable as Emperor Franz Joseph's long rule came to an end.

French influence had been weakened from (1) the Drefus case when a Jewish officer was falsely accused of spying for Germany, and (2) the suppression of the Catholic Church again. France too had been building up its forces.

Germany, under Kaiser Wilhelm II (Kaiser Bill) had a huge army and an even greater self-confidence, fostered by both Nietzsche's proclamation, "God is dead," and Darwin's launch of the theory "the survival of the fittest."

However, as we have seen, Germany had no intention of attacking Britain and in no way was it responsible for starting the war. Indeed, Bismarck *wanted to join forces with Britain*, Austria and Turkey to create a bulwark against Russian expansion.

Italy was politically unstable, even while Pope Pius X (1903-1914 – later St Pius X) was vigorously leading the fight against Modernism.

In short, throughout Europe, stability was breaking down.

Russia – The Tsars
The Tsars had tried to improve the living conditions of the serfs by giving them land and more freedom – however, granting this freedom began to lead to instability in Russian society.
The Tsars regarded Serbia (Russian Orthodox) as under Russian authority and this attitude antagonised Serbia's neighbour, Catholic Austria.

Lenin
Lenin was the brother of a man hanged for conspiring to kill the Tsar and, having read the works of Karl Marx, he resolved to set about changing the world.

Russian Japanese War
Russia tried to extend her possessions in the Far East – its main aim was to secure a warm water port on the Pacific Ocean – but Japan retaliated and won the Russo-Japanese War of 1904.

March on Winter Palace
Between 1904 and 1907, partly because, as we have seen, they wanted more freedoms and partly as a result of national defeat at the hands of Japan, the Russian population became restless. Many were shot by the Russian troops, notably in the march on the Winter Palace in 1905. To tackle this unrest, Tsar Nicholas II granted a constitution and established a Russian Parliament, the Duma.

Rasputin

Nicholas' influence was severely weakened by his wife Alexandra's fascination for the mystic and self-styled monk Gregori Rasputin.

The Start of World War I

Serbs seek to control Bosnia Herzegovina

While Austria-Hungary's occupation of Bosnia-Herzegovina had been beneficial for the inhabitants (Catholic and Muslim), nonetheless, Russian Orthodox Serbs in Bosnia-Herzegovina were determined to put an end to Catholic influence in what they considered to be Russian territory.

Sarajevo Assassination

When the heir to the Austria-Hungarian throne, Archduke Franz Ferdinand, visited Sarajevo, capital of Bosnia-Herzegovina, in June 1914, Gavrilo Princip, an Orthodox Serb who was also a Jew, as well as a member of the Black Hand secret society, assassinated him.

It may be considered extraordinary that a hitherto unknown assassin in Sarajevo should have triggered a world war – unless this event was *meant* to be the trigger for a pre-planned world war (a possibility that may not seem too absurd when one looks at how Britain had been building up its armed forces in preparation for such an event for the previous ten years) – and that *Britain effectively took the side of the assassin*, and sacrificed so many millions of lives in such a cause.

It is a little known fact that on 13th August 1914, Pope Pius X (now a canonised Saint) besought Emperor Franz-Joseph not to take revenge by attacking Serbia. The Pope went so far as to offer his own life in exchange for this earnest request, predicting that, if the request were not granted, he (Pius X) would die seven days later on 20th August. The Pope did indeed die on the predicted day, together with his trusted friend Cardinal Ferrata. In the case of the Cardinal, death was caused by poisoning, but the cause of the Pope's sudden and inexplicable death has never been diagnosed.

Finally, in this reflection, with Britain, Russia and France having signed an agreement to come to each other's aid if they were attacked, with Russia not being attacked, but being the aggressor, there is no way that Germany can be accused of *starting* the war. Indeed, the Kaiser begged Russia not to mobilise and only did so himself when Russia refused his request.

These extraordinary reflections apart, this is how the countries lined up:

Austria-Hungary	Serbia
Germany	Russia
Turkey	France
	Britain
	Australia
	New Zealand
	Japan
	USA

The Domino Effect

The alignment is sometimes explained as the "Domino Effect."
In reply to the assassination:

- Austria mobilised to attack Serbia

- Two days later, Russia mobilised to attack Austria
- Germany declared war on Russia (to defend Austria), but seeing Russia unbalanced and therefore of no immediate threat, first decided to move west to cross through Belgium and attack Russia's ally, France. They later began to attack Russia.
- Britain, having promised to protect France, declared war on Germany. Winston Churchill, First Lord of the Admiralty, imposed a blockade of all German seaports, with the aim of starving the German population into submission.
- Turkey joined Germany, hoping to get back some of its territory lost to Russia.

Alsace Lorraine
France immediately moved to occupy Alsace and Lorraine, the territory between France and Germany, which had been taken from France after the Franco-Prussian War.

Admiral Von Tirpitz
The German high fleet under Admiral Von Tirpitz was kept in port because of their fear of British sea power.

Germany attacks Russia
Germany opened up its Eastern Front to attack Russia, at the same time that German forces were advancing into France and heading for Paris on its Western Front. It was in Belgium and Northern France that it met the British Expeditionary Force (BEF). They first met at the Battle of the Marne, 1914. This confrontation resulted in stalemate with both sides digging themselves into trenches, a system of warfare that was to last four years.

Old Contemptibles
The Kaiser called the BEF a contemptible little army. After the war, those who survived were known as the "Old Contemptibles."

While on the subject of nicknames that have been applied to our fighting soldiers, the soldiers in the trenches in the First World War used to sing the self-mocking song "We are Fred Karno's army..." to the tune of Onward Christian Soldiers. Fred Karno was a famous comedian and this term was, and may still be, used to describe a chaotically organised group.

Battle of the Atlantic
This was the German campaign to prevent merchant ships from supplying the allies. Notable actions this year included:
Coronel – German victory
Falklands – Allied victory with four German ships sunk, including the *Scharnhorst* and *Gneisenau*.

1915   Gallipoli
With stalemate in Europe, Britain, with substantial Australian and New Zealand help (the ANZACs) decided to try to break the deadlock by attacking the "underbelly of Europe" at Gallipoli in Turkey in April 1915. This strategy was the responsibility of the British First Lord of the Admiralty, Winston Churchill. It proved to be disastrously ineffective against the Turkish defences under Ataturk, and the Allies had to withdraw later that year with appalling loss of life. Churchill had to resign from the War Cabinet.

Toc H
This is signallers' code for the letters T and H, which stand for Talbot House, a house at Poperinge near Ypres, in Belgium, where the Reverend "Tubby" Clayton started a refuge for soldiers from the war. After the war it became a movement for Christian service in the community, indeed Talbot House is still operating in Poperinge today.

Russia
In 1915, the situation in Russia grew worse as Nicholas II took charge of the army and Rasputin's influence began to direct the government.

Lusitania sunk
The sinking of this ship a few miles off the coast of Ireland, with the loss of nearly 1,200 lives, many of them US citizens, began to influence US opinion to join the war on the side of the allies. The ship had been carrying military armaments and had been assured by Churchill, who knew that German submarines were operating in the seas off Ireland, that it would be safe to sail to Liverpool. Some even hold that that the sinking of the Lusitania was orchestrated in order to bring the USA into the war.

Shackleton's Boat Journey
In 1915, Sir Ernest Shackleton's ship, *Endeavour*, was crushed in the South Polar ice. To save his crew, Shackleton led them in lifeboats over hundreds of miles of stormy seas to eventual safety. The perilous journey lasted many months, but every man was saved. The exciting story is one of the most impressive feats of leadership and risk-taking in modern history.

1916   Ireland
In 1916, during Easter week, the Irish Republican Brotherhood claimed independence from Britain, but this rising was cruelly put down by the British who, in 1920, used a new and temporary police force known as the Black and Tans. The famous Irish nationalist Sir Roger Casement was hanged for his part in the rising.

Battle of Jutland
This famous naval encounter between the German and British high fleets, in which the Germans inflicted heavier losses than the British and which is usually recorded as indecisive, resulted in the German fleet never putting to sea again.

The Battle of The Somme
On the Western Front in July 1916, the British Army lost over 600,000 men during the Somme offensive. This was a 140 day campaign against the Germans and intended to smash the German hold on France, but it resulted in remarkably little ground being gained.

Verdun
The Germans began a huge offensive against this salient, but, in spite of further appalling loss of life, did not take it.

Austrian Peace Effort
Following the death of Franz Joseph, Emperor of Austria-Hungary, his successor Charles of Austria, tried to end the war by offering territory to Kaiser Bill in exchange for a German ceasefire. The Germans chose to fight on.

Lawrence of Arabia
T. E. Lawrence became a guerrilla leader of the Arabs against the Ottoman Turks. With the Turks siding against Britain, Britain sent forces to Palestine to drive the Turks from Palestine. The removal of the Ottoman Turks from Syria and the resulting reduction of their influence in Palestine played a part in opening the way for later Jewish immigration into Palestine and the subsequent establishment of the State of Israel.

Prince Youssoupoff (or Yusupov)
Rasputin was murdered by a number of Russian noblemen, including Prince Felix Youssoupoff in 1916.

The first Tank
The tank was invented by the British soldier, Ernest Swinton.

British Summer Time
Daylight saving was first introduced this year.

1917   Paschendale
In 1917, the soldiers in the trenches were suffering from appalling conditions. A number of French soldiers mutinied, but General Haig reacted by ordering the Paschendale offensive, near Ypres in Flanders, which only resulted in further huge loss of life (400,000 casualties).

Vimy
Later that year, the Canadians were to storm the imposing Vimy Ridge close to Arras and Mons.

Commonwealth War Graves Commission
This year also saw the establishment of what is now known as the Commonwealth War Graves Commission, an organisation that tends nearly one million war graves and memorials around the world.

Fatima
During 1917, the Blessed Virgin Mary reportedly appeared several times at Fatima in Portugal. While only three small children (to whom she delivered a message of apocalyptic importance) witnessed the full apparition, thousands saw the miracle of the sun dancing in the heavens. It is now a place of pilgrimage.

The October Revolution
Following the abdication of Tsar Nicholas II in 1917 (ending the Romanov dynasty), Lenin, with financial backing from both New York and the German Government, took charge of the revolutionaries (Bolsheviks) in Russia. He was conveyed from Switzerland to Russia in a sealed train containing $10 million, the purpose of which was to undermine the Russian resistance (White Russians) towards the invading Germans, so that some of the latter could be conveyed to support the German troops on the Western Front. Thus the White Russians were unsuccessful and Lenin seized all church and private property, putting thousands to death including, in the next year, the Tsar and his family (the October Revolution).

Balfour Declaration
In a short letter from the British Foreign Secretary to Lord Rothschild, A. J. Balfour declared British support for the Zionists' call for a home for the Jews in the State of Palestine. As we have seen, Zionism is the political movement founded in the late 19th century, the aim of which was to establish a homeland for Diaspora Jews to return to Palestine, and thus to create a Jewish State. At the Versailles Peace Conference in 1920, Britain was granted the mandate to bring this about.

During the period of the British Mandate in Israel, Irgun and its breakaway movement, the Stern gang, both of them guerrilla groups, carried out a number of anti-British atrocities, notably Irgun's attack on the King David Hotel in Jerusalem in 1946.

Rodin dies
Auguste Rodin was a celebrated French sculptor. His most famous works include, *The Thinker*, *The Burgers of Calais*, and *The Kiss*.

Buffalo Bill dies
Born in 1846, William Cody had been a US army scout and Pony Express rider, supplying the men working on the US railroad with buffalo meat.

1918   America joins the War

The citizens and most of the US Congress were against joining the European war. They *had* been provoked by the sinking of the Lusitania, but, having observed the British blockade of German ports and the extreme shortage of food and suffering that was being inflicted on the German peoples, as well as other aspects of British naval strategy, they were not at all convinced that they should take Britain's side. However, President Woodrow Wilson wanted the USA to participate, so that he could be present at and play a leading part in the ensuing peace talks.

So, in 1918, American troops began arriving in Europe and joined the war effort. When Ludendorff, the German Commander, planned a major push through the trenches to capture Amiens, their attack failed when they met overwhelming numbers of US troops short of the city. Once the Germans were forced to halt their advance, the Allied troops regrouped and with both tank and air support, pushed the Germans back. The German army collapsed and this marked the start of the end of the war.

Austria was convulsed by revolution, the Emperor fled and the Kaiser abdicated.

Treaty of Brest Litovsk

This was a pact between (effectively) Germany and Austria-Hungary on one side, and Russia on the other, whereby they negotiated Russia's withdrawal from the war.

Armistice

By the time the Armistice was signed on 11 November, 8 ½ million men had been killed and 21 million wounded.

Not only had so many million soldiers and civilians lost their lives but a number of European countries also lost their monarchies as a result of World War I. Russia lost its Tsar, Austria-Hungary lost its Emperor, Germany lost its Kaiser and Turkey lost its Sultan. Greece and Spain would also lose their monarchies a few years later.

Chapter 10   Between the World Wars

1919   Versailles

Even though Germany hadn't really lost the war, Britain and France wanted to ensure that Germany was thoroughly punished at the Versailles Peace Conference in 1919. Indeed, Lloyd George and the French leader Clemenceau wanted to prevent Germany from ever being a force in Europe again. In addition, President Woodrow Wilson of the USA would not negotiate with any unelected leader such as Charles of Austria. As a result of this somewhat intransigent attitude, the seeds of the Second World War were laid in this conference.

The decisions taken included....
1.   **The creation of Yugoslavia and Czechoslovakia**
- Slav peoples such as Croats and Serbs were forced into the combined state of Yugoslavia
- Czechs and Slovaks were forced into another new state, Czechoslovakia, which also included thousands of Germans living in the Sudetenland
- The South Tyrol was added to Italy.

Slavs

The Slavs are the largest group of European people having a common ethnic and linguistic origin. They included Russians, Ukrainians, Belor-Russians, Poles, Czechs, Slovaks, Bulgarians, Serbs, Croats, Montenegrins and Macedonians.

2.   Reparation

Germany was forced to demilitarise the Rhineland and to hand back Alsace-Lorraine to France. They were also forced to pay huge reparations. The Germans deeply resented their treatment at the hands of the Versailles Peace Conference, seeing in the decisions made there developments that would only serve to further the cause of World Communism. The Germans therefore suspected and blamed the Communists for their resulting humiliation and bad treatment. Further to this, because the Communists in Russia were largely led by Jews, in German eyes Communism was therefore synonymous with Jewry. As a result, this resentment was to fuel German hatred for both Communists and Jews, and this would become a trigger for their ferocious attacks against them in later years.

All of the above unwanted decisions were to bring terrible trouble later. Indeed it has been said by historians that the decisions made at Versailles were made by men bereft of reason.

Nancy Astor

She was the first woman MP to be elected and take her seat in the British Parliament (in 1918, Constance Markievicz was elected for the constituency of Dublin St Patrick's, but as a candidate for Sinn Fein she did not take up her seat in Parliament).

Weimar Republic

In Germany, the 1919 elections brought the weak Weimar Republic to power which was to last until Hitler overthrew it in 1933. Its government met in the German town of Weimar. At this time there were revolutionaries in Germany, like Rosa Luxembourg and her Spartacus League, who, by stoking up revolution, wanted Germany to follow Russia's course towards Communism.

Amritsar Massacre

British troops in India killed 379 demonstrating, but unarmed, Sikhs without warning.

Alcock and Brown

These two British aviators, Sir John Alcock and Sir Arthur Brown, made the first non-stop transatlantic flight in a Vickers-Vimy aircraft.

1920   Prohibition
Prohibition, the name of the period when alcohol was banned in the USA, lasted from 1920 – 1933. It was never effective and the agents who tried to enforce prohibition were outnumbered by gangsters selling alcohol.

League of Nations
The League of Nations, based in Geneva, was established as an experiment in One World Government and in order to keep the world at peace, but the USA never joined and it never worked.

Cenotaph
This memorial, designed by Sir Edwin Lutyens, was erected in Whitehall in London.

Chatham House founded
The more formal name of this organisation is the Royal Institute of International Affairs, and its purpose is to create a prosperous and secure world. (See also the Council on Foreign Relations below.)

1921   Irish Free State
In 1921, the Irish Parliament, after the efforts of Michael Collins and Arthur Griffith, reluctantly agreed to the partitioning of Ireland. This involved the setting up of the Irish Free State, separated from the Northern six counties. The latter comprised Ulster which remained part of the United Kingdom of Great Britain and Northern Ireland, the somewhat lumpy entity that had been set up the year before. Michael Collins briefly became head of state but was killed in 1922. De Valera was a very prominent nationalist who became Prime Minister of Ireland (1932-48, 51-54, 57-59) and then President (1959-73).

Nazi Party established
In 1921, Adolph Hitler reorganised and renamed the National Socialist German Workers' Party (Nazi Party) which, as a result of the decisions taken against Germany at the Versailles Peace Conference, was intensely nationalistic and militaristic. The Nazis, as we have seen (see Reparation 1919), were not only anti-Communist and anti-Jewish (especially against non-Zionist Jews), but anti-Catholic too.

Mein Kampf
After the Munich Beer Hall Putsch, when Hitler tried, but failed, to seize power in Germany and form a national government, Hitler was put in prison where he wrote Mein Kampf ("My Struggle").

The Council on Foreign Relations
The "CFR" was founded in the USA under the shadow of Chatham House (see above) with the aim of establishing a World Government. One of its first activities was to hold secret meetings to establish a political union of all the countries of Europe. This is probably the earliest reference to the plan to establish a European Union much later in the century.

1923   BBC
The British Broadcasting Corporation began regular radio broadcasts.

Wembley
The FA cup final was first held at Wembley. This stadium was knocked down in the late 1990s and replaced with a new stadium on the same site that held its first match in 2007.

1924 The Soviet Union

In Russia, Lenin forced Communism on what was renamed the Soviet Union. This had disastrous results with many millions dying of starvation. In 1924, Stalin, who had defeated Trotsky, took over after Lenin's death. Thereafter the evils continued at a worse pace; at the same time the Communist International organisation (Comintern) began to spread this political cancer worldwide.

Dissidents who opposed Communism and many others were silenced by imprisonment in the Gulag, a system of prisons and Labour Camps where countless millions died or were executed between 1920 and 1990. This system witnessed the biggest mass murder in history.

Zinoviev Letter

Grigory Zinoviev, chairman of Comintern, wrote to British Communists urging them to start a revolution in Britain. However, in 1999 the British Foreign Office declared this letter to be a fake and merely part of the Tory attempt to prevent the Labour Party under Ramsay MacDonald winning the 1924 General Election. Nonetheless, Zinoviev said later that, if he had been asked to sign such a letter, he would have done so.

First Socialist Government in Britain

The Labour Party, led by Ramsey MacDonald, was elected to power (though as a minority government) following the demise of the Liberal Party and this happened as a result of two things:

- The Unionists had broken away from the Liberals to join the Conservative Party
- Lloyd George's refusal to impose a tax on land. This failure to impose the Land Values measure created such resentment amongst the working classes that they rejected Liberalism as being far too weak.

The Rise of Fascism

Elsewhere in Europe, Fascism began to spread. Fascism, inasmuch as it may be defined, means strong, dictatorial government without elections, as a bulwark against Communism and secret societies.

Mussolini came to power in Italy in 1922. He originated the Black Shirts Fascist Paramilitary Organisation. In Britain, Sir Oswald Moseley created the British Union of Fascists – another Black Shirt organisation.

Chemical pesticides

This was the first year that chemical pesticides were used.

1925 Locarno Pact

This agreement guaranteed the post-1919 frontiers between France, Belgium and Germany as well as demilitarisation of the Rhineland.

SS (Schutzstaffel) Established

The Nazi elite corps became the brutal German State Police.

1926 Television

The British electrical engineer and inventor John Logie Baird gave the first demonstration of television.

Gaudi dies

Antonio Gaudi y Cornet, the much celebrated Spanish architect, was born in 1852 and developed a flamboyant architectural style, notably in Barcelona.

1927   Menin Gate Memorial

This memorial, the largest memorial commemorating those who died in World War I, was built in Ypres over the road that led to nearby Paschendale. To this day, at 8pm every evening the traffic is halted and the "Last Post" sounded. It commemorates over 50,000 who were killed in that part of Belgium and for whom there is no known grave. Seventy four years later, by November 2001, the "Last Post" had been sounded 25,000 times, but, as may be noted to further emphasise the appalling loss of life that it commemorates, after seventy four years, by that time, it had been sounded only once for just half of those whose names are on the memorial.

1928   Thomas Hardy dies

He was a famous British novelist whose works feature Dorset and the West of England.

1929   Vatican City

In 1929, Mussolini, through the Lateran Treaty, gave the Papacy its own independent territory, Vatican City.

Maginot, Siegfried and Hindenburg Lines

The French War Minister, Andre Maginot, constructed the Maginot Line, a series of defence fortifications against the Germans. It extended from Switzerland to the English Channel. In 1940, the Germans simply broke through it at its weakest point.

The original Siegfried Line, also known as the Hindenburg Line, was built in 1916-17 by the Germans as a defence against the allies in World War I. However, when the Germans built a line parallel to the Maginot Line in the 1930s, the English called *this* the Siegfried Line. The Germans called it the Westwall.

1929-1930s   Great Depression

This was triggered by the 1929 Wall Street Crash in New York which resulted in grave economic difficulties and high unemployment in the USA and Europe. One of the most important protests against unemployment in Britain was the Jarrow March in 1936.

Penicillin first used in an operation

The use of penicillin was developed by Scottish bacteriologist Alexander Fleming. He is generally credited with the discovery of penicillin although there are a number of others who did a great deal more to promote its life-saving use than he did.

1931   British Commonwealth established

This is a loose association of 54 independent nations, most of which were formerly members of the British Empire. In 1947, it changed its name to the Commonwealth of Nations.

1932   Technicolor introduced in a Walt Disney cartoon

Hindenburg

The Nazi Party entered Parliament in large numbers in 1932 as a result of Hindenburg's weak and incompetent government. Hindenburg appointed Hitler as chancellor.

Sydney Harbour Bridge completed.

This bridge connected North and South Sydney.

Death of George Forrest

Forrest was arguably the most famous plant hunter and responsible for introducing many of the flowering woodland shrubs to be seen in British gardens today. He was born in 1873 and died while on his 7th expedition collecting Chinese Mountain Rhododendrons.

1933   Gestapo formed

The Gestapo was Nazi Germany's secret police. It was formed under the direction of Himmler.

Reichstag (German Parliament) burned down

First German Concentration Camp

The first German concentration camp was built at Dachau for Communists and other opponents of the new regime.

Third Reich proclaimed by Hitler

The chief architect of the Third Reich was Hitler's talented adviser, Albert Speer. It was to last from 1933 to 1945. Germans regarded the first Reich (German for "Kingdom") as being that of the Holy Roman Empire (962 – 1806); the second being that of the Hohenzollern Empire from (1877 – 1919). This declaration enabled Hitler to rule by decree with measures such as:

- The Nazi party was declared the only legal party
- Jewish businesses were to be boycotted
- Aryan couples were given cash incentives to have children (the word Aryan is defined below)
- What is little known is that Hitler offered to disarm totally if the other nations of Europe would do the same. Indeed every peace offer that Hitler made was scorned and rejected.

One of Hitler's aims was to make Germany great by uniting it with Czechoslovakia, Austria, Poland and Ukraine.

After the war, Speer was tried at Nuremberg, found guilty, said sorry and was released in 1966. He died of natural causes in 1981.

1934   The Master Race

In 1934, Hitler became President (as well as already being Chancellor), declaring that Germany, which had been the seedbed of Protestantism, was the Master race and that, once he controlled Europe, he would turn against both Jews and the Catholic Church. He believed that this master race was Aryan (basically the descendants of Noah's third son Japheth) and to match this belief (as we have seen) he developed his hatred and persecution of Jews, citing as justification his belief that they had too much control of the German economy. His racial hatred also extended to Arabs and Negroes.

Night of the Long Knives

At the end of June, Hitler ordered the political executions of the leaders of the Sturmabteilung (SA) a Nazi paramilitary organisation (associated with degeneracy and immorality) that threatened his power. The death toll is believed to be in the hundreds. Ernst Röhm, the SA's co-founder and Commander, was also executed on Hitler's orders.

Mao's Long March

This was the year in which Mao Tse-Tung, acting on the advice of agents of the Comintern, lead the Chinese Communists out and away from their base in Jiangxi in South China, a base they had been trying to defend. Nearly 100,000 men marched for a year to Yunnan in North West China (6,000 miles away) and nearly 70% of them died in rear guard actions against Guomindang, the Chinese National Party of the Republic of China.

Edward Elgar dies

This great English Catholic composer was born in 1857 and is associated with his home in the Malvern Hills, Worcestershire.

Marie Curie dies
This Polish scientist, who was born in 1867, discovered Radium. The Curie, the unit of measurement for radioactivity, is named after her.

Glyndebourne presents its first opera
This opera house in Sussex was opened by John Christie.

British Council
This organisation was established by the Government to represent British culture abroad, arranging visits and exhibitions by artists and performers.

Italy invades Abyssinia
Italy invaded Abyssinia (nowadays Ethiopia) from Eritrea – the purpose of this invasion was to further Mussolini's ambitions for an Italian Empire, as a successor to the Roman Empire. It was the first test of the authority of the League of Nations and its resulting ineffectiveness seriously weakened the League's standing.

Chapter 11   World War II

1935   German Rearmament, Hitler and Mussolini

While it is now generally believed that Hitler openly began to build a huge army in 1935 and, while the rest of Europe did very little except complain that this broke the Versailles Treaty, in fact Germany had no money with which to do this. Germany was neither preparing for war nor seeking one. By 1938, German armament production was lower than in Britain.

What is true is that Hitler had made Germany a powerful industrialised country and did so without any foreign loans – an achievement much resented by the international bankers. Britain even signed an agreement with Germany that allowed the German Fleet to be rebuilt, but not to a size any greater than 35% of the British Fleet.

In 1936, Hitler and Mussolini signed a mutual defence treaty and Germany and Italy became the Axis powers.

1936   Germany occupies the Rhineland

This invasion, in flagrant contravention of the Locarno Pact, was unopposed.

Television broadcasts

The BBC began regular TV broadcasting.

The Spanish Civil War
The Start

When the Spanish King Alfonso XIII abdicated in 1931, the atheistic Republican government that replaced him was violently anti-Catholic and, in 1936, all religious property was confiscated, churches were set alight and many priests and nuns were murdered. In other words, the purpose of the Communist-inspired Spanish Civil War was the destruction of the Catholic Church. The Communists were directed from Moscow.

Franco

On July 18th 1936, Generals Franco and Mola issued a proclamation against the Communist government and immediately received huge popular support. However, the highly industrialised region of Catalonia (capital city, Barcelona) was firmly against the Nationalist opposition that was led by Franco. The Catalans would provide fervent opposition to the later Franco regime.

In 1937, Franco merged all the anti-Communist elements, particularly the Falange party, into one Nationalist movement.

Franco and Hitler

Only Germany and Italy were prepared to help Franco, but Franco and Hitler were never on very friendly terms.

Franco reaches Madrid and the expression "Fifth Column"

The Nationalists declared war against the Communist Republicans on 21st July 1936 and the Spanish Civil War lasted three years until Franco marched triumphantly into Madrid in March 1939. During the siege of Madrid, the Nationalist General Emilio Mola, with four columns operating under his command said that he had a fifth column, of his sympathisers, inside the city.

Alcazar

The most famous incident of the war was the Republicans' unsuccessful siege of the Alcazar at Toledo, where in over two months they could not kill a single civilian.

Spain and World War II

Franco did not enter World War II because Spain could not afford another war and remained neutral. However, having received aid from Germany during the Spanish Civil War, Franco decided not to take arms against Germany. Partly as a result of this, Franco and the Spanish Catholic nationalists that supported them are, to this day, painted in a less favourable light than the Communist and Atheist republicans.

Hitler's Occupation of other parts of Europe

In 1936, Hitler reoccupied the Rhineland (territory that had been taken away from Germany at the Versailles conference) and, in 1938, Austria was absorbed into Germany (the Anschluss). So peaceful was the invasion of Austria that not a shot was fired.

In May 1938, Hitler marched into the Sudetenland (part of Czechoslovakia, which also had been taken from Germany at Versailles), where ¼ million Germans lived, and five months later he took the rest of the country.

1937   Churchill declares his admiration for Hitler

It is a little known fact that Churchill said that, if there were a war and our country were defeated, he hoped we should find a champion as indomitable as Hitler to restore our courage and lead us back to our place among the nations of the world.

1938   Munich Agreement

In 1938, the British Prime Minister, Neville Chamberlain, was assured by Hitler that the latter had no further ambitions in Europe; Chamberlain flew home with a piece of paper to this effect signed by Hitler, with Chamberlain declaring "Peace in our time." This policy of giving way to the demands of a dictator and hoping that such agreements will bring peace is called "Appeasement." However, knowing of Hitler's intentions with regard to Poland, Chamberlain assured the Poles, and warned Hitler that if Germany invaded Poland, Britain would come to Poland's aid. No-one was quite sure why Britain gave this assurance. Some said that it was to please President Roosevelt, because it would secure him the Polish-American vote. If this were the case, Roosevelt cruelly betrayed this same country through his later subservience to Stalin.

Kristallnacht (Night of Broken Glass)

Following a speech by Joseph Goebbels, in which, by referring to the murder in Paris of a German official by a Polish Jew, he incited Germans to take revenge, 91 Jews were killed in riots (pogroms) and much Jewish property was destroyed. This event, which stepped up the Nazi persecution of non-Zionist Jews, encouraged Zionist Jews to start leaving Poland; many headed for Palestine, shortly to be turned into the Jewish country of Israel. By September 1939, one half of Germany's half million Jews had emigrated.

1939   Hitler invades Poland

On 1st September 1939, after concluding the Ribbentrop Pact with Stalin, by which they reached a non-aggression agreement and divided Poland between the two countries, Hitler invaded the part of Poland that Germany claimed, conducting a Blitzkrieg (lightning war). It is correctly presented as a German attack, but what is seldom mentioned is that the Poles had been goading Germany for some time, so the invasion was in part a response to the Polish aggression; it was therefore not an entirely unprovoked invasion.

Once this happened, Hitler offered peace to the British government, but his offer was rejected.

The Ribbentrop Pact is an extraordinary development when one remembers that Hitler had put all of his energies into turning Germany into a bulwark *against* Russian Communism.

Declaration of War

On 3rd September 1939, Britain and France declared war on Germany, blockading German ports. This aspect, that it was Britain that declared war on Germany and not the other way around, is often overlooked. What is also overlooked is that Britain went to war to rescue Poland; and yet, after six years and with Britain on the winning side, Poland did *not* get its independence back; instead it was shackled to the Soviet Union. This is partly explained by the fact that, on 17th September, Russia invaded their part of Poland from the East.

What is also often overlooked is that, under the pact of mutual assistance to Poland, the British people assumed their government would also declare war on Russia, when it invaded Poland, but no such action was taken.

However, for the first six months there was little fighting (the Phoney War) and the British never offered Poland any direct aid. The fighting didn't really begin until 1940, when Hitler invaded Denmark, Norway, Holland and Belgium.

1940   Battle of the Atlantic

The Battle of the Atlantic in the Second World War was to last for the whole war. As in the First World War, it resulted from Germany's plan to prevent supplies reaching Britain. It began on 4th September, when the Germans sank the *SS Athenia*.

The British sank the German battleship *Bismarck* in 1941, which caused the Germans to step up their U-Boat patrols and nearly 800 of these submarines were to be sunk during the years that this battle lasted.

Dunkirk

The British Army (the British Expeditionary Force) which had gone to France at the start of the war, but had not experienced any fighting, found itself under attack in the late spring of 1940 and was pushed back to Dunkirk. Here, at the end of May 1940, and with the help of small craft from England, nearly 200,000 troops were rescued. Hitler could easily have completely destroyed the British Army at that point, but, for mysterious reasons that have never been made public, refrained from doing so.

Fall of France

Hitler then overran France with his army known as the Wehrmacht. However, he allowed Marshal Petain to govern the southern part of the country (the Vichy Regime) in return for an alliance with Germany. By this alliance, French armament factories would supply the German Army and thus enable Germany to continue the war for much longer than would otherwise have been the case.

Hitler again offered peace to Churchill, who by then had become Prime Minister, but Hitler's offer was rejected.

The British then destroyed the French Navy, attacking the French fleet at Mers el Kebir, killing 1,300 French servicemen, rather than allow French fighting ships to fall into German hands. This was known as Operation Catapult.

French Resistance

The French who objected to any alliance with Germany carried on guerrilla warfare against the Germans – this was called the Resistance Movement or the Free French. They regarded General de Gaulle, who had escaped to England, as their leader in exile. The French whom the Germans attempted to put into forced labour camps, but who escaped to the hills, were known as the

Maquis – after the thick scrub on the island of Corsica. Those who worked with and for the Germans were called the Milice.

While the Free French regarded de Gaulle as their leader in exile, in the years immediately following World War II, over one hundred thousand of them were brutally murdered by Communists. It was said that de Gaulle, a Communist sympathiser, regarded these brave patriots, who had been so loyal to him, as a threat to his plans.

Katyn Massacre
As we have seen, the German Army was followed into Poland by the Soviet Army from the East. The Russians occupied half of that country and murdered ten thousand Catholic officers at Katyn, deporting even more thousands to slave labour camps. It was not until 1989 that the British accepted the German protestations that it was not them, but the USSR, who had carried out the murders. Indeed the Germans called for an impartial investigation after the war to prove they were not guilty of this crime, but the British turned this suggestion down.

Hitler decides to invade Britain
Hitler tried to persuade Churchill to negotiate a peace treaty, but Churchill refused, whereupon Hitler planned an invasion of Britain called "Operation Sea Lion."

Battle of Britain
Hitler started by sending his Luftwaffe (air force) to bomb the British military bases, although it should be mentioned that, by this time, the British had already started bombing German civilians. This battle between the Luftwaffe and the Royal Air Force in August 1940 is called the Battle of Britain, a battle that Britain was to win.

Ultra
Hermann Goering, head of the Luftwaffe, believed it would take one month to invade Britain but he did not take into account the heroism of the RAF pilots. He also did not know that Britain possessed one of the German code machines called Enigma which contained the Ultra code. By this means, the British team of decoders, operating at Bletchley Park, near Milton Keynes, knew in advance not only how many German bombers had taken off, but also often what their target was as well. The British therefore won the Battle of Britain whereupon Hitler abandoned Operation Sea Lion.

Invasion of Norway
When Hitler invaded Norway, the right-wing Norwegian politician and friend of Hitler, Vidkun Quisling, offered himself as head of government. He won no support and thenceforth the term Quisling has been synonymous with traitor, although it should be mentioned that Quisling's stance was based on his wish to stop the spread of Communism to Norway.

The Invasion of Russia
Russia had shown aggression in 1940 by taking over Estonia, Latvia and Lithuania (a Catholic country which was hardest hit by the Russian persecution under Stalin). This prompted Hitler to launch...

1941   Operation Barbarossa
This began in June, 1941. Heading for Moscow, the German army reached within 30 miles of the capital, but was on an extended line, 1000 miles long. The usual explanation for Hitler's failure to take Moscow is that his troops were so extended that they proved a fatally weak obstacle for the Russian troops who forced the Germans into retreat by the end of January, 1942.

But there are a number of historians who say that the Germans had Moscow at their mercy but were prevented from inflicting the *coup de grace* by Hitler himself. They link this failure (to take

Leningrad and Moscow) to the equally inexplicable fact that Hitler allowed the British Expeditionary Force to escape at Dunkirk, when the British could so easily have been utterly defeated.

At the southern end of the German line lay Stalingrad. The Russians heroically and successfully defended this city in 1942, a resistance that was to prove a turning point of the war in the East.

So, by the end of 1942, Hitler had been beaten to a surrender in Russia with appalling loss of life on both sides.

Some say that the blame for Germany's defeat in the East was entirely down to Hitler. Hitler kept interfering, ordering his armies one way, then changing his mind and ordering the advance elsewhere (all to the disbelief of his generals). He forbade the troops to be properly supplied with adequate winter clothing and then forbade retreat until it was too late. Indeed his behaviour is now reckoned to have provoked the unsuccessful attempt on his life by the generals in 1944.

Atlantic Charter
In 1941, Churchill and Roosevelt met off the New Foundland Coast and called for a more equitable international economic system and the abandonment of the use of force.

Hitler and Greece
In the meantime, Italy had suffered disaster in Egypt and Greece. Indeed the Italian fleet had been defeated by the Royal Navy at Cape Matapan, off the southern coast of Greece.
The allies intended to invade the Balkans and develop bases from which to attack the German forces. When Hitler learned of this plan, he decided to foil it by ordering the German invasion of Yugoslavia and Greece.

Lend Lease
During this time, the USA began to provide economic aid partly to Britain and mainly to Russia which in total amounted to $42 billion. The dependence on US aid effectively led to Britain giving up important parts of its Empire.

Pearl Harbour
By this time, the German plan to dominate Europe was matched by a Japanese plan to dominate the Pacific. Japan had already been at war with China since 1937 and had occupied Manchuria in 1931 – this to protect Japan against the rise of Chinese Communism on its border. On 27th November 1936, Germany and Japan signed an alliance. Japan then decided to take revenge on the United States for its economic warfare against Japan. This economic warfare included a US embargo on all Japanese oil shipments, plus a total unwillingness on the part of the US to negotiate. So, on December 7th 1941, the Japanese air force, without any declaration of war, attacked the US Pacific fleet in Pearl Harbour, Hawaii, thus bringing the US into the war against Japan. As a result of this, Germany and Italy declared war on the USA. The US government then interned over 100,000 Japanese in concentration camps where conditions were extremely harsh. These people were never tried: many were the elderly, children and orphans, and they were not released until 1949.

Pearl Harbour is accepted as a Japanese attack on the USA. However, there is no doubt that this attack suited Roosevelt because in January, 1941, he had relayed a wish to Churchill that their two countries might wage war together.

1942   Singapore
The Japanese Army then spread violently and rapidly through Asia and the Pacific, taking, amongst others, Hong Kong by Christmas, 1941, and Singapore by mid-February, 1942. With

Singapore lost, the British had no naval base in the East from which to operate. After this defeat, British Ghurkha and Burmese guerrillas began to operate behind the Japanese lines, notably in Burma, under Orde Wingate who gave these soldiers the name "Chindits."

Beveridge Report

William Beveridge produced his report on "Social Insurance and Allied Services" which was to lead, in 1945, to the formal establishment of the National Welfare State and, in 1948, the foundation of the National Health Service.

Coral Sea

By May, 1942, the United States had recovered sufficiently from the disaster of Pearl Harbour and was able to respond to the Japanese onslaught; at the Battle of the Coral Sea, they were able to thwart the Japanese invasion of Australia.

Midway

The US victory at the Battle of Midway (June, 1942) was the turning point of the war in the Pacific.

Guadalcanal

The US victory at Guadalcanal, the largest of the Solomon Islands, after six months of jungle fighting, was a further consolidation.

El Alamein

In June, 1942, the Germans drove the British under Auchinleck out of the Libyan port of Tobruk. General Bernard Montgomery then took command of the British forces.

In October, 1942, General Erwin Rommel was defeated at the second battle of El Alamein by General Bernard Montgomery and Germany would always be retreating from this point in the war.

Dieppe Raid

In October 1942, a Canadian and British force of some 5,000 tried to establish a bridgehead at Dieppe in Northern France. More than 3,000 were killed, wounded or taken prisoner. This was a serious setback, but valuable lessons were learned from it for the Normandy Landings less than two years later.

1943   Landing in Sicily

By July 1943, the allies had forced the Germans back west along the North African coast and then over the sea into Italy. The allies followed them, landing on Sicily before proceeding towards the Italian mainland.

Dambuster Raids

Dams in the Ruhr were breached by the RAF. However, these famous raids by Bomber Command did little to stop German arms production.

Stalin is given Eastern Europe

At the Teheran Conference, Roosevelt and Churchill agreed to give Stalin Eastern Europe after the war, in exchange for Russian co-operation. Indeed it appears that at this conference it was decided to delay the ending of World War II to ensure that the Russian forces reached the Elbe and Berlin before the allies.

Fall of Mussolini

Mussolini was dismissed by King Victor Emmanuel III in July 1943 and then arrested. Italy then declared war on Germany and shortly afterwards surrendered.

The allies landed at Anzio on mainland Italy, near Rome, in September 1943.

Warsaw uprising
The Jews in Warsaw rebelled against the Germans, and many were put to death.

Computer
The first working computer was built in the USA.

1944   Normandy Landings
On 6th June 1944, the Allied invasion of France, under General Dwight Eisenhower (later US President) and Montgomery, began with the Normandy landings (D-Day). These successful landings then developed into a systematic and relentless forcing-back of the German Army into Germany. However, the war in Europe could have been ended a few weeks after D-Day had not Montgomery inexplicably refused to sanction the encircling of the German forces. As a result, the Germans escaped through the Falaise Gap and the war continued for another ten months.

Later that month the Russians moved back into Eastern Europe.

Operation Market Garden
In September, 10,000 allied paratroopers were dropped just north of Arnhem with a view to securing a bridgehead over the River Rhine in order to facilitate the invasion of Germany. The operation failed because the main army, coming from the south, failed to join up with the paratroopers. Indeed many paratroopers were killed or captured because they landed close to an awaiting German Panzer division. Many allied officers foresaw the grave danger the allied forces were going to be exposed to and tried to avert the disaster that would result from this hasty, ill-conceived and disastrous plan. The operation was a total failure.

V-1 and V-2 attacks
The Germans had developed two flying bombs during the war. The V-1 had been called a buzz bomb (the British referred to them as "doodlebugs") and carried nearly a ton of high explosive. It was powered by a noisy ramjet. Some 8,000 were fired at London between June, 1944, and March, 1945, killing over 5,500 civilians. The V-2, which carried about the same explosive force as the V-1, was powered by a rocket jet and thus was very fast and effectively silent – there was no warning sound prior to their explosion. Some 4,000 of these were fired on London. The rockets were developed by Werner Von Braun at the German rocket test centre at Peenemunde.

Battle of the Bulge
The German retreat was again temporarily halted, this time in December 1944, when the Germans launched a massive counter-attack in the Ardennes (the Battle of the Bulge). The fact that this action, like the extraordinary events at the Falaise Gap and Operation Market Garden, was allowed to delay the end of the war is now viewed as one of either deliberate or extraordinary incompetence on the part of the Allied leadership – the losses were quite unnecessary – and it only served to hold up the end of the war and allow Russia to take over more of Eastern Europe. However, this counter attack amounted to the final major offensive of the war by Germany, for it effectively exhausted what was left of the German forces.

Bretton Woods Conference
Both the World Bank and the International Monetary Fund were set up at this conference in New Hampshire.

There is evidence to suggest that, as a result of the Bretton Woods Conference and the subsequent lending of vast sums to developing countries, these countries are now so deeply in debt they are far worse off financially than they would have been without the loans. Indeed, many now think that this conference shifted power away from the hands of the nation states and into the hands of the transnational banks and other corporations.

1945   Yalta

In February 1945, the ailing President Roosevelt, advised by the Communist Alger Hiss, gave way to Stalin at the Yalta Conference. Stalin was given the control of Poland as well as the whole of Eastern Europe, dividing Communist territory from Western Europe by what Churchill called an "Iron Curtain." With Russia assured of such vast territorial gains, Stalin was free to make a thirty year pact with China that allowed the Communist red flag to fly unchecked in Manchuria, North Korea and other areas.

Richard Nixon, later to become US President, tried to expose what Hiss was attempting to achieve, during the Hiss Trial, which came about due to the revelations of former Communist, Whittaker Chambers.

At the earlier Conferences of Teheran (1943) and Potsdam (1945), the foundations for the wholesale abandonment of Eastern Europe to the Soviet Union had already been laid. This was a monstrous outcome, and particularly so if, as has already been mentioned, one considers that Britain entered the war to *preserve* Polish independence.

It has been said that it was at Teheran that Russia, not the West, won the war, and this as a result of Churchill's capitulation to Stalin's demands. Roosevelt even went so far as to say that he cared little if Eastern Europe became Communist.

It should be added that Stalin had no admiration for Churchill and, if anything, with Churchill a conservative, Stalin despised him. On the other hand Churchill would describe Stalin as a great man who gave him courage.

It was also at the Yalta Conference that Churchill agreed to repatriate to Russia many thousand Russians who had been forced to fight for Germany. This was a cruel betrayal of our allies because many of these soldiers were executed on their return to Russia, with the rest being transhipped to labour camps. And Britain was well aware that this would be their fate.

At the same time, if Churchill had not agreed to do this, Russia would not have released the Western allied troops they had gathered from German Prisoner of War camps.

This repatriation is known as Operation Keelhaul.

Roosevelt died in April and was succeeded by Harry Truman.

Saturation Bombing

The British and American bombers carried out a deadly policy of saturation bombing, of civilians (also known as area bombing and carpet bombing). Indeed, it had been them, and not the Germans, who first begun to bomb civilian targets, as early as 1940. The most outrageous example was the bombing of Dresden with appalling loss of life and suffering for the inhabitants who, for the most part, were non-German refugees. With the war effectively over by then, the bombing was for no military purpose.

German Surrender

On 30th April 1945, together with his mistress Eva Braun, it is claimed that Hitler committed suicide (although his body was never found) and, on 7th May, the German High Command surrendered at Luneberg Heath. The surrender could have been taken days earlier, but, as already intimated, some believe that the Allied generals prevented it happening, to give time for Soviet tanks to roll into East Germany.

Hiroshima & Nagasaki

The war in the Pacific lasted three more months. Japan had been trying to surrender before the two atomic bombs were dropped on Hiroshima and the Catholic city of Nagasaki. Their surrender was taken a few days later.

What is seldom mentioned is that the first person to develop atomic theory was Father Roger Boscovich, a Jesuit priest, physicist and polymath from Dubrovnik, in the 18th century, a fact well known and emphasised by such better known scientists as Faraday, Kelvin and Clark Maxwell.

Concentration Camps and the Holocaust

The Nazi regime had set up concentration camps, such as Auschwitz, Buchenwald, Dachau and Belsen, where many Jews, political dissidents, gypsies and other people were forcibly detained, mainly to work for the German war effort. When the Allies arrived at these camps at the end of the war, there were piles of corpses and starving inmates. The deaths of many Jews in these camps (Jewish authorities have reckoned the figure to be six million) has come to be known as the Holocaust.

A large number of Jews who survived the Nazi persecution were sent to live in Palestine, which would be renamed Israel in 1948. It is understood that this is why Germany still pays huge annual sums in reparation to finance Israel.

Pope Pius XII – Nazis and Jews

The Nazis were violently anti-Catholic. However, Pope Pius XII worked bravely and tirelessly in a practical way for his flock, the Jews and other Nazi victims. The Pope was not as outspoken as some might have wanted, but this was deliberate. If he had been forever condemning the Nazis, the fate of Jews and Catholics in German occupied territories would have been far worse. To give two examples of the stance the Church took, the Catholic hierarchy rescued 2,000 Jews from the Eichmann death march, and the Vatican arranged for hundreds of Jews to be hidden in German occupied Rome.

Jews thank the Catholic Church

At the end of the war, the Jewish hierarchy publicly thanked the Catholic Church for saving 400,000 of their number and for doing far more than any other church or institution ever did for their race.

The End of the British Empire

In 1942, Churchill had said "I have not become the King's first minister to preside over the liquidation of the British Empire." Yet, as a result of "winning" the Second World War, it was said, in 1952, by one of President Eisenhower's aids: "ten years ago the British took primary, political and military responsibility for the whole area Gibraltar east to Singapore. Since then they have given up most of the South East Asian empire, abdicated their position in Greece and Turkey, left Palestine and been thrown out of Iran. The US has supplanted Britain as the main naval power in the Mediterranean." If this is not a process of "liquidation of an empire," what is?

As Francis Neilsen says in his book *The Churchill Legend*, and after Churchill, the much celebrated war leader, had lost the 1945 general election: "What an end! What a triumph! Russia on the Elbe and a socialist government in Great Britain."

Europe after the War

The allies had been fighting to rid Europe of the menace of Hitler. Yet, having "won" the war, their reward was to see half of Europe bound in the chains of Communism, with the rest not only in ruins but dependant on money from the United States for survival. Some victory!

Chapter 12   After World War II

1945   United Nations

The United Nations was set up in 1945, ostensibly to prevent further wars, but it has been singularly ineffective in this role. Some fear that its real purpose is to assist in the creation of a One World Government, the so-called New World Order, a plan in line with Weishaupt's original ideas.

Germany divided

Under the Potsdam Conference (July-August, 1945) Germany was divided into four zones. These were occupied respectively by Britain, USA, France and the Soviet Union, with a view to reuniting Germany under a single government after early elections. However, the Soviet Union declared their zone a separate nation under their own domination, separating their territory, the German Democratic Republic (GDR) from the Federal Republic of Germany (West Germany). The GDR was controlled by the Stazi, an all-pervading system of state police and their informers, who tried to control the lives of everybody, with exceptional cruelty and repression.

Rudolph Hess and Nuremburg

Hess had landed in Scotland in 1941 with compromise peace proposals, but he was captured and held prisoner. At the Nuremburg war trials he was sentenced to life imprisonment in Spandau Prison, Berlin. After many years of being the only prisoner in Spandau, he died in 1972. Who was he, why was he held alone, and why was he never transferred? Some say that it was not Hess who was in Spandau, but a look-alike, and that the real Hess had been shot down before he got to Scotland by those who wanted the war to continue. Hess's wife was never allowed to see him in prison, permission apparently being refused by Hess himself.

The Nuremburg trials were a very strange and many say a disgraceful set of legal proceedings. Guilt was assumed at the outset. Defence lawyers were not permitted to cross-examine witnesses. Before the trials started, indeed at the Yalta Conference, Stalin called for 50,000 executions, regardless of the verdicts. An American judge was so disgusted by the illegalities he encountered that he resigned. And the Germans were held to account for obeying the laws of conventional warfare, while the Communists and some of the Allies who had flouted them fragrantly, were never tried.

Adenauer

The remaining sectors of Berlin and West Germany formed the Federal Republic of Germany (or West Germany) which, under Chancellor Konrad Adenauer, rapidly recovered into a powerful European force. In 1960, Adenauer agreed to finance the State of Israel to the tune of $50 million a year.

1946   Fulbright Scholars

US Senator, William Fulbright, an internationalist and strong supporter, indeed founder, of the United Nations, organised the Fulbright Act which provides grants for thousands of Americans to study overseas and for overseas students to study in the USA.

Italy becomes a republic

Death of John Maynard Keynes

Keynes was born in 1883 and promoted his economic theory that unemployment could be alleviated by government spending and deficit financing. He died at the time he was arranging a massive loan by the USA to Britain.

1947   Greece and the Communists

The Communists started civil wars in 1947 in Greece and Turkey, but the revolutionaries were defeated.

Tavistock Institute

This institute was founded to research business and organisational group behaviour.

Marshall Plan

This was an economic aid programme whereby the USA pumped $13,000 billion into Europe to help it recover and protect it against Communist takeover. It had the effect of softening up the economies that received the aid and, at the same time, allowing economies like Germany's to forge ahead, not on the foundation of so-called charity, but as a result of their own efforts and economically sensible strategies.

On top of this, the giving of Marshall Plan aid was dependant on economic co-operation between the European states. Indeed it is now seen to be the clear trigger for the eventual formation of the European Union and the replacement of the British Empire with what has become, in effect, an American Empire.

1948   Berlin Airlift

As we have seen, Berlin had itself been divided into four sectors and in July 1948 the Communists began the Berlin Blockade, halting road traffic into the city, hoping to starve out the Western occupants. The West then began the airlift of supplies to the city which the Soviet Union was unable to stop. It was so successful that the Soviets lifted the blockade in May 1949.

State of Israel

Israel was established in 1948 with the ending of the British mandate. It was immediately attacked by the Arab states. In the encounters which Israel won, Israel confirmed its independence and ruthlessly forced the original Arab occupants out of Palestine (renaming it Israel) into refugee camps in Gaza and the West Bank – an action the results of which persist today and still causes deep resentment in the Arab world.

What is usually forgotten is that until Israel was established in 1948, Arabs and Jews had been living side by side in prosperous harmony in Palestine for centuries. Palestine was a fruitful and productive region before the occupation of Israel, but these two characteristics have been not only devastated and severely curtailed by the unrest brought about by the imposition of this new state, but also overlooked and forgotten by the new inhabitants.

The Arab call for at least a separate Palestinian State is headed by Hamas, a political group of Sunni Muslims that was elected to power in Gaza in 2005, but which has, in part, pursued its aim with suicide bombings.

Mahatma Ghandi assassinated

This famous Indian Hindu leader had led India to independence, although he greatly regretted both the bloodshed as well as the fact of partition, with Pakistan and East Pakistan (now Bangladesh) becoming separate countries.

The Cold War

After the Second World War the Communists began to extend their influence throughout the world and the stand-off this initiated between the USSR and the West became known as the Cold War.

1949   China and Mao Tse Tung

This was the year of the Proclamation of the People's Republic of China. As a result of the overthrow of the last Emperor in 1912, since 1927 there had been a civil war between the Communists, under Mao Tse Tung, and the Christian Nationalists under Chiang Kai Chek. During the Second World War, Chiang defended China against the Japanese, while Mao continued to attack Chiang – as a result, the Nationalist forces were severely depleted.

Formosa

After the Second World War, Stalin poured money into Mao's coffers and by the end of 1949 Chiang had been driven off mainland China to the island of Taiwan (Formosa). The Chinese Communists slaughtered hundreds of thousands of civilians and outlawed religion.

National Parks began in the UK

NATO

North Atlantic Treaty Organisation was established for the collective defence of North America and Western Europe, particularly against the USSR.

1950   Korea

In January 1950, the Chinese, who controlled North Korea with Russian (i.e. Stalin's) support, launched an attack on independent South Korea. The North Koreans all but crushed South Korea before the US Marines and British forces arrived to help the South, and China came to the aid of the North. The ensuing war, which lasted until the peace talks in Panmunjon in October 1951, saw the battle line advancing and retreating more than once, and ended with the boundary between the two Koreas (the 38th Parallel) being redrawn where it had been before the war started.

During the war, the US General MacArthur, who had been an outstanding strategist in World War II, led the allied forces to the extent of defeating the North Korean Army. He then advocated operations against their Chinese allies, but, instead of being allowed to quash the Chinese belligerents, he was promptly dismissed, whereupon the Chinese rekindled the embers of the North Korean Army and, as has just been said, together they fought back and pushed the allies back to the 38th Parallel.

McCarthy

In the United States, the spread of world Communism was found to be rife within its own borders, but when Senator Joseph McCarthy announced that there were over two hundred Communists in the US government, the hearings that took place to root out "un-American activities," rather than resulting in the removal of Communists in the government, resulted in McCarthy himself being persecuted by the liberal press for creating a climate of fear in the USA. McCarthyism is now taken to mean a witch hunt, but there were many in the US who believed that what he was saying was true and there is much evidence to support it.

Death of Jan Smuts

Smuts, born in 1870, was South African Prime Minister and advocated strong links with Britain. This made him unpopular with Afrikaners, i.e. those of Dutch decent.

1951   Burgess and MacLean

Guy Burgess and Donald MacLean, two British Foreign Office officials, who were spying for the USSR, fled to Russia, followed by their associate Kim Philby.

The Mousetrap

The Mousetrap, by Agatha Christie, the world's longest running play (still running today) was first performed in London.

First Jet Liner
The British De Havilland Comet was the first jet plane to enter passenger service.

1953 Mount Everest Climbed
Mount Everest, 29,028ft high, was climbed by a British-led expedition under Sir John, later Lord, Hunt. The first two to reach the summit were Sir Edmund Hillary and Sherpa Tensing Norgay. Two British climbers, George Mallory and A. C. Irvine had gone missing in 1924, very near the top, but, to this day, nobody knows if they had actually reached it. Mallory's frozen body was found near the summit in 1999.

Critchell Down Scandal
This estate in England, which had been compulsorily acquired by the State during the war, rather than being returned to its original owners, was going to be sold to the highest bidder. But after the resignation of a government minister and a suicide of one of the residents of the estate, it was decided that, thenceforth, full market value must be paid for all such property compulsorily purchased by the State.

Bilderberg Group
This secret organisation was founded in 1953, and since then it has met in secret every year, at which it invites up-and-coming politicians and industrialists from all over the Western world to attend. Many observers, noticing the intense secrecy involved with the meetings, suspect (and indeed have evidence to support) that it is effectively a crash course for future members and leaders of other secret organisations believed to exert strong influence on world affairs, such as the Illuminati and the Council on Foreign Relations, etc.

1954 Four Minute Mile
Roger Banister broke this record at the Iffley Road running track in Oxford. His time was 3 minutes 59.4 seconds.

1955 Cyprus partitioned
In 1955, Greek Cypriots, under Archbishop Makarios, revolted against the British – he wanted the island united with Greece. This was to result, eventually in 1974, in the island being divided into a Greek South and a Turkish North. However, in 2005 the Turkish government recognised the legitimacy of the Greek government in the South – this being a requisite for Turkey's application to join the EU.

Einstein dies
Albert Einstein, who was born in Germany in 1879, proposed the revolutionary and still controversial Theory of Relativity in 1905. The theory is controversial because it predicts that if one clock is travelling at the speed of light, it will register time passing more slowly than one at rest. But if the Theory of Relativity be true, one cannot tell which clock is the one that moves because it *could* be the so-called stationary clock that is doing the travelling. But this would be preposterous having one clock going both faster *and* slower than the other. And, if the ether exists – and remember it has never been proved not to exist (see 1887) – then the clock at rest would *have* to be stationary (resting in and with respect to the ether) and then the Theory of Relativity would have been fatally undermined because that assumes that things move relative to each other. The concept of Relativity with respect to moving objects is neatly summed by asking a train conductor, "Does Manchester stop at this train?"

There are a number of scientists who believe the whole Theory of Relativity to be bogus. They say it relies on mathematical equations that not only have never been proved, but are actually un-provable. Indeed, in both 2007 and 2011 there appeared to be observable proofs that the theory no longer holds water.

1956   Invasion of Hungary

In post-war Hungary, the Communists were finding the Catholic spirit difficult to crush and on 24th October 1956, the USSR invaded Hungary with Soviet tanks arriving in the capital Budapest. The Russians utterly and ruthlessly crushed Hungary. The effect of this invasion, apart from the disaster it brought to Hungary, was to imply that, with the West doing nothing to stop the invasion, there was no power that was going to counter the power of Communism.

Suez Crisis

The United Nations paid no attention to the valiant Hungarians because they were concentrating on the Suez Canal where, the day before the invasion, Britain and France had bombed Suez in their futile attempt to prevent Egypt nationalising and blocking off the Canal. Egypt had taken this course because, with the US dropping their plans to finance the Aswan Dam, the Egyptian Prime Minister, Gamal Abdul Nasser, sought to replace that finance with the revenues he would enjoy from nationalising the Suez Canal. Britain and France also hoped to thwart the Egyptians from resisting the Israelis who used this crisis as a cover for invading Sinai. Britain and France themselves were humiliated and Israel withdrew.

First video recorder was launched

1957   Sputnik

USSR launched the first artificial earth-orbiting satellite.

Jodrell Bank

This was the world's largest steerable radio telescope and was built in Cheshire.

1958   The Common Market

The two Treaties of Rome, signed in 1957, established the European Economic Community (the European Common Market). Whilst known as the brainchild of Jean Monet, we now know that it was first proposed in occultist publications as early as 1914. The first signatories were Belgium, France, Italy, Luxemburg, the Netherlands and West Germany. The UK was not to join until 1973.

1959   Dalai Lama

The Dalai Lama is the spiritual leader of the Buddhists in Tibet. Tibetans believe him to be the reincarnation of his predecessor. In 1959, he fled into exile in protest against the Chinese annexation and oppression of Tibet. He continues to call for Tibetan liberation.

1960   Cuba

In 1960, after President Fidel Castro's dealings with the USSR, Cuba fell to the Communists. The next year Cuban exiles from the USA tried to invade Cuba, but were defeated at the Bay of Pigs.

1961   First man in space

The USSR puts, Yuri Gagarin, the first man in space.

Berlin Wall

In 1961, the Communists built the Berlin Wall (an armed barrier) to prevent East Germans fleeing to the West. They thus sealed the border between East and West Berlin.

1962   The Second Vatican Council

In the 1960s, a series of liberal resolutions were passed by an Ecumenical Council of the world's Catholic bishops, called the Second Vatican Council, which resulted in the wholesale modernisation of Catholicism. Many say that the church that emerged from this council, with its new doctrines, new morality and new way of saying Mass (that was radically different from that used for nearly 2,000 years, and against Catholic law and doctrine), etc., was, not the Catholic Church that began to operate at Pentecost, but an entirely new church.

Since this event, religious belief and the public sense of morality has collapsed catastrophically throughout the world, and most notably in the West.

The Second Vatican Council also gave "Liberation Theology" a huge boost. Communist revolutionaries in Latin America regard liberation theology as the spiritual version of Communism.

It is interesting to note that the (statistically negligible, but disproportionately reported) "child abuse scandal" involving priests, coincides not with what is usually presented as the "strict, oppressive" Church of before Vatican II, but very much with the sexual revolution and liberation of the 1960s and 70s, which *followed* the Second Vatican Council. It is a liberal problem, not a Catholic one.

Cuban Missile Crisis

When the USA discovered that the Soviets had built a missile base in Cuba, President Kennedy imposed a naval blockade against Soviet shipments to Cuba. The world appeared to hover on the brink of a nuclear war that would result if the weapons were not dismantled. However, Khrushchev did agree to dismantle the missiles in return for Kennedy agreeing not to attack Cuba and so long as the US dismantled their missiles in Turkey.

DNA

In 1962, Francis Crick of the Cavendish Laboratory in Cambridge and James Watson of the USA were awarded the Nobel Prize for medicine for discovering the structure of DNA (Deoxyribonucleic Acid).

1963   The Profumo affair

This scandal revealed that the Secretary of State for War, John Profumo, had slept with a showgirl named Christine Keeler who, in turn, had slept with a Russian spy. Profumo lied when subsequently questioned about it, which led to his resignation and also severely damaged the Macmillan government. Profumo devoted the rest of his life to charitable works in reparation.

President Kennedy was assassinated

Some extraordinary connections between Kennedy's and Lincoln's Assassinations		
	Lincoln	Kennedy
Elected to Congress	1846	1946
Elected President	1860	1960
Day of Assassination	Friday	Friday
How killed	Shot in head	Shot in head
Secretary's name	Kennedy	Lincoln
Name of successor	Johnson	Johnson
Successor born	1808	1908
Assassin born	1839	1939
Assassin's name. Both known by three names. Both names have fifteen letters	John Wilkes Booth	Lee Harvey Oswald
Place of assassination	Ford Theatre	Ford Lincoln car
Assassin's behaviour	Kills in a theatre, runs and hides in a warehouse	Shoots from a warehouse; runs and hides in a theatre
Assassin's fate	Killed before coming to trial	Killed before coming to trial
What was president doing a week before the shooting?	Visiting Monroe, Maryland	Visiting Marilyn Monroe

1964   Brazil
In 1964, Brazil overthrew a Communist government – a rare victory against Communism.

American Civil Rights Act
The Jim Crow laws, which segregated blacks from whites and which had been passed after the American Civil War, were effectively repealed by the Civil Rights Act which forbade racial discrimination and which President Johnson persuaded US Congress to pass.

1965   Vietnam War
In 1954, the French were forced to leave Vietnam when Dien Bien Phu fell to the Communists. This resulted in North Vietnam being given to the Communists while the South continued to be governed by the Catholic Ngo Dinh Diem. It was the USA that ousted Diem, who was subsequently assassinated, in 1963 resulting in chaos in South Vietnam. This chaos allowed the Communists from the North to step up their activity. In 1965, the US sent ground troops into South Vietnam. In spite of intense public opposition in the USA, the war lasted for 10 years until 1975 when the Communists overran the South. They also took Cambodia and Laos, inflicting high casualties while the US forces fled.

1967   Six Day War
In this war between Israel on the one side and Egypt, Syria and Jordan on the other, Israel captured the Golan Heights, the Eastern half of Jerusalem, the West bank of Jordan, the Gaza Strip and Sinai as far as the Suez Canal.

Operation Cyanide
During the Six Days War, the US sent an unarmed naval ship (*USS Liberty*) into Israeli waters, whereupon, on 8th June, 1967, the Israeli's attacked it, killing 34 sailors and disabling it with torpedoes. The boats and planes used by the Israeli forces were unmarked but had been provided by the US, to enable the Israelis to attack a US ship, but make it look as if it were an attack by Egypt.

Immediately after the attack, bombers were launched from *USS America* to drop *nuclear* bombs on Cairo in supposed retaliation. The planes were recalled on the orders of President Johnson before they could launch their attack.

The crew of the liberty were awarded the highest honours amid the greatest secrecy. This cover-up was most effective because few who lived through the war heard of the episode. It is held by some that, had the war against the Arabs (the Egyptians) started to go badly, the US-Israeli alliance could have blamed this attack on the Egyptians and would therefore have had the excuse to destroy the Egyptian capital Cairo, and thus bring about an Israeli victory. The war did not go badly for the alliance, but there seems little doubt that this secret plan existed.

Martin Luther King assassinated
This black civil rights leader was shot by James Earl Ray in Memphis, Tennessee, USA.

Che Guevara executed
In 1959, Guevara, from Argentina, had assisted Castro to gain power in Cuba by revolutionary means. He later became a symbolic South American revolutionary leader. His life ended trying to foment revolt in Bolivia.

1968   Prague Spring
Alexander Dubcek in Czechoslovakia initiated some liberal reforms, only for Soviet tanks to roll into his country and reverse them.

1969   Americans on the Moon
Neil Armstrong and Buzz Aldrin landed on the moon, although some 30 years later, there are persistent rumours that the whole thing was faked, as part of the propaganda war with Russia, during the Cold War.

1970   First Jumbo Jet

1971   Coco Channel dies
She was a French couturier, born in 1883, who brought simplicity back to women's clothing.

Publication of the Pentagon Papers
This year saw the publication of the *Pentagon Papers* which revealed the true involvement of the USA in Indochina (Vietnam), ever since 1945. It caused embarrassment to President Nixon who was seeking re-election in 1972 and wanted the material suppressed. At the time there was growing opposition to the US involvement in the Vietnam War and, until then, the public hadn't realised just how long the US had been interfering in that region.

Louis Armstrong dies
This world-renowned black trumpeter was born in 1900.

1972   Universal Time
Co-ordinated Universal Time began to be measured not by the moon or sun but by the oscillations of caesium atoms. This was formalised in 1986.

Watergate
A political scandal in the USA exposed senior members in the Republican Party as having broken into the Democratic headquarters (the Watergate Building in Washington). This, and the cover-up that followed, would result in President Nixon's resignation two years later.

Bloody Sunday
The British army in Northern Ireland fired on a banned civil rights demonstration and killed 13 people. This triggered the violent troubles in Ulster which only (apparently) began to ease when the Good Friday agreement was signed in 1998.

1973   Chile
In 1973, Chile overthrew the Communist government of Salvador Allende.

Yom Kippur War
Egyptian forces surprised Israel by crossing the Suez Canal and thereby regaining Sinai.

Trilateral Commission
This is the latest arm of what some believe to be a hidden administration behind global events. Following on from the formation of Chatham House, the Council on Foreign Relations and the Bilderberg Group, this was founded to coordinate the foreign policies of the USA, Europe and Japan.

Angola and Mozambique
In Africa, the USA refused to give aid to Angola and Mozambique, both of which fell to the Communists – as did Ethiopia.

Pablo Picasso dies
This famous Spanish artist was born in 1881.

W. H. Auden dies
This British poet was born in 1907. With C. Day Lewis, Louis MacNeice and Stephen Spender, they formed a group of left wing poets in the 1930s; by the end of his life Auden turned away from Marxism and favoured Christianity.

1974   Nixon resigns
President Nixon resigned over the Watergate revelations and his attempt to cover them up.

1975   Portugal
In 1975, Portugal provided another of the very few examples of a country reversing the trend and overthrowing a Communist government.

Pol Pot
In Cambodia (Kampuchea), Pol Pot, who commanded the Khmer Rouge, came to power and would lead the country until 1979. During his leadership about a quarter of the population were put to death (the "Killing Fields").

Death of P. G. Wodehouse
The comic writing of P. G. Wodehouse has led to him being described as the best writer of English in the twentieth century.

1976   Concorde enters service
This supersonic airliner, universally regarded for the beauty of its design, was withdrawn in 2003.

National Exhibition Centre in Birmingham opens

Deaths of Agatha Christie and L. S. Lowry
Agatha Christie is to this day still world famous for her detective stories. She was born in 1890.

Lowry was a British painter who painted (mainly) bleak scenes with matchstick people. He was born in Manchester in 1887.

1978   Liverpool Anglican Cathedral completed
It is the biggest cathedral in Britain and was designed in Gothic style by Giles Gilbert Scott, himself a Catholic. He also designed the (now almost entirely replaced) red telephone boxes.

1979   Afghanistan and Nicaragua
In 1979, Russian Communists invaded Afghanistan to support the Ghilzai government, but this encouraged a revolt against the Ghilzai and the Russians were defeated.

Communists also took control of Nicaragua.

Spain grants Autonomy to Basques
The Basques were very early settlers of Northern Spain and South West France. However, the Basques are republicans and want full independence. The political party supporting this goal is ETA, which wavers between causing violence and calling for ceasefires. In 2011, they seem to have called for a permanent ceasefire.

1980   Mrs Thatcher and Ronald Reagan
In the 1980s, Margaret Thatcher, Prime Minister of the UK (1979-1990), and Ronald Reagan, President of the United States (1981-1989), formed a close alliance that was instrumental in bringing about the end of the Cold War and the collapse of Communism, including giving aid to such groups as the Solidarity movement (Solidarnosc) in Poland.

1982   Falklands War

Argentina invaded the Falkland Islands, and occupied other British territories, in the South Atlantic, but they were defeated and forced to withdraw by the British within 2 months. These islands were named after Viscount Falkland when Captain John Strong landed there in 1690. They had first brought Britain to the verge of war in 1771 and there had also been an international incident in 1848. In 1914, after the German victory at Coronel, all available allied warships were assembled in the South Atlantic and, at the Battle of the Falkland Isles, the German fleet that had won at Coronel was sunk with just one ship escaping.

1984   Cabinet War Rooms

These underground and well-protected offices are where Churchill ran the British war effort during World War II. They were opened to the public this year.

1986   Gorbachev

In 1986, Mikhail Gorbechev took control of the USSR and began his double policy of Glasnost (Openness) and Perestroika (Restructuring). However, in spite of appearances to the contrary, the same people remained in power. As a result of his coming to power and from about this time, the countries that Russia had overrun began to try to escape the clutches of Communism and regain their independence.

Poland

In Poland, the non-Communist Lech Walesa was elected president. Poland was the first Communist country to elect a non-Communist leader.

Israel's Nuclear Arsenal

The London *Times* revealed the true extent of Israel's nuclear arsenal. Their source, Mordechai Vanunu, was imprisoned by the Israelis and, while subsequently released, remains under house arrest.

1988   Turin Shroud

The shroud was carbon dated. Three tests seemed to indicate that the shroud could be no older than 1260-1390, but subsequently experts have questioned the accuracy of the tests because they took no account of the effects caused by the fire in 1532, nor of the build-up of the bioplastic coating, which is a living bacterial build-up on the cloth. Both of these effects are known to give artefacts a misleadingly young age.

Further to this, in 2005, a new study refuted the 1988 findings for two reasons. One was that the piece of cloth tested in 1988 was not from the original shroud but from a piece sewn into it in the Middle Ages to repair it. The second was that the lack of lignin in the original cloth proves that it could easily be as old as 2000 years. This lack could never corroborate a date of only 700 or so years earlier.

1989   Germany is reunited and Communism appears to collapse in the Soviet Union

In 1989, the Berlin Wall was officially and dramatically demolished and the border between East and West reopened. In addition, Czechoslovakia held free elections. In 1990, Hungary followed East Germany, and at the same time all the other Soviet states were given back their independence. The independent states formed a loose grouping called the Commonwealth of Independent States (CIS).

However, granting independence did not go well:

Russia resisted the independence of Chechnya, a Muslim state lying between the Black and the Caspian Seas, and sandwiched between Russia and Georgia in the Caucasus Mountains, whose capital city is Grozny. It took Russia ten years to take back control of this troubled country. This conflict has occasionally spread into neighbouring Muslim Ingushetia.

Christian Georgia has also suffered much since independence, especially in connection with its long term wish to join the EU. Russia has resisted this move and has recognised the independence of South Ossetia and Abkhazia, both of which want independence from Georgia and have sizeable and rising Muslim populations.

Another troubled region concerns Nagorno-Karabakh. This lies to the south of Georgia and is a disputed area between Christian Armenia and Muslim Azerbaijan.

Hubble Space Telescope launched

1991   Gulf War
In 1990, Iraq, led by Saddam Hussein, invaded Kuwait. In 1991, British and American forces attacked Iraq (Operation Desert Storm) and successfully liberated Kuwait. At the same time, Hussein attacked the Kurds in Northern Iraq and forced 1million to flee.

The Kurds
The Kurds are a very ancient people who live in Iraq, Iran and Turkey. They are Sunni Muslims and predominantly agricultural. They have long wanted their own land. The most famous Kurd is probably Saladin. The Dervishes, who are also Muslims, live in this area as well. They are religious beggars and the Whirling Dervishes claim close community with their divinity, dancing dangerously with knives (the Arab equivalent is the Fakir, who may be Muslim or Hindu).

Maastricht Treaty
This treaty, building on the Single European Act of 1985, and introducing the plan for full European political union, was signed this year and later forced through the British Parliament amid great controversy. One reason for the controversy was because, amongst other things, this treaty ushered in European Regionalisation whereby the member countries would be (and now have been) divided up into European Regions with each Regional Assembly reporting not to national parliaments, but directly to Brussels. In due course this system of Regionalisation is set to see the closure of all European national governments, with just one seat of European national government at Brussels. Whilst this closure hasn't happened yet, the following are already organised or are about to be organised on a European regional basis:
- Fire
- Police
- Ambulance
- Voting in European elections
- Telephones
- Health services
- Planning

And it is likely that a great deal more will follow.

These assemblies were very unpopular in Britain, and were replaced by Regional Development Agencies in 2010..

1992   End of Yugoslavia
Yugoslavia split into the independent states of Slovenia (principally Catholic), Croatia (Catholic), Serbia (Russian Orthodox), Bosnia-Herzegovina (Muslim) and Macedonia (Greek Orthodox). Modern Yugoslavia consists of Serbia, Vojvodina and Montenegro, all of which are Russian Orthodox. However, at the same time, all these states contain elements of other types of Slav, and there was huge unrest with many atrocities and much blood spilt, mainly in Bosnia-Herzegovina.

Kosovo

Also within Serbia is the province of Kosovo, mainly peopled by Albanians who are Muslim and who wish to unite Kosovo with Albania. The real problem is that Serbia has clearly established rights to control Kosovo, where there are many Orthodox Shrines. So Serbia formally annexed Kosovo for the benefit of its Orthodox peoples. Notwithstanding this, there has been continuing violence and atrocities, including a short war in 1999, in which Serbia was forced to give up control of Kosovo. Kosovo has since sought independence from Serbia and indeed proclaimed it in 2008.

Czechoslovakia split up

In this same year (1992) Czechoslovakia split up into the Czech Republic and Slovakia.

1993   Fermat's last theorem solved

Andrew Wiles solved Fermat's famous last theorem which Pierre de Fermat had resolved in about 1650, but never written down.

1994   Mandela becomes President of South Africa

After 46 years, the Apartheid regime ended. Having been released from prison after serving a 26 year sentence for sabotage and other offences, Nelson Mandela became the President of South Africa.

The Channel Tunnel opens

1997   Turin Shroud

The Turin Shroud was, once again, saved from fire.

Diana Princess of Wales killed in car crash in Paris

1998   US "Stonehenge" discovered

On a building site in Florida, a set of circular rock carvings, 38 feet across, was discovered. This is probably North America's oldest man-made artefact – there are very few man-made structures in the USA which predate Christopher Columbus – and it is reckoned to be 4,500 years old. Its discovery happens to take us neatly back, more or less, to where our story began.

Later Notes

2000   Unrest in Jerusalem
The authorities in Israel began to make overt moves to rebuild the Jewish temple on Temple Mount near Mount Zion, by placing on a lorry a large foundation stone intended for this purpose. This caused a significant increase in the continuing troubles between Jews and Arabs in Israel (Intifada).

2001   World Trade Centre Towers destroyed and Pentagon attacked
On 11th September, it was reported that four commercial airliners were hijacked in Eastern USA by Muslim extremists. Two planes were seen to fly into the World Trade Centre towers in New York, and, after a short fire, both buildings collapsed.

A third plane badly damaged the Pentagon in Washington, the fourth crashed into open country. About three thousand lives were lost. The USA, with British assistance, blamed the attacks on the extremist Muslim Al Qaeda movement (led by Osama Bin Laden) who were supported and protected by the Taliban regime in Afghanistan, but who, until now, had not been considered one, coherent group (indeed, this status appears to have been attributed to them as a result of these attacks, to the mutual advantage of Bin Laden's followers – for it made them seem a much greater menace than they in fact were – and the US government, to justify their subsequent aggression and wars). Both Al Qaeda and the Taliban demand a separate state for the Palestinians. However, both factions denied having had anything to do with the attacks. Nonetheless, the US and Britain attacked Afghanistan, in revenge, and the Taliban government collapsed and went underground.

2002   Euro replaces the individual currencies of most European nations
By 2011, the currency was in serious trouble as a result of economies of the Eurozone countries pulling in different, and sometimes opposite, directions. Those countries, such as Greece, that were in uncontrollable deficits were being constantly bailed out by the nations that had larger and more stable economies. In 2012, this instability and vast drain on nations' funds continues, with Spain now requiring a bailout, as well as Greece, with other countries likely to follow.

2003   Second Gulf War
The British and Americans overthrew the Iraqi regime run by Saddam Hussein in a short war. They maintained that he was a threat to world peace by holding an arsenal of "Weapons of Mass Destruction" and the West was determined to remove him.

Many suspected, and not without reason, that the real reason for the invasion was to secure Iraq's oil deposits for Western use. Of particular note was the failure by the invading forces to uncover any so-called Weapons of Mass Destruction (WMDs), which had been the pretext for the invasion in the first place.

There was a further and related mystery, involving the apparent suicide in the summer of 2003 of Dr David Kelly, who had inspected the weapons held in Iraq and both knew and declared that Saddam Hussein had no weapons worthy of a US/British invasion. He is reported to have committed suicide shortly after revealing that the intelligence report on which the decision to go to war had been based, and which declared that Iraq possessed weapons of mass destruction that were capable of delivery within 45 minutes, had been "sexed up." Many believe that the paucity of the evidence that he committed suicide suggests that he was actually murdered before he could undermine the British government's credibility any more.

2004   Madrid Bombings

The Spanish Judiciary concluded that Al Qaeda (or an "Al Qaeda-inspired terrorist cell") was responsible for the killing of over 200 people with bombs that were apparently set off to punish the West for their actions in Iraq, despite no direct Al Qaeda involvement ever being established.

Indian Ocean Tsunami

About 300,000 were killed when a very powerful earthquake in the Indian Ocean triggered a number of tsunamis (tidal waves) that devastated the ocean's coastline.

2005   London Bombings

On 7th July, over 50 people were killed by four bombs in London – an attack that appeared to copy the Madrid bombings of fifteen months earlier.

2006   Iran develops its own nuclear arsenal

Iran has continued to develop nuclear technology, claiming its use was for domestic energy production only, but widely believed to be for the creation of nuclear weapons; a development that caused much concern to the West. Indeed the problem of Iran's nuclear ambitions played its part in the month-long war that raged in Southern Lebanon in 2006 between the Israeli army and Hezbollah forces, backed by Iran, in which 1,200 people (mostly Lebanese Christian civilians) were killed.

Litvinenko's murder

Former Russian KGB employee, Alexander Litvinenko, who had fled to the West, was killed by nuclear (Polonium) poisoning in London. No-one could establish who had done it, but it had all the hallmarks of a KGB (now called FSB) killing.

2007   Death of Milton Friedman

Friedman was born in 1912 and coined the economic theory which challenged Keynes' version, known as Deficit Financing and which claims that governments can spend their way out of trouble. Friedman maintained that governments should manage their economies by controlling the money supply (Monetarism). Margaret Thatcher was a follower of Friedman.

It is little known that Monetarism was first described by a Parisian Catholic called Nicholas Oresme, who died in 1382. Oresme said that governments should not interfere with the Money Supply at all.

Einstein's theory disproved?

Two German physicists claimed to have found photons that break the speed of light. If this is proved, Einstein's theory of relativity, which requires an infinite amount of energy to propel an object at more than 186,000 miles a second, will be in tatters. Evidence that this does indeed happen was produced in 2011, when it seemed that neutrinos generated at the Large Hadron Collider in Switzerland travelled to Italy at a speed in excess of the speed of light.

And in 2011 this claim seemed to have been proved when neutrinos were apparently observed to travel faster than light.

Treaty of Lisbon

This treaty, which had been called the European Constitution but had been rewritten and was now called the Treaty of Lisbon, was signed in 2007, ushering in a federal Europe and further destruction of the powers of the individual European national governments. It had been rejected by the French and Dutch electorate, and was rejected the following year by the Irish voters, but this did not stop the Brussels bureaucrats from proceeding with implementing the provisions of this self-amending treaty.

2008   Election of first black US President
Barak Obama was elected amidst great and world-wide public adulation, though it should be noted that he is of mixed race, and does not have roots in the US Civil Rights movement.

2009   Credit Crunch
While the recession caused by the Credit Crunch had begun in 2007, when banks started getting into serious financial difficulties, it was in this year that the severe effects of the resulting recession began to be noticed.

2011   Japanese Tsunami
The North East Coast of the main Japanese island of Japan was inundated by a Tsunami which was caused by one the largest earthquakes ever recorded. Many thousands of lives were lost.

Arab Spring.
In 2011, first of all the government in Tunisia fell, then in Egypt, and then Libya (aided by the West). The reason given for these uprisings was the overthrow of the apparently tyrannical and unelected regimes that were in place in these countries. However, it should be noted that, in each instance, the people do not seem to be more democratically or peacefully governed under their new regimes, and violent unrest abounds.

In the case of Libya, Colonel Gaddafi is always portrayed as a despot but, while this is not generally known, he governed his people well with a benevolence that is unheard of in European countries. Free electricity for all citizens, subsidies of $50,000 for newlyweds to buy their first home, and a debt-free economy: all at the hands of Gaddafi. However, despite decades of Western backing, he too (another leader of a country rich with oil and opposed to the State of Israel) was deposed, and, in this instance, murdered, denying him a trial in which he could have said much to expose his dealings with the West.

2012   Unrest in Syria
There is also great unrest in Syria, with terrorist uprisings, supported by the West, against its government, which happens also to be opposed to the State of Israel.

2013   Rise of UKIP
The U K Independence Party, founded in 1993, and which campaigns for the United Kingdom to withdraw from the European Union, gains 25% of the national vote in local elections.

Part Two
History notes
Contents

Preamble
Part I Pre-Norman History
Part II Norman History

Part III Plantagenet History

Part IV The Houses of Lancaster and York

Part V Tudor History

Part VI Stuart History

Part VIII The House of Windsor

218. Lord Palmerston
219. Garibaldi
220. Franco Prussian War
221. Gladstone
222. Disraeli
223. General Gordon
224. Jameson Raid
225. Boer War
226. Boxer Rebellion
227. Local Councils
228. Joe Chamberlain
229. Edward VII
230. George V
231. World War I
232. Suffragettes
233. Lord Balfour
234. Russian Revolution
235. Lloyd George
236. Stanley Baldwin
237. General Strike
238. Edward VIII
239. World War II – causes
240. World War II – start
241. World War II – North African Campaign
242. World War II – in general

Part Two
History Notes
Preamble

Pre-Roman Britain

We tend to be taught that British History began with the coming of the Romans – and indeed that they were the first bringers of civilisation to these islands. However, and as those who study Celtic history will tell you, the Romans, like the members of any usurping empire (or would-be empire) were not popular; they dealt ruthlessly with the people they found there and, being the victors, left them with a history that suppresses what happened before they arrived. This is why we all tend to know so little about pre-Roman Britain.

So what do we know?

Let's see what we may have heard of from this period. If we take the earliest period, the Stone Age, we might have heard of Kent's Cavern (perhaps) in Torquay. If we move into the Bronze Age, we find the hut settlements, barrows and Stonehenge. In the Iron Age we have probably heard of the many examples of hill forts, like Maiden Castle in Dorset, and we might have heard of the sailor, Pytheas the Greek, who visited Britain. But not much else.

What else is there to know? Well, there are some important names and events, and this preamble is an attempt to mention the interesting ones and thereby to fill in some of the gaps in our pre-Roman historical knowledge from which most people seem to suffer.

As the World History section relates, it was the people we now call the Celts who first occupied the island of Britain. Now, whilst few historians agree on dates, there is a general consensus that there was a general migration of people in a north-westerly direction across the continent of Europe during the second millennium BC. Those who settled in the British Isles, as we say, were Celts. These were the people who built or erected the great Bronze Age structures like Stonehenge.

The first event that has been recorded was the arrival of Brutus from Troy in the thirteenth century BC (please note that he is not the same Brutus that we associate with Julius Caesar). He was the grandson of Aeneas, a cousin of the Trojan King, and he escaped from Troy after the Greeks had destroyed it. At that stage, the island of Britain was known as Albion, but Brutus changed the name to Britannicus. While he landed at Totnes, he founded and made his capital city London, which he called Trinovantum (New Troy). He divided the island between his sons Locrinus, Camber and Albanactus. Locrinus received (roughly) what we now call England, Camber was given Wales (hence Cambria, Cambrian Mountains etc.) and Albanactus received the part that is now Scotland, which was then named after him and called Albany. Brutus's second-in-command was called Corineus, and, in reward for his services, Brutus gave him the land we now know as Cornwall.

What this implies is that the British are part Celtic and part Trojan.

Shortly after Brutus's arrival, Humber, King of the Huns, attacked Britain, but was defeated. He drowned in the estuary that bears his name.

There were apparently nearly 100 kings of Britain after Brutus and we do not plan to give their names here. What we will do is select a few names from the list with their rough dates because their existence may interest you.

1050BC King Ebraucus, who gave his name to what we now know as York (Ebor)

1000BC King Leil, who gave his name to Carlisle

?900BC King Leir, who gave his name to Leicester, and on whose life Shakespeare based his famous play

?400BC King Belinus, who gave his name to Billingsgate in London

?50BC King Lud, who renamed Trinovantum, London, and gave his name to Ludgate in London

(55BC Roman Landings)

At this point, the British History Notes section takes over, as indeed do the sections on Scotland and Wales in Country by Country. However, the following British kings reigned *after* the Romans invaded, and they may be of interest:

125AD King Sulgenius. It was during his reign that the Romans built Hadrian's Wall.

3rd C AD King Cole (or Coel) who founded Colchester and is believed to be the father of Helena, the mother of the Emperor Constantine.

?4th C AD King Maximianus. He took control of what was then known as Armorica in northern France and renamed it Second Britain, hence we get the name of Brittany.

449AD King Vortigern, who let in the Saxons.

?6th C AD King Arthur, about whom many famous legends have been invented. We have no way of knowing how much of his story is true, but he is reckoned to have ruled not just Britain, but, in addition, Ireland, Scotland, Iceland, Norway, Denmark and most of the northern part of France. He is reputed to have been mortally wounded at the Battle of Slaughter Bridge in Cornwall.

Shortly after King Arthur we link up with King Egbert whose name appears at the top of the list of English Kings and Queens in the Appendix.

As has already been mentioned, for a brief summary of the histories of Scotland, Wales and Ireland please refer to their entries in the Country by Country section.

History notes
Introduction

These notes, unlike the first section (which perhaps can be read or skimmed), are simply the bullet points of the key events of British history (as well as some events that are not strictly British history, but are closely enough related to it to be included here) and are intended to represent the essential elements of British history between the Romans and the end of World War II (British history thereafter is covered in <u>World History: The Story So Far</u>). These notes may be helpful to the student who wishes to remind himself of the essential points about a person, place, event or activity in British history.

PART I
PRE-NORMAN HISTORY

1.   Roman Landings
- 55BC, the Romans landed at Deal in Kent.
- Their leader was Julius Caesar.
- The Britons wore paint called Woad.
- The Romans only stayed a few days.
- Next year, 54BC, there was another short invasion.
- Julius Caesar was assassinated in 44BC.

2.   Roman Invasion
- Invasion, AD43.
- There was no fighting when they landed.
- Later, Romans were victorious at Rochester and Colchester, which became their capital town.
- They advanced through Britain capturing Maiden Castle and many other places.
- They built very straight roads.
- They used a "tortoise" (or "testudo") formation with their shields, when attacking.

3.   Roman Baths
- Every Roman town had baths.
- They were for health and cleanliness – not swimming.
- A visit was a social occasion.
- Baths had different temperatures:
  Frigidarium – coldest
  Tepidarium – tepid
  Caldarium – hottest.
- After bathing, oils were rubbed into the skin, to replace the natural oils.

4.   Boadicea
- AD 60, King Prasutagus died.
- The Romans arrested his widow, Boadicea.
- She led her tribe, the Iceni, in revolt against the Romans.
- Many other Britons joined her.
- They resented the powerful Romans.
- The rebels took the towns of Colchester, St Albans and London.
- The Roman commander marched from Wales and defeated the Britons.

5.   Hadrian's Wall

- Emperor Hadrian ordered the wall to be built: it was finished in 122.
- It was 73 miles long and stretched from Wallsend-on-Tyne to Bowness, near Carlisle.
- It kept out the Picts, the inhabitants of Scotland.
- Every mile there was a mile castle.
- Between the mile castles there were two turrets.

6.   Religion under the Romans

- The Romans worshipped many gods, including, gradually, the ruling emperor.
- Their gods included Jupiter, Juno, Vesta, Mars, Venus, Diana and Janus.
- The Romans punished all who refused to worship their gods.
- The Emperors Nero (AD64) and Diocletian (AD300) persecuted Christians most fiercely.
- Many Christians were thrown to the lions or burnt or crucified.
- In AD313, the Emperor Constantine converted to Christianity and Christians were allowed to worship freely thereafter.

7.   Saxon Invasion

- In 449, King Vortigern invited two Saxon chiefs, Hengist and Horsa to defend Britain against raiders.
- The Saxons admired Britain and took over the land.
- They had come from Germany, together with Angles and Jutes
- The Romans had returned to Rome shortly after 400 to defend the rest of their empire.
- The Saxons were heathens and they killed the priests and destroyed the Christian Churches.
- The Saxon gods were:

	The god of:
Woden	Wednesday
Thor	Thursday
Freya	Friday (Woden's wife)
Tiu	Tuesday
The Sun	Sunday
The Moon	Monday.

8.   St Augustine

- The Saxons were heathen, but King Ethelbert's wife Bertha was a Christian from France.
- Pope Gregory saw some slaves in Rome that had been brought from Britain.
- It was surprising for him to see children with fair hair and he asked who they were.
- When he heard they were Angles he replied that they were "not Angles, but angels."
- He sent Augustine to Ethelbert, who arrived in 597.
- Ethelbert was instructed and became a Christian.
- Augustine became the first Archbishop of Canterbury.
- Christianity spread throughout the land, although the Celtic churches in the western fringes of the British Isles already practicsed Christianity, it having been introduced there shortly after Christ's Resurrection (the Saxon invasion never affected it).
- St Martin's Church in Canterbury is where Bertha heard Mass before Augustine arrived.

9.   Synod of Whitby

- St Patrick had been responsible for the conversion of Ireland to Christianity by 450 (the Church that then already existed in Britain is called the Celtic Church, and was in fact the Catholic Christianity brought to Britain during the time of the Romans, which was maintained by Britain's Celtic fringe – British bishops were present at the Council of Arles in 314, and at Ariminum in 359, for instance).
- Britain was no longer Christian due to the Saxon persecution.

- In 563, an Irish monk, Columba, sailed from Ireland to Iona to set up a monastery.
- In 597, Augustine landed in Kent, but when in 604 he died, many lapsed from the Faith.
- In 635, Oswald, King of Northumbria, wanted the Word of Christ spread to his people.
- He sent for Aidan in Iona, who, with a band of monks, set up a monastery at Lindisfarne.
- As they began to preach, it became apparent that the Celtic Church and St Augustine's Church (i.e. the Church of Rome) had different dates for Easter.
- In 664, at Whitby (the Synod of Whitby), it was agreed to follow the Roman Church in this and other disciplinary matters.
- St Hilda was the first Abbess of Whitby.
- Caedmon was a monk at Whitby – famous for his poetry.

10. Venerable Bede

- He was a historian, one of the first.
- He died in 735.
- He wrote "An Ecclesiastical History of the English People" – finished in 731 (still in print).
- He was a monk at Jarrow.

11. Vikings

- In 790, the Vikings attacked the east coast of Britain.
- They came from Norway and Denmark.
- They murdered everyone, especially Christians. They destroyed the churches.
- The land they occupied, governed by their laws, was called Danelaw.
- The British prevented some of the attacks by paying the Vikings Danegeld – i.e. money, etc. – to go away. It didn't work.

12. King Alfred

- Alfred is the only king to be called 'The Great'.
- He became King in 871.
- He defeated the Vikings under Guthrum, whom he persuaded to become a Christian.
- He held his parliament (or Witan) at Winchester.
- Alfred was King of Wessex, and he defeated Guthrum at Ethandune (Edington).
- They signed the Treaty of Wedmore dividing the country along Watling Street (i.e. Danelaw – Vikings to the north, Wessex to the south).
- Alfred died in 899.
- He was crowned at Winchester. The Burnt cakes episode followed his defeat at Chippenham.
- Other Danes, under the pirate Hastinga, attacked England, but Alfred won by draining the Thames.
- He founded the Royal Navy, the Army, Tower of London, many monasteries and schools, and a legal system.
- He divided England into counties.

13. Offa's Dyke

- In the 8th Century, King Offa of Mercia, who was so powerful that he called himself King of the English, built a ditch to keep out the Welsh.
- It ran from the Dee to the Severn.
- It ran for 140 miles.
- It was 15 metres wide and can still be seen in many places.

14. Ethelred the Unready

- He was half-brother to St Edward the Martyr.
- Edward was 12 on becoming King and was murdered at Corfe Castle aged 15 in 978.

- Ethelred, aged 10, did not murder his half-brother, his advisors did. Thus he usurped the Throne.
- Ethelred was a weak king and in the hands of his advisors.
- He tried to buy off the Danes by paying them money (Danegeld) to stop their attacks, but, "If once you have paid him the Danegeld, you never get rid of the Dane" (Kipling).
- In 1013, the Danes under Sweyn overran England and Ethelred fled to Normandy.

15. King Alfred to King Harold
- King Alfred died in 899 and was buried in Winchester.
- His son Edward and grandson Ethelstan recaptured most of Danelaw.
- Ethelstand became King, succeeded by Edmund, then Eadwig.
- King Edgar then reigned over all England from 959-975.
- In 980, Viking attacks began again, but Ethelred the Unready bought them off with Danegeld.
- In 1013, Sweyn Forkbeard defeated Ethelred who fled to his brother-in-law in Normandy.
- When Sweyn died, Ethelred returned with his son, Edmund Ironside. Sweyn's son, Canute, fled to Denmark.
- When Ethelred and Edmund died, Canute returned to become King in 1016.
- Canute rebuilt many churches and went to Rome on a pilgrimage.
- When he died, Ethelred's son, St Edward the Confessor, came from France to be King. He built Westminster Abbey.
- When he died in 1065 he said Harold, an earl's son, should be King; but Harold Hardrada and William Duke of Normandy both had other ideas.

16. King Canute
- King Canute reigned from 1017-1035.
- He was a great king, but was not the Saint Canute of the same period.
- He was a Viking.
- He was elected King after Ethelred's death.
- He married Ethelred's widow, Emma of Normandy.
- He ruled much of northern Europe.
- He went on a pilgrimage to Rome.
- He was buried at Winchester.

17. St Edward the Confessor
- 1042-1066.
- He was a monk at heart.
- He planned Westminster Abbey.
- He lived in Normandy during Canute's reign.
- He had wanted to go on pilgrimage to Rome, but the Pope bade him build Westminster Abbey instead.
- He refused to pay Danegeld.
- He levied no taxes, paying for all public expenses himself.
- His reign was of unbroken peace.
- He is buried in Westminster Abbey.

18. King Harold
(For family tree see Appendix 17a)
- In 1051, Edward promised the English crown to William.
- Harold vowed to agree to this.
- Earl Godwin, Harold's father, ran the country for Edward.
- When Edward died, Harold took the crown, being crowned the day after Edward died.
- Tostig also claimed the throne and asked Harald Hardrada to assist him.

- They were defeated by King Harold at Stamford Bridge in Yorkshire.
- Meanwhile William had landed at Pevensea on 28th September 1066.
- King Harold marched 250 miles to meet William outside Hastings.
- King Harold was killed at the Battle of Hastings on 14th October 1066.

PART II
NORMAN HISTORY

19 Battle of Hastings

- 14th October 1066, 9.30am, Normans threw spears at the English, who threw stones back.
- The whole Norman army advanced, but failed to break through. The Bretons on the left retreated, the English attacked them, but were killed by the Normans at the bottom of the hill.
- A rumour that William had been killed led to him removing his helmet, to show he was still alive. The Normans fell back to regroup, whereupon the English attacked, but this time many were killed.
- The Normans then outnumbered the English. They attacked and won.

20 William I

- He reigned from 1066-1087.
- He organised the Doomsday Book, in 1086.
- He died fighting in France.
- He is buried at Caen.
- He united the country of England.

21. Hereward the Wake

- Was an Englishman who fought against the Normans after the Conquest.
- He lived near Peterborough.
- He joined with the Danes and burned Peterborough.
- In 1071, William the Conqueror attacked and defeated Hereward at Ely.

22. Norman Influence

- Norman Castles: there are many fine examples still standing, especially the Tower of London and Dover Castle.
- Church-building began (though Saxon churches already existed) and a few Norman churches still survive.
- Monasteries & Cathedrals, such as Exeter and Salisbury.
- Buildings were now made of stone, not wood.
- Domesday Book. Dioceses were formed, the counties had already been drawn up during Alfred's reign.
- Quarrying began and so did tin mining – especially on Dartmoor.
- Bayeux tapestry dates from this time.
- Saints' names were chosen instead of old English ones.
- Certain place names are Norman.
- England was forged into one nation.

23 The Norman Heritage (1066 – 1200)
Changes in England after the Conquest

- Saints' names were used instead of old English personal names.
- We also note that funny sounding place names (Ashby de la Zouche) are Norman, being a mixture of Old English and Norman. Also ...cester lost its chester. We get ...ville, ...ew. Not only was there a strong French influence but the administration was done in Latin.

- Buildings began to be built of stone. Hence quarrying, to build the cathedrals and monastic institutions, and tin mining, particularly on Dartmoor.
- Towns expanded, particularly those with Norman castles, for example London (the Tower of London) and places like Launceston and Okehampton.
- Church-building began on a large scale.
- Dioceses were mapped out (the counties already had been).
- England was forged into one nation (although Wales was not defeated).

24   Domesday Book
- When King William arrived in England there were few records.
- He did not know how much land he ruled.
- He sent men all over the country to write down all the facts.
- Some of the people were angry because they did not want the King to know what they owned.
- They did not dare give the King's men wrong answers for fear of punishment.
- 1086 is the date of the Domesday Book and King William died in 1087.

25   Death of William II
- William the Conqueror had 3 sons, Robert, William and Henry.
- Robert displeased his father and so, when William I died, the crown passed to William.
- William II was not popular and became cruel.
- One day, when out hunting, he was hit in the chest by an arrow (now marked by the Rufus Stone in the New Forest).
- Walter Tyrell, a close friend of the King, rode away after the death, but swore he was innocent.
- Was it an accident or murder?
- William II was succeeded by his brother Henry I.
- William II had a red complexion and was nicknamed Rufus.
- He reigned from 1087-1100.

26   Henry I
- He was brother to William II.
- He reigned from 1100-1135.
- He was known as Beauclerc, because he was so well-educated.
- He might have been involved in William II's death.
- His son, William Adelin, was drowned in the White Ship on 25th November, 1120, which led to a succession crisis and a period of civil war called "The Anarchy."
- He introduced the post of Chancellor of the Exchequer.
- He imprisoned his brother, Robert, for 28 years.
- He wanted his daughter, Matilda, to reign after him but his nephew thought otherwise.
- He died of a surfeit of lampreys..

27   St Anselm
- He was born in Italy.
- He lived from 1033-1109.
- He was a monk at Le Bec Hellouin (Benedictine).
- He succeeded Lanfranc as Archbishop of Canterbury.
- He advised William II, but his advice was not always taken and this was particularly the case in 1100 when Henry I ordered him to consecrate William Giffard Bishop of Winchester. Initially Anselm refused, an action which formed a part of the Investitures Dispute, but he later gave way. In due course Giffard was to restore Winchester cathedral with great magnificence.

28   **King Stephen**
- Reigned from 1135-1154.
- He had promised Henry I that he would support Henry's daughter Matilda.
- When he took the crown, Matilda waged civil war against him.
- On separate occasions they had each other imprisoned.
- His reign is referred to as "nineteen long winters".
- When he died, Matilda's son Henry became King Henry II.

PART III
PLANTAGENET HISTORY

29.   **Henry II and St Thomas Becket**
- In mediaeval England, the Church and the State were very close.
- Henry II had appointed St Thomas Becket as his Chancellor (the Head of the Law).
- Thomas Becket and the King were close friends..
- In order to control the Church more closely, Henry appointed Thomas Archbishop of Canterbury.
- Thomas accepted, but, at the same time, resigned as Chancellor.
- This made the King cross.
- Thomas was lenient in his dealings with errant priests – too lenient, according to the King.
- The King asked for the priests to be dealt with by the civil courts. Thomas gave way but left England.
- When Thomas returned, he preached a sermon attacking heretics and some of his congregation complained about this to the King.
- The King replied: "Who will rid me of this turbulent priest?" and four knights understood this to mean that they should murder Thomas (1170), which they then did.
- Henry was aghast at the murder and walked barefoot to Canterbury, to pray at the spot where he was killed. A magnificent shrine was then erected in Canterbury Cathedral, but Henry VIII later destroyed it.

30.   **Henry II**
- He reigned from 1154-1189.
- His mother was the Empress Mathilda.
- He began the House of Plantagenet (from the Latin for the common broom shrub, worn by Geoffrey Anjou in his hat).
- He married Eleanor of Aquitaine, daughter of German King Henry V and wife of French King Louis VII.
- When he married, he controlled a large part of Europe from the Cheviots to the Pyrenees.
- He reorganised the country after the civil wars of Stephen's reign and was very powerful.
- He revised the law and made landowners pay scutage (shield money) for his army.
- His wife rebelled against him and she was imprisoned for 15 years at Salisbury.
- His successful reign was marred by the murder of St Thomas Becket.

31   **Richard I and the Crusades**
- Richard I was the eldest son of Henry II. He inherited the crown in 1189.
- Jerusalem was controlled by Muslims, whose leader was Saladin.
- The Pope granted indulgences to all who went on a Crusade to free Jerusalem.
- Richard led the Third Crusade, which landed at Jaffa and he joined the French King Philip Augustus.
- They captured Acre, and won the Battle of Arsuf in 1191.
- Richard never reached Jerusalem, but returned home.
- He was killed fighting in France, in 1199.
- Of his ten years on the throne, he spent just six months in England.

32. **First Crusade**
- It took place from 1095-1099 (William Rufus' reign).
- They assembled at Constantinople in 1096.
- They crossed Turkey (Anatolia and Taurus Mountains) in 1097.
- They captured Antioch (1098).
- They captured Jerusalem (1099).
- Peter the Hermit wandered through Europe preaching (advertising) the Crusade.
- The name Crusade comes from the Latin *crux* = cross.
- It was the most important and successful Crusade.

33. **Crusades – History of Jerusalem**
- After the Crucifixion, Jerusalem was destroyed by the Romans in AD70.
- They built a new city and banned the Jews from it.
- In 614, it was captured by the Persians.
- In 638, a long period of Arab rule began.
- It was held by the Crusaders between 1099 and 1187 (the Second Crusade, 1145-1149, resulted from the fall of the first Crusader state, Edessa).
- In 1917, it was governed by Great Britain.
- In 1948, the British left and the Jews took over.

34. **The Third Crusade**
- The Crusaders, while based in Jerusalem, had been attacking the Muslims.
- The Muslims, led by Saladin, got their revenge by winning the Battle of the Horns of Hattin in 1187.
- A few weeks later, Jerusalem fell and the remains of the True Cross were lost.
- Europe responded by sending the Third Crusade (or Crusade of the Kings), 1189-1192.
- The German contingent, under Emperor Frederick Barbarossa, turned back after he had drowned at Seleucia.
- King Richard I of England and King Philip II of France joined forces to attack Acre.
- After they had beaten Saladin at the Battle of Arsuf (1191), Saladin gave permission for Christians to visit Jerusalem.
- Richard, who saw Jerusalem, but never entered it, did not besiege it because he had no water supplies and, even if he had taken it, with Saladin's great forces in Palestine, he would never have been able to hold it.
- He left for home, was shipwrecked and imprisoned in Austria, only to be released after his faithful minstrel Blondel had found him and a ransom paid.
- Richard was not popular because he levied high taxes to pay for the Third Crusade.
- While Richard was away, his brother John tried to take over the country.
- Richard was very headstrong and upset both King Philip and the Duke of Austria.
- He is buried with his parents at Fontrevault.

35. **Pilgrimage**
- It is a purifying thing to visit the bodies of the Saints and, above all, the places of martyrdom.
- It remits sins and is a penance. It helps to develop character.
- An early English ballad says:
  "They bear with them no manner of thing
  That was worth a farthing
  No cattle, no gold, no fee
  But meekly they asked their meat
  Wherever they might it get
  For Holy Charity."

- Pilgrims wore a special smock and hat, carried a stick and wore pilgrim signs, which often enabled them to pass through hostile land. Pilgrims to Canterbury wore a bell or the head of a Saint on a brooch. Their wallet was their scrip.
- Both Canterbury and Winchester have grown as a result of their being places of pilgrimage.
- Pilgrims often dictated the course of roads. They wore out a path from the sea coast to Canterbury.
- Crusades arose from the idea of pilgrimage to the Holy Land.
- Miracle plays are derived from returning pilgrims acting out their pilgrimage for the benefit of those unable to visit the shrine, etc. (vide Oberammergau).
- International Communications owe an enormous debt to pilgrimages. Pilgrimages were the only reasons that led people to visit another country peacefully.
- An exceedingly large number of foreigners came to visit the tomb of the Holy Blissful Martyr, St Thomas of Canterbury. Pilgrims often carried "the mails". Pilgrims caused wayside inns to be set up.
- Religious orders were founded to protect pilgrims (Knights Templar).
- Dangers/Scandals of Pilgrimages:
  It is wrong to   (a) insist that pilgrimages are necessary for salvation
                         (b) go on a pilgrimage and neglect home duties
                         (c) go on a pilgrimage and live wantonly.
- Particular Pilgrimages:
(a) Westminster (St Thomas Becket suggested the building of the magnificent shrine to St Edward the Confessor)
(b) Canterbury
- Birthplace of Anglo-Saxon Christianity
- Scene of Martyrdom of St Thomas Becket
- Henry VIII only declared himself head of Church of England after he had personally attacked St Thomas and strongly discouraged pilgrimages
- Chaucer says one should visit in Spring "the Holy Blissful Martyr for to seek"
(c) Winchester
- Had been the spiritual centre of England until the martyrdom of St Thomas
- St Swithin
(d) Salisbury
- There is a prayer for pilgrimage in the Sarum Missal.
- St Osmund.
- For pilgrimages to Canterbury, pilgrims would gather in Winchester, Dover and London.
- Some pilgrims went in search of miracles and cures.

36. King John
- He was Henry II's youngest son.
- He reigned from 1199-1216.
- He divorced his first wife and lived with Isabella of Angouleme.
- He was fat, greedy and unjust.
- He signed Magna Carta which was the forerunner of English Justice.
- He lost most of his lands in France.
- He is often considered to have been England's worst King.
- He even lost his treasure while crossing a river near The Wash.

37. Magna Carta
- Magna Carta is regarded as the beginning of English Justice.
- King John had made himself unpopular by imposing heavy taxes on the barons.
- The main tax was called scutage or shield money to pay for the army.
- The taxes were so heavy that the barons decided to make war on the King

- Only seven Barons took the King's side.
- The King saw that he was outnumbered and he agreed to grant the barons the laws and liberties they wanted.
- On 15th June 1215, at Runnymede, near Windsor, on the River Thames, he signed the great charter and thus the barons took over many of the responsibilities the King had formerly enjoyed.
- The main points were:
(a) No taxation without representation (i.e. the taxpayers would have some say in how their taxes should be spent)
(b) Habeas Corpus ("that you may have the body"). This meant that nobody could be imprisoned without a fair trial.

38   Simon de Montfort

- He was a Frenchman who married King Henry III's sister.
- He was chosen by Parliament to lead their side in the quarrel with the King.
- Parliament wanted to limit the King's power.
- In 1264, Simon defeated and captured Henry III at the Battle of Lewes.
- But in 1265, Simon was killed when he was defeated at the Battle of Evesham.
- He is heralded as the first champion of parliamentary democracy.

39   Henry III

- Henry III reigned from 1216-1272.
- He was the eldest son of King John.
- Aged only 9 at his father's death, he was brought up by priests.
- He had a great love for churches and art (Salisbury Cathedral was built during his reign).
- He rebuilt Westminster Abbey and the shrine of St Edward the Confessor.
- He tried to regain the French possessions his father had lost and he became very unpopular for the heavy taxes he raised.
- The Barons, under Simon de Montfort, rebelled, but were eventually defeated at the Battle of Evesham in 1265.
- He is regarded as having been weak, but his reign ended with the country very peaceful.
- During his reign, the first time Parliament was held, Canterbury Cathedral was finished, and many statues and stained glass windows created.

40   Monks and Friars

- Monks lived in monasteries, usually Benedictine (i.e. followers of the Rule of St Benedict).
- Friars wandered the country, either as Dominicans (Blackfriars) who preached the Gospel and fought heresy, or as Franciscans (Greyfriars) who preached and were strong advocates of poverty.
- Friars lived in friaries, but moved between different friaries, rather than remaining in a single one.

A typical day in a Monastery

Something akin to this:

Midnight	Matins
1.00am	Lauds
1.30am	Bed
6.00am	Prime
6.30am	Chapter – spiritual instruction/discussion & Parliament – business discussion
7.00am	Mass for workers and priest's private Masses
7.30am	Light breakfast (mixtum)
	Work and/or Lectio Divina (spiritual reading)

9.00am	Tierce
9.15am	Conventual High Mass
10.00am	Work
12.00pm	Sext
12.15pm	Dinner (and recreation)
3.00pm	None
3.15pm	Work
6.00pm	Vespers
6.30pm	Collation (supper)
7.30pm	Compline
8.00pm	Bed

41   Chivalry

- In the middle ages men were taught to live in accordance with three main aims:
       Strength in war
  Devotion to religion
  Good manners.
- This was called the Age of Chivalry, mainly from the 11th-15th Centuries.
- Chivalry comes from chevalerie or armoured knights on horseback.
- Boys, at the age of 7, would become pages in noble households, learning riding, singing, good manners, music, Latin, French, reading and writing.
- At age 14 they would become squires to a knight, learning to be soldiers and helping their knight to manage all his affairs including his horses.
- At age 21, if they could afford it, they became knights and were granted land in return for military service.
- They kept fit by taking part in Tournaments.

42   Influence of the Church

- The monasteries dominated the countryside, usually Benedictine (the model for them originating in Monte Cassino).
- The monks kept records of all that happened – they were historians.
- They copied the writings of the learned men from earlier centuries – hence illuminated manuscripts.
- They organised the first hospitals.
- They welcomed strangers and looked after the poor and needy.
- They organised the teaching of children.
- They organised higher education and Universities (Oxford & Paris).
- They taught the best farming methods.
- They built the wonderful cathedrals (Norman and Gothic).
- St Dominic founded his order of Preachers (Dominicans), of great learning.
- The holy life of poverty and looking after the poor was taught by St Francis of Assisi.
- Morality, doctrine, philosophy, theology and spiritual matters were taught by St Thomas Aquinas (a Dominican).
- St Clare founded an order of nuns.
- Those who wished to live a stricter monastic life did not find it in the great Benedictine monasteries and so they joined the Cistercian order, a more rigorous observance of the Rule of St Benedict (from Citeaux in France), at places such as Fountains Abbey and Rievaulx.
- The leader of the mediaeval Church in England (after the Pope, that is, who was head of the universal Church) was the Archbishop of Canterbury. Since the Reformation, the monarch has been the head of the Church of England, which replaced the Catholic Church. Thus in those days the Church maintained greater independence from the

Crown. Nonetheless the Pope did give certain religious duties to the monarch, who could influence the appointment of bishops.

- Thus, government was strong and efficient because Church and State worked closely together.
- When the Church and the monarch disagreed, there were bound to be difficulties, as the martyrdom of St Thomas Becket shows, but these difficulties were relatively infrequent.

43 The relationship between England and France in the Middle Ages

- English and French affairs were closely connected because the first Kings of England were also Dukes of Normandy.
- They lost Normandy in 1204, but continued to be involved with France, because they had other lands in the south.
- But by 1453, all French lands, except Calais, had been lost.
- Nonetheless, the two countries traded with each other, in wine and wool.

44 Crafts and Guilds

- Workers in each trade formed organisations called guilds (from Old English, geld = payment).
- Those workers with special skills belonged to a craft guild.
- They would meet in the guildhall – such as in Plymouth and Tavistock.
- Workers in the same trade usually worked near each other. In York, the butchers worked in The Shambles.
- The guilds insisted on high standards.
- The Church insisted on just prices.
- A worker wanting to join a craft guild first became an apprentice, then a journeyman (because he could do a day's work) and then...
- After making a "Masterpiece", if the masters of the guild accepted it, he became a skilled craftsman.
- The guilds would perform mystery plays to entertain and teach the people in the town.
- Each guild performed acts of charity:
- (a) looking after sick members
- (b) looking after widows and children
- (c) praying for the souls of their members
- (d) supporting their local church/guild chapel/chantry.

45 Fairs and Markets

- The word "fair" comes from the Latin *feria* for "day" (holy day).
- They were held in church grounds on the days of their local saint's feast, or other holydays.
- Tradesmen from far and wide would come to sell their goods.
- Tavistock's Goosey Fair (for example) comes from the 13th Century.
- Fairs were held from time to time throughout the year, and the tradesmen, sometimes from abroad, would travel from town to town for the different fairs.
- The word "market" comes from the Latin *mercatus* = merchant.
- Markets were (and still are) held regularly every week or month.
- In town markets, local tradesmen and farmers, etc., set up stalls to sell their goods.
- The town is paid a sum, for the space a stall occupies, by the stall-holder.

46 Feudalism

- Feudalism is a system of ownership of land.
- Large estates were called manors and the noble in charge was called a lord.
- The lord would allow certain men to hold their land in return for serving in the lord's army when required. This man was called a vassal.

- The ceremony at which the vassal was granted the land was called "homage".
- Those who worked on the land were called serfs or villains.
- The serfs lived in poor houses clustered near the lord's castle – hence village.
- The lord sometimes granted the inhabitants of a village or town freedom to organise life in the town as they wished. The details were recorded in a Charter.

47   Knighthood

- In battle, a squire would be knighted by being touched on the shoulder with a sword (dubbed).
- In preparation for a peacetime dubbing he would:

    (a)   serve his lord at dinner
    (b)   have his head shaved
    (c)   bathe
    (d)   be reminded of his duties
    (e)   spend the night in prayer
    (f)   confess his sins to a priest
    (g)   hear Mass
    (h)   dress in rich clothes
    (i)   receive sword and spurs – signs of knighthood
    (j)   be dubbed.
    These were called Knights of the Bath.

- Some knights formed themselves into religious orders, such as Knights Hospitallers (to feed, shelter and heal pilgrims) or Templars (to protect the Christian shrines and churches in Jerusalem, as well as the Temple, and protect pilgrims).
- Knights belonging to no order are Knights Bachelor.

48   Norman Castles

- The Normans built Motte and Bailey Castles.
- Castles were usually built on hilltops.
- If they were on flat ground they would have a moat and drawbridge.
- When the castle was attacked, everyone would gather inside.
- The enemy might win by starving them out, or knocking the walls down with a battering ram.
- Defending a castle was easier because the defendants could be protected as they fired arrows or poured boiling lead on their attackers.
- Life in a castle was not very comfortable for most therein.

49   Gothic Style

- It originated in France in the 12th Century.
- It is marked by: pointed arches, graceful columns, tall spires and decorations (tracery).
- Gothic buildings in Britain date from 1200-1500.
- This period is divided into:
(i)   Early English – simple design – Salisbury
(ii)   Decorated – decorations – Exeter
(iii)   Perpendicular – more solid – Eton College.
- The earliest example of gothic architecture in England is at Canterbury Cathedral.
- The most famous gothic cathedrals are Notre Dame in Paris and at Chartres.
- Most gothic sculpture was destroyed at the Reformation.

50   Transport and Travel
- In mediaeval times, travellers used the old Roman Roads – none had been built since.
- Few carts existed, so goods were carried by pack horse.
- Wealthy people rode, the rest walked.
- Travel was dirty and dangerous.
- Ships were used for transport, now that the rudder had been invented. They were also much larger vessels and could sail against the wind.

51   Tournaments
- Tournaments were held to keep the knights fit, as well as for entertainment. They included:
- (a)   Jousting – 2 knights on horseback charging each other with blunt lances;
- (b)   Tilting – a knight would charge a model (manikin) soldier, hit him with a lance and try to avoid being hit by a bag of sand which would swing around behind him;
- (c)   A melee – pitched battle between knights;
- (d)   A list – long wooden enclosure for a joust.
- Tournaments could be very dangerous.

52   Parliament
- Parliament, from the French word Parler – to speak, began shortly after Magna Carta.
- Before then, the King had made the laws and raised taxes.
- The Church tried to influence the King, but when they disagreed, problems arose (viz. St Thomas Becket).
- When Henry III, son of King John, tried to raise heavy taxes, the barons under Simon de Montfort rebelled.
- de Montfort imprisoned the King and summoned the first parliament in 1265.
- In 1295, a different form of parliament was summoned called the Model Parliament.
- Not only were Knights called to Parliament, but also representatives from the towns, and two knights appointed from each shire. These formed the House of Commons.
- The House of Commons was responsible for raising taxes. This is why the House of Commons is more important.
- As war became more expensive, the House of Commons became even more important.

53   Battles
- There are four principles to be followed when fighting a battle:
  - (a)   concentrate on the enemy's weak spot
  - (b)   surprise – pretend to do one thing, then do another
  - (c)   co-operation – your men must all work together
  - (d)   mobility – you must all be able to move quickly.
- There is also luck to be expected.
- At the Battle of Hastings in 1066:
  - (a)   Harold's forces were exhausted
  - (b)   William arrived at the battle sooner than Harold expected
  - (c)   Luck – the Normans twice fell back to regroup, the English followed, thinking the Normans were retreating. The Normans turned and killed them (Harold was killed by a stray arrow).
- At the Battle of Evesham, 1265:
  - (a)   De Montfort had put himself in a trap and Edward seized on the opportunity
  - (b)   The Welsh spearmen on De Montfort's side began to escape
  - (c)   De Montfort could not move
  - (d)   Luck – the heavy rain made fighting more difficult.
- At the Battle of Bannockburn, 1314:
  - (a)   The English were tired and in a bad position with no retreat

(b)   The English did not all fight well together
(c)   The English could not use their archers.

54   Weapons

Up to 1400	1400 onwards
Chain mail	Armour plate
Warhorses	Warhorses
Sword	Sword
Large shield	Small shield
Battleaxe	Longbow
Feudal unpaid army	Paid professional soldiers
Scutage paid for other soldiers	Explosives
-	Thicker walls needed for castles
-	Heavy canons were made –Mons Meg
-	More expensive
-	More taxation needed to pay for wars
-	Parliament had to give authority for taxes to be raised
-	Parliament became more and more powerful

55   Edward I

- He reigned from 1272-1307.
- He was the son of Henry III.
- When his wife Eleanor of Castile died at Grantham, her body was taken to London and wherever it rested Edward erected a beautiful cross.
- He took the Stone of Scone to Westminster Abbey. Scone was where the Scottish kings were crowned and Edward was thus trying to unite Scotland under his rule.
- He created his eldest son, later Edward II, Prince of Wales, thus uniting Wales under his rule.
- He introduced the long bow from Wales into his army and built magnificent castles in Wales.
- He went on a Crusade.
- He reformed much of the law and agreed that parliament must approve tax-raising measures.
- He was called "Longshanks" and "the Hammer of the Scots" for his victories over Scotland.
- He is called Edward I because he was the first Edward to reign in England after the primogeniture system was established by the Normans (hence St Edward the Confessor is not called Edward I).

56   Welsh Castles

- Castles were built along the Welsh border, such as Flint and Caerphilly.
- They were also built around the coast at Conway, Beaumaris, Caernarvon and Harlech.
- Edward I used these magnificent castles and others to keep the Welsh in order.
- Edward declared war on Llewellyn, Prince of Wales, in 1276, because he would not pay homage.
- To fight the war he built castles around the coast and on hilltops.
- In 1277, Llewellyn surrendered.
- In 1282, Llewellyn rose again but was killed near Builth at the Battle of Orewin Bridge. After that, Edward expanded his castle-building programme.
- These castles are the greatest mediaeval structures in Britain after the Cathedrals, etc.

57   Marco Polo
- Marco Polo was the world's first famous explorer.
- His journey lasted 25 years from 1271 to 1296.
- He visited Central Asia, China and Japan.
- The Chinese Emperor at the time was called Kublai Khan.

58   Towns
- Towns, though they grew in importance, during the Middle Ages were small.
- In the year 1300, only 60,000 people lived in London, compared with 7 million today.
- Fire was a great danger in the towns, where wooden houses and workshops were close together.

59   Castles
- Castles were used for protection when there was a battle.
- The army attacking the castle would use ladders, battering rams, mantlets and mangonels.
- People in the castle would use hot pitch and fire arrows.
- Kings and barons lived in them for protection.
- Sometimes the people inside would be starved out.

60   Battle of Bannockburn
- After Edward I's death in 1307, the Scottish King, Robert the Bruce, began to drive the English out of Scotland.
- By 1314, Stirling Castle was the only English outpost in Scotland.
- When the English arrived near the castle to relieve it, Sir Henry de Bohun rode forward to kill the unprotected Bruce, but Bruce killed him.
- The two sides fought all day and the English camped close to the Forth that night.
- The next day, 24th June, Robert charged the English who were hemmed in and unable to use their Archers.
- When the Scottish small folk, local farmers, etc., appeared at the end of the day, the English will was broken and the battle lost.

61   Edward II
- He reigned from 1307-1327.
- He married Queen Isabella, daughter of Philip IV of France.
- He lost Bannockburn, 1314.
- He was murdered (gruesomely) on the order of his wife at Berkeley Castle.
- He was buried at Gloucester Cathedral.

62   The Black Prince
- He was the son of Edward III.
- He was brave, and a tough soldier who won many battles for his father.
- He died before Edward III and so never became King.
- His tomb is in Canterbury Cathedral.
- He was born in 1330 and joined the Hundred Years War in 1346.
- Edward, the Black Prince, "won his spurs" at Crecy in 1346. The French cavalry and crossbowmen were no match for the English long bow.
- He is called the Black Prince from the colour of the livery worn by his retainers.
- In 1361, he married "the Fair Maid of Kent," Princess Joan.
- In 1356, he won the Battle of Poitiers and captured the French King.
- In 1376, he died.

63 Edward III

- Edward III reigned from 1327-1377.
- He was married to Philippa of Hainault.
- He imprisoned his mother at Castle Rising for 28 years.
- He began the Hundred Years War in 1338:
  (a)   to gain French crown
  (b)   to expand the wool trade
  (c)   to expand the wine trade.
- He won the following battles:
  (a)   Sluys, 1340
  (b)   Crecy, 1346 – with longbows
  (c)   Poitiers, 1355.
- In 1348, the Black Death ravaged the country and killed his daughter Joan.
- His campaigns, while successful, never resulted in him gaining the French throne.
- He rebuilt Windsor Castle and created the Order of the Garter.
- His most famous sons are:
  (a)   The Black Prince
  (b)   John of Gaunt.

64 The Black Death

- In 1348, terrible plague swept Europe from China.
- It was carried by rats travelling in merchant ships.
- Sufferers could die within hours.
- It was highly contagious.
- It affected the groin, armpits and skin. It could cover a man with black boils.
- Many priests died giving the last rites. With the religious houses needing replacement priests, many were poorly trained and their poor standard is thought to have been used popularly, and largely retrospectively, to justify the Reformation.
- Nearly half the British population died.
- Afterwards, in 1351, there were many fewer men to work the land and these demanded higher wages which led to the Peasants' Revolt in 1381. It also led to the end of the Feudal system.
- In the 14th Century, there were no drains and little attention was paid to personal hygiene.
- Fleas are believed to have spread the disease from the rats.
- With more work to be done, the villains began to wander from their lords, seeking others to whom they might pay rent – rather than working for them.
- Pope Clement VI gave permission for laymen to minister to the dying during the Black Death.

65 The Peasants' Revolt

- Took place in 1381.
- It was led by Wat Tyler and John Ball – a priest.
- John Ball said, "When Adam delved and Eve span, who was then the gentleman?"
- The march on London resulted from a combination of factors:
  (a)   Black Death (1348) had led to great depression
  (b)   Tyler & Ball taught that rebellion would bring riches to the poor
  (c)   The Hundred Years War had led to a poll tax which everyone had to pay equally.
- Wat Tyler was killed when the peasants reached London, but the King, Richard II, bravely quietened the masses.
- With their leader dead, the crowd went home, but the poll tax was abolished and the peasants were given more freedom and money.

- During the revolt, Wat Tyler's men murdered the Archbishop of Canterbury in St John's Chapel in the Tower of London.
- In the 1980s, a Poll Tax (this time it was called the Community Charge) was reintroduced, causing riots and unrest, but it too failed and was abolished in 1993.

66 What Mediaeval England has given us:

- Gothic Cathedrals and churches, such as Canterbury, York, Westminster Abbey and Salisbury
- Monasteries, such as Fountains, Tintern, Lindisfarne
- Education for the masses, which began with a very logical approach to teaching methods.
- Universities, which began with more students per capita than ever since.
- Parliament – Magna Carta – democracy
- Hospitals
- Local government – town charters
- Roads – through pilgrimages and trade (wool)
- Farming methods
- Landlord & tenant system – feudalism
- Science – which began to advance, and was encouraged.
- Great treatises on Theology and Philosophy – Summa Theologica, St Thomas Aquinas
- Stained glass windows
- Trades organised and governed
- Mystery plays
- Great paintings – Giotto
- Libraries
- Great Latin hymns
- Dante's Inferno
- Advancement of women – St Clare's Nuns, St Elizabeth
- Law organised into courts
- Great castles – Windsor, Caernarfon, Corfe, Chepstow
- Exploration
- Charities
- Real community life
- Insurance.

67 Richard II

- He reigned from 1377-1399.
- He was the son of the Black Prince.
- He bravely stood against the Peasants' Revolt and stopped it.
- His uncle was the Duke of Lancaster, John of Gaunt.
- He married Anne of Bohemia, who died, and, later, Isabella, but had no children.
- He was unpopular with Parliament because he ignored it.
- Henry Bolingbroke, John of Gaunt's son, took Parliament's side and imprisoned Richard.
- In 1399, Richard abdicated and died (was he murdered?) in 1400.
- Henry Bolingbroke became Henry IV.
-

PART IV
THE HOUSES OF LANCASTER AND YORK

68 The Hundred Years War

- The war lasted spasmodically from 1337 until 1453.
- It began in the reign of Edward III.
- There were few great battles and the French were victorious in the end.

- Since 1066, English Kings had been Dukes of Normandy, and, under Henry II, England had controlled large areas of France. The French resented this and the Hundred Years War was their means of getting rid of the English.
- The war began when Philip VI of France attacked the English in Aquitaine. Edward III sent two armies, one to Aquitaine and the other to Northern France.
- Because the English were successful, the French sent a large army, in 1346, to northern France, to stop their advance. The English defeated them at Crecy.
- In 1356, the French were again defeated at Poitiers, but with Edward III old, the Black Prince ill, and France with a new young King, the tide then turned.
- In 1415, England had a new King in Henry V and he defeated the French at Agincourt and gained control of most of northern France, including Paris.
- In 1431, the martyrdom of St Joan of Arc, coupled with weak English leadership, gave the French new courage.
- The French gradually pushed the English out of France, finally defeating them at Formigny in 1450.

The Main Dates:
1340   Battle of Sluys – English Naval Victory
1346   Battle of Crecy – English victory by longbow
1356   Battle of Poitiers – English capture French king
1415   Battle of Agincourt – English victory by longbow
1450   Battle of Formigny – French victory

69   The Battle of Crecy, 26th August 1346
- The English defeated a much larger French army.
- It was one of the major battles of the Hundred Years War.
- Edward III claimed the French throne.
- The French Army was led by Philip VI and pursued the English, who crossed the Somme near Abbeyville.
- Edward had Welsh and English longbows.
- Philip had Genoese crossbows – which had to be rewound.
- Many French fought on horses, so when their horses were killed they were unable to get up and fight in their armour.
- There was a violent thunderstorm.
- The Black Prince sent to his father for help. His father replied "let the boy win his spurs."
- Edward then marched on Calais.

70   John of Gaunt
(For his family tree see Appendix 17b)
- He lived from 1340-1399.
- "Gaunt" was how the English pronounced Ghent in Belgium, where he was born.
- He fought in the Hundred Years War, but not very successfully.
- His first wife bought him the Dukedom of Lancaster. He was thus father of the Lancastrians in the Wars of the Roses.
- His second wife, Constance of Castile, gave him and his successors close unity with Spain.
- His fame is really because he was father and grandfather, etc., of three kings, although not a king himself.

71   Henry IV = Bolingbroke
- He reigned from 1399-1413.
- He organised the abdication of his first cousin Richard II.

- The main event in his life was when the Earl of Northumberland, his son Hotspur and the Archbishop of York rose against him. Henry IV defeated them at the Battle of Shrewsbury in 1403.
- It was his dirty work in organising the abdication of Richard II that led to the Wars of the Roses in 1455.

72   Owen Glendower

- He lived from 1359-1416.
- He was of royal Welsh blood.
- A local argument grew into a revolt against the English (1400).
- Owen's forces attacked many Welsh castles, many surrendered, but Caernarvon, with 28 men, held out.
- In 1405, Prince Henry, later Henry V, slowly began to defeat him.

73   Henry V

- He reigned from 1413-1422.
- He tried valiantly to pursue Edward III's right to the French throne.
- His greatest victory was winning the Battle of Agincourt in 1415.
- This brave King died of dysentery when he was 35.

73   Lollards

- Lollards were the first of what may be termed Protestants (there were many heretics prior to them).
- Their leader was John Wycliffe who died in 1384.
- They protested against:
  (i)   the Pope's powers
  (ii)   confession of one's sins to a priest
  (iii)   the wealth of the Church
- They were thus also heretics.
- Many were burned at the stake.
- When Wycliffe died, his followers, under John Hus, kept the movement alive. This contributed to a movement that was to become the Reformation.
- There was a small rebellion in 1414.

75   Battle of Agincourt

- It took place in 1415.
- 6,000 Englishmen, under Henry V, defeated 20,000 Frenchmen.
- The English longbow men, who were highly skilled, were far more effective than the heavily armoured French knights.
- Agincourt is in northern France.

76   St Joan of Arc

- She was burned at the stake in 1431.
- She received visions while at home that the English, who were besieging Orleans in France, would be defeated and that the Dauphin would be crowned.
- After questioning her, the Dauphin agreed to let her dress as a boy in armour.
- She set out for Orleans with the French army and relieved the siege.
- During this siege the French attacked a convoy bringing provisions to the English forces and the French were defeated at what is known as the Battle of the Herrings.
- The Dauphin, Charles, was crowned in Rheims in 1429.
- The war continued; Joan was captured by the English and burnt at the stake for(unfounded) heresy, as a result of a partisan trial (later annulled), much being made of

her wearing men's clothes, which she argued was necessary for her role in battle, behind enemy lines, but also to preserve her chastity.
- She died a holy death gazing on a crucifix, was exonerated and canonised. She is patron of France.

77   Henry VI
- He reigned twice: 1422-1461 and 1470-1471.
- He was crowned King of France (as well as England), but this title disappeared in 1435.
- His reign is muddled and dominated by the Wars of the Roses (1455-1485).
- He founded Eton College and King's College, Cambridge.
- His reign was interrupted by Edward IV, his third cousin and a great-great grandson of Edward III.
- He was imprisoned in the Tower of London from 1465-1470.
- He was executed while saying his prayers.

(See also Wars of the Roses.)

78   The Wars of the Roses
(For family tree see Appendix 17d)
- The wars started in 1455, when Henry VI's third cousin Richard Duke of York challenged him for the throne at the first Battle of St Albans. Henry VI lost, thus giving York the crown.
- Henry VI was a devout King who had suffered a stroke. While he was ill, Richard had been protector. Now he was better, Richard did not want to hand control back.
- Henry VI soon escaped the clutches of the Duke of York and his main supporter, the Earl of Warwick.
- In 1460, Warwick defeated Henry at Northampton and Richard appeared free to keep the throne.
- But Richard was killed by supporters of the Queen (Margaret).
- Warwick was then defeated at the second Battle of St Albans.
- Warwick fled to Hereford and defeated the Queen's forces at Mortimer's Cross in 1461, whereupon Owen Tudor, a supporter of Henry VI, was beheaded.
- Owen Tudor had married Henry V's widow, Queen Margaret, and was grandfather of Henry VII.
- The defeat at Mortimer's Cross, was a defeat for Henry VI and so Edward (Richard Duke of York's son) was crowned Edward IV .
- After his Coronation, Edward and Warwick marched north and defeated Queen Margaret's forces at Towton in 1461.

Summary (1455-1461)
- Richard challenges Henry VI.
- They fight four battles, Richard is killed.
- Henry is defeated and Richard's son Edward becomes Edward IV giving victory to the House of York.
- Subsequent events and discoveries were to prove that Edward was illegitimate.

79   Paston Letters
- These represent correspondence between the Paston family from 1422-1509.
- They are a unique collection of papers which describe life in mediaeval England.
- They show how unsettled English life was during the Wars of the Roses.

80   Warwick the King Maker
- The Earl of Warwick was very powerful.
- He began by supporting Richard Duke of York and was thus a supporter of Edward IV.
- However, by 1470, Edward was growing unpopular, because he asked too much of his supporters. They turned against him and he was forced to surrender.
- Warwick tried to run the country but failed to gain support. He thus released Edward IV, but it was Edward who took control, not Warwick.
- Warwick & Clarence (Edwards's brother) tried to oppose Edward by stirring up rebellions, but they failed and fled to Normandy.
- Once there, they resolved to enlist the support of Henry VI who was in the Tower.
- When Warwick & Clarence returned, Edward was unable to resist them and it was Edward's turn to flee to France (1470).
- When Edward IV returned in 1471, with Richard (III), Warwick was unable to muster enough support, Clarence joined Edward, and Edward reclaimed the throne, putting Henry VI back in the Tower.

81   Printing and other discoveries
- Printing began in China (perhaps) long before it came to Europe.
- It was brought to England by an Englishman, William Caxton, who became interested in it in Belgium, in 1476.
- The reason he was so successful in introducing it into England is because he worked for Edward IV's sister.
- Thus Caxton did not invent printing, but he encouraged its use.
- The most famous European book of the 15th century is the Guttenberg Bible. There is a copy at Eton College and one on public display at the British Library (and P. G. Wodehouse says there is one in the library at Blandings Castle!).
- Other important discoveries: the compass; gunpowder.

82   The Mediaeval Town
- Towns grew up mainly because of trade.
- Many were established near bridges or crossroads.
- Some towns were granted a charter for running their own affairs.
- The main trade was in wool and wine.
- Inns were built for travelling traders and pilgrims.

83   Edward IV
- He reigned from 1461-1483.
- He was the victor of the Wars of the Roses.
- His claim to the throne was based on the fact that Henry IV had no right to take it from Richard II. However, subsequent discoveries, including some in 2002, have clearly indicated that Edward IV was himself illegitimate.
- During his reign, printing began – William Caxton.
- He was secretly married before he married Elizabeth Woodville. His children were thus illegitimate and it is this that caused Richard III so much trouble.

84   Richard III
(For family tree see Appendix 17d)
- He reigned from 1483-1485.
- Richard was Edward IV's younger brother.
- Edward IV's widow, Elizabeth Woodville, wanted her illegitimate son, Edward V to reign. Richard, knowing this to be impossible, kidnapped the boy to protect him.
- Richard took the title of protector.

- He appointed Lord Hastings to be his Chancellor, but when Hastings plotted with the Queen, Richard ordered his execution.
- It was then announced that Edward V and Richard Duke of York were illegitimate and so Richard himself was therefore the rightful heir to the throne.
- Richard's defenders say that he arranged for the two little princes to be kept safely in the Tower, which was a royal palace rather than a prison, but…
- Shortly after Easter 1484, they were never seen alive again.
- Richard's son, Edward, died in 1484 and so, apart from Richard III himself, there was no heir to the throne. So Richard's 5th cousin and Henry V's grandson, Henry Tudor, planned to challenge Richard for the throne.
- He landed in 1485 at Milford Haven and met and defeated Richard at Bosworth that year.
- How the main players were related:

85   Battle of Bosworth
- It was fought in 1485.
- Henry Tudor, with no strong claim to the throne, opposed Richard III, having landed at Milford Haven.
- Lord Stanley, with a large private army, was asked by Richard to help him. Richard apparently threatened Stanley's son with death if he didn't help.
- Stanley decided to support Henry. However, even then, the battle was very even. But when Richard was killed, his cause was ended and his followers fled.
- Henry was crowned unofficially on the Battlefield as Henry VII.
- He consolidated his claim to the throne by marrying Elizabeth of York, daughter of Edward IV.

PART V
TUDOR HISTORY

86   King Henry VII   1485-1509
- Henry Tudor, the first of the House of Tudor.
- By marrying Elizabeth of York, daughter of Edward IV, he united the Houses of York and Lancaster.
- He was not popular, but everyone liked the Queen.
- He entertained huge numbers and his lavish living must surely have influenced his son, Henry VIII.
- His claim to the throne was very remote, but after the death of Richard III, and by marrying Elizabeth, no one was able to prevent him becoming King.
- He ignored Parliament, but still managed to collect a vast sum of money to give to his son when he died.
- Henry had a Lord Chancellor and Archbishop of Canterbury called John Morton who developed a two-pronged argument that supported the raising of taxation; it was called Morton's Fork. The argument goes thus: if you have an extravagant lifestyle, this proves you have enough money to pay the tax, whereas if you have a parsimonious one, this shows that you can also pay the tax because you have set enough money aside to do so.

87   Lambert Simnel and Perkin Warbeck
Perkin Warbeck
- He was hanged, drawn and quartered in 1499 for pretending to be Richard, Duke of York.
- In 1498, he had landed at St Michael's Mount and reached Taunton with a large force before Henry VII could stop him.
Lambert Simnel
- Was crowned in Dublin as Edward VI in 1487.

- He was defeated at Stoke Field (Notts) and became a servant of Henry VII but was later executed.
- His backers tried to pretend he was Clarence's son (encouraged by the boy's tutor, the priest Richard Simon).

88   Great Tudor Explorers

- In 1453, the overland trade route to the East was closed by the Turks. They captured Constantinople.
- In 1498, Vasco da Gama (Portuguese) reached India by sailing around Africa.
- In 1492, Christopher Columbus, an Italian, but paid by the Spanish King, reached America by sailing across the Atlantic Ocean. He initially thought he had reached India.
- The Pope then announced that all newly discovered land found west of the Azores belonged to Spain, and to the east belonged to Portugal (hence Brazil being Portuguese).
- John Cabot, from Venice, paid by Henry VII in 1497, crossed the Atlantic and reached Newfoundland. He was lost in his ship in 1498 on his second trip.
- The Portuguese nation became famous for naval explorers, due to the influence of Prince Henry the Navigator.
- In 1486, Bartholomew Diaz rounded the Cape of Good Hope (then called the Cape of Storms).
- The Mohammedans, resenting this navigating success, attacked the Portuguese in 1509, at sea, but lost. After this, the Christian merchants controlled the seas.
- Other English explorers included Gilbert and Frobisher, who visited Newfoundland and Labrador.
- Sir Walter Raleigh (step=brother of Gilbert) founded Virginia, which he named after Queen Elizabeth.
- Sir Richard Grenville also visited Virginia in 1585, but angered both the Indians and the Spaniards by capturing their galleons.
- Virginia was not successfully colonised until 1607.

89   Christopher Columbus

- Columbus was born at Genoa in about 1453.
- After the fall of Constantinople, the overland route to Asia was closed, and Genoa became much less important as a seaport.
- Columbus approached the Spanish with his suggestion of finding a route to Asia by sailing west. The Spanish were fighting the Moors and were not free to accept the offer until after their victory in 1492.
- Columbus sailed in 3 ships, Santa Maria, Pinta and Nina. In October 1492 he reached San Salvador.
- He called the natives Indians, because he thought he had reached India. We now call the islands the West Indies.
- In all, he crossed the Atlantic four times, but the Spanish regarded him as a failure because he never reached India.
- Columbus was always supported by King Ferdinand and Queen Isabella.

90   Followers of Columbus

- America was probably named after Amerigo Vespucci, the first man to declare that it was not Asia.
- Because Cabral, a Portuguese, had landed in Brazil, it became the only country south of the USA to speak Portuguese – all the rest speak Spanish.
- Magellan sailed south and around South America into the Pacific Ocean, so called because it was calm. The straits between the Continent and Tierra del Fuego are named after him.

- While Magellan was killed in the Philippines, a small number of his sailors reached Portugal and thus became the first men to sail around the world..

91 Spain's Explorers
- In 1513, the Spanish discovered the Pacific Ocean and Florida.
- In 1519, Hernando Cortes discovered Mexico and the Aztecs, whose leader was called Montezuma.
- Pizzaro discovered the Incas in Peru and their capital Cuzco.
- Ferdinand de Soto explored the southern part of what is now the United States as far as the Mississippi and Coronado reached the Grand Canyon.
- The explorers were always accompanied by missionary priests (mostly friars) and San Francisco began as a mission with a church, a school and a workshop.
- It is due to these missionaries that Latin America became Catholic.
- The Spanish did not exterminate the Indians, like the English did, in their colonies.

92 Elizabethan Sea Dogs
- Sir John Hawkins made money from shipping slaves illegally from Africa to America.
- Sir Francis Drake was a pirate who captured ships and stole gold and silver. He was the first Englishman to sail around the world and, it would appear, stealing as he went!
- Drake and Hawkins were cousins.
- Drake's ship was the Pelican, but he renamed it the Golden Hind.

93 Henry VIII
- He reigned from 1509-1547.
- He was called Defender of the Faith by Pope Leo X for his paper defending the seven sacraments and criticising Luther.
- He married his brother's widow, Catherine of Aragon, with the Pope's permission.
- When she failed to produce a son, he, with no real cause, doubted whether his marriage to her was valid.
- His six "wives" were:
  - Catherine of Aragon – divorced
  - Anne Boleyn – beheaded
  - Jane Seymour – died
  - Anne of Cleaves – divorced
  - Catherine Howard – beheaded
  - Catherine Parr – survived.
- Thomas Cardinal Wolsey failed to get the Pope to annual Henry's marriage to Catherine of Aragon and was sacked as Chancellor.
- Wolsey was succeeded by Sir Thomas More, but More (later St Thomas More) was executed for refusing to accept Henry as head of the Church.
- More was succeeded by Thomas Cromwell who was executed for arranging the marriage with Anne of Cleaves, and this in spite of his work "dissolving" the monasteries.
- Cromwell was succeeded by Cranmer.
- Before his fall, Henry's appearance was very impressive. He was tall, good looking, richly clothed and with a red beard. He would hear three Masses a day; he loved hunting, music and tennis. Later, he was obese and degenerate.

94 The Court of Star Chamber
- It was the room where the King and his council would meet.
- It was called Star Chamber from the stars on the ceiling.
- It began in the reign of Edward III.
- It was the senior court of the land.
- Henry VII used it to keep his nobles under control.
- It was subject to its own rules, was unpopular, and Parliament abolished it in 1641.

- In the reign of Henry VIII, Cardinal Wolsey made great use of the Court of Star Chamber, tending to treat his opponents badly.

95 Battle of Flodden

- Henry VII married his daughter Margaret to James IV of Scotland, in order to unite both countries.
- But the English in the north kept on raiding the Scottish borders.
- When Henry VIII went to war with France in 1513, James decided it was the best time to teach the northern English a lesson.
- They marched from Edinburgh and stopped near Flodden with an army of over 30,000 men (some say up to 60,000).
- The Earl of Surrey marched north with 25,000 men and placed his soldiers behind the Scots, cutting off their retreat.
- In the battle, many Scots were killed, including King James IV of Scotland.

96 Field of Cloth of Gold

- It was held in 1520 just south of Calais.
- It was a grand "picnic" at which Henry VIII and Francis I made friends.
- A temporary palace and 2,800 tents were erected.

97 Henry VIII's Family Tree

(See Appendix 17 c)

98 16th Century Ireland

- In 1541, Henry VIII declared himself King of Ireland.
- The Irish, remaining Catholic, resisted Henry's imposition.
- Henry flooded northern Ireland with English settlers, and in 1601 the Irish army was defeated at Kinsale.
- However, the English could never get the Irish to give up their Catholic Faith.

99 Reformation

- This essentially began with Luther in Germany in 1512.
- He attacked the Pope and indulgences.
- Henry VIII began by opposing Luther and was given the title "Defender of the Faith" by the Pope for his resistance to Protestantism. However, when Clement VII refused to allow Henry to divorce, Henry assumed papal authority in England for himself and to this day British monarchs claim the title, "Defender of the Faith."
- Once Henry had made himself the equivalent of the Pope, he decided he must have all the Church's land and property as well.
- Thus the Reformation in England began, in part, with greed. Once the Church was no longer loyal to the Pope, other people began to change the religion as they pleased. Hence the many, fragmented variations of Protestantism.

100 Defender of the Faith

- In 1521, Pope Leo X gave Henry VIII the title *Fidei Defensor* (Defender of the Faith).
- This was a reward for Henry's paper written in defence of the seven sacraments. Martin Luther had violently attacked them in 1520. The seven sacraments are, Baptism, Confirmation, the Holy Eucharist, Confession, Matrimony, Holy Orders and Extreme Unction (the Last Rites).
- Later in his reign, Henry was to abuse this privilege after his break with Rome by continuing to use the title, and all succeeding monarchs have done the same since.

101 Cardinal Wolsey

- Cardinal Wolsey became both chancellor to Henry VIII and the Pope's personal representative in England. He was thus very powerful and immensely rich.
- It was he who built Hampton Court.
- When Wolsey failed to get Pope Clement VII to annul Henry's marriage to Catherine of Aragon, Henry sacked him.
- He was on his way to London to stand trial when he died at Leicester in 1530.

102 Anne Boleyn

- Anne Boleyn was probably Henry's own daughter.
- She was crowned in 1533, but executed in 1536.
- It was Henry's lust for Anne that led to the Protestant Reformation in England.

103 St John Fisher

- He was a Cardinal and Bishop of Rochester.
- He opposed and resisted Henry VIII's divorce from Catherine of Aragon, for which he was tried for treason.
- He was martyred on Tower Hill on 22nd June 1535 (the same year as St Thomas More). He too is a canonised saint.

104 The Act of Supremacy

- In 1534, Henry VIII made himself Supreme Head of the Church of England.
- Henry threatened members of parliament with execution if they did not pass the Act establishing this.
- In 1535, Sir Thomas More, Henry's chancellor, was indeed executed for failing to support the King.
- More's acknowledgement of the supremacy of the Pope led to his martyrdom. "My Lord," the saint said at his trial "for one bishop of your opinion, I have a hundred saints of mine."

105 St Thomas More

- He was a pious statesman.
- He succeeded Wolsey as Lord Chancellor.
- He resisted Henry VIII's divorce and refused to acknowledge Henry as head of the Church in England.
- He was beheaded on 7th July 1535.

106 Thomas Cromwell

- He became friendly with Henry VIII by joining the enemies of Wolsey.
- It was he who persuaded Henry to take the title of Supreme Head of the Church of England.
- The dissolution of the monasteries was organised by him as part of his aim of abolishing papal authority.
- He fell from his high office (chancellor) when Henry lost interest in Anne of Cleaves, whom Cromwell had chosen.
- He was beheaded on Tower Hill in 1540.

107 "Dissolution" of the Monasteries

- Once Henry had assumed power over all the Catholic Church in England, it was obvious he would claim ownership of all its possessions.
- He thus sent visitors to the monasteries commanding them to snoop around and note down all their possessions.

- Any monks who showed they were against the King's divorce were sent to the Tower or forced out of their monasteries.
- The silver, gold and lands, etc., were all taken over by the King.
- Cranmer became Archbishop of Canterbury, the first married one – and the first Protestant one (Protestants protest against the authority of the Pope) – and Cromwell became Chancellor.
- Cromwell and Henry were quite ruthless. They executed any who opposed them, whether abbots, monks or lay people.
- The smaller religious houses were closed and sold in 1536; the larger ones in 1539 (nearly 1,000 in all). The monks and servants were simply expelled. The lands and treasures, where they were not appropriated by the King, passed to those who had helped him. (One of these families was the Russells, who became Dukes of Bedford. It appears that they had originally been a Jewish family from Portugal called Rossel.)

108   Pilgrimage of Grace
- It was led by Robert Aske in 1536, in opposition to Henry VIII's break with Rome and the dissolution of the monasteries.
- The whole of Yorkshire rose in rebellion.
- They took York, but when they reached London, Aske was arrested and executed.
- A similar rebellion began in Devon and Cornwall, under Edward VI, called the Prayer Book Rebellion, in 1549 (demanding the restoration of the Latin Mass). It too was crushed and thousands were killed.

109   The Jesuits
- The Society of Jesus was founded by St Ignatius of Loyola in 1534.
- The Society was founded and used to counter the effects of Luther (Germany), Calvin (Switzerland), Knox (Scotland), and Henry VIII (England) – i.e. the Protestant reformers.
- Jesuits are soldiers of Jesus, who take a fourth vow of special, direct service to the Pope (in addition to vows of poverty, chastity and obedience).

110   On a visit to Hampton Court one can see:
- Kitchens
- Cellars
- Private Royal apartments
- Fountain Court
- Cardinal Wolsey's rooms with paintings of Tudors
- State apartments, Great Hall, Chapel
- Tennis Courts – Royal Tennis was invented in France
- Maze
- Royal Toys

111   The Book of Common Prayer
- In 1549, the Book of Common Prayer was introduced in English.
- The Act of Uniformity made its use compulsory and abolished the Latin Mass.
- It was written by Cranmer.
- It led to the Prayer Book Rebellion in Devon and Cornwall in 1549.
- In 1552, a revised version was printed.

112   Edward VI
- He reigned from 1547-1553, dying at the age of 15.
- On his accession, and to enforce his father's claim to spiritual supremacy in England, at the age of nine he was declared, in effect, "pope" of England, with authority and power to legislate on all spiritual matters. This meant that...

- During his reign the Protestant religion was further enforced by his uncle, Edward Seymour, Duke of Somerset (Protector Somerset).
- Edward wished for the crown to be passed on his death to the Protestant Lady Jane Grey.
- During his reign (1549) the Book of Common Prayer was produced by Archbishop Cranmer.
- Somerset was Lord Protector of all England, but was sacked for supporting the suffering peasants and executed in 1552. His place was taken by the Duke of Northumberland.

113   Queen Mary

- She reigned from 1553-1558.
- She is known, quite unjustly, as "Bloody Mary" (as a result of Protestant propaganda).
- When she came to the throne, Catholicism was immediately restored. No laws needed to be passed to achieve this, and it was enthusiastically re-endorsed by the English people.
- She married Philip II, the King of Spain, whose son by an earlier marriage was Don Carlos.
- Philip persuaded Mary to go to war with France, the result of which was that Calais, the last English possession in France, was lost in 1558.
- The Protestants then rose in rebellion against her. They were led by Thomas Wyatt. The rebellion failed.
- Under Cardinal Pole's advice, the heretical bishops, Latimer and Ridley, were burned at the stake.
- She is called "Bloody" because during her reign 287 Protestants were put to death. However, not only were such executions a part of every monarch's reign at the time (and must be viewed in this context), she herself was never in favour of them; the decisions being forced on her by her advisers who themselves became Protestants in the next reign, that of Queen Elizabeth (who is far more deserving of the epithet "bloody" in her treatment of Catholics).

114   Lady Jane Grey

- She was the great-niece of Henry VIII and a Protestant who, after the death of Edward VI, reigned for nine days in 1553.
- She was planted on the throne by her father-in-law, the Duke of Northumberland, who had been Edward's main adviser.
- She, her husband and Northumberland were all executed when the country rebelled in favour of the King's Catholic daughter Mary.

115   Archbishop Cranmer

- He was Archbishop of Canterbury under Henry VIII.
- He was burned at the stake in 1556 under Mary.
- He died an unrepentant Protestant.

116   Queen Elizabeth

- She reigned from 1558-1603.
- She was the daughter of Anne Boleyn, and therefore quite possibly the product of incest because Anne Boleyn's mother had been one of Henry VIII's mistresses.
- She outlawed the Catholic Faith, killing many Catholic priests and lay people. Cuthbert Mayne was the first priest to die for the Faith in her reign (in Launceston).
- She executed Mary Queen of Scots in 1587.
- Her main adviser was William Cecil.
- She fined all who refused to attend Protestant services (these people are called recusants).
- Those who wanted the church to become even more Protestant were called Puritans.

117   Mary Queen of Scots

- She was born in Scotland in 1542.
- When her father died, six days later she went with her mother, Mary of Guise, to live in France.
- In 1558, having married the Dauphin, she became Queen of France.
- When the King of France died in 1560, she returned to Scotland.
- In 1565, she married Lord Darnley.
- In 1567, Darnley was killed. Mary was suspected of being involved, mainly due to the existence of the eight so-called "Casket Letters," which appeared to show her complicity in the death of Darnley. Whether they were forgeries or not, Mary eventually fled to England.
- Once in England, Elizabeth feared Mary's rightful claim to the throne (Europe said Elizabeth was illegitimate with no right to the throne, whereas Mary was effectively next in line). Mary was imprisoned and, after nineteen years, Elizabeth signed her death warrant. She was executed at Fotheringhay Castle. She never abandoned her Catholic faith.

118   Spanish Armada

- Relations between England and Spain grew worse as a result of Drake's exploits.
- The main reason for the Armada sailing was to restore the Catholic Faith to England.
- The main reason the Armada was defeated was the wind allowing Drake to send fire ships into it.
- The Spanish galleons that could, fled around Scotland, but more than 10,000 Spaniards lost their lives.
- In 1587, Drake delayed the Armada by sailing into Cadiz harbour and attacking galleys – singeing the King of Spain's beard.
- The Armada sailed in 1588, under the Duke of Medina Sidonia.
- Those Spaniards who landed in Britain or Ireland were treated with great cruelty.

119   Poor Laws

- Up until the Reformation, the Catholic monasteries looked after the poor, the sick, the elderly and the schools.
- When the monasteries were closed in 1536, the poor people had nowhere or no-one to look after them, instigating a period of great poverty and suffering.
- The state then began to collect money to provide for them. Thus the welfare state began.

120   Pope St Pius V

- He reigned from 1566-1572.
- He codified (standardised) the Latin Mass for all time.
- He excommunicated Elizabeth I for tyranny towards Catholics.
- His prayers and the saying of the Rosary are said to have won the Battle of Lepanto in 1571.
- He was extremely devout and a much revered Pope.

121   Renaissance (1300 – 1500)

- In Roman times, Constantine moved his capital city from Rome to Byzantium.
- He renamed it Constantinople and it became a splendid Catholic centre.
- In 1453, when it fell to Islam, the Greek scholars fled to Italy where their influence began the Renaissance or "rebirth."
- Famous artists from this time include: Leonardo da Vinci, Raphael, Michelangelo, Giotto, Fra Angelico/Bellini.
  Sculptors: Donatello, Cellini. Writers: Dante, Petrarch, Erasmus, St Thomas More.

PART VI
STUART HISTORY

122   Parliament & King

- Henry VIII had worked closely with Parliament, forcing it to agree with his proposals. This actually made Parliament more important after he died.
- This importance increased as the monarch needed to ask more and more for money.
- Eventually in Charles I's reign, he had such determination to act as he wished ("the divine right of kings") that between 1629 and 1640 he ruled without Parliament – the Eleven Years Tyranny.
- After the Civil War, the King simply could not rule (he would have no money to do so) without Parliament. Parliament, from then on, called the tune.

123   James I

- He reigned from 1603-1625.
- He had been King James VI of Scotland and, on succeeding to the English throne, he united both countries.
- He believed in the divine right of kings, which meant he would hardly listen to his Parliament. He was called the "Wisest Fool in Christendom."
- His intimate friend, George Villiers, Duke of Buckingham, was given power and money by James.
- The most notable event in his reign was the Gunpowder Plot in 1605.
- The "King James Bible" was published in 1611.
- James' first cousin, Arabella Stuart, was favoured by some to become monarch instead of James.

124   Gunpowder Plot

- When James I became King, Catholics hoped that, in memory of his mother, Mary Queen of Scots, James would give back their freedoms.
- When he refused, the story goes that a group of Catholics led by Robert Catesby, resolved to blow up King, Lords and Commons, in the 1605 State Opening of Parliament.
- The plan, it is claimed, had been that with the King dead, English Catholics would appeal for help to Spain and put Princess Elizabeth (James's daughter) on the throne.
- But one of the group lost his nerve and warned the Council of the supposed plot (the Monteagle letter).
- The Houses of Parliament were searched, the gunpowder discovered and the culprits arrested and executed.
- The result of the Gunpowder Plot was an increase in hatred towards Catholics.
- There is significant evidence that the plot, or parts of it, were a deliberate hoax, designed to discredit Catholics and justify their persecution.

125   Tunnage & Poundage

- When James I came to the throne, Parliament voted him the customs duties (tunnage and poundage) for his income.
- Once they belonged to James, he thought he could increase them, but Parliament refused.
- The judges, whom James had appointed to settle the issue, agreed with James and so James dismissed his Parliament in 1611.
- The next Parliament (1614) was dismissed almost as soon as it had met and was called the Addled Parliament.

126 Voyage of the Mayflower
- The "Pilgrim Fathers" were Puritans, (extreme Protestants) who sailed to America in 1620 to be free to practice their religion.
- They sailed from Plymouth, but some of their number came from Holland.
- They landed at Plymouth Rock, Massachusetts, and called their colony New England.
- New York's first name was New Amsterdam, but it was later renamed New York in honour of James, Duke of York, who was to become King James II.
- The journey to America was very rough.

127 George Villiers, Duke of Buckingham
- He was an intimate friend ("favourite") of King James I.
- James thought so highly of him that he gave to him, rather than Parliament, the job of running the country between 1617 and 1628.
- He was unpopular and murdered at Portsmouth in 1628 by a man called Felton.

128 Sir Walter Raleigh
- He was born in Devon in 1554.
- He is supposed to have laid his cloak over a puddle so that Queen Elizabeth I did not get her feet wet.
- His half-brother was Sir Humphrey Gilbert and his cousin Sir Richard Grenville.
- He led an expedition to what is now North Carolina.
- He brought tobacco to England and potatoes to Ireland.
- He organised the defence of Devon against the Spanish Armada.
- When James I came to the throne, Raleigh was unpopular and after an unfair trial he was imprisoned and beheaded in 1618.

129 The Thirty Years War
- This was fought between Austria and Spain (Catholic) and Germany (Protestant).
- James's daughter was driven out of Germany and the English wanted to declare war on Spain.
- James did not want war and forbade Parliament to discuss it.
- When Spain refused to allow Charles to marry their King's daughter, Parliament was so indignant that war was declared on Spain.
- The war lasted from 1618-1648.
- The main result of the Thirty Years War was the devastation it wrought on the whole of Germany.

130 Charles I
- He reigned from 1625-1649.
- He married Henrietta Maria, a Catholic.
- He perpetuated his father, James I's belief in the divine right of kings.
- This belief led to the English Civil War and his execution.
- For eleven years (1629-1640) he ruled without Parliament.
- He appointed William Laud, Archbishop of Canterbury, a tough "high church" Anglican.
- Vicars who refused to obey Laud were tried by the Court of High Commission, lay-people by the Court of Star Chamber.

131 Cardinal Richelieu
- He ruled France as Chief Minister (essentially the first prime minister) from 1624 to 1642, being appointed by King Louis XIII.
- He made France very powerful, but sided with Protestants whenever they were likely to help the French cause.
- He was ruthless and unpopular.

132   Holy Roman Empire
- It grew out of the remains of the old Roman Empire.
- Charlemagne was the first Holy Roman Emperor, crowned in 800.
- Charlemagne was a great Catholic and he gave life to the idea that all Catholics should be subject to one King.
- After his death the next emperor was King of Germany.
- The Emperors were often in dispute with their lesser rulers and even with the Pope.
- By the 15th Century, the emperors belonged to the family of Habsburg.
- The Empire was gradually lessened by internal wars – particularly the Thirty Years War between Protestants and Catholics – and the title Holy Roman Empire was abolished in 1806.

133   The Petition of Right
- The Petition of Right was drawn up in 1628 declaring that it was illegal to raise taxes without consent of Parliament and to imprison people without trial.
- Charles I agreed to this.

134   Ship Money
- Ship Money was a tax the King could legally raise in time of danger. A port could either pay money or supply a ship to defend the land.
- In 1637, John Hampden refused to pay Ship Money because Parliament had not approved it. He was tried in court, but lost his case.

135   Covenanters
- In 1638, Archbishop Laud tried to impose the English Prayer Book on Scotland.
- The Scots rebelled, signed a covenant (hence covenanters) and Charles's army signed the peace treaty of Berwick without fighting a battle.
- The Scots complained that the Prayer Book was not Protestant enough.

136   The Short Parliament
- In 1640, Charles summoned Parliament to raise money for an army.
- The Commons refused to support the King until their own grievances had been remedied.
- The King refused, and dissolved Parliament.

137   Sir Thomas Wentworth, Earl of Strafford
- He was an adviser to Charles I.
- Strafford opposed Parliament, which passed an Act of Attainder, calling for his death without any trial.
- Charles, in fear of the mob, gave way and signed the Act and so Strafford was beheaded.

138   The Long Parliament
- This met in November 1640.
- It was led by John Pym.
- It:
  - (i)   organised Strafford's execution
  - (ii)   abolished the Court of Star Chamber
  - (iii) abolished the Court of High Commission
  - (iv)   abolished Ship Money
  - (v)   said Parliament must meet every three years (the Triennial Bill).
- Its members also included John Hampden and Oliver Cromwell.
- Those who wanted to reform the Church of England were Roundheads, those who did not, Cavaliers.

- When the Irish Catholics rebelled, Parliament needed an army. If the army had Charles's support, Parliament feared he would use it to attack them, so Pym drew up the Grand Remonstrance, attacking the King and removing his powers. This was passed and Parliament summoned its own army.
- Charles reacted by marching on Parliament with 400 soldiers to arrest the five leaders – Hampden, Holles, Haselrig, Pym and Strode.
- But they had escaped before Charles arrived. He is quoted as saying, "I see the birds have flown."
- Charles went to York and both he and Parliament began to raise their armies for the Civil War.
- Parliament appointed the Earl of Essex as General and ordered the Earl of Warwick to seize the navy.
- In the Self-denying Ordinance, Parliament decided that no member of either house might take military command.

139   The Battle of Edgehill
- Charles I raised his army at Nottingham in 1642.
- One of his main officers was Prince Rupert of the Rhine.
- They met the Parliamentary Army at Edgehill in October 1642 and routed it.
- This gave the King Oxford, which became his headquarters.
- During 1643, most of the battles went the King's way.

140   The Battle of Marston Moor
- In early 1644, the Scots marched south and, together with the Parliamentary Army, besieged the King's forces in York.
- Prince Rupert marched north and arrived at Marston Moor. The siege was instantly lifted.
- Sir Thomas Fairfax charged the Royalist Army. To begin with the Roundheads did badly, but Oliver Cromwell regrouped his forces and attacked the Cavaliers from behind.
- It became the Roundheads' first major victory.
- However, it did not dishearten the Cavaliers who won further victories, especially at Lostwithiel.
- These caused the reorganisation of the Roundheads into the New Model Army under Sir Thomas Fairfax and Oliver Cromwell.

141   Civil War (Generally)
- Not everyone fought in the war but nearly everyone suffered.
- The soldiers were badly paid.
- Houses were often looted.
- There was much anti-Catholic propaganda.

142   Civil War Ends
- The New Model Army turned the whole war by winning the Battle of Naseby (1645).
- Nine months later, the King surrendered at Oxford (1646) and the war was over.
- The King was taken from Holmby House in Northamptonshire to Hampton Court Palace by Cornet Joyce, but in 1647 he escaped to the Isle of Wight.
- Many people rallied to the King's cause, including the Scots. The Scots were defeated at Preston (1648) and Cromwell also subdued the English Royalists throughout the south of England and Wales.
- This ended the Second Civil War and Oliver Cromwell began the moves that were to lead to the execution of King Charles.
- What was left of Parliament imposed heavy fines on all who had supported the King.

143   Oliver Cromwell
- After the Civil War, Parliament refused the soldiers their back-pay.
- Cromwell, who had been a very successful general in the Civil War, saw his chance and supported the soldiers.
- The Army marched on London, forced eleven members of Parliament to leave, and offered terms to the King.
- The terms were that everyone, except Catholics, might worship freely and the King must share power with Parliament. The King refused.
- The King's refusal led to the brief Second Civil War in 1648. Once Cromwell had won this war, he decided the King must die.
- This made Cromwell hated and he was never able to rule without force.

144   Death of Charles I
- After the arrest of the King, Parliament still had a majority that would never consent to the King's death.
- Cromwell sent Colonel Pride with a force of soldiers to Parliament to arrest 50 members and bar entry to nearly 100 more (Pride's Purge).
- The members left behind became known as the "Rump Parliament."
- The King was then tried, but he refused to plead, because he said they had no right to try him.
- The King was sentenced and was executed on 30th January 1649.

145   The Commonwealth
- When this began it was very unpopular. Both Scotland and Ireland claimed Charles II as their ruler.
- Cromwell went to Ireland and suppressed the Royalists ruthlessly. He killed thousands at the sieges of Drogheda and Wexford.
- Scotland crowned Charles II; Cromwell went north and defeated the Scots at Dunbar, taking Edinburgh in 1650.
- The Scots regrouped, went south to invade England, but Cromwell caught them and defeated them at Worcester in 1651.
- The Levellers, a party in Parliament, wanted to do away with rank. Cromwell was against this, and while Parliament was sitting he ordered his troops to pull the Speaker from his chair and lock the doors.
- The Rump having been dismissed, Cromwell organised a Parliament called "Barebones," but this was soon dissolved and Cromwell became Lord Protector.

146   The First Dutch War
- During the English Civil War, the Dutch had built up their trade.
- However, Charles I and the Rump had built up the English Navy.
- When, in 1651, Parliament declared that all ships should salute the English flag in the channel, the Dutch declared war, which they lost in 1654.
- Cromwell then set about attacking Spanish shipping (because it was Catholic) and defeated the Spanish at the Battle of the Dunes, near Dunkirk, in 1658.
- Blake was Cromwell's naval leader.

147   Charles II
- He reigned from 1660-1685.
- After the unpopularity of the Commonwealth, he was a very welcome monarch.
- During his reign the following events took place:
  - 1662   Prayer book was published
  - 1665   The Plague*
  - 1666   Fire of London*

1667   Defeat by the Dutch*

- The country was short of money and Charles was financed by Louis XIV (the Sun King) in return for English army help.
- He is known as the "Merry Monarch" and he died a Catholic.
- He was invited to reign by "The Sealed Knot" – a secret royalist association.
- Having been invited to reign, Charles II had much less power over Parliament than his father.
- * These three events (above) caused widespread discontent and Charles found it easier to run the country with a group that came to be called a Cabal rather than Parliament
- The word Cabal comes from:
  Clifford, Arlington, Buckingham, Ashley Cooper and Lauderdale.

148   Clarendon Code
- These were laws passed in 1661, establishing the Anglican Church as the Church of England.
- Neither Clarendon nor Charles II agreed with them.
- By the Code, all other religions were suppressed.

149   Second Dutch War
- England's rivalry with Holland over trade led to war breaking out again in 1664.
- It went badly for England and when peace seemed likely, all the naval ships retreated to Chatham in 1667.
- At this the Dutch sailed up the Medway, broke into the harbour, burned four battleships and towed away the flag ship, the Royal Charles.
- The sailors, having not been paid, made no effort to stop them.

150   Declaration of Indulgence
- In 1672, this was issued by Charles thus setting aside the laws against Catholics and non-conformists.
- Charles did not dare help one side without the other.
- After the Third Dutch War, which he had lost, Charles needed money and asked Parliament to convene to vote it for him.
- Parliament met and cancelled the Declaration. Instead they passed the Test Act which dismissed all Catholics in government service (this included James, Duke of York).
- In 1685, James II issued a Declaration of Indulgence and ordered it to be read out in all churches. Seven bishops refused and were arrested and tried, but found not guilty.

151   The Third Dutch War
- Louis XIV wanted to extend France's borders to the Rhine.
- To do this he invaded the Spanish Netherlands in 1672, with English forces to help him.
- The Dutch beat him by flooding the land and defeating the English Navy off the coast of Suffolk.

152   The Great Plague
- The Great Plague (1665) was similar to the Black Death.
- It affected London the worst.
- It was brought by fleas on black rats and ended when brown rats drove them out.
- The Great Fire of London destroyed many plague infested houses.

153   The Great Fire of London
- It began on 2nd September 1666, in Pudding Lane, and lasted until 5th September.
- Catholics were falsely suspected of starting it.
- The Monument was built to commemorate the fire.

- St Paul's and many churches, as well as 10,000 houses, were destroyed.
- The houses were rebuilt in brick.
- Sir Christopher Wren rebuilt St Paul's and many city churches.
- It was after this fire that throughout England fire precautions began to develop.

154 Science & Learning in Restoration England
- Williams Harvey described the circulation of the blood.
- Robert Boyle discovered Boyle's law for gases.
- Isaac Newton laid down laws which explained the movement of stars.
- Samuel Pepys, the diarist, was president of the Royal Society and Clerk of the Acts of the Navy.
- With theatres being reopened, many new plays were staged.
- Newspapers such as "The Tattler" and "Spectator" began.

155 Whigs and Tories (i)
- In the second half of Charles II's reign, Charles's heir was his Catholic brother James.
- This worried the country and it was proposed that Charles's illegitimate son, the Duke of Monmouth, should succeed.
- Charles did not want this and, with bribes from Louis XIV, he kept Monmouth's supporters quiet.
- Monmouth's supporters then rallied around the Earl of Shaftsbury and became known as Whigs.
- Thus Whigs were anti-Catholic.
- The party that united around Charles was known as Tories, whose name came from a band of Irish brigands.

156 The Popish Plot
- It was invented by Titus Oates. He gossiped that Catholics were plotting to murder Charles, put James on the throne, land a French army and massacre leading Protestants.
- From 1678, at least 15 innocent Catholics were executed on Oates's false accusations, and scores of others accused and persecuted.

157 Exclusion Bill
- This Bill, which was never passed by Parliament, would have prevented James II from becoming King (1680).

158 The Rye House Plot
- This was a Protestant plot to murder Charles as he returned from racing at Newmarket.
- Rye House is 20 miles (or so) north of London.
- The plot was ruined in 1682 by a fire at Newmarket which caused the King to return home early.

159 James II
- He reigned from 1685-1688.
- He became a Catholic and was thus the last Catholic King of England.
- He was an accomplished naval officer.
- On succeeding to the throne, he was faced with the invasion by his Protestant illegitimate nephew, the Duke of Monmouth.
- He defeated this invasion at the Battle of Sedgemoor (1685).
- After the battle, many Protestants were tried by Judge Jeffries who hanged so many that his trials were known as the Bloody Assizes.
- James tried to run the country with his Catholic supporters and resisted seven Protestant bishops who opposed him,

- It was this aspect of his monarchy that so infuriated a small group of influential Protestants that they invited James's brother-in-law, William, to become King instead.
- William of Orange landed at Torbay in 1688, whereupon James's supporters deserted him. James and his family had to flee the country.
- It was because he was a Catholic that James was deposed and it wasn't Parliament, but a group of Protestants, who arranged for William to become King. The end of James's reign is known as the "Glorious Revolution."

160 William and Mary

- They reigned from 1688-1702.
- Neither had first claim to the throne and, unlike monarchs, their only title was that they ruled by Act of Parliament.
- James II's son, James, a Catholic, was the true heir, and to prevent him succeeding, Parliament passed the Act of Settlement (1701) forbidding any Catholic from becoming King.
- James II's son was called the Old Pretender..
- When James II died, Louis XIV recognised James, the son, as King James III of England. This so infuriated the Whigs that they supported William in his wish to go to war with France.
- This war is called the War of the Spanish Succession and England's famous general was the Duke of Marlborough.
- William died when his horse tripped over a mole hill, after which the English Catholics raised their glasses and toasted "the Gentleman in Black Velvet."

161 The Glorious Revolution

- James II's first wife, who died, had been a Protestant. His daughter (Mary) had married William, Prince of Orange, and ruler of Holland. Both were Protestants.
- His second wife was a Catholic who bore him a son, his first, in 1688.
- The Protestants feared this son, a Catholic, because he was heir to the throne. A scurrilous rumour was put about that he wasn't James's son, but had been smuggled into the palace in a warming pan.
- Thus frightened, a small group of Protestants encouraged William and Mary to come and claim the throne.
- When Louis XIV invaded Germany, William could see that Holland was under no threat and so he sailed, landing at Torbay in November 1688.
- When William had landed with his Dutch army, James's supporters deserted him. James sent his wife, Mary of Modena, and son out of the country and soon followed himself. As he left he deliberately threw his royal seal into the River Thames.
- William didn't really want to become King (he was already King of Holland), but he didn't want to be junior to his wife, who was to become Queen. He agreed to rule jointly with her.
- Parliament restricted both the powers and the income of William and Mary, and thus Parliament became the true source of government. A law was passed (the Triennial Act) which meant elections to the House of Commons had to take place every three years.

162 The Massacre of Glencoe

- Although the Kings of England had been Kings of Scotland as well since 1603, the two countries were quite separate.
- Therefore it was necessary for William to be recognised as King of Scotland as soon as possible.
- Certain Scottish nobles vowed not to acknowledge William as King. Although they won the Battle of Killiecrankie (1689) their leader, Bonny Dundee, was killed and the movement died out.

- To ensure all Highland Chiefs were loyal to William, they were required to take an oath before New Year's Day 1692. The MacDonalds of Glencoe were accidentally a few days late taking the oath.
- William ordered the Campbells to punish the MacDonalds. After arriving in Glencoe, and behaving very warmly towards the MacDonalds, the Campbells suddenly murdered 38 of them and drove them from their land.

163   Darien Scheme
- The Scots wanted to found their own colony on the Isthmus of Darien, not far from Panama.
- The English were trading overseas, so why not the Scots?
- The Spanish drove the Scots away from Darien in 1700, and the English, having no wish to upset Spain, refused to help them.

164   The Act of Union
- In 1707, the English and Scottish Parliaments were merged.
- Scotland had long been at odds with England and, on the death of Queen Anne, threatened to make its own choice of kings.
- England, fearing this possibility, agreed to surrender her trading monopoly and accepted 45 members and 16 peers.
- No alteration was made to the Scottish legal system.
- Thus began the United Kingdom of Great Britain.

165   Bank of England
- It was founded in 1694.
- It began by lending £1.2 million at 8% interest to the government to pay for King William's war. (This was William's attempt to defeat the French between 1689 and 1697 and thus prevent a Catholic king returning to England. It was also known as the War of the League of Augsburg.)
- The loan and the bank were meant to last for ten years only, but the bank and its debt are now 300 years old.
- The debt the government still owes is called the National Debt.
- The government has bought the bank and through it issues bank notes and coins.
- It is in Threadneedle Street in the City of London.

166   The Battle of the Boyne
- After James II had escaped to France, he resolved to regain the English throne with Irish help.
- In 1689, he landed in Ireland with French troops. The Irish were delighted to help him and together they laid siege to Protestant Londonderry.
- William landed in Ireland and defeated his father-in-law at the Battle of the Boyne in July 1690.
- Following this, the whole of Ireland was conquered by the English and, in spite of promises to the contrary, all Catholics were treated with great harshness. They could neither sit in Parliament nor vote. They could not become soldiers, sailors or teachers, and they were not allowed to hold land on a large scale.

167   Act of Settlement
- When it looked as if William and Mary and Anne would all die without providing an heir to the throne, the Whigs (traders and financiers) wanted to ensure Catholic James II and his successors were not restored to the throne.
- The Whigs were more powerful than the Tories because they controlled the Bank of England which was owed £1.2 million by the government.

- Thus, in 1701, while the Whigs were not in government, they were powerful enough to pass the Act of Settlement giving the crown to the Protestant descendants of James I, known as the House of Hanover.

168   Queen Anne
- She reigned from 1702-1714.
- She had 14 children, but none lived beyond the age of 11.
- Her great and intimate friend was Sarah Churchill, wife of the Duke of Marlborough.
- During her reign, the great worry was that the Jacobites would want James II's son, a Catholic, to become King. Thus Parliament amended the Act of Settlement to pass the crown to Protestant Hanoverians.

169   The War of the Spanish Succession 1700-1711
- This war was a continuation of the War of the League of Augsburg (1689-1697) which was King William's successful attempt to subdue Louis XIV and prevent him returning James II (Catholic) to the English throne.
- In 1700, King Charles II of Spain died childless. He left all his empire to the grandson of Louis XIV, thus giving France considerable power and renewing the opportunity of restoring a Catholic king to England.
- France eased her way into Holland, excluded England and Holland from Spanish trade, and recognised James II's son, James Edward, as King of England.
- The war began in more earnest in 1702, and the Duke of Marlborough led the English forces. The first great English victory was at Blenheim in 1704.
- The French needed to fight the Austrians because, since Charles II's death, the Archduke claimed the Spanish throne.
- In order to worry the French (i.e. take their mind off attacking the Austrians) the English sent a fleet to the Mediterranean. This fleet took Gibraltar and Minorca.
- Having beaten the French, Marlborough pushed them back into France defeating them three more times at:
  - Ramilles 1706
  - Oudinarde 1708
  - Malplaquet 1709.
- As a result of the Treaty of Utrecht, 1713, Philip of Anjou became King of Spain, the Spanish Netherlands were given to Austria, and England, keeping Gibraltar and Minorca, was given Nova Scotia and Newfoundland, improved trading rights, and thus had become a world power.

PART VII
HANOVERIAN HISTORY

170   George I
- He reigned from 1714-1727.
- He spoke no English and left the business of government to a group of ministers called a Cabinet.
- The main politician of his reign was Sir Robert Walpole.
- The two main events of his reign were the Jacobite Rising of 1715 and
- The collapse of the South Sea Company of 1720 (known as the South Sea Bubble).

171   Riot Act
- In 1715 there was considerable unrest caused by the opposition in England to "German George."
- This led Parliament to pass the Riot Act giving magistrates increased powers.
- It was effectively another anti-Catholic measure.

172   The 1715 Rising

- The time for the supporters of James III, the Old Pretender, to rise in revolt, was as soon as George I had arrived.
- Those who rallied to James's support were known as Jacobites.
- The Jacobites were preparing their invasion in France, but after Louis XIV had died, the Duke of Orleans, who was Louis XV's regent, sided with the English and thus kept them informed of the Jacobite plans. One of the Duke's successors was to be the main instigator of the French Revolution.
- When the Jacobites landed in England, they were defeated at Preston.
- In Scotland under the Earl of Mar (Bobbing John), they drew the Battle of Sheriffmuir
- None of this helped James III, and the rising collapsed.
- The Whigs were so shocked by the rising that they passed the Septennial Act extending the life of their Parliament by four more years.

173   South Sea Bubble

- In 1717, the South Sea Company took over the National Debt and was going to pay for this debt by successful trading in the South Seas.
- The dream of vast profits from the South Seas led others to set up other companies for such trading.
- Thousands of people flocked to buy shares and this rush pushed the prices of shares up by 1000 per cent.
- Eventually, confidence in future profits collapsed and the shares in the companies became worthless – the Bubble burst.
- A man of great financial ability was needed to put the country on its feet again and Robert Walpole (Whig) came to power in 1721 and stayed there for 21 years.

174   Whigs and Tories (ii)

- The Whig party began late in the seventeenth century and drew its support from men engaged in trade and finance.
- The Tories formed themselves in opposition to the Whigs and represented the landowners, the Church of England, and above all the House of Stuart (i.e. James III).
- The Whigs favoured the House of Hanover and their rise to power coincided with both the founding of the Bank of England as well as the return of the Jews to England. The Jews sided with the Whigs who opposed Catholic James III.
- The Whigs, under Robert Walpole, were all powerful in the first half of the eighteenth century.

175   Sir Robert Walpole

- He was "a big Whig."
- He was a very powerful financier in the way he ran the country – promoting trade by borrowing money.
- He borrowed money from the supporters of the House of Hanover.
- He is thought of as being the first Prime Minister of Great Britain.
- He was strongly anti-Jacobite.

176   George II

- He reigned from 1727-1760.
- The main events of his reign were
    - i.   War with Spain known as the War of Jenkins' Ear (1739)
    - ii.   The War of the Austrian Succession (1743-48) and the Treaty of Aix-La-Chapelle
    - iii.   The Seven Years War (1756-1763)
    - iv.   The '45 Rebellion and Bonny Prince Charlie

     v.   Foundation of the Indian Empire and Black Hole of Calcutta
     vi.   Capture of Quebec and the conquest of Canada.
- This war-faring King was the last British King to lead his troops into battle (at Dettingen in 1743).

177   The War of Jenkins' Ear
- Ever since the Treaty of Utrecht (1713), the Spanish had attacked British ships in revenge for Britain's improved trading rights.
- When Captain Jenkins, in 1739, told the House of Commons that Spaniards had boarded his ship and cut off his ear, the members replied by declaring war on Spain.
- It was a short and unsuccessful war, subsumed into the War of Austrian succession, ending in 1748.

178   War of Austrian Succession
- In 1740, Frederick the Great of Prussia seized Silesia from the Austrian ruler Maria Teresa.
- George II, sensing Hanover was threatened, went to Maria Teresa's help.
- In 1743, he won the Battle of Dettingen, but in 1745, the French, under Marshal Saxe, defeated the British at Fontenoy.
- The war ended at the Peace of Aix-la-Chapelle (1748), which allowed Frederick to keep Silesia, but forced France to acknowledge the Protestant monarchs of England and to expel Bonny Prince Charlie.

179   The 1745 Rising
- Thirty years after his father's attempt to regain the crown for the Stuarts, Bonny Prince Charlie decided to try again.
- He landed at Glen Finnan (west coast of Scotland) and within a month had reached Edinburgh where he defeated the English at Prestonpans.
- On entering England, he found the people much less supportive – they had grown used to the Hanoverian kings – and, after reaching Derby, Bonny Prince Charlie realised he had to retreat.
- The English, under the Duke of Cumberland (son of George II), chased after him and defeated him at Culloden in April 1746.
- The defeated Scots were treated with great cruelty by Butcher Cumberland, but after an exciting escape Bonny Prince Charlie sailed to France.
- This rising ended all Jacobite hopes of unseating the Hanoverian kings.

180   The Seven Years War (Generally)
- This lasted from 1756-1763 and involved Britain, Prussia, Austria and France. In the previous war (the war of Austrian Succession), Austria had sided with Britain, but, Britain having failed to keep Silesia for Austria, this time Austria sided with France, and Britain fought with Prussia to protect both Hanoverian interests as well as British naval interests around the world.
- In 1756, the French seized Minorca. Admiral Byng was sent to relieve the island but failed and was executed "pour encourager les autres."
- British morale was very low and William Pitt (the Elder), also known as the Great Commoner, came to the rescue.
- Most of the fighting was led by Clive in India and Wolfe in Canada. The British were victorious and added huge new territories with which to trade.

181   The Seven Years War in India
- The British, in their war with the French, wanted to rid India of French factories.
- India was a valuable trading area and, by attacking the French, Britain hoped to increase her own trading opportunities, both in India and the rest of the Far East.

- The British, under Robert Clive, defeated the French at Plassey in 1757 and thus, through the trading activities of the East India Company, controlled most of India, particularly Bombay, Bengal, Madras and Calcutta.

182   The Black Hole of Calcutta
- This was an incident in the Seven Years War.
- In 1756, Calcutta, an English trading post, was attacked and taken by the Nawab of Bengal.
- The Nawab was on the side of the French.
- A group of over 150 Europeans were locked in a small guardroom overnight and by the next morning 43 had died.
- This became known as the Black Hole of Calcutta.
- Clive recaptured Calcutta in 1757.

183   The Seven Years War in Canada
- The French had a colony in Canada, and General Wolfe was sent by William Pitt the elder to subdue it.
- The key to success lay in whoever controlled Quebec.
- Wolfe decided to attack the French forces under Montcalm by first of all capturing the Heights of Abraham above Quebec.
- Wolfe succeeded in this by a risky and daring expedition. He took Quebec in 1759, but died in the battle.

184   The East India Company
- In 1600, some London merchants set up this company to handle the trade of spices and silk in India.
- They set up a factory in Bombay, and when Charles II married Catherine of Braganza, a Portuguese princess who owned Bombay, the British hold on India was strengthened considerably.
- In 1757, the French, who also had factories in India, fought the British under Robert Clive. The British won the Battle of Plassey and thus gained the rich province of Bengal.
- The East India Company administered most of India and was in charge of handling events such as the Indian Mutiny in 1857.
- The company ceased to exist in 1873.

185   George III
- He reigned from 1760-1820.
- He was the first George to be brought up speaking English and was urged to "be a king" by his tutor.
- He tried to regain some of the powers lost by his predecessors. He had the right to appoint ministers and lay down policy, but Parliament had to approve his actions.
- MPs who wished to hold office, such as Walpole, both Pitts, etc., had not only to catch the King's notice, but to ensure that their own policies were supported by enough MPs for them to be able to govern.
- He is famous for losing the American Colonies.
- His second son, Frederick Duke of York, was Commander in Chief of the army and it is of him that the nursery rhyme "The Grand Old Duke of York" was written, concerning his tactics on the hill at Cassell, just south of Dunkirk.
- His chief ministers were Lord North and William Pitt, the Younger.
- When he became senile, his son, George IV ran the country as Regent.

186   The Stamp Act
- In 1765, the British Parliament passed the Stamp Act which made all legal documents in the North American colonies subject to a tax. British legal documents already had to be taxed.
- The colonists refused to pay the stamp duty and burned the papers because they said the British Parliament could not make them pay tax without them returning any MPs to the British Parliament.
- The Stamp Act was repealed in 1766, but Parliament passed another Act declaring its right to make laws for the colonies.
- These two Acts made the American colonists so rebellious that they, in turn, led to the American War of Independence.

187   The Boston Tea Party
- The tax imposed on tea in 1773 was very unpopular in North America.
- A large body of men, who resented paying tax on tea, disguised themselves as Red Indians and boarded three tea ships in Boston Harbour. They threw hundreds of smashed crates of tea into the sea and this protest is known as the Boston Tea Party.

188   The American War of Independence
- The disgruntled Americans rebelled in 1775 and were supported by France and Spain (in 1783, Britain was forced to accept their independence).
- There were 13 British colonies that rebelled.
- The reasons for the war were as follows:
    - (a) The American colonists were 3,000 miles from Britain and did not like being ordered about by a Parliament in which they had no representation.
    - (b) The Seven Years War in America, while successful, had cost Britain dearly and she looked to the colonists for help in payment. The colonists did not like paying for this war.
    - (c) See notes on Stamp Act and Boston Tea Party.
- To counter the British, the colonists set up their own parliament and protested against British treatment. In return, Lord North sent even more troops to America.
- The first shots were fired in 1775 at Lexington.
- In 1776, Congress made its Declaration of Independence and appointed General George Washington its Commander in Chief.
- Part of the British troops surrendered at Saratoga in 1777 and the rest at Yorktown in 1781.
- At the Treaty of Paris in 1783, Britain accepted American Independence, but due to a brilliant victory by Admiral Rodney over the French just before the treaty, Britain retained most of her other gains. (The treaty is also known at the Treaty of Versailles.)

189   Declaration of Independence
- It was drawn up by Thomas Jefferson.
- It was based on Tom Paine's writings.
- It was signed on 4th July 1776.
- It stated that all men are created equal and that governments exist to guarantee life, liberty and the pursuit of happiness.
- 4th July is celebrated every year in the USA as Independence Day.

190   The Armed Neutrality
- During the American War of Independence, not only did France and Spain support the Americans, but Russia, Denmark and Sweden formed an alliance to protect their shipping.
- This alliance, the Armed Neutrality, was formed to prevent England attacking their ships as well as the French and Spanish ships..

191   The French Revolution

- The French Revolution broke out in 1789 because (we are told) the people were both poor and oppressed. However the suffering they endured as a result of the revolution only served to make their lot considerably worse.
- The French Parliament (the States General) had not met for 175 years and the King, Louis XVI, ruled France through his own favourite statesmen.
- Louis wanted to call a meeting of the States General (consisting of nobles, clergy and the rest of the people). The rest of the people demanded a constitution for France and when the King, nobles and clergy refused, the rest formed their own Parliament, the National Assembly.
- The National Assembly published a document, the "Declaration of the Rights of Man." The riots which broke out in support were organised by the Duke d'Orleans. The National Assembly took charge, the Bastille was stormed, and the Royal Family taken from Versailles to Paris.
- The Royal Family tried to escape, but were caught at Varennes. This act turned many of the people against them.
- The mob burst into the Tuilleries, where the King was imprisoned, and the National Assembly dethroned him.
- The Austrians invaded France to rescue the King in 1792, but were defeated at Valmy. (General Lafayette had also tried, but failed).
- After a general election, the new assembly (called the Convention) began the Reign of Terror. Louis XVI and Marie Antoinette were sent to the guillotine as were hundreds of others.
- The mild members of the Convention (Girondists) were executed, and the remainder (Jacobins) ruled France violently under Danton, Marat and Robespierre.
- People lost their property, the Church lost its land, many churches were destroyed, and many priests and people were condemned to death without trial.
- Eventually, France sickened of this bloodshed, Marat was murdered in his bath by Charlotte Corday and the other two leaders were guillotined.
- In this weakened state, in 1799, Napoleon Bonaparte seized power and became Emperor of France (crowning himself in 1804).
- Encouraged by the success of the Revolution in destroying the French Church and Monarchy, the leaders wanted to make the French Empire bigger and they were (by 1799) already at war with Britain and Spain.

192   Napoleonic Wars

- England had been at war with France since the time of the French Revolution (1793), when the Convention offered help to all nations that wanted to overthrow their kings.
- This war was marked by four British naval victories: the Glorious First of June (1794), the Battles of Cape St Vincent and Camperdown (1797), and the Battle of the Nile (1798). It was ended in 1802 at the Peace of Amiens.
- When Napoleon crowned himself Emperor in 1804, he had already invaded Hanover and this act caused Britain to declare war against France, especially as France was threatening to invade England from Boulogne.
- Austria and Russia sided with Britain, but Napoleon defeated them both at Austerlitz in 1805.
- Later that year, Napoleon's successes were checked by Nelson's famous victory at Trafalgar.
- Napoleon, having defeated the Prussians at Jena in 1806, issued the Berlin Decrees, forbidding any country to trade with Britain. Britain stood alone as all her allies had been defeated.

- Napoleon then made his own brother King of Spain, at which the Spanish rebelled and British troops went to Portugal to assist Spain.
- Russia refused to carry out the Berlin Decrees, so Napoleon invaded Russia in 1812 and defeated them at Borodino. While the Russians retreated, they destroyed the crops as they went (scorched earth policy) and although Napoleon entered Moscow, the Russians soon burnt it down and the French had to retreat, returning home with only 5% of their army alive.
- Napoleon was defeated at Leipzig in 1813 and in 1814 he fled to Elba.
- In 1815 he returned to France only to be defeated at Waterloo – after this he was banished to St Helena until he died in 1821.

193 The Peninsular War
- This lasted from 1808-1814, when Napoleon placed his brother on the Spanish throne and the Spanish rebelled.
- Britain decided to send troops to Lisbon and to attack the French from there. Due to the incompetence of two elderly generals, the British were forced to retreat to Corunna in 1809 and escape by sea (Sir John Moore's retreat).
- Later in 1809, the British landed again, under Wellington. The British had the following advantages:
  - (a) favourable geography
  - (b) command of the sea
  - (c) Spanish guerrillas
  - (d) Wellington's ability.
- Wellington advanced into Spain, defeated the French at Talavera, but was unable to remain safely in Spain and retreated to Lisbon building the defensive fortification lines of Torres Vedras behind him.
- Wellington's first victories came at Badajoz, Cuidad Rodrigo and Salamanca which enabled him to enter Madrid in 1812.
- In the same year, Napoleon found himself in difficulties in Moscow and so, from Madrid, Wellington pushed north and defeated the French, first at Vittoria and finally in France at Toulouse.

194 Emancipation of Catholics & The Gordon Riots
- In 1778, the Catholic Relief Bill was passed repealing some of the more oppressive laws against Catholics. Priests could say Mass again and Catholics buy and sell property.
- As a result, feeling against Catholics grew, and shouts of "No Popery" were raised everywhere.
- This culminated in the Gordon Riots in London, led by Lord George Gordon in 1780. The mob ransacked areas of London, burning Catholic chapels and order was only restored by the aid of 10,000 troops.
- 500 of the mob were killed and 25 executed, but Gordon was freed.

195 Peterloo Massacre
- In 1819, a peaceful meeting in Manchester (St Peter's Fields) was broken up by soldiers wielding swords (this was before the days of police).
- Eleven were killed and 600 wounded.
- It became known as the Peterloo Massacre after St Peter's fields and the Battle of Waterloo four years earlier.
- The meeting was to call for the reform of Parliament.

196 Industrial Revolution
- This began in the eighteenth century and marks the change from people working at home to working in factories.

- The first invention of note was James Watts' improved steam engine in 1782. This was closely associated with -
  Kay's Flying Shuttle – weaving faster
  Hargreaves' Spinning Jenny – making yarn
  Cartwright's Power Loom – wool and cotton.
- All the inventions needed steel and heat from burning coal to shape the steel. Thus at the hub of the Industrial Revolution lay the iron and coal industries.
- Manchester became the capital of the cotton industry and Birmingham of the metal trades. The countryside began to empty.
- Houses were needed quickly and cheaply and were thus put up with little thought, giving rise to row upon row of dreary housing and numerous sanitation problems.
- Better transport was soon needed and James Brindley was one of the first canal builders. By 1800, the enormous network of canals linking the important towns had begun to grow.
- John McAdam invented tarmac and Rennie and Telford built better bridges.
- George Stephenson built a steam engine, the Rocket, that could move on rails, and in 1825 the first railway line opened between Stockton and Darlington. Within 20 years, all the main towns were connected by railway and the canals began to fall into disrepair
- Next came steam ships which replaced sailing ships. The first was the Comet on the River Clyde.
- With machinery doing so much work, women and children worked long hours in the factories until the Factory Acts introduced more humane practices.
- Factory workers formed themselves into Trade Unions, although it was not until 1871 that Trade Unions were allowed to help the workers legally.
- The Industrial Revolution saw a population shift from the open south to the industrial north of England.

197   Important People of the 18th Century

- William Pitt the Elder.
  - He opposed Sir Robert Walpole and came to power in 1756, successfully directing the Seven Years' War.
  - Sympathy for the French Revolution was his undoing.
- Jane Austen
  - She lived from 1775-1817.
  - She was one of the greatest English novelists. Her most famous book is *Pride and Prejudice*.
  - She declared her strong sympathies for the Catholic Faith (and quite possibly died a Catholic).

199   Spencer Perceval

- He was Prime Minister from 1809 to 1812, when he was assassinated by John Bellingham in the lobby of the House of Commons.

200   Duke of Wellington

- He lived from 1769-1852.
- He is most famous for leading the victorious British Armies during the Peninsular War (1808-1814) and at Waterloo in 1815.
- He was Prime Minister from 1828-1830, favoured Catholic Emancipation, but opposed electoral reform.
- He is known as the Iron Duke and is Britain's best known soldier.
- He is reputed to have said that the Battle of Waterloo was won on the playing fields of Eton.

- When Queen Victoria asked him how to get rid of the small birds that lived in the Great Exhibition building, he replied "Sparrowhawks, Ma'am."

201   Slave Trade

- A slave is a person who is owned completely by another person. Slaves were bought and sold like any other property.
- The ancient Greeks and Romans had slaves, and in 73BC a gladiator called Spartacus led a rebellion of slaves.
- The Negro slave trade, which began in the 15th Century, involved shipping slaves from Africa (who had been sold by their chiefs) to Brazil, the West Indies and North America. They were used to cultivate the land.
- Thanks in part to William Wilberforce, the Slave Trade was forbidden in 1807 by England, and in 1833 slavery was abolished in all British Colonies.
- In the USA, after the publication of Uncle Tom's Cabin, the Northern States decided against slavery. The Southern States were still in favour, and this division led to the American Civil War in 1865, which the North won.

202   George IV

- He reigned as King from 1820-1830, but he had already been Prince Regent since 1811, when his father George III became incapable of ruling.
- He is known as the Prince of Pleasure; he ran up enormous debts and was very fat and very unpopular.
- His first and only true marriage was to Mrs Fitzherbert, a Catholic, but the state did not recognise it and insisted he marry his Protestant cousin Caroline of Brunswick, whom he never liked – he did not even invite her to his coronation.
- He built the Royal Pavilion at Brighton and the term Regency is given to the furniture and buildings of this period.

203   Cato Street Conspiracy

- This was a conspiracy, led by Thistlewood, to blow up the Cabinet in 1820.
- It failed and the leaders were arrested in Cato Street.
- The conspirators were against government policy which included parliamentary reform and Catholic emancipation.

204   Charles Dickens

- He lived from 1812-1870.
- He is one of the greatest English novelists.
- His books include: The Pickwick Papers
                       David Copperfield
                       Oliver Twist
                       Great Expectations
                       A Tale of Two Cities
                       Barnaby Rudge (set during the Gordon Riots).

205   William IV

- He was George IV's younger brother and reigned from 1830-1837.
- The main event of his reign was the passing of the Great Reform Bill.

206   The Great Reform Bill

- Parliament was full of members who had been elected by very few votes. Very few people had the right to vote and some large towns had no representatives.
- Some members represented "rotten boroughs" with no inhabitants at all, like Old Sarum.

- But Parliament, having seen the disasters brought on France by the French Revolution, did not favour reform, thinking it too was revolution.
- The first Reform Bill was defeated in 1831.
- Two other Reform Bills were also defeated in 1831, but eventually the Duke of Wellington persuaded the House of Lords to accept it and the bill was passed, the King signing it in 1832.
- The chief provisions were:
  (1) a much fairer distribution of seats
  (2) many more people having the vote.

PART VIII
THE HOUSE OF WINDSOR

207 Queen Victoria

- She reigned from 1837-1901.
- She married Albert of Saxe-Coburg who died in 1861.
- Famous events during her reign:
  The Chartists
  Income Tax introduced
  Great Exhibition
  Crimean War
  Indian Mutiny
  American Civil War
  Franco-Prussian War
  General Gordon in the Sudan
  Highland Clearances
  County & Parish Councils
  Boer War
  Her own Diamond Jubilee.

- Famous people:
  Sir Robert Peel
  Lord Palmerston
  Gladstone
  Disraeli.

208 Chartists

- After the passing of the Great Reform Bill, the London Working Men's Association was formed, which drew up a charter calling for:
  (a)   Every man to have a vote
  (b)   Equal-sized constituencies
  (c)   Anyone to be eligible to stand for Parliament
  (d)   MPs to be paid
  (e)   Annual elections.
- Parliament refused to agree and the more extreme Chartists in 1836 led an armed revolt.
- Many Chartists died in this unsuccessful revolt and, as a result, a monster petition of 2 million signatures was prepared. This was seized and many names discovered to be forgeries.
- In spite of their failure, within 70 years the first four demands became law.

209   Income Tax
- While income tax had been first introduced in 1799 to finance the Napoleonic wars, in 1842 Sir Robert Peel introduced income tax of 7d in the pound on all who earned more than £150 a year.
- It was meant to last three years, but in 1845 it was renewed and the British public have been paying it ever since.

210   The Highland Clearances
- After their crushing at Culloden (1746), the Scottish Highland chiefs lost their faith and their integrity.
- They began to realise that, if only they were to rid their vast estates of the Highlanders, they could use the land for sheep and therefore make more profit.
- In the early nineteenth century the Highlanders were forced out of their homes (which were immediately set on fire) and then onto ships for America and Canada.

211   Sir Robert Peel
- He was Prime Minister once during Queen Victoria's reign.
- He eventually supported Catholic emancipation.
- He is the originator of the Conservative Party.
- He founded the Metropolitan Police Force in London, in 1829, and is the reason policemen are still called Bobbies.
- He repealed the Corn Laws in 1846.

212   Corn Laws
- After years of bad harvest, in 1815, Parliament forbade the importation of cheap corn to protect British farmers. The laws were called the Corn Laws.
- This meant the poor could never afford bread and there were great shortages.
- Peel repealed the Corn Laws in 1846, which allowed cheap imports, although these were to seriously damage British agriculture as well as British industry generally.

213   Factory Act
- In 1833, the first Factory Act was passed which provided that:
  - (a)   no children under the age of nine could work in factories
  - (b)   children under 13 should work for no more than 8 hours a day
  - (c)   women and those under 18 should work for no more than 12 hours a day.
- It was introduced by the Earl of Shaftsbury.

214   New Postage Scheme
- In 1840, postage stamps were introduced.
- Rowland Hill, afterwards Sir Rowland, persuaded the government to reduce the postage to 1d on letters between all places in the United Kingdom.
- Rowland Hill's suggestion was not only accepted, but followed by every other civilized country in the World.

215   Great Exhibition
- This was held in 1851 at the suggestion of Prince Albert.
- It was the first ever great trade exhibition.
- Manufacturers from all over the world brought and exhibited their goods.
- It was held in a huge glass palace (Crystal Palace) which was built in Hyde Park, but later removed to Crystal Palace in south London.

216 Crimean War

- In 1853, Tsar Nicholas I of Russia claimed he should protect all Christians in the land ruled by Turkey, but Turkey ignored his claim.
- The Tsar sent troops to protect the Christians and Turkey declared war, but the Russians destroyed the Turkish fleet in the Black Sea.
- Britain and France, fearing Russia would become too powerful, sent troops to attack the Crimea.
- The British won the Battle of Alma in 1854, but failed to take the main city of Sebastopol.
- The Russians then besieged Balaclava. During the siege, the Charge of the Light Brigade took place at which British Cavalry attacked the wrong guns and suffered appalling casualties.
- The last main battle saw another British victory at Inkerman.
- The war ended in stalemate because atrocious weather and inefficient provisioning caused heavy British casualties.
- The war is famous for the nursing work of Florence Nightingale, but credit should also be given to Sister Bridgeman and the Catholic Sisters of Mercy.

217 Indian Mutiny

- In 1857, Indian Sepoys (Indians serving in the British Army) tried to throw out the East India Company and regain independence for India.
- One aspect of Indian resentment against the British was the use by the British of cow fat in rifle bullets – the cow in India is a sacred animal to the Hindus.
- The mutiny broke out in Delhi which was captured by the Indians. The British, Europeans and Sikhs then laid siege to the town which they recaptured after four months.
- There were other sieges at Cawnpore and Lucknow. The British recaptured both, but with dreadful loss of life to the civilians inside.
- The fighting finished in 1858, but from then on India was ruled by the British Government and not the East India Company.

218 Lord Palmerston

- He was a famous Prime Minister.
- He was a Whig who was also famous as a foreign minister, particularly colonising Hong Kong for Great Britain, taking control of it from the Chinese.

219 Garibaldi

- He was a brilliant soldier who fought to unite Italy in the middle of the nineteenth century.
- The climax of his efforts came in 1861, when his victories enabled King Victor Emmanuel to become the first King of a United Italy. Previously, Italy had been made up of separate smaller kingdoms.

220 Franco-Prussian War

- It lasted for six months during 1870/71.
- The Prussian Prime Minister, Otto von Bismarck, who had already defeated Austria in 1866, wanted to increase Prussian power by creating a united German State. However, he knew France would never accept this idea and so he had to defeat France in war in order to remove French opposition.
- The French declared war when they could not get a Prussian prince to agree not to become King of Spain. If one had become King of Spain, France would have been surrounded by Prussians.
- Having begun the war, the French army lost every battle and eventually Paris was taken.

- As a result of losing the war, France lost Alsace and Lorraine to Germany and became a humiliated European state.

221 William Gladstone

- He was four times Prime Minister during Queen Victoria's reign – but the Queen did not like him.
- He was originally a Conservative under Sir Robert Peel, but, due to his liberal ideas, particularly trying to abolish Income Tax, he broke away from the Conservatives to form the Liberal Party in 1868.
- His main failure was his inability to get the Home Rule for Ireland Bill passed in the House of Commons. Had he succeeded, the problems of Northern Ireland in the 20th Century might not have arisen.
- He died in 1898.

222 Benjamin Disraeli

- He was probably the most famous Victorian Prime Minister.
- He wrote novels – particularly Coningsby.
- He was a Jew who became a Christian.
- His main rival was William Gladstone.
- He bought all the shares in the Suez Canal in 1875.
- He died in 1881.

223 General Charles Gordon

- He is famous for his exploits in China and the Sudan.
- He is mainly remembered for organising the Sudan, being made Governor General in 1877. He wiped out the slave trade there.
- He was a devoted Evangelical, who visited the sick and set up a boys' club in Kent, though apparently some of his beliefs were rather eccentric (including in reincarnation).
- In 1884, while trying to lead the defeated Egyptian army out of the Sudan, he was besieged in Khartoum. He was killed two days before British troops came to relieve him.

224 Jameson Raid

- During the nineteenth century, British settlers dominated South Africa running it as a Cape Colony. The Dutch, called Boers, resented this and crossed the Vaal River to form their own Transvaal Republic, or South African Republic, in 1840.
- The British Government in 1880 annexed Transvaal which led to fighting in which the Boers were victorious.
- Shortly after gold and diamonds were discovered in the Transvaal and, in order to protect this find, the Boers refused to allow non-Boers any rights.
- Dr Jameson led an armed force to protect the so-called outlanders in Transvaal, but President Kruger forced him to surrender at Krugersdorp.
- The raid led to bad feeling between the British and the Boers and culminated in the Boer War (1899-1902).

225 The Boer War

- This war lasted from 1899-1902.
- It resulted from the ill-feeling caused by the Jameson raid, but in essence it was caused by the rivalry over gold and diamond mines at Kimberley.
- Until 1900, the Boers were winning the war under leaders such as Jan Smuts.
- When Lord Kitchener arrived, the British began to win. They recaptured Kimberley and relieved the towns of Mafeking and Ladysmith. President Kruger left South Africa and, while the war then ended, the Boers continued fighting as guerrillas until 1902, when they finally surrendered.

- The British did not treat the Boers at all well, especially in the concentration camps they devised for the women and children, where many thousands died. In reparation, Britain gave £3million to help rebuild the country.

226   Boxer Rebellion
- In 1894, China was heavily defeated by Japan.
- European nations arrived in China to seize ports and naval bases through which to trade with China.
- The Chinese rebelled against them, to drive out the foreign devils, but they failed.
- This failure led to the end of the Manchu Dynasty and the start of Chinese nationalism.

227   Local Councils
- County Councils were set up to run the counties in 1888.
- Parish Councils were set up in 1894.

228   Joe Chamberlain
- He was a strong Liberal politician who, in 1891, was so opposed to Gladstone's Home Rule Bill that he broke away from the Liberal Party to form the Liberal Unionists (the Liberals were in favour of Home Rule for Ireland).
- In due course, Joe Chamberlain's party merged with the Conservative Party to be called the Conservative and Unionist Party.
- It was this movement that ensured that Northern Ireland remained under British control as part of the United Kingdom.

229   Edward VII
- He reigned from 1901-1910.
- His reputation was that of a fun-loving, but naughty King.
- During his reign, Kaiser Wilhelm (Kaiser Bill), his own nephew, whom he thoroughly disliked, built up German arms in preparation for World War I.

230   George V
- He reigned from 1910 -1936.
- He married Princess Mary of Teck who died in 1953.
- The main events of his reign were:
  World War I
  Suffragettes
  Balfour Declaration
  General Strike
  The loss of the Titanic.
- It was he who began the Royal Christmas broadcasts.

231   World War I
- It lasted from 1914-1918.
- It began when the heir to the Austrian throne was murdered by a Serb at Sarajevo, in Serbia, which Austria had seized.
- The Austrians attacked the Serbs.
  Russia defended Serbia.
  Germany therefore attacked Russia.
  France came to Russia's aid.
  Germany entered Belgium to attack France.
  Britain defended Belgium.
  It was an example of the Domino effect.

- The war was fought in three main areas:
  - a) The Western Front (West of Germany)
  - b) The Eastern Front (East of Germany)
  - c) The Middle East.
- The German advance on France was halted by their defeat at the Battle of the Marne. Both sides dug trenches and stayed more or less stationary until the end of the War.
- The British tried to break the deadlock in 1916 by attacking the German trenches in the Battle of the Somme. Haig was in charge but, using too few tanks, the allies lost 615,000 casualties and the Germans 650,000.
- When the Germans attacked Verdun in 1916, the French counter-attacked and eventually regained most of their lost ground.
- In 1917, Haig attacked Ypres, but this battle, like the Somme, only ended in huge casualties, mainly at Paschendale.
- The Eastern Front saw fighting between Russia and Germany, but not with trench warfare. Turkey joined the German forces and, in order to help Russia, Churchill decided to send British, Australian and New Zealand troops to knock Turkey out of the war. They landed at Gallipoli on 25th April 1915, but failed to make any real headway and were withdrawn in January 1916. This area is called the Underbelly of Europe.
- One of the main purposes of World War I was to push the Turks out of Palestine. With the help of Laurence of Arabia, who enlisted Arab support, General Allenby took Jerusalem in 1917 and from then until 1948 Palestine was under British control.
- In 1917, the Russian Revolution caused a complete allied collapse on the Eastern Front. This released Germans to fight on the Western Front and allowed them to attack US shipping with their submarines and U-Boats. This caused America to join the war and the extra troops soon gave the allies the upper hand.
- Around the world the British Navy was attacking German colonies and this explains why there was fighting off the coast of South America, at the battles of Coronel and the Falkland Islands.
- The two main fleets met at the Battle of Jutland in 1916. The fact that the German High Fleet never put to sea again afterwards emphasises the importance of this British victory.
- World War I saw the start of air warfare. The Germans used airships called Zeppelins to start with, but both sides eventually used fighters, bombers, reconnaissance planes and even aircraft carriers.
- Eventually the Germans were starved of food and lost heart over the war. Their leaders signed the Armistice (surrender) on 11 November 1918.
- Germany lost all its colonies at the Treaty of Versailles. The Austrian Empire was shredded by the creation or enlargement of Czechoslovakia, Poland, Romania, Yugoslavia, Estonia, Latvia and Lithuania.
- At the end of the war, all the countries, except the United States, formed the League of Nations to keep world peace. This, together with the Treaty of Versailles, was organised by Woodrow Wilson, Lloyd George and Clemenceau.
- Finally, the German fleet was taken by the British to Scapa Flow in the Orkneys and sunk.

232 Suffragettes

- These were the campaigners, mainly women, for votes for women (women's suffrage).
- They were active, sometimes violently, between 1900 and 1918, when most women were given the vote.
- Their most famous leader was Emmeline Pankhurst and the most famous demonstration in favour of female suffrage was when Emily Davidson killed herself by throwing herself in front of the horses in the 1913 Derby.

233 Balfour Declaration (Lord Balfour)

- He was Conservative Prime Minister from 1902-1905.

- In 1917, as foreign minister, he was the author of the Balfour Declaration whereby the British Government promised to establish a Jewish home in Palestine, thus forcing the Arabs out of their own country.
- This led to the modern turbulent State of Israel.

234   Russian Revolution

- This was organised by Lenin and Trotsky in 1917 and resulted in the murder of Tsar Nicholas II and all of his family, bringing to an end the Russian Royal Family.
- Lenin organised the factory workers into Soviets or Councils, which were run by the Bolshevik Party. In 1918, the Bolsheviks were renamed Communists.
- Those who opposed the new Communist Government were called White Russians.
- Lenin was able to organise the revolution because World War I had taken all the workers away from the farm land and into the army. Thus the Russian people were very short of food and prepared to revolt against the Tsar.
- When Lenin died in 1924, he was succeeded by Stalin who was in power until 1953.

235   Lloyd George

- Lloyd George, a Welshman, succeeded Herbert Asquith as Prime Minister in 1916.
- Earlier, as Chancellor of the Exchequer, he introduced Old Age Pensions and National Insurance.
- He was also Minister for War before becoming Prime Minister.
- He attended the Treaty of Versailles.
- He resigned as Prime Minister in 1922.

236   Stanley Baldwin

- He became Prime Minister (Conservative) in 1923 and was in office, with a small interruption, until 1937.
- He was Prime Minister during the General Strike .
- He was also Prime Minister when Edward VIII abdicated.
- The interruption to his rule was caused by Ramsay Macdonald (Labour) who led a national government from 1931 – 1935..

237   General Strike

- This occurred in 1926, when the whole British work force went on strike for 10 days.
- Stanley Baldwin was Prime Minister and during its course, with no newspapers, the government published the British Gazette.

238   Edward VIII

- He was the only monarch to give up the throne voluntarily.
- He succeeded his father, George V, in January 1936, but abdicated in December 1936 on his choice to marry Wallis Simpson, a divorcee.
- As head of the Church of England, it was decided, the monarch could not do this.
- He was a popular man, much given to the welfare of his subjects, and his abdication caused a great deal of unhappiness in the country.
- The man who most opposed the marriage was Stanley Baldwin.

239   World War II

The Causes of the War
- Many Germans believed that they could have continued fighting after 1918.
- The German nation was humiliated at the Treaty of Versailles and had to give up much of its own territory.
- Germany thus deeply resented the way it had been treated, and particularly the economic hardship it suffered in the 1920s.

- This was the seedbed into which Adolph Hitler was planted. He became Fuhrer in 1933 and was resolved not only to regain the lost German territory, but for Germany to become the greatest power on earth.
- This explains why Germany invaded or occupied parts of Austria, Czechoslovakia and Poland, which had been German and in which Germans were living.
- To begin with, Great Britain and France allowed Hitler to edge back into former territories, but in 1938, at Munich, Hitler agreed to move no further. Neville Chamberlain, British Prime Minister, thought Hitler would keep his word.
- When Hitler moved into Poland, and especially because Great Britain had promised to defend Poland, Great Britain declared war in 1939.
- It was obvious throughout the 1930s that Germany was preparing for war because of its massive rearmament.
- Hitler was the head of the Nazi Party – the National Socialist German Workers Party.
- Following Hitler's example of expansionism, in Italy Mussolini marched troops into Ethiopia and Japan invaded Manchuria. These countries formed the Axis powers.
- The League of Nations was powerless to prevent the Axis powers' operations and was considered to be quite ineffective.

240   The Start of the War

- The war really began on 3rd September 1939, when Germany invaded Poland. Two weeks later, the USSR also invaded Poland, Estonia, Latvia and Lithuania.
- The British troops that went to France were not faced with Germans and thus it became known as "the Phoney War."
- The French defences running north/south against Germany were known as the Maginot Line.
- In 1940, the Germans moved into Norway and Denmark, Belgium, Holland and Luxembourg.
- The British troops were trapped and had to escape from the beach at Dunkirk – 346,000 were picked up, partly by pleasure craft from England.
- Hitler then moved into France which fell on 22nd June 1940.
- Winston Churchill became Prime Minister.
- Hitler then decided to invade England and began by bombing airfields and posts, but the British Spitfire and Hurricane RAF fighters were so successful in shooting down these bombers and sinking the barges collecting troops on the other side of the Channel that Germany was forced to give up its invasion plans. This air battle, fought between August and October 1940, is known as the Battle of Britain.
- The Germans then restricted their attacks to bombing English cities and in London this was known as the Blitz. In 12 months, nearly 100,000 civilians were killed or wounded.

241   World War II – the North African Campaign

- Much of North Africa was under Italian control and when, in June 1940, Italy joined Germany in the war, their fresh and complete army was able to begin enlarging their hold on North Africa.
- In the autumn of 1940, the Italians invaded Egypt from Libya, but British forces under Wavell pushed them back.
- In 1941, the Germans fought down through Yugoslavia, Albania, Greece and Crete, leading to Germany landing in Libya to assist the Italians (the German leader was Rommel).
- The Germans advanced towards Egypt, taking Tobruk in 1941. Wavell was not to blame because his forces had been severely depleted by Churchill who had moved half of his army to Greece. Nonetheless Wavell was replaced by Auchinleck, who was also successful, but made to take the blame for a later reversal of fortune. Auchinleck was replaced a few months later by Montgomery (Monty). The British hit back under

Montgomery with the 8th Army in October by winning the crucial battle of El Alamein in 1942.

- From this point on the Germans were on the retreat, and in May 1943 they surrendered in North Africa.
- From El Alamein the eighth army pushed the Germans west along the North African coast and north through Sicily and up the Italian mainland. Italy surrendered in September 1943 and Rome was taken in June 1944. It was a turning point in the war.

242   World War II in General

- Once Hitler had conquered central Europe, he resolved to crush the USSR.
- He reached Moscow in December 1941, but the cold, and Russian armies, prevented him from controlling the USSR.
- By January 1943, the Russians were able to drive the Germans home and this was how the Russians re-entered Poland and Romania.
- On 7th December 1941, the Japanese attacked Pearl Harbour in Hawaii, thus forcing the US into the War.
- Japan then took control of most of the western edge of the Pacific, including Hong Kong and Singapore.
- After the Germans had lost the Graf Spee in 1939, and the Bismarck in 1941, their naval efforts centred around U-boat attacks on merchant ships taking food from North America to Britain and the USSR.
- Meanwhile the RAF began heavy bombing raids on industrial German cities.
- Between 1941 and 1945 escorted allied merchant ships delivered vital supplies to Archangel and Murmansk. They were known as the Arctic Convoys.
- Once the Americans had joined the war, their strength of numbers began to push the Japanese out of their conquered territories in the Pacific. The British pushed the Japanese out of Burma.
- On 6th June 1944, a huge allied landing in Normandy under General Eisenhower pushed the Germans back to Paris and eventually to Germany itself.
- Meanwhile the Germans had been sending pilotless flying bombs – V1s (like an aeroplane) or doodlebugs and V2s (rockets) – to London and these caused over 50,000 casualties.
- The allies' advance up through Italy, coupled with both their push east across northern Europe from Normandy as well as the Russians advancing west towards them, forced Germany to surrender in May 1945.
- It is claimed Hitler committed suicide, and Churchill, Roosevelt and Stalin met at Yalta in the Crimea to organise the peace treaty.
- Japan could only be made to surrender after the US had exploded atomic bombs over Hiroshima and Nagasaki in August 1945.
- Russia took over most of Eastern Europe and East Germany, forcing a huge tract of land to become Communist – this lasted until 1990.
- The German and Japanese leaders were tried for war crimes and many executed.
- Some famous German leaders were Rommel, Goering and Himmler.
- Over 350,000 British were killed in the war and in total over 35 million elsewhere.

For important historical events after World War II, please turn to "The Story so far" into which the essential parts of British history for this subsequent period has been woven.

Part Three
Country by Country
Contents

Afghanistan

Albania

Algeria

Antarctica

Arctic

Argentina

Armenia

Australia

Austria

Bahamas

Bahrain

Balearic Islands

Bangladesh

Barbados

Belgium

Belize

Bolivia

Bosnia-Herzegovina

Brazil

Brunei

Bulgaria

Burma (See Myanmar)

Cambodia

Cameroon

Canada

Chile

China

Columbia

Crete

Croatia

Cuba

Cyprus

Czech Republic

Denmark

Ecuador

Egypt

Estonia

Ethiopia

Finland

France

Georgia

Germany

Greece

Holland (see Netherlands)

Hungary

Iceland

India

Indonesia

Iran

Iraq

Ireland

Israel (Palestine)

Italy

Jamaica

Japan

Jordan

Kazakhstan

Kenya

Korea, North & South

Kuwait

Laos

Latvia

Lebanon

Liberia

Libya

Liechtenstein

Lithuania

Luxembourg

Macedonia

Malaysia

Malta

Mexico

Monaco

Mongolia

Morocco

Myanmar (formerly Burma)

Namibia

Nepal

Netherlands

New Zealand

Nicaragua

Nigeria

Norway

Oman

Pakistan

Palestine

Panama

Papua New Guinea

Paraguay

Peru

Philippines

Poland

Portugal

Punjab

Romania

Russia (Russian Federation)

Saudi Arabia

Scotland

Seychelles

Singapore

Slovak Republic
Slovenia
South Africa
Spain
Sri Lanka
Sudan
Sweden
Switzerland
Syria
Taiwan
Thailand
Tunisia
Turkey
Uganda
Ukraine
United Arab Emirates
United Kingdom
United States of America
Uruguay
Vatican City State
Venezuela
Vietnam
Wales
Yemen
Yugoslavia
Zaire
Zambia
Zimbabwe

Country by Country

Date	Event

Afghanistan

Date	Event
4th C BC	The country was part of the Persian Empire.
7th C AD	The country became Islamic.
1747	The country became independent.
	Afghans are split between two tribal groups of Pashtuns (formerly Pathans). One is the rural and middle class, Durranis; the other is the fiercely religious Ghilzai whose homelands stretch into Pakistan. In 1775, the Durranis moved their capital from Ghilzai Kandahar to Kabul, from which city they ruled, enlisting foreign help whenever they could.
1839-42	Afghan War. British fought to prevent Russian and Ghilzai threat to their interests in India. Britain lost all three wars.
1878-80	Second Afghan War (see above).
1919	Third Afghan War (see above).
1963	Constitutional Monarchy established.
1973	Monarchy overthrown.
1979	Russian Communists invaded Afghanistan to support the Ghilzai government, but this encouraged a revolt against the Ghilzai and the Russians were defeated.
1985	Mujahaddin ("Holy Warriors") guerrillas (sometime known as Afghan rebels) fought Russians.
1986	Partial Russian withdrawal, leaving country run by pro-Soviet Najibullah. The US then supported the Ghilzai-run Taliban government and their ally, Osama bin Laden.
1988	Non-Communist government established.
1992	Najibullah overthrown and Islamic law introduced.
1996	Taliban took over, starting to create an extreme Muslim state. The word Taliban means "students."
2001	After attack on World Trade Centre in New York (etc.) US & Britain attack Afghanistan and defeat Taliban although a few years later, while the country is nominally governed by Durranis under the corrupt President Karzai, the Taliban are back and in effective control of most of the country. Mainly Muslim.

Albania

Date	Event
To 4th C AD	It was a Roman province and known as Epirus.
To 1347	It was under Byzantine rule.
Next 100 years	It was over-run by Bulgarians, Serbs, Venetians and Turks.
1468	It became part of the Ottoman Empire.
1822	Death of Ali Pasha. Some of the deeds of this tyrannical ruler are recorded in Lord Byron's poem "Childe Harold" and his death forms the basis of Alexandre Dumas's novel "The Count of Monte Christo".
1912	It became independent.
1946	It became Communist.
1990	Opposition parties allowed, so too religion.

| 1991 | Labour government elected. |
| | Mainly Muslim. |

Algeria

To 5th C AD	It was ruled by Carthage and then by Rome.
396-430	St Augustine lived at Hippo.
6th C	Vandals took over.
7th & 8thC	It was ruled by Byzantium.
9th C	It was invaded by Arabs.
15th/16th C	Spain tried to take over.
16th C	Ottoman Empire took over.
18th C	It became a pirate state.
1830	France colonised the country.
1940	The country struggled for independence.
1962	Independence achieved despite violent opposition by the secret army (OAS), which caused widespread disruption in both Algeria and France. Algeria's first president was Ahmed Ben Bella.
1992	Military take control.
	Mainly Muslim.

Antarctica

1773	Found by Captain Cook.
1911	Roald Amundsen reaches South Pole.
1959	Arctic Treaty signed by countries with rival claims to land, which has governed the continent since.

Arctic

9th - 10th C AD	Vikings colonised Iceland and Greenland.
1909	Robert Peary reached North Pole.
	Territories divided between various countries in Northern Hemisphere/Arctic Circle.

Argentina

Pre-16th C AD	It was inhabited by South American Indians.
16th C	It was first visited by Europeans.
1536	Buenos Aires founded.
1776	Country became a Spanish Viceroyalty.
1810	Revolt against the Spanish.
1816	Independence achieved.
1946-1955	Peron became dictator after military coup.
1951	Peron's first wife Evita tried to stand for vice-president, but was opposed.
1952	Eva Peron died and Peron was overthrown.
1973-4	Peron returned to rule, but died next year. His 3rd wife Isabel succeeded him.

1982	Argentina temporarily occupied the Falklands Isles, precipitating short war with Britain.
1990	Argentina restored full diplomatic relations with Britain, which in recent years have become strained once more.
	Mainly Catholic.

Armenia

1828	After centuries of Mongol, Ottoman and Persian rule it was acquired by Russia.
1915-1916	¾ of its population were massacred by the Turks, with the rest displaced. This is known as the Armenian Massacre or Armenian Diaspora.
1918	It became an independent republic from Russia.
1920	It was occupied by the Red Army.
1988	Demonstrations took place, in favour of independence for Nagorno-Karabakh.
1988	Severe earthquake killed 25,000.
1989-1991	Civil War with Azerbaijan.
	Armenian Christians.

Australia

1606	First reported sighting of continent by the Dutch.
1770	Captain Cook occupied and claimed New South Wales as a British colony.
1850s & 1880s	Gold Rushes.
1825	Tasmania claimed.
1829	Western Australia founded.
1836	Southern Australia founded.
1851	Victoria founded.
1859	Queensland founded.
1901	Became Commonwealth of Australia (British monarch remains sovereign Head of State).
1911	Site for Canberra acquired. Became Australian Capital Territory.
1915	Gallipoli landings where many ANZACs are killed.
1941	Call for help by USA ended special relationship with Britain.
1970	Japan became chief trading partner.
1975	Papua New Guinea became independent.
	Mainly Protestant.

Austria

Before 14 BC	It was occupied by Celts.
14BC	It became part of the Roman Empire.
5th C AD	It was occupied by Goths, Vandals, Huns, Avars and Lombards.
9th C	Charlemagne established East Mark, to become nucleus of Holy Roman Empire.
1273	Rudolph of Habsburg seized country.
	From then to 1918 this family provided most of the Holy Roman Emperors.
1526	It controlled Bohemia and formed a bulwark against the Turks.
1697	Hungary was liberated from Turkish control and incorporated into Austrian dominion.

1740	Maria Theresa becomes Archduchess of Austria and Queen of Hungary.
1740-48	War of Austrian Succession.
1848	Revolutions between mixed nationalities of Austria Hungary.
1867	Archduke Franz Joseph established dual monarchy of Austria-Hungary.
1878	Under Treaty of Berlin, Austria given administration of Bosnia and Herzegovina.
1908	Austria annexed Bosnia and Herzegovina.
1914	Archduke Franz Ferdinand assassinated in Sarajevo and Austria attacks Serbia.
1918	Austria-Hungary defeated and last Habsburg emperor overthrown.
1934	Chancellor Engelbert Dollfuss, who tried to establish Austria on Catholic principles, was assassinated.
1938	Austria incorporated into Germany (Anschluss).
1955	Independence of Austria recognised.
	Mainly Catholic.

Bahamas

1492	It was reached by Christopher Columbus.
1717	It became a British Crown Colony after being the centre of piracy.
1964	It achieved home rule.
1973	It became fully independent from Britain, but retained the British monarch as sovereign Head of State.
	Mainly Protestant.

Bahrain

	Bahrain is an island in the Persian Gulf.
Pre-16th C AD	An Arab Monarchy.
16th C	It was under Portuguese control.
1602	It was dominated by Persia.
1783	It became a Sheikdom.
1861	It became a British Protectorate.
1968	Bahrain, with Qatar and the Trucial States, became the Federation of Arab Emirates.
1971	Qatar and Trucial States withdrew and Bahrain became independent.
	Mainly Muslim.

Balearic Islands

From 123 BC	It became a Roman Colony.
1009 -1232	They were under Moorish control.
1343	They were captured by Aragon and thereafter under Spanish control.
	Mainly Catholic.

Bangladesh

Prior to 1947	See India.
1947	It was formed into Eastern Pakistan (Muslim) on partition of British India.
1947-1971	See Pakistan.
1971	It became independent.

1975	Mujibar Rahman assassinated.
1981	Maj-Gen Zia ur Rahman assassinated.
	Mainly Muslim.

Barbados

Before 1627	It was inhabited by Arawak Indians.
1627	It became a British Colony.
1961	It became independent, retaining the British monarch as sovereign Head of State.
	Mainly Anglican.

Belgium

Prior to 15BC	Belgae were ancient Celtic peoples.
15BC	It was run by Romans and called Belgica.
3rd C	Overrun by Franks.
	Under Charlemagne, country became centre of Carolingian dynasty.
11th C	There were seven feudal states.
15th C	States run by Dukes of Burgundy.
1477	Country passed into Habsburg control.
16th C	Country passed into Spanish control, then back to Austria.
1830	It became independent.
1914 & 1940	It was invaded by Germany.
1949	It became a founding a member of the Council of Europe.
	Mainly Catholic.

Belize

Before 17th C	It was run by Mayans.
17th C	It was colonised by the British, as British Honduras.
1964	Self-government achieved.
1973	It became Belize.
1981	It became independent, retaining the British monarch as sovereign Head of State.
	Mainly Catholic.

Bolivia

Before 1538	It was part of Inca civilization.
1538	It was conquered by Spain.
1825	It was liberated by Simon Bolivar.
1952	Nationalist Revolutionary Movement came to power.
1964	Military Junta overthrew Nationalist President Estenssoro
	Overwhelmingly Catholic.

Bosnia-Herzegovina

| 1878 | It was controlled by Austria (formerly part of the Ottoman Empire). |
| 1918 | It was incorporated into Yugoslavia. |

1941	It was occupied by Nazi Germany.
1990-1994	There was great unrest as Serbia tried to take over.
1992	It became independent.
	Mainly Muslim.

Brazil

Before 1500	It was occupied by various South American Indians.
1500	It was colonised by the Portuguese.
1808	Napoleon invaded Portugal, the King moved Capital from Lisbon to Rio.
1822	It became independent.
1888	Slavery abolished.
1889	Monarchy abolished.
1930	Dictatorship until 1945.
	Overwhelmingly Catholic.

Brunei

From 15th C	It was an Islamic Sultanate.
1888	It became a British Protectorate.
1941-5	It was occupied by Japan.
1963	The proposal to join Malaysia was abandoned.
1971	It became self-governing.
1984	It became independent.
	Mainly Muslim.

Bulgaria

Roman times	It was originally Thrace and Moesia.
6th C	It was occupied by Slavs.
7th C	Bulgars arrived from Asia.
865	It adopted Eastern Orthodox Christianity.
From 11th C	Ruled by Byzantium, then Turkey.
1908	It became independent.
World War I	It was allied with Germany.
1923	It became fascist.
1934	It had a dictatorial monarchy.
World War II	It was allied with Germany, but occupied by Russia.
1946	Monarchy abolished.
1991	End of Communism.
	Mainly Eastern Orthodox Christian.

Burma (See Myanmar)

Cambodia

| 6th to 15th C | It was occupied by Khmers. |

1863	It became a French Protectorate (becoming part of French Indochina in 1887).
World War II	It was occupied by Japan.
1953	It became independent.
1975	Communist Khmer-Rouge took over.
1978	Vietnamese invade.
1987	Vietnamese withdraw.
	Mainly Buddhist.

Cameroon

1472	It was first visited by Europeans.
1884	It became a German protectorate.
after 1918	France governed 80% of the country.
1946	It became a UN Trust territory.
1960	It became independent.
	More Christian than anything else (35% Catholic).

Canada

2000BC	Inuit Eskimos began settling territory.
1000AD	Vikings arrived.
1497	John Cabot arrived.
1608	Quebec founded.
1763	France ceded Canada to Britain.
1791	Canada divided into French speaking Lower Canada and British Upper Canada.
1793	Mackenzie reached the Pacific by land.
1840	Upper and Lower Canada united.
1905	Territories (Alberta and Saskatchewan) join the Dominion.
1914-18	Canadian troops fight for the Allies.
1931	It became independent, retaining the British monarch as sovereign Head of State.
1939-45	Canadian troops fight for the Allies.
1949	New Foundland joins Confederation.
1950-53	Fights in Korean War.
	Christian (more Catholic than Protestant).

Chile

Pre-15th C AD	It was occupied by Araucanian Indians.
15th C	It was invaded by Incas.
1520	Magellan arrived.
1541	Santiago founded, then colonised by Spain.
1818	It became independent.
1970	Salvador Allende (Communist) was elected.
1973	General Pinochet took over. Allende killed.
1982	Pinochet supported Britain over Falklands War.
1983	Violent opposition to Pinochet.

| 1988 | Referendum forces Pinochet out of power. |
| | Overwhelmingly Catholic. |

China

c2800-2200BC	Age of Sage Kings (Agricultural).
to 1500BC	Xia Dynasty (Irrigation).
to 1066BC	Shang Dynasty (Writing and Calendar).
to 221 BC	Zhou Dynasty (time of Confucius 559-479).
to 206 BC	Qin Dynasty (Great Wall of China and Terracotta army, discovered in 1974). Qin is pronounced "Chin", hence the word "China". Qin was the first Emperor of China. He merged all seven rival kingdoms to form the united country of China for the first time.
to 220 AD	Han Dynasty (Buddhism introduced).
to 581	Three Kingdoms (Taoism introduced and includes Jin Dynasty).
to 618	Sui Dynasty (Barbarian invasions stopped).
to 907	Tang Dynasty (Sculpture, painting and Poetry).
to 960	Five Dynasties and Ten Kingdoms (Printing invented).
to 1279	Song Dynasty (Mongol invasions and Marco Polo – see History Notes).
to 1368	Yuan Dynasty (Beginning of Mongol rule and Kublai Khan).
to 1644	Ming Dynasty (Mongols expelled, Peking flourished as capital).
to 1912	Qing (Ching) Dynasty (Boxer Rebellion. Last (boy) emperor deposed).
to 1949	Major political upheavals led to Communist rule.
1925 - 1949	Challenges to Communists by Chaing Kai-shek.
1935-45	Long March to north west to escape Kai-shek led to Mao Tse Tung.
World War II	It opposed Japan.
1946-49	Civil War (ends at Nanking Battle. Kai-shek flees to Taiwan)
1949	Yangtze Incident when British firgate, Amethyst, on a friendly visit to Nanking, was attacked, some crew were killed, and the ship grounded for 3 months. It later escaped.
1954	It adopted a Soviet-style regime.
1966-69	Cultural Revolution set back against move to Capitalism.
1972	President Nixon visited China.
1989	Student Demonstrations with 2000 being killed in Tiananmen Square.
	Officially Atheist, but nearly all religions there, including 6m Catholics.

Colombia

Pre-16th C AD	It was occupied by Chibcha Indians.
16th C	It was conquered by Spain.
1538	It formed a colony called New Granada.
1886	It became independent.
1949	Civil War.
	Overwhelmingly Catholic.

Crete

	Crete is the largest Greek island in the east Mediterranean.
Pre-1500 BC	It was occupied by Minoan Civilization.
	Then occupied by the Romans.
	Then the Byzantines.
	Then the Venetians .
	Then the Turks.
1913	It was annexed by Greece (the Cretan State).
1941	It was captured by the Germans.
1944	It was retaken by the allies.
	Greek Orthodox.

Croatia

	Serbo-Croatian country in central Europe.
6th-9th C AD	Croats arrived.
818	Duchies of Dalmatia and Pannonia founded.
1538	Croatian Military Frontier founded.
1918-1991	It formed part of Yugoslavia.
1941	It became Nazi puppet state.
1945	It returned to Yugoslavia.
1990	Communists defeated by democrats led by Tudjman.
1991	Krajina succeeded and country declared independence.
1993	Country tried to re-adopt Krajina.
	Croats are Catholic and Serbs are Orthodox.

Cuba

Before 1492	It was occupied by Arawak Indians.
1492	Columbus visited.
1511	It became a Spanish colony.
1523	Slaves brought from Africa to replace depleted Indians.
1886	Slavery abolished.
1898	Cuba ceded to USA at end of Spanish-American War.
1933	Batista seized power until 1944.
1952	Batista returned to power.
1953 and 56	Castro tried to replace Batista.
1959	Castro, with the aid of Argentinian revolutionist Che Guevara, deposed Batista. He was in power until 2008.
1960	US assets seized without compensation. Diplomatic relations broken off.
1961	Unsuccessful Bay of Pigs invasion by USA. Cuba becomes Communist.
1962	Soviet missiles installed but dismantled (the Cuban Missile Crisis).
1991	All soviet troops withdrawn.
	85% Catholic.

Cyprus

Before 8thC BC	It was part of the Greek Empire.
8th C BC	It was part of Assyrian Empire.
	Then Babylonian, Egyptian and Persian Empires.
58BC	It was seized by Rome.
395AD	It was ruled by Byzantium.
1191	It was taken by England in the Third Crusade.
1489	It was annexed by Venice.
1571	It became part of the Ottoman Empire.
1878	It was administered by Britain.
1925	It became a Crown Colony.
1955	Civil War against the British. Enosis wanted unification with Greece.
1956	Archbishop Makarios was the rebel leader and was deported.
1959	Makarios returned and became President.
1960	Independence achieved.
1963	Turks set up their own government in Northern Cyprus.
1974	Military Coup deposed Makarios and Turkish army sent to North Cyprus.
	Island divided this way ever since.
	Greek Orthodox in South, Muslim in North.

Czech Republic

Before 1918	It was under Habsburg domination
1918	Czechoslovakia became an independent republic after the break-up of the Austro-Hungarian Empire.
	Originally it was Bohemia, Moravia, Silesia and Slovakia.
1948	Communists assumed power.
1969	Socialist Republic created.
1989	Communist party stripped of powers.
1991	Pressures for Czech and Slovak separation became evident.
1992	Creation of separate Slovak state, the Slovak republic – i.e. back to how they previously were.
	75% Catholic.

Denmark

5th & 6th C AD	Danes migrated from Sweden
8th to 10th C	They were pirates until Harold Bluetooth established Christianity. (It was Bluetooth's skill in communicating with his people that made the people who developed wireless technology name it after him.)
1014-1035	King Canute ruled Denmark, Norway and England.
1397	Denmark, Norway and Sweden united.
1449	Sweden broke away.
1460-1863	It was under Schleswig Holstein, fiefdom of the Holy Roman Empire.
1536	Lutheranism established.
1807	British bombarded Copenhagen and seized the fleet to save it from Napoleon. This action drove Denmark into the arms of France.

1855	Death of Kierkegaard, Danish founder of the philosophy of existentialism. This was a philosophical and atheistic theory emphasising a person's freedom to determine his or her own development through acts of the will.
1863	War between Denmark and Germany over which country controlled Schleswig Holstein, the area that lies between them (the Schleswig Holstein Question).
1866	The Duchy of Schleswig Holstein was annexed to Prussia.
World War I	Neutral.
1940-5	It was occupied by Germany.
1945	Iceland's independence recognised.
1948	Home Rule granted to Faeroe Isles.
1949	It became founding member of NATO.
1973	It joined the EEC.
1992	It rejected the Maastricht Treaty, but accepted it in 1993.
2000	It rejected the Euro.
	97% Lutheran.

Ecuador

15th C	It was conquered by Incas.
1532	It was conquered by Spain.
1822	It was liberated by Antonio Jose de Sucre.
1830	It became independent.
1875	Catholic President Garcia Moreno assassinated by Freemasonic conspiracy.
1895	Liberal Revolution.
	Since then it has been a troubled country.
	95% Catholic.

Egypt

3110-2884BC	Early Dynastic Period I. Major ruler Menes. Unification of Upper and Lower Egypt.
2884-2780BC	Period II. Memphis founded.
2780-2680BC	Old Kingdom Period III. Snefru was major ruler
2680-2565BC	Period IV. Cheops major leader. Imhotep built step-pyramid and pyramids at Giza built.
2565-2420BC	Period V.
2420-2258BC	Period VI.
2258-2225BC	First Intermediate Period VII & VIII.
2225-2134BC	Period IX & X.
2134-2000BC	Period XI.
2000 - 1786BC	Middle Kingdom Period XII.
1786 - 1570BC	Second Intermediate Period XIII - XVII Egypt liberated by Theban dynasty.
1580BC	High point of ancient Egypt.
1570 - 1342BC	New Kingdom Period XVIII major leaders Amenhotep, Thutmose I - IV, Akhenaton (who married Nefertiti), Tutankhamum.
1342 - 1200BC	Period XIX. Major leaders Ramses I & II.
1321BC	Temples at Karnak and Abu Simbel built.
1200-1085BC	Period XX Ramses III.

1085 - 945BC	Period XXI.
945 - 745BC	Period XXII Libyan Dynasty.
745 - 718BC	Period XXIII Nubian Dynasty.
718 -712BC	Period XXIV.
712BC - 663BC	Period XXV Invaded by Assyrians in 666.
663 - 525BC	Period XXVI.
525BC	It became a Persian province.
525 - 405BC	Period XXVII.
405 - 332 BC	Periods XXVIII - XXX.
332BC	Conquest by Alexander the Great.
30BC	Death of Cleopatra, last of Macedonians and conquest by Romans.
1AD	Jesus exiled at Heliopolis.
641	Conquest by Arabs.
1250	Mamelukes seize power.
1517	It became part of Ottoman Empire.
1978-1801	It was occupied by Napoleon.
1859-69	Suez Canal built.
1882	It was occupied by Britain.
1914	It was declared a British Protectorate.
1922	Independence achieved.
1936	Farouk became King.
1946	All British troops withdrawn.
1952	Farouk overthrown.
1953	Nasser declared a republic.
1956	Nasser nationalised Suez Canal. Britain attacked, but was forced to withdraw.
1967	Six Day War sees Israel occupy Sinai and Gaza.
1970	Nasser died and was succeeded by Anwar Sadat.
1973	Lost territory regained in Yom Kippur War.
1981	Sadat assassinated.
1984	Mubarak elected, but he was ousted in the "Arab Spring" of 2011.
	95% Sunni Muslim 5% Coptic Christian.

Estonia

1st C AD	It became an independent state.
13th C	It was controlled by Teutonic Knights.
1561	Sweden took control of the North, with Poland controlling the South.
1625	Sweden ruled whole country.
1710	Russians took over.
19th C	Struggle for independence began.
World War I	Germany took over.
1939	Germans agreed that Russia should take over.
1940	Russians did indeed take over.
1941-44	Germany took over again.
1944	Russians regained control.

| 1991 | It became independent again. |
| | Lutheran. |

Ethiopia (formerly Abyssinia)

11C BC	Having been subject to Egypt it became independent.
4th C AD	Coptic religion introduced.
7th C	Islam gradually took over, but monarchy remained Christian.
1889	Country reorganised with Italian support.
1930	Haile Selassie became Emperor.
1935-41	It was occupied by Italy in support of Christian population. Haile Selassie fled to Britain, until 1941.
1974	Haile Selassie deposed, bringing to an end the world's oldest Christian monarchy, and USSR adopted country as an ally.
1977	Ethiopia fought off Somali rebels in Eastern Ogaden Province.
1980 onwards	Severe droughts brought famine in which millions died.
1993	It became independent again.
1994	Northern Province of Eritrea became independent.
	Sunni Muslim 45%, Ethiopian Orthodox Christian 40%.

Finland

1C BC	It was inhabited by Lapps.
12th C	It was occupied by Sweden.
Next 200 yrs	Sweden and Russia fought over the country.
1809	Country invaded by Russia.
1917	It became independent.
1939	It was defeated by the USSR.
1941	It allowed German troops in to bombard Russia.
1944	Armistice concluded with Russia.
	Mainly Lutheran.

France

5th C BC	Gaul, as it then was, was invaded by Celts.
51BC	Conquest by Julius Caesar.
2nd C AD	Christianity introduced to Brittany from south west England.
5th C AD	Germanic tribes invaded, as Roman Empire dissolved.
500 to 750	Clovis accepted Christianity and made Paris his capital. He introduced Salic law, after the Salian Franks, which barred women from inheriting land or thrones. Country became anarchic under Merovingians (Clovis' successors).
750	Pepin re-established order and founded the Carolingian dynasty.
800	Charlemagne made France centre of the Holy Roman Empire, becoming its first Emperor.
912	Normandy was given to Rollo, an invading Viking.
11th C	Capets became a powerful family around Paris.
1337-1453	Hundred Years War saw English expelled.
1453	Burgundy and Brittany annexed.

1503-1697	Wars with Spain over supremacy in western Europe.
1592-98	Protestantism (Huguenots) caused civil wars.
1633-48	Richelieu and Mazarin secured Alsace and France became a leading power in Europe.
1638-1715	Louis XIV, the Sun King.
1701-14	War of Spanish Succession.
1710-1774	Louis XV.
1754-1793	Louis XVI.
1756-58	War of Austrian Succession.
1756-63	Seven Years War saw loss of Canadian colonies to Britain.
1789-99	French Revolution.
1793	Louis and Marie Antoinette executed.
1785-1795	Louis XVII.
1799-1815	Napoleonic Wars.
1804	Napoleon crowned himself Emperor.
1814	Bourbon Monarchy restored with Louis XVIII.
1830	Louis Philippe is crowned.
1848	Second Republic established.
1848	Republicans overthrew the Constitutional Monarchy after brief Civil War.
1852 -70	Louis Napoleon, Napoleon's nephew, became Napoleon III, but this ended with...
1870-71	Franco Prussian War – France defeated and Third Republic established.
1863-64	Colonisation of Indo-China (Vietnam, Cambodia and Laos). Became independent in 1954.
1914	France sided with the Allies.
1940	Germany occupied France. It allowed a puppet dictatorship under Petain.
1944	France liberated by Allies – start of Fourth Republic.
1956	Morocco and Tunisia received independence. Algeria in 1962.
1958	de Gaulle started 5th Republic.
	90% Catholic.

Georgia

4th C AD	Christianity introduced.
12C	Golden Age of prosperity.
1555	Country divided between Persia and Turkey.
Early 19thC	Control passed to Russia.
1918	Country became independent.
1936	It became a separate Soviet Republic.
1990	Country became independent again.
1992	President Gamsakhurdia was overthrown by armed rebels and Edward Shevardnadze became President.Georgian troops fought rebels in Abkhazia and South Ossetia, who wanted to separate from Georgia. Russia supported the separatists.
1994	The economy collapsed and Georgia joined the Commonwealth of Independent States.

| 1995 | South Ossetia and Abkhazia were granted autonomy. |
| 2008 | Further war between Georgia and Russian-backed South Ossetia and Abkhazia. Mainly Georgian Orthodox Church – they broke away from Russian Orthodoxy in 1917. |

Germany

4th C AD	Germanic peoples from Scandinavia settled near the Rhine.
8th C	Charlemagne imposed Christianity on Saxony, and united it with France.
9th C	Germany was separated from France.
10th C	They began colonising Slav lands east of the Elbe.
1521	Diet of Worms saw Catholics confronting Luther.
1618-48	Thirty Years War destroyed Germany's cultural & economic life.
1740-86	Brandenburg-Prussia reached its military height.
1806	Germany was reunited by Napoleon as the Confederation of the Rhine.
1848	Unsuccessful revolutions.
1871	German Empire formed by Bismarck. William II of Prussia became Emperor (Kaiser Bill) and made Germany predominantly Protestant.
1914-18	World War I was, in part, caused by German rivalry with Britain, Russia and France.
1918	Emperor (still Kaiser Bill) overthrown by the Social Weimar Republic.
1922-24	Rampant Inflation.
1923-29	Germany fell close to revolution which was averted by Hitler taking power with the Nazis, on the pretext of their violent hatred of Communism. It was at this stage that the persecution began of both Catholics and Jews.
1933-39	Unemployment was solved by vast rearmament, with ruthless suppression of all opposition.
1939-45	Germany invaded neighbouring countries, but was ultimately defeated.
1945-52	Country divided and, in 1949, was partitioned into Communist East and Democratic West.
1957	Germany was a founder member of European Economic Community.
1961	Berlin Wall built.
1969	Willy Brandt became Chancellor.
1974	Helmut Schmidt became Chancellor.
1982	Helmut Kohl became Chancellor.
1989	Berlin Wall removed and countries reunited.
	42% Protestant, 35% Catholic.

Greece

1980 BC	Ionians, members of the Hellenic peoples, invaded from the North East.
1600 - 1200BC	Minoans from Crete were main influence.
14th C BC	Achaeans overran Greece.
13th C BC	Victorious wars against the Trojans.
1100BC	Dorians invaded.
1100-800BC	Spartans became most influential people in Greece.
750-500BC	Greeks traded successfully.
545BC	Persians invaded.

490 BC	Persians invaded again under Darius, but were defeated at Marathon.
480 BC	Persians invaded again under Xerxes, but were defeated at Thermopylae and Salamis.
461-429 BC	Pericles tried to make all Greeks into Athenians.
421-404BC	Peloponnesian War - Spartans defeated Athenians.
5th C BC	Socrates and Plato.
378-371BC	Thebes took over Greece.
358-336BC	Philip of Macedon.
323BC	Philip of Macedon's son, Alexander the Great, died, after extending the empire enormously.
212BC	Romans began to intervene in Greece.
146BC	Rome annexed Greece.
529AD	Emperor Justinian closed the University of Athens.
14th C AD- 1821	Greece came under Turkish rule.
1686-1715	Greece run by Venetians.
1829	Greece became independent.
1912-1913	Balkan Wars saw most of Greece's ancient territory returned.
1941-44	Germany overran Greece.
1946	Royalists defeated Communists.
1967	Royal family removed.
1974	Restoration of monarchy rejected in referendum.
1981	It became a member of the EEC.
1992	Greece recognised independence of Macedonia.
2011	Greek deficit led to major crisis in Euro currency.
	Greek Orthodox 97%.

Haiti

	N.B. Haiti shares the island of Hispaniola with the Dominican Republic
1492	It became a Spanish colony. Many slaves were imported from Africa.
1697-1804	It was gradually ceded to France; at the end of this period it gained its independence. It is the only black country to successfully gain its independence from a slave rebellion.
1915-1934	It was occupied by the USA.
1957	Papa Doc Duvalier came to power and was succeeded by his son. He enforced rule with his violent henchmen, the Tonton Macoutes.
1971	Duvalier's son was known as Baby Doc. Both are known for their brutal regime.
1990	Jean Bertrand Aristide became president.
2010	Massive earthquake devastated country, killing approx. 220,000 (neighbouring Dominican Republic completely unaffected).
	Catholic 80%. Voodoo widely practised.

Holland (see Netherlands)

Hungary

Pre-Roman	It was occupied by Celts.
Post-Romans	Germanic invaders came in.
9th C	Asian invaders established a Magyar kingdom.
997-1038	St Stephen became Hungary's first King.
1396	Turks began to invade.
1526	Turks finally took control of south and centre of country.
End of 17th C	Habsburgs drove out Turks, whereupon Hungary came under Austrian rule.
1848-9	Revolution tried to drive out Austrians.
1867	Austro-Hungarian Empire established.
World War I	Hungary fought with Germans.
1918	Empire collapsed and Hungary became independent.
1919	Hungary ruled by Communist Bela Kun.
1920-44	Regency ruled by Admiral Horthy.
1946	Russians imposed Stalinist regime.
1956	Hungarian uprising overturned by Soviet tanks.
1980's	Democratisation gradually began.
1989	Border opened with Austria.
1991	Last Soviet troops departed.
	67% Catholic, 25% Other

Iceland

874	First occupied by Norse settlers.
1000	Christianity adopted.
1263	Iceland submitted to authority of Norway.
1380	Norway and Iceland fell under Danish rule.
1814	Norway became independent, but Iceland remained under Danish rule.
1944	Iceland voted for complete independence.
1976	"Cod War" with Britain, which Iceland won.
1979	200 mile exclusion zone announced.
1985	Iceland declared itself a nuclear-free zone.
	95% Lutheran.

India

2500-1600BC	Indus Valley first occupied.
1500BC	Aryans, militant horse-riding nomads, invaded from north west, and Brahmanism, an early form of Hinduism, began.
500BC	Buddhism began.
321-184 BC	Mauryan emperors unified subcontinent.
300-500	Gupta Dynasty.
11th & 12th C	Muslim adventurers began to raid.
14th & 16th C	Islam became main religion of north and middle of India – Deccan plateau.
16th C	Dutch, French and British established trading posts on the coast.
1528-1858	Mogul emperors.
1756-63	Seven Years War. British overcame their French trading rivals.

1857-8	Indian Mutiny ended the rule of the East India Company, which was transferred to Britain. British rule was called the Raj and lasted until 1947. It was also known as the Indian Empire, with Queen Victoria becoming Empress of India.
1885	Congress Party founded as a focus for nationalism.
1915-47	Resistance to British rule, organised by Gandhi.
1947	India divided into India (Hindu) and Pakistan (Muslim). Independence achieved.
1964	Death of Nehru and border war with Pakistan.
1966	Indira Gandhi became Prime Minister.
1971	War with Pakistan led to creation of Bangladesh (formerly East Pakistan).
1984	Indira Gandhi assassinated and son Rajiv elected.
1990	Central rule imposed in Kashmir, following violence from separatist Muslims.
1990	Violence in Punjab.
1991	Rajiv Gandhi assassinated.
	80% Hindu, 10% Muslim and 2.5% Christian.

Indonesia

2500-500BC	Asians displaced Melanesians.
700-1000AD	Two Hindu empires took over.
13th C	Islam became main religion.
16th C	British and Dutch trading active.
1595	Holland took over (Dutch East Indies).
1816	Became a formal Dutch colony.
1920s	Sukarno led rise of Nationalism.
1942	Japan invaded.
1945	Sukarno proclaimed independence.
1963	Western New Guinea ceded by Holland to Indonesia.
1965-66	Sukarno orders massive retaliation against Communist insurgents.
1975	Terrorists seize Dutch train claiming independence for South Moluccan Islands.
1976	Forced annexation of Portuguese East Timor by Sukarno.
1986	Forced transportation of people to settle outlying islands, notably Irian Jaya.
1988	Sukarno elected for fifth term.
	88% Muslim, 10% Christian and rest mainly Buddhist.

Iran

	The name comes from Aryan, Indo-Europeans who lived between India and Europe. Hitler called anyone with white skin, fair hair and blue eyes Aryan, but this was a misnomer.
1600BC	Country overrun by Medes and Persians.
550BC	Cyrus the Great, a Mede, took power and conquered Babylon and other countries.
334BC	Alexander the Great conquered Persia, passing it onto his descendants, the Seleucids.
3rd C BC	Country overrun by Parthians.
226AD	Sassanid Empire until Mohammed.
633-641	Arabs conquered country for Islam.
1037-1055	Seljuk Turks took over. Seljuks are Tartars, descended from Genghis Khan. They later formed the Ottoman Empire.

12 & 13th C	Mongols took over.
1380	Tamerlane unified the country.
1499-1736	Safavid Dynasty ran country.
1736 - 47	Nadir Shah.
1747 - 1925	Qajar Dynasty.
18th C	Russia threatened country, taking Georgia and much of Armenia.
World War I	British and Russian forces occupied the country, to keep control of oil fields.
1925	Colonel Reza Khan was crowned Shah.
World War II	British, US, Indian and Russian forces occupied the country to secure its oil fields. They caused the death of tens of thousands of Iranians as they purloined food supplies for their troops.
1951	After foreign forces had left, oil fields were nationalised.
1953	With US backing, Shah took control.
1978	Ayatollah Khomeini organised resistance to Shah.
1979	Shah left Iran, revolutionaries seized power and took hostages from US embassy.
1980	Start of Iran-Iraq war, over Shat-al-Arab waterway between two countries.
1981	US hostages released.
1988	Talks with Iraq.
1989	Khomeini called for death of British author Salman Rushdie. Secret oil deal with Israel revealed.
1990	Peace with Iraq.
1991	1 million Kurds fled from Iraq to Iran.
	92% Shiite Muslim.

Iraq

	Formerly known as Mesopotamia
	It was the centre of the Sumerian, Babylonian and Assyrian Empires.
114AD	It was conquered by Romans.
266-632	It was ruled by Sassanids.
633	It was overrun by Moslem Arabs.
1065	It was taken over by Turks.
1258	Mongol invasion.
1401	Baghdad destroyed by Tamerlane.
1533	It was annexed by Suleiman the Magnificent – the country became part of Ottoman Empire in 1638.
1920	It was placed under British administration.
1921	The country became known as Iraq.
1932	It became fully independent.
1933	King Faisal died.
1958	With Jordan they formed the Arab Federation. Monarchy overthrown and became republic.
1979	Saddam Hussein, a Sunni Muslim, took power. He belonged to the Ba'athist party, a political organisation that urged the creation of a united Arab nation.
1980	War with Iran.

1988	Chemical weapons used against Kurds.
1990	Invaded and annexed Kuwait.
1991	Forced to withdraw from Kuwait by British and US forces. Kurds, Marsh Arabs in the Euphrates delta, and Shi'ite Muslims brutally suppressed.
2003	Invaded by USA and Britain over false claim of weapons of mass destruction. Saddam Hussein captured and later executed. US and British occupied country. 65% Shi'ite Muslim 30% Sunni Muslim (though many claim more).

Ireland

3rd C BC	It was invaded from Europe by the Gaels.
432 AD	Christianity introduced from Britain by St Patrick.
5th & 6th C	It sent missionaries to Europe.
800	Danes began to invade – Christianity was just maintained in isolated places such as Skellig Michael, a rocky island off the coast.
1014	Danes defeated by Brian Boru at Clontarf.
1167	Anglo-Norman invaders arrived, but English control confined to the Pale, the area around Dublin.
16th C	English conquest, settlement (plantation) and imposition of Protestantism.
1610	Plantation of Ulster.
1649	Irish revolt cruelly suppressed by Cromwell.
1689-91	Another revolt cruelly suppressed with Catholic majority held down by penal laws.
1739-41	Irish Famine killed 1.5 million (approx. 38% of population).
1782	Irish Protestants rebelled against English rule and were granted Irish Parliament.
1798	Irish rebellion in shadow of French Revolution.
1800	English Prime Minister forced Irish parliament to vote itself out of existence by Act of Union.
1846-51	Great Famine caused 1.5 million to emigrate, mostly to USA.
1880	Movement for Home Rule. Gladstone supported, but was defeated by British parliament.
1914	Home rule was conceded, but delayed by World War I.
1916	Easter Rising. Nationalists seized Dublin Post Office and proclaimed republic. This was suppressed and the leaders executed.
1918-21	Guerrilla Warfare by Irish Republican Army led by Michael Collins.
1921	Ireland partitioned into Irish Free State and Northern Ireland.
1937	Independence achieved.
1949	Ireland left the Commonwealth and became the Republic of Ireland.
1972-1998	Sectarian unrest dominated life in Northern Ireland. Since then the situation has been more settled. 94% Catholic.

Israel (Palestine)

1230BC	Canaan invaded by Philistines and renamed Palestine.
1043BC	King David proclaimed King of the Israelites
1030BC	Philistines were removed and David made Jerusalem his capital.
922BC	Palestine was split into Israel in the North and Judah in the South.

721BC	Israel conquered by Assyrians; it was renamed Samaria, with only a few Jews remaining.
587BC	Judah was conquered by the Babylonians. Jews went into exile and their Temple was destroyed.
538BC	Jews allowed to return.
332BC	Conquest by Alexander the Great.
168BC	Seleucids overran Palestine, but by 141BC Maccabean revolt had restored Jewish independence.
63BC	Roman conquest of Palestine.
33AD	Crucifixion and Resurrection of Jesus Christ.
70AD	Jerusalem destroyed by Romans, and Jews were dispersed (Diaspora). The second Temple was destroyed, all except the Western (Wailing) Wall.
638	Muslim conquest of Palestine made it a target for Crusades.
1517	Palestine conquered by Ottoman Turks.
1880-1914	Jewish immigration increased sharply following pogroms in Russia and Poland.
1897	First Zionist Congress. Jewish home called for in Palestine.
1909	Tel Aviv, first all-Jewish town in Palestine, founded.
1917	Balfour Declaration expressed British government's support for Jewish home in Palestine.
1917-18	Turks driven out of Palestine.
1922	Palestine placed under British mandate.
1936-39	Arab revolt against Jewish immigration.
1937	Peel Commission recommended partition of Palestine into Jewish and Arab states.
1939-45	Jews and Arabs served in allied forces.
1946	Arab riots against British.
1947	Partition approved.
1948	Israel proclaimed, after Jewish campaign of terrorism against British.
1948	Palestinian Arabs were displaced as Jews and Egyptians assumed most of Palestine.
1964	Palestine Liberation Organisation formed and began guerrilla war.
1987	Intifada (popular rising against Israel) began.
1993	Palestinians given degree of autonomy in Gaza & West Bank. Phased withdrawal of Israeli troops.
2000	Jews appeared to attempt to begin rebuilding the Temple, which caused peace negotiations to cease.
2005	Jewish Settlements in Gaza closed and destroyed.
2008/9	Israel attacked Gaza trying to crush the influence of Hamas. Over 1,000 Palestinians were killed, with approximately a dozen Israeli deaths.
	83% Jewish, with Sunni Muslims, Christians and Druze.

Italy

4th & 3rd C BC	Inhabitants (Etruscans, Latins, Sabines, Greeks and Gauls) were united under Romans.
476AD	Final extinction of Roman Empire. Italy then attacked by Lombards and Ostrogoths.
8th C	Papal power rises. Lombardy in the north is annexed by Charlemagne.

9th - 12th C	Events in Italy overshadowed by relationship between Holy Roman Empire and Papacy.
	During this time Italian cities seized the opportunity of converting themselves into self-governing republics.
by 1300	There were 5 major powers in Italy: Milan, Florence, Venice, the Papal States and Naples.
1494-1559	This muddled situation saw Naples and Milan falling under Spanish rule.
1700	Austria secured Milan, and Naples fell under the Spanish Bourbon dynasty.
1796-1814	France ruled Italy and united it.
1814-1861	Muddled situation again with a number of revolutions.
1859	Austrians expelled from Lombardy. Garibaldi overthrew Neapolitan monarchy.
1861	Victor Emmanuel II proclaimed King of unified Italy.
1869	Land purchased on Red Sea.
1869-89	Italy occupied Eritrea.
1896	Attempts to seize Ethiopia were thwarted.
1900	King Umberto assassinated.
1914-18	Italy entered the war as a result of Masonic pressure.
1922	Mussolini came to power with Fascist regime.
1935-6	Conquest of Ethiopia.
1943	Defeat in Africa and the allied invasion of Sicily resulted in Mussolini's downfall.
1943	New Government declared war on Germany.
1946	Monarchy replaced by Republic.
1954	Trieste divided between Italy and Yugoslavia.
1978	Prime Minister Aldo Moro kidnapped and murdered by Red Brigade terrorists.
	100% Catholic (state religion).

Jamaica

1494	Christopher Columbus arrived.
1509-1655	It was occupied by Spain.
1655	It was captured by the British.
1944	Self-Government introduced.
1962	Independence achieved, retaining British monarch as sovereign Head of State.
	70% Protestant, with Rastafarian.

Japan

600BC	First Emperor recorded.
4th C AD	Yamoto dynasty unified warring classes.
5th C	The art of writing introduced from Korea.
6th C	Buddhism also introduced from Korea and Chinese culture was generally accepted.
12thC	First Shogunate – military government. These lasted until 1867. Mogul invasions repulsed.
1542	Portuguese traders arrived.
1549	Christianity introduced by St Francis Xavier.
1609	Dutch traders arrived.

1624	Spanish expelled, due to worry that Catholicism would lead to conquest by Spain.
1630	Portuguese expelled, followed by total Christian persecution.
1630	Only Dutch allowed to trade. No Japanese allowed to leave Japan.
1853	USA re-opened trade relations.
1867	Last Shogun resigned with executive power vested in Emperor.
1889	New constitution launched base on German model.
1894	War with China gave Japan control of Formosa (Taiwan) and Southern Manchuria.
1910	Japan annexed Korea.
1902	Japan formed alliance with Britain.
1904-5	Japan defeated Russia and won control of southern half of Sakhalin.
1914-1918	Japan sided with Allies and afterwards won control of German islands in North Pacific.
1920	Japan advanced towards democracy.
1932	Election of semi-Fascist government. A Japanese puppet monarchy was established in Manchuria.
1937	War with China resumed and carried on until World War II.
1941	Japan entered World War II by attacking US fleet at Pearl Harbour.
1946	Defeat saw Japan surrendering Formosa and Manchuria.
1958	Japan joined U N. It still agitates for the return from Russia of islands immediately to the north.
	Shinto, Buddhism and (small minority) Christianity, with 30% claiming personal religious faith.

Jordan

4thC BC-106AD	The Kingdom of Jordan occupied by Nabataeans, whose capital was the Edomite city, Petra.
106AD	Occupation by Romans.
7th C	Petra destroyed by Arabs.
1099-1187	It was part of the Crusader Kingdom of Jerusalem.
1187	Palestine (the West Bank of present day Jordan) became part of Ottoman Empire.
1812	The ruins of Petra were rediscovered.
Post-WWI	Placed under British Administration.
1923	The rest of Jordan, known as Transjordan, became responsible for its own affairs.
1946	Jordan achieved independence from Britain.
1948	West Bank claimed by the new state of Israel and attacked by Arab nations.
1949	Peace was restored, but Jordan had occupied part of the West Bank.
1950	The whole of the West Bank was annexed by Jordan.
1952	King Hussein took throne.
1958	Jordan & Iraq formed Arab Federation, but only for five months, when Iraqi monarchy was overthrown.
1967	Israelis captured the West Bank and occupied it. Jordan still tried to administer it.
1985	Jordan and Yasser Arafat put forward peace proposals.

1988	Jordan passed its claim to administer West Bank to Palestine Liberation Organisation.
2000	King Hussein died.
	Sunni Muslim 92%, Christian 8%.

Kazakhstan

1920	It became an autonomous republic within the USSR (formerly governed as part of Russian Empire, prior to that, a nomadic region on the Silk Road).
1936	It became a full union republic within the USSR.
1960's	Large influx of Russians made Kazakhs minority in their own land.
1991	Kazakhstan joined Commonwealth of Independent States.
	Mainly Muslim.

Kenya

8th C AD	African tribes occupied Kenya, which had previously been under Arab occupation.
15th & 16thC	It was under Dutch rule.
1895	It became a British Protectorate.
1920	It became a British Colony.
1950	Mau Mau campaign for independence began.
1953	Kenyatta imprisoned.
1956	Mau Mau campaign defeated and Kenyatta released.
1964	It achieved independence.
	Protestant 38%, Catholic 28%, Indigenous beliefs 26%, Muslim 6%.

Korea, North & South

2333BC	Foundation of Korean state.
1122-4th C BC	It was under Chinese rule.
688AD - 1000	Korean peninsula unified under Buddhist rule.
1392	Korea became a vassal of China.
16th C	Invaded by Japan.
1905	Korea treated by Japan as a protectorate.
1910	Annexed by Japan.
1945	Japanese in Korea surrendered. Occupying forces (Russia and US) formed a division at 38th Parallel.
1950	North Korea invaded the South to unite the country under Communist rule.
1953	Korean War ended with division still in same place.
1972	Reunification talks began.
1979	Assassination of President Park (leader of South).
1980	Reunification talks broke down.
1985	North Korea grew even closer to USSR.
1988	South Korea held Olympic Games.
	Religion in North is traditionally Buddhist, but is curtailed by state.
	Religion in South is Buddhist, Confucian and Chondokyo, with Christianity, 28%.

Kuwait

Post-16th C AD	It was part of the Ottoman Empire.
1756	Kingdom of Kuwait founded.
1899	Britain made treaty and gave it status of self-governing protectorate.
1938	Oil discovered.
1961	Kuwait achieved independence.
1990	Iraq invaded Kuwait, but Kuwait was liberated the next year by US and British forces.
	Sunni Muslim 45%, Shi'ite 30%

Laos

4-5th C AD	It was under Chinese influence.
6-11th C	It was under Indian influence and adopted Buddhism.
12-13th C	It was part of the Khmer Empire.
13th C	It was invaded by the Lao from Thailand.
14th C	It became independent.
17th C	First visited by Europeans.
1893-1945	It was a French Protectorate.
1946	France re-established control after brief Japanese incursion.
1950	It was granted semi-autonomy.
1954	It achieved independence.
1954-73	Civil War between royalist Prince Phouma and Communists under Pathet Lao, backed by North Vietnam.
1960	Pro-Western government established.
1960s	Massive US bombardment.
1973	Ceasefire gave 2/3 part to Communists, but 2/3 of population flocked to Royalist cause.
1988	Vietnamese forces withdrew.
	Buddhist 85%.

Latvia

9th C	Viking invasions.
13th C	Teutonic knights invaded, but were resisted until 1230 when they took control.
by 1562	Poland and Lithuania had taken over most of the country.
1621	Sweden conquered the north of the country.
1710 - 1800	Russia took control.
WWI	Germany invaded.
1917	Russia again took control.
1918	Germany took control again until they withdrew and Russia was again in control.
1940	It was incorporated into the USSR.
1941-44	Germany invaded again.
1944	Russia again took control.
1990	Communist power abolished.
1991	Independence achieved.
1992	Russia pulled forces out.
	Mostly Lutheran or Catholic, with Orthodox.

Lebanon

5th C BC	It was occupied by Phoenicians.
1st C BC	It was under Roman control and Christianity began to take over.
635	Muslims arrived.
16th C	It was part of the Ottoman Empire.
1920 - 41	It was administered by France.
1944	Independence achieved.
1948-9	Joined in first Arab War against Israel. Palestinian refugees settled in the South.
1958	Christian Maronite Church formed Phalange Militia, becoming largest political group in Lebanon.
1964	Palestine Liberation Organisation formed in Lebanon.
1971	PLO expelled from Jordan and formed headquarters in Lebanon.
1975	Civil war between Christians and Muslims.
1976	War ends with Syrian-dominated force controlling much of the country.
1976	Conclusion of civil war resented by Christians.
1978	Israel invaded South Lebanon in search of PLO.
1979	Part of South Lebanon declared independent.
1979	Iranian Revolutionary Guard Troops entered Lebanon to spread revolution amongst the Shi'ite population.
1982	Palestinians withdrew and formed base in Tunis. Hezbollah (an Iranian Shi'ite group) was formed in Lebanon.
1984	Syrian forces entered Beirut and Western hostage-taking by Hezbollah began.
1990	Hostage releases began.
1991	Treaty of co-operation signed with Syria.
1993	Israel attacked Hezbollah in South Lebanon.
2005	Syrian forces withdrew. (Cedar Revolution.)
2006	Israel again attacked Hezbollah in South Lebanon, mostly affecting Christians. 33% Shi'ite, 24% Sunni Muslim, 40% Christian (Maronite & Orthodox) & 3% Druze. (Druze - Monotheist sect whose members believe a 10th C Caliph is God. They draw from Christian and Muslim doctrine.)

Liberia

19th C AD	Land bought by American philanthropists as a settlement for liberated slaves.
1847	Independence proclaimed.
1909	Country went bankrupt and was reorganised by US army officers.
1980	Coup put Africans in power.
	Animist 65%, Muslim 20%, Christian 15%.

Libya

5th C BC	It was occupied by Phoenicians.
	Then Greece, Rome, Byzantium and Islam.
16th C	It was part of the Ottoman Empire.
1911	It was occupied by Italy.
1934	It was renamed Libya.
1942	Divided into three provinces.

1951	It became independent.
1969	Colonel Khaddhafi (Gaddafi) deposed the King in coup.
2011	West backed and armed rebellion, resulting in overthrow and murder of Col. Gaddafi.
	Sunni Muslim 97%.

Liechtenstein

	It lies between Switzerland and Austria and is one of the world's richest countries.
1342 AD	It became a sovereign state.
1719	It became known as Liechtenstein.
1923	It was united with Switzerland in a customs union.
	87% Catholic, 8% Protestant.

Lithuania

12thC AD	It became an independent state.
13th C	Teutonic knights were successfully repelled. Lithuania extended its borders nearly to Moscow.
1386	Lithuania joined with Poland.
1569	The two countries became a single state.
1795	Russia took control of both countries.
1831 and 1863	Two revolts to gain independence failed.
World War I	Lithuania was invaded by German troops.
1918	Lithuania declared its independence, but was subsumed by Russia.
1919	Soviet forces were overthrown by Germans, Poles and Lithuanians. Democracy was established.
1920-39	Province of Vilnius declared independence.
1939	Lithuania came under Soviet influence and incorporated into USSR in 1940.
1941	German occupation.
1944	USSR took over again, but Lithuanians fought on for independence.
1988	Movement for autonomy was established.
1989	Communist monopoly of power abolished.
	Predominantly Catholic.

Luxembourg

1354	It became a duchy within the Holy Roman Empire.
1482	It came under Habsburg control.
1797	It was ceded with Belgium to France.
1815	It became a Grand Duchy and was ruled by the King of the Netherlands.
1830	Luxembourg revolted against Dutch rule and part of it became independent with Belgium.
1848	The rest of Luxembourg became independent.
1948	With Belgium and the Netherlands it formed the Benelux Customs Union and thus became a forerunner and founder member of the EU.
	97% Catholic.

Macedonia

338BC	It gained control of Greece under Alexander the Great.
146BC	It became a Roman province.
1912-13 AD	It was divided between Serbia, Bulgaria and Greece.
1918-1993	Serbian part became part of Yugoslavia.
1941-44	It was occupied by Bulgaria.
1980	Nationalism became popular after death of Tito.
1991	The word "Socialist" was dropped from its name.
1992	It became independent, but Greece objected to the name, which is still used by part of Greece.
	Macedonian Orthodox Christian.

Malaysia

9th-14th Cs AD	It was part of the Buddhist Empire of Sri Vijaya, followed by Muslim incursions.
1511	Portuguese brought Catholicism.
1641	Dutch ousted the Portuguese.
1786	Malaysia came under British control.
1818-24	Brief return to Dutch control.
1826	It became a British colony (British Malaya).
1963	Federation of Malaysia formed with Saba & Sarawak (in Borneo) and Singapore.
1965	Singapore seceded from federation.
1969	Anti-Chinese riots in Kuala Lumpur.
1987	Malay-Chinese relations further deteriorated.
	Islam is official religion, with Buddhist, Hindu, Christian minorities, and local beliefs.

Malta

870AD	Having been run by Phoenicians, Greeks, Carthaginians and Romans, it fell to Arabs.
1090	Norman Count Roger of Sicily conquered Malta.
1530	It was handed to the Knights of St John of Jerusalem.
1565	After a Turkish attack it was refortified.
1798	Malta was surrendered to Napoleon.
1814	Malta was annexed to Britain and became a leading naval base.
World War II	After its heroic defence, the island was awarded the George Cross.
1947	It became self-governing.
1964	It became independent.
1974	It became a republic.
1979	British military base closed.
	98% Catholic.

Mexico

	Early civilisations include: Mayan, Olmec, Toltec, Mixtec, Zapotec.
1520	Montezuma killed during Spanish Conquest.
1535	Mexico became vice-royalty of Spain.

1810	Struggle for independence began.
1821	Spanish rule ended.
1846-48	Mexico lost war with and territory to USA.
1848	Mayan revolt suppressed.
1864-67	Emperor Maximillian of Austria was Emperor of Mexico.
1913-1925	Democratically elected president was violently removed from office by a civil war instigated from the USA. Religious orders were banned and Catholicism was ruthlessly suppressed, with 300 churches, convents and religious orders forced to close. Crosses were removed from graves and ninety priests were murdered. This religious war is hardly ever mentioned today, even in Mexico.
1985	Earthquake in Mexico City.
	97% Catholic.

Monaco

12th C	Monaco became a Genoese possession, having been part of the Holy Roman Empire.
1297	It was ruled by the Grimaldi family.
1542-1641	Monaco became a Spanish Protectorate.
1797	It was annexed to France.
1814	Independence from France was established.
1815	Monaco became a protectorate of Sardinia.
1861	Protectorate reverted to France.
1940	It was occupied by Italy.
1943	It was occupied by Germany.
1945	Liberation.
1949	Prince Rainer inherited the crown.
	95% Catholic.

Mongolia

1206 AD	Genghis Khan united the country's nomads to form the Mongol Empire.
1689	Mongolia became part of China.
1912	Mongolia became autonomous.
1915	Chinese influence again took over until...
1921	Russia removed Chinese.
1924	It adopted the Soviet system of government.
1946	Independence achieved.
1990	Mongolia democratised with free multi-party elections.
	No official religion.

Morocco

10th-3rd C BC	Coastal plains occupied by Phoenicians, rest occupied by Berber tribes.
5th C AD	Vandals took over.
6th C	Visigoths took over, and then...
7th C	Arabs arrived.
11th C	Almoravids united Morocco with Spain and Tunisia.
15th C	Portugal occupied port of Ceuta, but was defeated.

1912	Morocco was divided into French and Spanish protectorates.
1956	Independence achieved.
1957	Sultan restyled as King.
	Sunni Muslim 99%.

Myanmar (formerly Burma)

638AD	Peoples who arrived from Tibet called themselves Burmese.
1287	Kublai Khan's grandson arrived, destroying its pagan dynasty. When he withdrew, anarchy reigned.
1490-1750	Toungoo tried to maintain control.
1752	Alaungpaya formed the capital at Rangoon.
1824-26	Burmese war with Britain, and Britain gained control of coastal regions.
1852	British annexed Lower Burma in Second Burmese War.
1886	British gained control of Upper Burma in third Burmese War.
1937	It became a crown colony within the Commonwealth.
1942-45	Japanese occupation.
1948	Independence achieved and left Commonwealth.
1962	Army coup.
1989	Martial Law imposed and name of country changed to Myanmar. Human rights abuses abound.
2010	Aung San Suu Kyi, the opposition leader held in house arrest for thirteen years, was released.
2012	Aung San Suu Kyi elected to Lower House and took up seat.
	85% Buddhist.

Namibia

1884	Germans occupy country with exception of Walvis Bay, a British Cape Colony.
1920	Country mandated to South Africa.
1990	Independence achieved.
	Lutheran 51%, 19% Catholic, rest other protestant sects.

Nepal

1768	Nepal united under one kingdom
1815-16	Gurkha War resulted in country becoming a buffer state between India and China.
	Since this date, Nepalese have been recruited to the British Army as the Gurkhas.
1923	Independence achieved.
1951	Monarchy restored.
1981	Elections held for Parliament.
2001	Most of Royal family murdered by King's brother.
	Hindu 90%.

Netherlands

| 51BC | Land south of Rhine previously occupied by Celts and Germanic peoples, was united by Romans. |

7 & 8th C AD	The Francs followed, and then the Saxons, and then they paid allegiance to the Holy Roman Emperor.
15th C	The country passed to the Dukes of Burgundy.
1504	The Spanish Habsburgs took over.
1568	The Dutch rebelled against Phillip II of Spain.
1648	Dutch republic recognised by the treaty of Westphalia.
17th C	The Dutch led the world in trade and founded an empire in both the East and West Indies.
17th C	Rivalry between the Dutch and the British led to three naval wars (1652-4, 1665-7, 1672-4).
1713	War between the Dutch and France ended with the Dutch exhausted and ruined.
1795	Batavian republic formed.
1806	Napoleon made his brother, Louis, King of Holland.
1810-3	Holland was annexed to France.
1815	Congress of Vienna united North Netherlands and also confirmed Belgium as independent from Holland.
1940-5	Brutal occupation by Germany.
1947	Joined Benelux customs union.
1992	Maastricht Treaty on European political and monetary union ratified.
	40% Catholic, 31% Protestant.

New Zealand

Pre-14th C AD	It was occupied by Polynesian Maoris.
1642	Dutch Explorer, Abel Tasman tried to land, but was prevented.
1769	Captain Cook explored the coasts.
1815	British Missionaries arrived.
1840	By Treaty of Waitangi, Maoris accepted British sovereignty.
1845-7	First Maori revolt.
1853	Self-government achieved.
1860-72	Second Maori revolt.
1877-84	Introduction of male suffrage.
1893	Introduction of female suffrage.
1907	It achieved Dominion status.
1931	It was granted independence, retaining the British monarch as sovereign Head of State.
	50% Protestant, 15% Catholic.

Nicaragua

1522	First Europeans arrived and it became Spanish.
1821	It was united with Mexico.
1838	It achieved full independence.
1926-33	It was occupied by US Marines.
1936	Start of near dictatorship by Somoza family.
1962	Sandinista formed to fight against Somoza rule.
1979	Somoza government ousted by Communist Sandinistas.

1982	US Government promoted subversive action against Sandinistas.
1987	Central American peace agreement signed by Nicaragua.
1988	Hurricane left 180,000 homeless.
	95% Catholic.

Nigeria

700BC	Evidence of first occupation.
15th C AD	British and other slave traders raided the coasts.
1861	Lagos bought by British.
1900	Two protectorates set up: North (Muslim) and South (Christian).
1914	Both halves united.
1960	It became independent.
1967	Conflict over oil revenues led to declaration of independence of Ibo state of Biafra.
1970	Surrender of Biafra and end of war.
	Muslim 50%, Christian 40%, local religions 10%.

Norway

Pre-8th C AD	Norway was originally inhabited by Lapps, but then invaded by Goths.
8th -11thC AD	Norway's Vikings raided many parts of Europe.
11thC	Christianity introduced.
1217	Monarchy introduced.
1380	Norway united with Denmark by marriage.
1397	Sweden joined the union.
1523	Sweden broke away.
1814	Norway was ceded to Sweden, but Norway was reluctant to accept this arrangement.
1905	Norway achieved full independence.
1940-45	Occupied by Germany.
	94% Lutheran.

Oman

7th C	Muslims vitalised whole of Arabia with Islamic faith.
1508-1658	Country was Portuguese possession.
1658-1744	Country ruled by Persia.
By early 19th C	Country was most powerful in Arabia. It ruled Zanzibar until 1861.
1951	Independence achieved.
1965	Popular front has been working for the overthrow of Sultan.
	Religion is Muslim of various strands.

Pakistan

1947	Pakistan formed a separate country from India when the latter gained its independence.
1956	It was proclaimed a republic.
1971	Secession of East Pakistan to independent Bangladesh.
1979	Former Prime Minister Bhutto executed.

1986	Free elections returned Bhutto's daughter Benazir as Prime Minister.
1988	General Zia, who introduced a strict Islamic legal code was killed in plane crash.
1990	Army mobilised in support of Muslim separatists in Kashmir.
2007	Benazir Bhutto assassinated during the country's general election campaign.

75% Sunni Muslim, 20% Shi'ite Muslim, 4% Hindu (Christian minority heavily persecuted).

Note: There is a tribe living in the Hindu Kush, the tall mountain range in northern Pakistan, called the Pashtun or Pathans, who speak the Pashto language. They are devout Muslims, farmers and warriors. The area where they live is also known as the North West Frontier and it controls the Khyber Pass to Afghanistan.

Palestine

1235BC	Israelites escaped from Egypt, reached "The Promised Land" and named it Canaan.
1230BC	Philistines occupied Canaan and renamed it Palestine.
C1000BC	King David formed a united Kingdom of Israel.
922BC	Israel split into Israel in the north and Judah in the south.
587BC	Babylonians conquered country and took Israelites into exile until 536BC.
539BC	Palestine became part of Persian Empire.
332BC	Alexander the Great conquered Palestine.
168BC	Maccabean revolt restored independence.
63BC	Conquest by Romans.
33AD	Crucifixion and Resurrection of Jesus Christ.
70AD	Romans destroyed Jerusalem and the Jews dispersed.
636	Land conquered by Muslim Arabs.
1516	Conquest by Ottoman Turks.
1880-1914	Jewish immigration increased after pogroms in Russia and Poland.
1897	Jews called for permanent home in Palestine.
1909	Tel Aviv, the first all-Jewish town, built.
1917	Balfour declaration.
1922	Palestine placed under British control.
1936-39	Arab revolt against Jewish immigration.
1939-45	Arab and Jewish forces fought for allies in WWII.
1946	Immigration restrictions created resentment amongst Jews who revolted.
1948	Jewish state of Israel proclaimed, following Jewish terrorism against British.
1967 & 1973	Arab-Israeli wars saw Jews gaining much territory and displacing many Palestinian Arabs.
1964	Palestine Liberation Organisation formed and guerrilla war began.
1987	Intifada began against Israeli occupation.
2000	Jewish plans to rebuild Temple in Jerusalem caused greatly increased violence

There are 1 m Arabs in the West Bank, East Jerusalem & Gaza Strip, 1.2 m in Jordan, 3/4m in Israel, and 3m in Lebanon. 1m in US.

75% Muslim (mainly Sunni), 8% Christian, 17% Israeli Jews, in Palestinian territories.

Panama

1502AD	Panama visited by Columbus and it became Spanish until independence.
1572-95	Spanish Settlements sacked by Francis Drake.
1698-1701	Scottish settlers built Fort St Andrews.
1822	Independence achieved from Spain, but joined Gran Colombia.
1903	Full independence achieved, but USA bought rights to build the Canal and was given control of it.
1977	Full control of Canal transferred to Panama.
1989	Unrest in country with state of war with the USA. The US invaded and restored the allegiances it needed.
	93% Catholic.

Papua New Guinea

	A Short History of the eastern half of the Island
2500BC	Records of early system of farming by immigrants from Indonesia.
1526AD	Portuguese first Europeans to arrive.
1821	East India Company took control of western half and it became part of the Dutch East Indies.
1884	South East claimed by Britain, North East by Germany, but only until the end of World War I.
1905	British part transferred to Australia.
1921-42	Eastern part held as a League of Nations Mandate.
1942-45	It was occupied by Japan.
1975	Independence achieved from Australia. British monarch retained as sovereign Head of State.
	63% Protestant, 31% Catholic.

Paraguay

1526AD	Sebastian Cabot arrived.
1537	Spanish founded Asuncion.
1600-1767	Jesuits administered most of the country.
1767	Spanish expelled and it became a viceroyalty of Peru.
1776	It became part of viceroyalty of Buenos Aires.
1811	Independence achieved.
1865-70	Territory lost to Brazil, Argentina and Uruguay.
1932-35	Territory gained from Bolivia.
	97% Catholic.

Peru

1200AD	Chimu culture flourished, but gradually overtaken by Incas.
1531	Pizarro arrived.
1533	Execution of last of Inca emperors, Atahualpa.
1541	Pizarro assassinated.
1824	Peru achieved independence.
1849-74	Massive Chinese immigration as manual labour to collect guano.

| 1945 | Peru declared war on Germany. |
| | Subsequent unsettled history of switching between military and civilian rule. 90% Catholic. |

Philippines

1542	Named Philippines by Spanish explorers.
1565	It was conquered by Spain.
1898	It was ceded to the USA after Spanish-American War.
1935	It was granted self-government.
1942-45	It was occupied by Japan.
1946	Independence achieved from the USA.
1965	Marcos elected president.
1986	Marcos overthrown by Corazon Aquino.
1991	Mount Pinatubo erupted.
	84% Catholic.

Poland

10th C AD	Polish tribes were Christian.
1241	Mongol hordes devastated the country, allowing German and Jewish refugees to settle.
1331	First Polish Parliament met.
1386-1572	Poland became a great power and the largest country in Europe, taking over Byelorussia and Ukraine.
1569-1776	Poland was united with Lithuania.
1581	Stephen Bathory defeated Ivan the Terrible.
1683	John Sobieski forced the Turks to raise the siege of Vienna.
Mid 17th C	Poland was utterly defeated by Russia, Sweden and Brandenburg.
1772, 1793, 95	Poland partitioned and lost so much territory that its name disappeared from the map.
1815	Congress of Vienna reconstituted parts of Poland as a kingdom under the Tsar.
1918	Poland was revived as an independent republic.
1939	German invasion and occupation.
1940	Katyn Massacre of 14,500 Poles by Russia, which admitted responsibility in 1989.
1944	Germans driven out by Russian forces.
1945	Polish boundaries redrawn by Potsdam conference.
1947	Communist republic proclaimed.
1980	Solidarity emerged as independent trade union.
1981	General Jaruzelski imposed Martial Law.
1984	Amnesty for political prisoners.
1989	New pluralist constitution formed.
1990	Lech Walesa elected president.
	95% Catholic.

Portugal

11thC	Portugal originated as a country subject to Leon in Spain.
1128	It became an independent monarchy.
1260	Moors expelled.
13th C	The Cortes (parliament) began to take control of taxation.
1294	Treaty with England signed.
1373	Alliance with England established.
1497	Vasco da Gama explored the African coast and reached the sea route to India.
1500	Cabral reached Brazil.
1580	Philip II of Spain seized the crown; the Portuguese rebelled and...
1640	...The House of Braganza took the throne.
1668	Portuguese independence recognised.
1700-1713	Portugal fought with Britain in the War of the Spanish Succession.
1807	France invaded Portugal, but was driven out by the British in the Peninsular War.
1910	Republic proclaimed by Freemasons.
1917	Apparition of Blessed Virgin Mary to three shepherd children at Fatima.
1928-68	Dictatorship of Salazar who removed Masonic influences.
1975	African colonies became independent.
1988	Portugal joined EEC.
	97% Catholic.

Punjab

1849	Britain annexed Punjab.
1845-6, 1848-9	Sikh Wars led to Punjab state where land was given by Britain to Indians who had fought for Britain.
1947	At the Partition of India, Punjab was divided into Pakistani West Punjab (Muslim) & Indian East (Sikh & Hindu).
1947	There was huge loss of life as Indians fled to their appropriate state.
	Lahore is capital of East Punjab, Amritsar of West.

Romania

	Originally formed by migrants from the immediate south - a region originally known as Thrace.
275AD	Goths invaded.
6th - 12th Cs	It was overrun by Huns, Bulgars and Slavs.
15th & 16th Cs	Country fell to Ottoman invaders.
1829-56	Russia took control.
1861	Country first became known as Romania. Previously it was two states, Moldavia and Walachia.
1877-78	Russo-Turkish war led to Romanian independence.
1913	In the Second Balkan War, Romania fought against Bulgaria.
1914	Romania was occupied by Germans.
1918	Romania received Bessarabia, Bukovina and Transylvania and became the largest Balkan country.
	Romania benefited enormously from the dismemberment of the Habsburg empire.

1940	Romania again occupied by Germany and much of the newly gained territory was given up.
1946	The King was forced to abdicate by Communists.
1989	President Ceausescu executed.
1990	Gradual liberalisation of country.
	Romanian Orthodox 80%, Catholic 6%.

Russia (Russian Federation)

9th -10th Cs AD	Vikings overran Russia.
988	Country united by Christian base at Constantinople.
1223	Mongols overran southern part of country.
1462-1505	Ivan the Great expelled the Mongols and united the North West.
1547	Ivan the Terrible became the first Tsar and colonised Siberia.
1613	Michael became the first Romanov Tsar.
1667	Cossack revolt was put down.
1682-1725	Peter the Great formed capital at St Petersburg, introduced Western education & took the Baltic seaboard.
1762 - 96	Catherine the great annexed Crimea, and took White Russia.
1798	Napoleon failed to take Moscow.
1827-9	Russia began to dominate the Balkans.
1853-56	Crimean War.
1861	The poor condition of the peasants is claimed as the seedbed of discontent leading to Marxist revolution.
1877-78	Balkan War with Turkey.
1904	Russian occupation of Manchuria led to war with Japan. Japan won.
1905	Tsars had to cede powers to the Duma (Parliament).
1914	Russian-German rivalries led to World War I.
1917	October revolution led to the killing of the Tsar and his family. Lenin became Russian leader.
1917-20	White Russians unsuccessfully waged civil war on the Red revolutionary army led by Trotsky.
1922	Stalin became the new leader.
1939-45	In World War II, Russia (USSR) withstood huge German onslaught, but with enormous loss of life.
1991	What was formerly known as Russia, Capital at Moscow, became the Russian Federation under Yeltsin.
1993	New constitution approved.
	Russian Orthodox.

Saudi Arabia

18th C	Nejd Desert fell to Turkish control. At this time the land was known as the Hejaz.
After WWI	It was only now that nationalism in the Arabian peninsula began to emerge.
By 1926	King Ibn Saud had fought off all other Arab claimants, becoming undisputed King of the Hejaz.
1932	The country was established.

1975	King Feisal was assassinated.
	Sunni Muslim.
	Note: The Wahhabiyyah is the name of a Muslim sect calling for strict observance of the rules laid down in the Koran and the Kingdom of Saudi Arabia has adopted these rules.

Scotland

2nd Millen. BC	Celts reached the British Isles and a number of tribes of Celts occupied what is now Scotland.
	When Brutus, King of Britain, died, he gave the northern part to his son Albanactus. Scotland was known as Alba or Albany. At that stage the tribe of Scots lived in Ireland.The Scots may have got their name from one of their leaders having married an Egyptian princess called Scota.
1st C AD	Roman invasion of Britain.
	The Romans called the people from Alba, Picts, because they wore paint. This was the time when the defensive Brochs were built. Examples remain at Glenelg and Carloway.
83AD	The Romans defeated the tribes of Albany at the Battle of Mons Graupius.
	The Romans prevented the Picts from penetrating far into England by building...
122	.....Hadrian's Wall from Carlisle to Newcastle and then...
142	...The Antonine Wall from the Forth to Clyde estuaries. The tribe immediately north of the Antonine Wall was the Caledonii – hence the word Caledonia/Caledonian.
After 1st C AD	With the Picts suppressed, the Scots began to leave Ireland and settle in Scotland.
	The Scots spoke Gaelic, a language that is believed to have originated in Mesopotamia.
400AD	Scotland was united and attacked England as far as London.
5th/6th Cs	Christianity introduced from Ireland. Columba reached Iona in 563AD.
9thC	Attempts were made to unite Scotland. Kenneth MacAlpin was the first King of Scotland.
9th C	Scotland was united as one country – the Declaration of Scone.
1266	Scotland gained the Hebrides from Norway at the Treaty of Perth.
1296	English defeated at Stirling Bridge.
1314	English defeated at Bannockburn by Robert the Bruce.
1320	Declaration of Arbroath at which the Scots claimed their independence from England.
1328	Scottish independence recognised.
1371	First Stuart King (Robert II).
1513	James IV killed by English at Flodden.
1540/50s	John Knox introduced Calvinism.
1542	Mary Queen of Scots becomes Queen of Scotland as a baby.
1560s	Queen Mary in Scotland.
1568	Mary flees to England for safety, but she is imprisoned.
1587	Mary is beheaded by order of Elizabeth I of England.
1592	Presbyterianism established.
1603	James VI became James I of England, in addition – Union of Crowns.
1651-60	Cromwell's forces defeated Scotland.
1689	Battle of Killiecrankie.

1707	Act of Union between England and Scotland.
1715	Rebellion under Earl of Mar failed.
1745	Rebellion under Bonny Prince Charlie failed. His forces were utterly defeated at...
1746	... The Battle of Culloden.
18th/19th C	Highland Clearances.
1998	Scottish Parliament re-established.
	Mainly Presbyterianism and Catholicism.

Seychelles

1500	It was probably first visited by Portuguese.
1744	It became a French Colony.
1814	It was ceded to Britain after the end of the Napoleonic Wars.
1903	It became a Crown Colony.
1975	Internal self-government achieved.
1976	Independence achieved.
	90% Catholic.

Singapore

1819	It was leased as a trading post to the British East India Company.
1858	It passed to the British Crown.
1942	It was invaded and occupied by Japan.
1945	Japanese forces removed.
1959	Independence achieved.
1965	It became an independent republic.
	Buddhist, Toa, Muslim, Hindu, Christian.

Slovak Republic (Slovakia)

906-1918	It was under Magyar domination.
1918	Independence achieved from Austro-Hungarian Empire. Joined Czechs to form Czechoslovakia.
1948	Communists assumed power.
1993	Slovak republic became sovereign state.
	60% Catholic.

Slovenia

1918	It was united with Croatia and Serbia (having been part of the Austro-Hungarian Empire; its history being dominated by the Habsburgs).
1929	It became part of Yugoslavia.
1991	Independence declared.
	Catholic.

South Africa

| 1488 | Cape of Good Hope rounded by Bartholomew Diaz. |
| 1652 | Dutch East India Company founded Cape Town. |

1795 & 1806	Britain occupied Cape Town.
1814	Britain purchased the hinterland.
1824	British settled in Natal.
1836	Great Trek – the Dutch, wishing to escape from British rule, occupied Transvaal and Orange Free State.
1854	Orange Free State became independent.
1856	Natal became a separate colony.
1867	Diamonds discovered at Kimberley.
1877-81	Britain attempted to occupy Transvaal, but was defeated in the first of the South African Wars.
1886	Gold discovered in Transvaal.
1896	Jameson Raid. British moving into Transvaal failed to overthrow Dutch government.
1899-1902	British won Boer War against the Dutch colonists.
1910	Union of South Africa (Cape of Good Hope, Natal, Orange Free State, Transvaal and, what is now, Namibia).
WWI & WWII	South Africa fought with the allies.
1948	Beginning of Apartheid.
1964	In Sharpeville (in the north east), a riot of blacks was controlled by the massacre of 69 demonstrators.
1961	Union became a republic and withdrew from the Commonwealth.
1964	Nelson Mandela, leader of African National Congress was imprisoned for sabotage and leading opposition to Apartheid.
By 1980s	300,000 blacks had been resettled in Black Townships. These included the Bushmen of the Kalahari and Hottentots who come from south of the Zambezi river. In some cases, these enforced population movements were in order to leave the land free for diamond-mining by the government.
1986	South Africa waged war with guerrillas in Botswana, Zambia and Zimbabwe.
1988	Namibia's independence recognised.
1990	Mandela released.
1991	Repeal of remaining Apartheid laws.
1994	Mandela installed as President.
	Dutch Reformed Church 40%, Anglican 11%, Catholic 8%.

Spain

Pre-Roman	Land occupied by Celts, Basques and Iberians. Phoenicians and Greeks had also established colonies.
5th C BC	Carthaginians dominated.
200BC	Conquered by Romans.
5th C AD	Visigoths set up a kingdom in Spain with permission of Rome.
711	Invasion by Moors.
1250	All of Spain had been reconquered, except Granada.
1479	Ferdinand of Aragon and Isabella of Castile united all Spain except Granada.
1492	Granada was reconquered.
Mid 16th C	By the time of Philip II, and through explorations at sea, Spain became very powerful.
1535	Naples was annexed to Spain.
1580	Portugal was annexed to Spain. Charles I inherited the Netherlands.

1588	After the defeat of the Armada, Spain's influence began to weaken.
1713	By end of the War of Spanish Succession, Spain lost Naples, Sicily, Milan, Netherlands and Gibraltar.
1808	France occupied Spain.
1814	With British help (the Peninsular War), France was removed from Spain.
1810-1830	Spain lost its American Colonies.
1898	In the Spanish-American War, which Spain lost, Cuba and the Philippines were ceded to the US.
1923-30	Supporters of the Monarchy failed to preserve it and a republic was set up by freemasons.
1936	Communist reforms resulted in one hundred Catholic Churches in Madrid being burned; other church property was seized and priests were forced to pay the government for the use of their own churches. As a result of this persecution, Civil War was started by Franco, as a Nationalist campaign against the Communists who had murdered seven thousand priests – in spite of the huge odds against them, the Nationalists won, but, ever since, it is the Communists who have been portrayed as the virtuous.
1947	Franco announced that the Monarchy would be restored at his death.
1975	Franco died and the Bourbon Monarchy was indeed restored.
	99% Catholic.

Sri Lanka (Ceylon)

To 550BC	It was occupied by aborigines called Vedda.
550BC	It was conquered by Sinhalese from North India.
3rdC BC	Island became world centre for Buddhism.
1st 1550 yrs AD	Spice Trade brought Arabs and Europeans who called the island Ceylon.
1505	Portugal established a settlement.
1658	Settlers from the Netherlands arrived.
1796	British settlers arrived.
1802	Ceylon became a crown colony.
1802-1948	Immigrant Tamils (Hindus) from South India arrived to work in tea and rubber plantations.
1948	Independence achieved, but it remained a British dominion.
1956	Prime Minister Solomon Bandaranaike decreed that only Sinhalese was to be spoken in universities.
1956-9	The resulting Tamil riots ended in Bandaranaike's assassination.
1959-77	Bandaranaike's widow ruled intermittently as Prime Minister.
1972	Socialist Republic of Sri Lanka proclaimed.
1976	Tamils called for independent Tamil state in the North.
1982	State of emergency after Tamil terrorism.
1991/2	Sri Lankan army and civilians massacred Tamil Tigers.
	Buddhist 69%, Hindu 15%, Moslem 8%, Christian 7%.

Sudan

	It was originally known as Nubia and ruled by Egypt.
6thC	Inhabitants converted to Coptic Christianity.
15th C	Inhabitants converted to Islam, following take over by Arabs.

1820	Egypt took over again.
1885	Revolt led to Khartoum being held by Mahdi. General Gordon killed.
1896-98	Anglo-Egyptian force under Lord Kitchener defeated Mahdi.
1955	Civil war between Muslim North and non-Muslim South.
1956	Sudan achieves independence from both Egypt and Britain.
1970	Reunion with Egypt agreed in principle.
1971	Sudan became one-party (socialist) state.
1983	Islamic Law introduced.
1987	Civil war between elected government and Sudan People's Liberation Army.
1988	Severe flooding forced SPLA to sue for peace.
1990	Civil war flared up again.
2004 - 5	Civil war between Chinese-backed Janjaweed (Arab gunmen, commissioned by the Sudanese government) and the settled African farmers. This brought death and suffering to hundreds of thousands in the Darfur region, and was caused mainly by Sudan's oil reserves in that quarter.
2011	South Sudan became an independent nation in its own right.
	Sunni Muslim 73%, Animist 18%, Christian 9% (in the South).

Sweden

4000BC	First evidence of inhabitation.
800-1060AD	Swedish Vikings sailed mainly east and founded Novgorod.
12th C	Country accepted Christianity.
12th-14th C	Finland brought Sweden under its rule.
1397-1520	Sweden, Norway and Denmark were united under Danish rule.
1520	Gustavo Visa elected King of Sweden and founded the dynasty that ruled until 1818.
16th -18th C	Territorial ambitions led to failure and impoverishment.
1809	Sweden lost Finland to Russia.
1814	Annexed Norway.
1905	Union with Norway dissolved.
1818	New dynasty established.
1914-45	Neutral in both World Wars.
2003	Sweden rejected joining the Euro.
	Lutheran 95%.

Switzerland

Roman times	The Romans called the inhabitants of Switzerland Helvetians or Transalpine Gauls.
1291	Three cantons formed a league to defend liberties against the Holy Roman Empire.
1513	This number grew to 13 cantons.
1523-29	Urban cantons accepted the Reformation, but rural areas remained Catholic.
1648	Treaty of Westphalia gave full independence to Switzerland from the Holy Roman Empire.
1798-1815	Following invasion by the French, a Helvetic Republic established centralised government.

1815	Congress of Vienna guaranteed Swiss neutrality. Switzerland received Geneva and 21 other cantons.
1848	Civil War led to greater centralisation.
1874	Principle of the referendum introduced.
1986	Switzerland rejected membership of United Nations.
	Catholic 50%, Protestant 48%.

Syria

	Ancient Syria occupied by various small kingdoms. They were all subdued by the Assyrians.
2500-612BC	Assyrian Empire which ended in 612BC with destruction of their capital, Nineveh. Sumerian was their religion.
6th C BC	Babylonian occupation.
5thC BC	Persian occupation.
4th C BC	Macedonian occupation.
300BC	Antioch founded.
300BC - 636AD	It formed part of Roman and Byzantine Empires.
636	Syria was conquered by Saracens. (Saracen was the Greek and Roman term for Muslim.)
Middle Ages	Syria was the battleground for many of the Crusader conflicts.
1516-1918	Syria was part of the Ottoman Empire.
1918-19	Syria was occupied by French and British troops.
1920	Syria was placed under French mandate.
1946	Syria became independent.
1949	Military rule imposed.
1958	Merged with Egypt to form United Arab Republic.
1961	UAR disintegrated.
1967	Six Day War and loss of territory to Israel.
1973	Yom Kippur War – Israel consolidated its presence in Golan Heights.
1991	Syria fought against Iraq in Gulf War.
2011	The country was beset by western-backed rebels seeking to topple President Bashar al-Assad
	Sunni Muslim 74%, Other Islamic Sects 16%, Christian 10%.

Taiwan

15th C AD	It was settled by China. At this stage it was known as Formosa.
17th C	It was briefly occupied by the Dutch.
1895	It was ceded to Japan.
1945	It was regained by China.
1949	It became the refuge of Chinese nationalists (under Chiang Kai-shek) who were fleeing Mao Zedong.
1949-71	They were recognised by the USA as the legitimate government of China.
1991	End of civil war with China declared.
	Officially atheist.

Thailand

4000BC	First evidence of inhabitation.
1350AD	It was united as a kingdom (Siam).
1511	It was reached by Portuguese traders.
17th C	It was reached by the British and Dutch.
1855	Treaty established Britain as paramount power in the region.
1896-1904	It was recognised as the official buffer zone between British Burma and French Indochina.
1932	Constitutional monarchy established.
1939	Name changed from Siam to Thailand.
1941-44	Occupation by Japan.
1972	Withdrawal of Thai troops from South Vietnam.
	Buddhist 95%, Muslim 4%.

Tunisia

8thC BC	It was founded as Carthage by Phoenicians.
7thC AD	It became an Arab country.
1574	It became part of the Ottoman Empire.
16th-19thC	Its coast was known as the Barbary Coast and renowned for its pirates.
1881	It became a French protectorate.
1955	It achieved self-government.
1956	Independence achieved.
2011	The "Arab Spring" resulted in the government being replaced.
	Sunni Muslim 95% plus Jewish and Christian.

Turkey

6thC AD	The Turks originally came from Mongolia.
7thC	They adopted Islam.
1055	The Seljuk Turks established an empire in Asia Minor and the Ottoman Turks entered their service.
1299	Osman I founded an empire of his own and overran Asia Minor.
1354	They captured Gallipoli.
1453	They captured Constantinople.
1480	They were masters in the Balkans.
by 1550	They had conquered Egypt, Syria, Mesopotamia, Arabia, Tripoli and most of Hungary.
1571	They took Cyprus.
1669	They took Crete.
1683	The Turks were defeated before Vienna.
1699	They lost Hungary.
1774	Russia ousted them from Moldavia, Walachia and the Crimea.
1821	Greece threw off Turkish rule.
1854-6	The British fought on the Turkish side in the Crimean War.
1878	Turkey lost Bulgaria, Bosnia and Herzegovina.
1911	Italy seized Tripoli.

1912	Turks were expelled from Albania and Macedonia.
1914-8	Turkey, having joined on the losing German side in World War I, lost Syria, Arabia, Mesopotamia and Egypt.
1919	Kemal Ataturk became president and defeated Italian, French and Greek forces.
1923	Turkey became independent.
1974	Turkish forces sent to protect Turkish interests in Cyprus.
	Sunni Muslim 98%.

Uganda

1894-1962	British Protectorate.
1962	It joined the Commonwealth under Milton Obote.
1971	Obote overthrown by Idi Amin.
1972	All Asians were expelled and fled to Britain. Hundreds of thousands of opponents were killed.
1978	Amin forced to leave the country.
1980	Obote returned to power.
1993	King of Buganda reinstated as formal monarch.
	33% Catholic, 33% Protestant, 16% animist.

Ukraine

$10^{th}/11$ C	The state founded on Kiev (the Kievan Rus) was extremely powerful and influential, its "Golden Age" beginning with Prince Vladimir the Great's conversion to Christianity.
Until 20th C	Period of foreign dominance (largely Russian).
1918	Independent republic proclaimed.
1920	It was overrun by the Soviet army.
1921	Poland allotted charge of Ukraine.
1932-3	Famine caused death of 7.5 million.
1941-44	It was under Nazi control.
1944	Soviet control re-established.
1945	It became founder member of the United Nations.
1986	Chernobyl nuclear reactor disaster.
1991	Independence declared.
	Orthodox, with Catholic Uniate.

United Arab Emirates

1952	Seven sheikdoms set up the Trucial states under British protection.
1960s	Trucial states became very wealthy due to discovery of large oil deposits.
1971	It became known as United Arab Emirates.
	96% Muslim.

United Kingdom

Pre 1707	See other histories, especially History Notes, and Country by Country histories of Scotland and Wales.
1707	Act of Union between England and Scotland.

1721	Robert Walpole became first Prime Minister.
1783	Loss of American Colonies.
1801	Act of Union united Ireland to Union.
1914	Irish Home Rule bill introduced to Parliament.
1920	Home Rule Act incorporated Northern Ireland (Ulster) into United Kingdom.
1921	The rest of Ireland became a dominion.
1937	Ireland became the Irish Free State or Eire.
1956	Suez Crisis.
1972	Direct Rule on Northern Ireland imposed.
1973	UK joined European Economic Community.
	60% Protestant, 8% Catholic.

United States of America

1492	Official date of Christopher Columbus's "discovery" of the Americas.
1620	Puritan "Pilgrim Fathers" landed on Plymouth Rock, from Britain.
1692	Salem Witch Trials – when 20 people were executed in Massachusetts for witchcraft.
1776	Declaration of Independence from Britain.
1789	Washington elected as first president.
1803	Louisiana purchase.
1812-14	War with England as a side effect of Napoleonic Wars.
1819	Florida purchased from Spain.
1836	Battle of the Alamo – Texas won from Mexico.
1841	First Wagon train left Missouri for California.
1846-48	Mexico lost Arizona, California, Colorado, Wyoming, New Mexico, Texas and Utah to USA.
1848-9	California Gold Rush.
1860	Lincoln elected president.
1861-5	Civil War.
1865	Slavery abolished and Lincoln assassinated.
1867	Alaska bought from Russia.
1890	Battle of Wounded Knee, the last major battle with the Indians.
1898	War with Spain. Spain lost Philippines, Guam & Puerto Rico. Independence for Cuba, Hawaii annexed.
1917	USA entered World War I.
1924	Indians made citizens.
1920-33	Prohibition, when alcohol was declared illegal. Bootlegging was illegal distribution. Mafia developed.
1929	Wall Street Crash.
1933	Roosevelt's New Deal.
1941	Japanese attack on Pearl Harbour led to US entering World War II.
1945	USA dropped bombs on Hiroshima and Nagasaki to end World War II.
1947	Taft Hartley Act restricted the power of Trade Unions.
1950-53	Korean War. McCarthy tried to expose Communists working in the USA.
1954	Civil rights legislation introduced.

1955	Rosa Parks arrested for sitting in the "whites only" area of a bus – this essentially started the black Civil Rights movement.
1958	First US satellite in orbit.
1961	Abortive invasion of Cuba led to Bay of Pigs fiasco.
1963	President Kennedy assassinated.
1965	Malcolm X, a black nationalist leader, was assassinated by Muslims who regarded him as a traitor.
1964-75	US involvement in Vietnam War.
1969	US put man on moon – or was it a clever hoax?
1973-74	Watergate scandal led to President Nixon's resignation.
1979-80	Iranian hostage crisis.
1981	First Space shuttle flight.
1986	Iran Contra affair. The plan involved the illegal payment of money to Nicaraguan Contra rebels from the sale of weapons to Iran.
1987	Presidents Reagan and Gorbachev signed nuclear non-proliferation treaty.
1989	Presidents Reagan and Gorbachev ended Cold War in Malta conference.
1989	The Supreme Court allowed States some control over abortion, overturning the Rowe vs. Wade decision which had left women free to decide.
1991	Gulf War against Iraq.
2001	World Trade Centre towers attacked and destroyed (supposedly by Arabs supporting the Palestinian cause). Subsequent wars in Afghanistan and Iraq.
	85% Christian (1/4 of those are Catholic)

Uruguay

1624	Country settled by Spain.
1680	Country settled by Portugal.
18th C	Spain secured all the territory.
1814	Spanish rule thrown out by Jose Artigas.
1820	Brazil threw out Artigas.
1825	Uruguay declared independence, although this is not recognised until 1853.
1936	Civil War.
1960s-70s	Marxist revolution by Tupamaros guerrillas.
	66% Catholic.

Vatican City State

1377	Popes first take up residence in the Vatican.
1929	Lateran Treaty recognised sovereignty of the Pope.
1985	Catholicism no longer the state religion.
	100% Catholic.

Venezuela

1498	Columbus visited Venezuela.
1520	First Spanish settlement.
1811	Rebellion against Spain led by Simon Bolivar.
1830	Independence gained.
	96% Catholic.

Vietnam

208BC	Country founded under Chinese over-lordship.
111BC - 939	It was under direct Chinese rule.
1288	It defeated the forces of Kublai Khan.
16th C	European traders arrived.
1802	Country united under one dynasty.
1858-84	France conquered the country, joining Laos, Cambodia and Annam as French Indochina.
1940-45	It was occupied by Japanese forces.
1946	War of independence started by Vietminh against French control.
1954	French defeated at Dien Bien Phu and Vietnam divided along 17th Parallel.
1963	First President of South Vietnam, Ngo Dinh Diem (a Catholic), assassinated.
1964	US troops entered war.
1973	Paris peace agreement.
1975	Saigon entered by Communist troops from the North.
1978	Vietnam invasion of Cambodia.
1989	Boat people leaving Vietnam murdered by Thai pirates.
	Buddhist, Taoist, Confucian and Christian (mostly Catholic).

Wales

2nd Millen. BC	Celts reached British Isles and a number of tribes of Celts occupied what is now Wales. When Brutus, King of Britain, died, he gave Wales to his son Kambri – hence Cambria and Cymru.
1st C AD	Roman invasion of Britain. The Welsh tribal leader, King Caradog (Caractacus) with the Ordovices and Silurian Tribes were defeated. The Romans built the fortress at Caerleon on Usk.
200	Christianity adopted.
450 – 600	Wales became a stronghold of Christianity, when the pagan Saxons invaded. The Welsh were united against the occupiers of England.
800	Welsh were pushed back into Wales and behind the frontier established between the Rivers Dee and Severn by Offa, King of Mercia (Offa's Dyke).
11th & 12th C	Normans pressed to invade Wales, but resisted by Llewellyn I and II.
1277	Edward I accepted by the Welsh as overlord. Edward began to build magnificent Castles.
1284	Edward I completed the conquest of Wales.
1294	Revolt against the English put down by Edward I.
1350 - 1500	A number of uprisings against the English, most notably by Owen Glendower.
1485	Henry Tudor, a Welshman, became King Henry VII of England.
1536 - 43	Acts of Union united England and Wales. Wales adopts Protestantism.
18th C	Non-conformism firmly established in Wales.
19th C	Mine and Steel workers were strong supporters of Chartism.
1966	Wales returns its first Plaid Cymru MP to Westminster.
1999	National Welsh Assembly established in Cardiff.

Yemen

2nd Millen. BC	Kingdom founded.
	Later ruled by Egypt, Rome and Ethiopia.
628	Islam adopted.
1538-1630	Part of Ottoman Empire.
1962	North Yemen broke away and formed Yemen Arab Republic (YAR).
1967	South Yemen Republic founded after Civil War and then joined an association with Aden.
1971-72	War between South Yemen and YAR.
1990	Both parts reunited as the Republic of Yemen.
	Sunni Muslim 63%, Shiite Muslim 37%.

Yugoslavia

BC	It was under Greek and Roman Empires, but later invaded by Slavs.
Middle Ages	The countries which eventually formed Yugoslavia were independent states. Serbia was the largest.
14&15th C	Conquered by the Turks, except Montenegro, with Croatia & Slovenia, joining the Habsburg Empire.
1878	Serbia threw off Ottoman yoke.
1912-13	Serbia grew as a result of Balkan Wars.
1918	Croatia and Slovenia released by Habsburgs. Kingdom of Croats, Serbia and Slovenes formed.
1929	Name of Yugoslavia adopted.
1941	It was invaded by Germany.
1945	Communist constitution adopted under Marshall Tito.
1948	It split with USSR.
1980	Tito died.
1991	Slovenia and Croatia declared independence, but fighting continued.
1992	Bosnia-Herzegovina became independent. Montenegro voted to remain part of Yugoslav republic.
1993	Macedonia became independent.
	41% Eastern Orthodox, Catholic 12%, Muslim 3%.

Zaire

15th Century	Portuguese explorers arrived and gave it its name.
1870's	Interior explored by Stanley and Livingstone.
1885	It was named Congo Free State by the King of Belgium who partly financed the exploration.
1908	Belgium annexed the country to prevent atrocities, calling it the Belgian Congo.
1960	Independence achieved, but civil war broke out between Katanga and central government.
1963	Katanga war ended.
1971	Country became the Republic of Zaire.
1972	Katanga renamed Shaba.
1974	Foreign-owned businesses seized.
1977	Congolese forces wanting Shaba as an independent state from Zaire invaded from Angola.

1978	Second unsuccessful invasion from Angola.
	Christian 70%, Muslim 10%.

Zambia

18th C	Country visited by Portuguese traders.
1851	Livingstone exploration.
1924	It became Northern Rhodesia as a British protectorate.
1964	Independence achieved, as Zambia, under Kenneth Kaunda.
1976	Support for the patriotic front in (Southern) Rhodesia.
	Christian 66%, Animist, Hindu and Muslim.

Zimbabwe

300AD	Evidence of Bantu speaking peoples.
1200	Mashonaland, now East Zimbabwe, was a major settlement of Shona people.
16th C	Portuguese explorers visited the country.
1837	Matabele peoples settled in Western Zimbabwe – called Matabeleland.
1889	Whole country named Rhodesia. It was divided into Northern and Southern Rhodesia in 1911.
1923	It became a self-governing British colony.
1961	ZAPU formed by Joshua Nkomo to try to gain independence.
1962	ZAPU declared illegal.
1963	ZANU formed, led by Robert Mugabe.
1964	Ian Smith became Prime Minister and imprisoned both Nkomo and Mugabe.
1965	Smith declared unilateral independence (UDI).
1966-8	Abortive talks to try to settle the matter.
1974	Nkomo and Mugabe released.
1979	Smith governed country with Abel Muzorewa, but Nkomo and Mugabe disagreed.
1979	Lancaster House conference in London established peace.
1980	Independence achieved. Country named Zimbabwe with Mugabe as Prime Minister.
1981-2	Rift between Nkomo and Mugabe.
1984	Zanu PF declared a one party state.
1985	Troops sent to Matabeleland to quell insurrection.
1987	White Roll seats in Parliament abolished. Mugabe was appointed both President and Prime Minister.
1989	ZANU and ZAPU merge.
2002	Mugabe evicts all white farmers (killing some who resisted) and, in the following years, this brings the economy to its knees with little criticism and no effective opposition from the West. This strange behaviour may be explained by the fact that Zimbabwe has some of the richest deposits of gold in the world, with the West heavily involved in Zimbabwe's mining companies.
	Christians, Animists and Muslims.

Appendices:

Appendices

1. British Kings and Queens:
English Monarchs

Saxons and Danes:

Egbert	802 - 39
Ethelwulf	839 - 58
Ethelbald	858 - 60
Ethelbert	860 - 5
Ethelred	865 - 71
Alfred the Great	871 - 99
Edward the Elder	899 - 924
Athelstan the Glorious	924 - 39
Edmund	939 - 46
Edred	946 - 55
Edwy the Fair	955 - 9
Edgar the Peaceful	959 - 75
Edward the Martyr	975 - 8
Ethelred II (the Unready)	978 - 1016
Edmund Ironside	1016
Canute	1016 - 35
Harold I (Harefoot)	1035 - 40
Hardecanute	1040 - 2
St Edward the Confessor	1042 - 66
Harold II	1066

House of Normandy:

William I (the Conqueror)	1066 - 87
William II (Rufus)	1087 - 1100
Henry I	1100 - 35
Stephen	1135 - 54

House of Plantagenet:

Henry II	1154 - 89
Richard I (Lionheart)	1189 - 99
John	1199 - 1216
Henry III	1216 - 1272
Edward I (Longshanks)	1272 - 1307
Edward II	1307 - 27
Edward III	1327 - 77
Richard II	1377 - 99

House of Lancaster

Henry IV	1399 - 1413
Henry V	1413 - 22
Henry VI	1422 - 61 & 1470 - 71

House of York

Edward IV	1461 - 70 & 1471 - 83
Edward V	1483
Richard III	1483 - 5

House of Tudor

Henry VII	1485 - 1509
Henry VIII	1509 - 47
Edward VI	1547 - 53
Mary	1553 - 8
Elizabeth I	1558 - 1603

British Monarchs

House of Stuart

James I (James VI of Scotland)	1603 - 25
Charles I	1625 – 49
Commonwealth	*1653 – 59*
Charles II	1660 - 85
James II	1685 - 88
William III (and Mary II, d. 1694)	1688 - 1702
Anne	1702 - 14

House of Hanover

George I	1714 - 27
George II	1727 - 60
George III	1760 - 1820
George IV	1820 - 30
William IV	1830 - 7
Victoria	1837 - 1901

House of Saxe-Coburg

Edward VII	1901 - 10

House of Windsor

George V	1910 - 36
Edward VIII	1936
George VI	1936 - 52
Elizabeth II	1952 -

Willie, Willie
A rhyme to help you remember the order in which British Kings and Queens have reigned:

Willie, Willie, Harry, Stee
Harry, Dick, John, Harry Three,
One Two Three Neds, Richard Two,
Henry Four, Five, Six, then who?
Edward Four, Five, Dick the bad,
Harry's twain and Ned the lad,
Mary Bessie, James the vain,
Charlie, Charlie, James again.
Will and Mary, Anna Gloria,
Four Georges, William and Victoria.
Edward Seven and Georgie Five,
Edward Eight and Liz alive.

And to help you remember the royal houses:

No plan like yours to study history wisely.

Viz:
Norman
Plantaganet
Lancaster
York
Tudor
Stuart
Hanover
Windsor

2. British Prime Ministers

Con = Conservative, Lib = Liberal, Lab = Labour, Coal = Coalition

Robert Walpole	Whig	1721 - 42
Spencer Compton	Whig	1742 - 3
Henry Pelham	Whig	1743 - 54
Thomas Pelham	Whig	1754 - 6
William Cavendish	Whig	1756 - 7
Thomas Pelham	Whig	1757 - 62
John Stuart	Tory	1762 - 3
George Grenville	Whig	1763 - 5
Charles Watson Wentworth	Whig	1765 - 6
William Pitt (the Elder)	Whig	1766 - 7
Augustus Henry Fitzroy	Whig	1767 - 70
Lord North	Tory	1770 - 82
Charles Watson Wentworth	Whig	1782
William Petty	Whig	1782 - 3
William Henry Cavendish	Coal	1783
William Pitt (the Younger)	Tory	1783 - 1801
Henry Addington	Tory	1801 - 4
William Pitt (the Younger)	Tory	1804 - 6
William Wyndham Grenville	Whig	1806 - 7
William Henry Cavendish	Coal	1807 - 9
Spencer Percival	Tory	1809 - 12
Robert Banks Jenkinson	Tory	1812 - 27
George Canning	Tory	1827
Frederick John Robinson	Tory	1827 - 8
The Duke of Wellington	Tory	1828 - 30
Charles Grey	Whig	1830 - 4
Viscount Melbourne	Whig	1834
Robert Peel	Con	1834 - 5
William Lamb	Whig	1835 - 41
Robert Peel	Con	1841 - 6
Lord John Russell	Lib	1846 - 52
The Earl of Derby	Con	1852
George Hamilton Gordon	Peelite	1852 - 5
Henry John Temple	Lib	1855 - 8
The Earl of Derby	Con	1858 - 9
Viscount Palmerston	Lib	1859 - 65
Lord John Russell	Lib	1865 - 6
Earl of Derby	Con	1866 - 8
Benjamin Disraeli	Con	1868
William Ewart Gladstone	Lib	1868 - 74
Benjamin Disraeli	Con	1874 - 80
William Ewart Gladstone	Lib	1880 - 5
Marquis of Salisbury	Con	1885 - 6
William Ewart Gladstone	Lib	1886
Marquis of Salisbury	Con	1886 - 92
William Ewart Gladstone	Lib	1892 - 4
Earl of Rosebery	Lib	1894 - 5
Marquis of Salisbury	Con	1895 - 1902
Arthur James Balfour	Con	1902 - 5
Henry Campbell-Bannerman	Lib	1905 - 8

Herbert Henry Asquith	Lib & Coal	1908 - 1916
David Lloyd George	Coal	1916 - 22
Andrew Bonar Law	Con	1922 - 3
Stanley Baldwin	Con	1923 - 4
James Ramsey MacDonald	Lab	1924
Stanley Baldwin	Con	1924 - 29
James Ramsey MacDonald	Lab	1929 - 31
James Ramsey Macdonald	National Gov	1931 - 5
Stanley Baldwin	National Gov	1935 - 7
Arthur Neville Chamberlain	National Gov	1937 - 40
Winston Leonard Spencer Churchill	Coal	1940 - 5
Clement Richard Atlee	Lab	1945 - 51
Winston Leonard Spencer Churchill	Con	1951 - 5
Robert Anthony Eden	Con	1955 - 7
Maurice Harold Macmillan	Con	1957 - 63
Alec Frederick Douglas-Home	Con	1963 - 4
James Harold Wilson	Lab	1964 - 70
Edward Richard George Heath	Con	1970 - 74
James Harold Wilson	Lab	1974 - 6
Leonard James Callaghan	Lab	1976 - 9
Margaret Hilda Thatcher	Con	1979 - 90
John Major	Con	1990 - 7
Anthony Charles Lynton Blair	Lab	1997 - 2007
James Gordon Brown	Lab	2007 - 2010
David William Donald Cameron	Con/Lib Coal	2010 -

3. Scottish Kings and Queens

Malcolm II	1005 - 34
Duncan I	1034 - 40
Macbeth	1040 - 57
Lulach	1057 - 58
Malcolm III	1058 - 93
Donald III (Donald Bane)	1093 - 4
Duncan II	1094
Donald III (Donald Bane)	1094 - 7
Edgar	1097 - 1107
Alexander I	1107 - 24
David I	1124 - 53
Malcolm IV (the Maiden)	1153 - 65
William I (the Lion)	1165 - 1214
Alexander II	1214 - 49
Alexander III	1249 - 86
Margaret (Maid of Norway)	1286 - 90
Interregnum	1290 - 2
John Balliol	1292 - 6
Interregnum	1296 - 1306
Robert the Bruce	1306 - 29
David II	1329 - 71
Robert II	1371 - 90
Robert III	1390 - 1406
James I	1406 - 37
James II	1437 - 60
James III	1460 - 88
James IV	1488 - 1513
James V	1513 - 42
Mary Queen of Scots	1542 - 67
James VI	1567 - 1625

(Scottish and English Kingdoms thereafter united)

4. Holy Roman Emperors

(N.B. some of these dates overlap)

Charlemagne (Charles I)	800 - 14
Louis I (the Pious)	814 - 40
Civil War	840 - 3
Lothair I	843 - 55
Louis II	855 - 75
Charles II (the Bald)	875 - 7
Interregnum	*877- 81*
Charles III (the Fat)	881 - 7
Interregnum	*887 - 91*
Guido of Spoleto	891 - 4
Lambert of Spoleto	892 - 8 (jointly)
Arnulf	897 - 9
Louis III	901 - 5
Berengar I	905 - 24
Conrad I	911 - 18 (jointly)
Henry I (the Fowler)	919 - 36
Otto I (the Great)	936 - 73
Otto II	973 - 983
Otto III	983 - 1002
Henry II	1002 - 24
Conrad II	1024 - 39
Henry III	1039 - 56
Henry IV	1056 - 1106
Rudolf of Rheinfelden	1077 - 1080 (jointly)
Hermann	1081 - 93
Conrad II	1093 - 1101
Henry V	1106 - 25
Lothair II	1125 - 37
Conrad III	1138 - 52
Frederick I (Barbarossa)	1152 - 90
Henry VI	1190 - 7
Philip of Swabia	1198 - 1208
Otto IV	1198 - 1214
Frederick II	1215 - 50
Henry Raspe	1246 - 7
William Count of Holland	1247 - 56
Conrad IV	1250 - 4
Great Interregnum	*1254 - 73*
Richard of Cornwall	1257 - 72
Alfonso of Castile	1257 - 75
Rudolf I	1273 - 91
Adolf	1292 - 8
Albert I	1298 - 1308
Henry VII	1308 - 13
Frederick III	1314 - 26
Louis IV (the Bavarian)	1314 - 46
Charles IV	1346 - 78
Wenceslas	1378 - 1400
Rupert I	1400 - 10
Sigismund	1410 - 37

Albert II	1438 - 9
Frederick III	1440 - 93
Maximilian I	1493 - 1519
Charles V	1519 - 56
Ferdinand I	1556 - 64
Maximilian II	1564 - 76
Rudolf II	1576 - 1612
Mathias	1612 - 19
Ferdinand II	1619 - 37
Ferdinand III	1637 - 57
Leopold I	1658 - 1705
Joseph I	1705 - 11
Charles VI	1711 - 40
Interregnum	*1740 - 2*
Charles VII	1742 - 5
Francis I	1745 - 65
Joseph II	1765 - 90
Leopold II	1790 - 2
Francis II	1792 - 1806

5. Popes

Peter	33 - 64
Linus	64 - 76
Anacletus	76 - 90
Clement I	90 - 99
Evaristus	99 - 105
Alexander I	105 - 117
Sixtus I	117 - 127
Telesephorus	127 - 137
Hyginus	137 - 140
Pius I	140 - 154
Anicetus	154 - 166
Soter	166 - 175
Eleutherius	175 - 189
Victor I	189 - 198
Zephyrinus	198 - 217
Calixtus	217 - 22
Urban I	222 - 30
Pontian	230 - 5
Anterus	235 - 6
Fabian	236 - 50
Cornelius	251 - 3
Lucius I	253 - 4
Stephen I	254 - 7
Sixtus II	257 - 8
Dionysius	259 - 68
Felix I	269 - 74
Eutychian	275 - 83
Caius	283 - 296
Marcellinus	296 - 304
Marcellus I	308 - 9
Eusebius	310
Miltiades	311 - 14
Sylvester	314 - 35
Mark	336
Julius I	337 - 52
Liberius	352 - 66
Damasus I	366 - 84
Siricius	384 - 99
Anastasius	399 - 401
Innocent I	402 - 17
Zosimus	417 - 18
Boniface I	418 - 22
Celestine I	422 - 32
Sixtus III	432 - 40
Leo I (the Great)	440 - 61
Hilarius	461 - 8
Simplicius	468 - 83
Felix III (Felix II was an anti-pope)	483 - 92
Gelasius	492 - 6
Anastasius II	496 - 8
Symmachus	498 - 514
Hormisdas	514 - 23
John I	523 - 6

Felix IV	526 - 30
Boniface II	530 - 32
John II	533 - 5
Agapetus I	535 - 6
Silverius	536 - 7
Vigilus	537 - 55
Pelagius I	555 - 61
John III	561 - 74
Benedict I	575 - 79
Pelagius II	579 - 90
Gregory I (Gregory the Great)	590 - 604
Sabinian	604 - 6
Boniface III	607
Boniface IV	608 - 15
Deusdedit	615 - 18
Boniface IV	619 - 25
Honorius I	625 - 38
Vacant seat	638 - 40
Severinus	640
John IV	640 - 42
Theodore I	642 - 9
Martin I	649 - 55
Eugene I	655 - 7
Vitalian	657 - 72
Adeodatus	672 - 76
Donus	676 - 78
Agatho	678 - 81
Leo II	681 - 3
Benedict II	684 - 5
John V	685 - 6
Conon	686 - 7
Sergius I	687 - 701
John VI	701 - 5
John VII	705 - 7
Sisinnus	708
Constantine	708 - 15
Gregory II	715 - 31
Gregory III	731 - 41
Zacharias	741 - 52
Stephen II	752 - 57
Paul I	757 - 67
Stephen III	767 - 772
Adrian I	772 - 795
Leo III	795 - 816
Stephen IV	816 - 817
Paschal I	817 - 824
Eugene II	824 - 827
Valentine	827
Gregory IV	827 - 844
Sergius II	844 - 847
Leo IV	847 - 855
Benedict III	855 - 858
Nicholas I	858 - 867
Adrian II	867 - 872

John VIII	872 - 882
Marinus I	882 - 884
Adrian III	884 - 885
Stephen V	885 - 891
Formosus	891 - 896
Boniface VI	896 - 897
Stephen VI	896 - 897
Romanus	897
Theodore II	897
John IX	898 - 900
Benedict IV	900 - 903
Leo V	903
Christopher	903 - 904
Sergius III	904 - 911
Anastasius III	911 - 913
Lando	913 - 914
John X	914 - 928
Leo VI	928 - 929
Stephen VII	929 - 931
John XI	931 - 935
Leo VII	936 - 939
Stephen IX (VIII)	939 - 942
Marinus II	942 - 946
Agapetus II	946 - 955
John XII	955 - 963
Leo VIII	963 - 964
Benedict V	964
John XIII	965 - 972
Benedict VI	973 - 974
Benedict VII	974 - 983
John XIV	983 - 984
Boniface VII	984 - 985
John XV	985 - 996
Gregory V	996 - 999
Sylvester II	999 - 1003
John XVII	1003
John XVIII	1003 - 1009
Sergius IV	1009 - 1012
Benedict VIII	1012 - 1024
John XIX	1024 - 1033
Benedict IX	1033 - 1045
Sylvester III	1045
Gregory VI	1045 - 1046
Clement II	1046 - 1047
Damasus II	1048
Leo IX	1049 - 1054
Victor II	1054 - 1057
Stephen IX	1057 - 1058
Benedict X	1058
Nicholas II	1058 - 1061
Alexander II	1061 - 1073
Gregory VII	1073 - 1085
Victor III	1086 - 1087
Urban II	1088 - 1099

Pascal II	1099 - 1118
Gelasius II	1118 - 1119
Calixtus II	1119 - 1124
Honorius II	1124 - 1130
Innocent II	1130 - 1143
Celestine II	1143 - 1144
Lucius II	1144 - 1145
Eugene III	1145 - 1153
Anastasius IV	1153 - 1154
Adrian IV (Nicholas Breakspear)	1154 - 1159
(The only English Pope)	
Alexander III	1159 - 1181
Lucius III	1181 - 1185
Urban III	1185 - 1187
Gregory VIII	1187 - 1191
Celestine III	1191 - 1198
Innocent III	1198 - 1216
Honorius III	1216 - 1227
Gregory IX	1227 - 1241
Celestine IV	1241
Innocent IV	1243 - 1254
Alexander IV	1254 - 1261
Urban IV	1261 - 1264
Clement IV	1264 - 1268
Vacant Seat	1268 - 1271
Gregory X	1271 - 1276
Innocent V	1276
Adrian V	1276
John XXI	1276 - 1277
Nicholas III	1277 - 1280
Martin IV	1281 - 1285
Honorius IV	1285 - 1287
Nicholas IV	1288 - 1292
Celestine V	1294
Boniface VIII	1294 - 1303
Benedict XI	1303 - 1304
Clement V	1305 - 1314
John XXII	1316 - 1334
Benedict XII	1334 - 1342
Clement VI	1342 - 1352
Innocent VI	1352 - 1362
Urban V	1362 - 1370
Gregory XI	1370 - 1378
Urban VI	1378 - 1389
Boniface IX	1389 - 1404
Innocent VII	1404 - 1406
Gregory XII	1406 - 1415
Vacant Seat	1415 - 1417
Martin V	1417 - 1431
Eugene IV	1431 - 1447
Nicholas V	1447 - 1455
Calixtus III	1455 - 1458
Pius II	1458 - 1464
Paul II	1464 - 1471

Sixtus IV	1471 - 1484
Innocent VIII	1484 - 1492
Alexander VI (Borgia)	1492 - 1503
Pius III	1503
Julius II	1503 - 1513
Leo X	1513 - 1521
Adrian VI	1521 - 1523
Clement VII	1523 - 1534
Paul III	1534 - 1549
Julius III	1550 - 1555
Marcellus II	1555
Paul IV	1555 - 1559
Pius IV	1559 - 1565
Pius V	1566 - 1572
Gregory XIII	1572 - 1585
Sixtus V	1585 - 1590
Urban VII	1590 - 1591
Innocent IX	1591
Clement VIII	1592 - 1605
Leo XI	1605
Paul V	1605 - 1621
Gregory XV	1621 - 1623
Urban VIII	1623 - 1644
Innocent X	1644 - 1655
Alexander VII	1655 - 1667
Clement IX	1667 - 1669
Clement X	1670 - 1676
Innocent XI	1676 - 1689
Alexander VIII	1689 - 1691
Innocent XII	1691 - 1700
Clement XI	1700 - 1721
Innocent XIII	1721 - 1724
Benedict XIII	1724 - 1730
Clement XII	1730 - 1740
Benedict XIV	1740 - 1758
Clement XIII	1758 - 1769
Clement XIV	1769 - 1774
Pius VI	1775 - 1799
Pius VII	1800 - 1823
Leo XII	1823 - 1829
Pius VIII	1829 - 1830
Gregory XVI	1831 - 1846
Pius IX	1846 - 1878

(Pius IX instigated the First Vatican Council in 1870)

Leo XIII	1878 - 1903
Pius X	1903 - 1914
Benedict XV	1914 - 1922
Pius XI	1922 - 1939
Pius XII	1939 - 1958

John XXIII	1958 - 1963

(John XXIII instigated the Second Vatican Council, 1962 - 1965)
Subsequent to Vatican II:

Paul VI	1963 - 1978

John Paul I	1978
John Paul II	1978 - 2005
Benedict XVI	2005 - 2013
Francis	2013 -

6. Rulers, etc., of France

House of Capet

Hugh Capet	987 - 996
Robert II (the Pious)	996 - 1031
Henry I	1031 - 1060
Philip I	1060 - 1108
Louis VI (the Fat)	1108 - 37
Louis VII (the Young)	1137 - 1180
Philip II (Augustus)	1180 - 1223
Louis VIII	1223 - 1226
Louis IX (Saint Louis)	1226 - 1270
Philip III (the Bold)	1270 - 1285
Philip IV (the Fair)	1285 - 1314
Louis X	1314 - 1316
John I	1316
Philip V	1316 - 1322
Charles IV	1322 - 1328

House of Valois

Philip VI	1328 - 1350
John II	1350 - 1364
Charles V	1364 - 1380
Charles VI	1380 - 1422
Charles VII	1422 - 1461
Louis XI	1461 - 1483
Charles VIII	1483 - 1498
Louis XII	1498 - 1515
Francis I	1515 - 1547
Henry II	1547 - 1559
Francis II	1559 - 1560
Charles IX	1560 - 1574
Henry III	1574 - 1589

House of Bourbon

Henry IV	1589 - 1610
Louis XIII	1610 - 1643
Louis XIV	1643 - 1715
Louis XV	1715 - 1774
Louis XVI	1774 – 1792
First Republic	*1792 – 1804*
Emperor Napoleon I	1804 – 1814

Bourbon Restoration

Louis XVIII	1814 - 1824
Charles X	1824 - 1830
Louis Philippe	1830 – 1848
Second Republic	*1848 – 1852*
Emperor Napoleon III	1852 - 1871

(End of French Royal Dynasties)

Third Republic	*1871 – 1940*
Vichy Government	*1940 – 1944*
Provisional Government of *The French Republic*	*1944 – 1946*
Fourth Republic	*1946 -*

7. Presidents of the United States of America

1.	George Washington		1789 - 97
2.	John Adams	Federalist	1797 - 1801
3.	Thomas Jefferson	Democratic Republican	1801 - 9
4.	James Madison	Dem-Rep	1809 - 17
5.	James Monroe	Dem-Rep	1817 - 25
6.	John Quincy Adams	Dem-Rep	1825 - 9
7.	Andrew Jackson	Dem	1829 - 37
8.	Martin Van Buren	Dem	1837 - 41
9.	William Henry Harrison	Whig	1841
10.	John Tyler	Whig	1841 - 5
11.	James Knox Polk	Dem	1845 - 9
12.	Zachary Taylor	Whig	1849 - 50
13.	Millard Fillmore	Whig	1950 - 3
14.	Franklin Pierce	Dem	1953 - 7
15.	James Buchanan	Dem	1857 - 61
16.	Abraham Lincoln	Rep	1861 - 5
17.	Andrew Johnson	Rep	1865 - 9
18.	Ulysses Simpson Grant	Rep	1869 - 77
19.	Rutherford Birchard Hayes	Rep	1877 - 81
20.	James Abram Garfield	Rep	1881
21.	Chester Alan Arthur	Rep	1881 - 5
22.	Stephen Grover Cleveland	Dem	1885 - 9
23.	Benjamin Harrison	Rep	1889 - 93
24.	Stephen Grover Cleveland	Dem	1893 - 7
25.	William McKinley	Rep	1897 - 1901
26.	Theodore Roosevelt	Rep	1901 - 9
27.	William Howard Taft	Rep	1909 - 13
28.	Thomas Woodrow Wilson	Dem	1913 - 21
29.	Warren G. Harding	Rep	1921 - 3
30.	Calvin Coolidge	Rep	1923 - 29
31.	Herbert Clarke Hoover	Rep	1929 - 33
32.	Franklin Delano Roosevelt	Dem	1933 - 45
33.	Harry S. Truman	Dem	1945 - 53
34.	Dwight David Eisenhower	Rep	1953 - 61
35.	John Fitzgerald Kennedy	Dem	1961 - 3
36.	Lyndon Baines Johnson	Dem	1961 - 69
37.	Richard Milhous Nixon	Rep	1969 - 74
38.	Gerald Rudolph Ford	Rep	1974 - 7
39.	James (Jimmy) Earl Carter	Dem	1977 - 81
40.	Ronald Wilson Reagan	Rep	1981 - 89
41.	George Herbert Walker Bush	Rep	1989 - 93
42.	William (Bill) Jefferson Clinton	Dem	1993 - 2001
43.	George W. Bush	Rep	2001 - 2009
44.	Barak Hussein Obama	Dem	2009 -

8. Tsars, etc., of Russia

Grand Dukes of Moscow:

Daniel	1283 - 1303
Yuri	1303 - 25
Ivan I Kalita	1325 - 41
Semeon	1341 - 53
Ivan II	1353 - 9
Dmitri I Donskoy	1359 - 89
Vasily I	1389 - 1425
Vasily II	1425 - 62
Ivan III (the Great)	1462 - 72

Rulers of all Russia:

Ivan III (the Great)	1472 - 1505
Vasily III	1505 - 33
Ivan IV (the Terrible)	1533 - 47

Tsars of Russia:

Ivan IV (the Terrible)	1547 - 84
Fedor I	1584 - 98
Boris Godunov	1598 - 1605
Fedor II	1605
Dmitri II (the False)	1605 - 6
Vasily IV (Shuisky)	1606 - 10
Civil War	*1610 - 13*

(House of Romanov)

Mikhail (Michael Romanov)	1613 - 45
Alexi I Milhailovich	1645 - 1676
Fedor III	1676 - 82
Peter I (the Great)	1682 - 1725
(Peter the Great jointly with Ivan V 1682 - 1696)	
Catherine I	1725 - 7
Peter II	1727 - 30
Anna Ivnova	1730 - 40
Ivan VI	1740 - 1
Elizabeth Petrovna	1741 - 62
Peter III	1762
Catherine II (the Great)	1762 - 96
Paul	1796 - 1801
Alexander I	1801 - 25
Nicholas I	1825 - 55
Alexander II (the Liberator)	1855 - 81
Alexander III	1881 - 94
Nicholas II	1894 – 1917

Soviet Union Presidents:

Kamenev	1917
Sverlov	1917 - 19
Kalinin	1919 – 46

General Secretaries:

Stalin	1922 - 53
Malenkov	1953

Kruschev	1953 - 64
Brezhnev	1964 - 82
Andropov	1983 - 4
Chernenko	1984 - 5
Gorbachev	1985 – 91

Presidents of the Russian Federation:

Yeltsin	1991 - 99
Putin	1999 - 2008
Medvedev	2008 - 2012
Putin	2012 -

9. Chancellors of Germany

Bismark	1871 - 90
Graf von Caprivi	1890 - 4
Chlodwic	1894 - 1900
Von Bulow	1900 - 9
Von Bethmann Hollweg	1909 - 17
Von Herfling	1917 - 18
Prince Max	1918
Ebert	1918
Scheidemann	1918 - 20
Muller	1920
Ferenbach	1920 - 1
Wirth	1921 - 2
Cuno	1922 - 3
Streseman	1923
Marx	1923 - 5
Luther	1925 - 6
Marx	1926 - 8
Muller	1928 - 9
Bruning	1929 - 32
Von Papen	1932
Schleicher	1932 - 3
Hitler (Führer from 1934)	1933 - 45
Adenauer	1949 - 63
Erhard	1963 - 6
Kiesinger	1966 - 9
Brandt	1969 - 74
Schmidt	1974 - 82
Kohl	1982 - 98
Schroeder	1998 - 2006
Merkel	2006 -

10. European Union Treaties

Name	Date effective	Powers taken from member states and other notes
European Iron and Steel Communities Treaty (Treaty of Paris)	1952	Lapsed in 2002.
European Economic Community Treaty (Treaty of Rome)	1958	Took Treaty of Paris towards a Common Market.
Euratom	1958	Covered atomic energy.
Treaty establishing a Single Council and Single Commission (Merger Treaty)	1967	Repealed by Treaty of Amsterdam.
Treaty of Luxembourg	1971	Covered Budgetary measures.
Brussels Treaty	1977	Set up Court of Auditors.
European Elections	1978	Set up Elected European Parliament.
Single European Act	1987	Set up • Single Market • Established Qualified Majority Voting (QMV) • Converging National Legislation.
Maastricht Treaty	1993	Established the EU and set up • Common Foreign and Security policy • Justice and Home Affairs • Economic and Monetary Union.
Treaty of Amsterdam	1999	This treaty • Amended Maastricht • Extended QMV • Incorporated Schengen which passed control of national borders to EU.
Treaty of Nice	2003	Enlargement of the EU Common Defence Policy.
Treaty of Lisbon	2009	The EU treaty (constitution) ushering in the European Union as a country in its own right.

11. **Controls taken from Member States by the European Union, as at 2001. The proportions (taken from the European Journal) have increased since the date these were measured.**

Powers of Legislation	Proportion taken by the EU	Proportion of legislation initiated by EU
Free Movement of Goods	100%	100%
Customs Union	100%	100%
Movement of Workers	50%	
Freedom to Provide Services	70%	
Competition Policy	80%	80%
Trade Relations	80%	90%
Agriculture	90%	90%
Fisheries	90%	90%
Transport	60%	60%
Environment	80%	80%
Taxation	20%	
International Development	50%	50%
Social Policy	50%	50%
Working Time Directive	40%	
Employment		40%
Regional Policy	50%	50%
Consumer Protection	50%	40%
Public Health	50%	50%
Industrial Policy	70%	
Energy		40%
Company and Business Law	30%	30%
Energy	20%	
Nuclear industry	90%	
External Relations and Defence	30%	30%

12. The Modern Olympic Games

	Athens	1896
	Paris	1900
	St Louis	1904
	London	1908
	Stockholm	1912
	Antwerp	1920
	Paris	1924
	Amsterdam	1928
	Los Angeles	1932
	Berlin*	1936
	London	1948
	Helsinki	1952
	Melbourne	1956
	Rome	1960
	Tokyo	1964
	Mexico	1968
	Munich	1972
	Montreal	1976
	Moscow	1980
	Los Angeles	1984
	Seoul	1988
	Barcelona	1992
	Atlanta	1996
	Sydney	2000
	Athens	2004
	Beijing	2008
	London	2012
Proposed:	Rio de Janeiro	2016

*It was at the Berlin Olympics that Hitler instigated the parading of the Olympic torch through the host country prior to the games taking place.

13. Rulers of the Roman Empire

N.B. Julius Caesar was not a Roman Emperor. He was a general and statesman whose career marked the end of the Roman Republic. He was murdered in 44BC and after his death the Republic was run by Mark Anthony who was defeated by Octavian at the Battle of Actium in 31BC. Mark Anthony committed suicide in 30BC.

Augustus (previously known as Octavian)	27BC - AD14
Tiberius	14 - 37
Caligula also known as Caius	37 - 41
Claudius I	41 - 54
Nero	54 - 68
Galba	68 - 9
Otho	69
Vitellius	69 (the Year of the Four Caesars)
Vespasian	69 - 79
Titus	79 - 81
Domitian	81 - 96
Nerva	96 - 8
Trajan	98 - 117
Hadrian	117 - 38
Antoninus Pius	138 - 61
Marcus Aurelius	161 - 80
(Lucius Verus jointly with Marcus Aurelius 161 - 9)	
Commodus	180 - 92
Pertinax	193
Didius Julianus	193
Septimus Severus	193 - 211
Caracalla	211 - 17
(Geta jointly with Caracalla	211 - 12)
Macrinus	217 - 18
Heliogabalus	218 - 22
Alexander Severus	222 - 35
Maximin	235 - 8
Gordian I & II, Balbinus, Pupienus	238
Gordian III	238 - 44
Philip	244 - 9
Decius	249 - 51
Hostilianus	251
Gallus	251 - 3
Aemilianus	253
Valerian (and below)	253 - 60
Gallienus	253 - 68
Claudius II	268 - 70
Aurelian	270 - 5
Tacitus	275 - 6
Florianus	276
Probus	276 - 82
Carus	282 - 3
Carinus (and below)	283 - 5
Numerianus	283 - 4
Diocletian (and below)	284 - 305
Maximian	286 - 305

Constantius I	305 - 6
Galerius	305 - 10
Maximin	308 - 13
Licinius	308 - 24
(Emperor in the West)	
Maxentius	306 - 12
Constantine I (the Great)	306 - 37
Constantine II	337 - 40
Constans	337 - 50
Constantius II	337 - 61
Magnentius	350 - 53
Julian (the Apostate)	361 - 3
Jovian	363 - 4
Valentinian I	364 - 75
Valens	364 - 78
Grantian	375 - 83
Maximus	383 - 8
Valentinian II	375 - 92
Eugenius	392 - 4
Theodosius I (the Great)	375 - 95
Arcadius	395 - 408
Theodosius II	408 - 50
Marcian	450 - 7
Leo I	457 - 74
Leo II	474
Honorius	395 - 423
Maximus	409 - 11
Constantius III	421
Valentinian III	425 - 55
Petronius Maximus	455
Avitus	455 - 6
Marjorian	457 - 61
Libius Severus	461 - 5
Anthemius	467 - 72
Olybrius	472
Glycerius	473 - 4
Julius Nepos	474 - 5
Romulus Augustus	475 - 6

14. Shiite and Sunni Muslims

Who fits in where?

Who	Sunni	Shiite
Al-Qaeda	✓	
Hamas	✓	

Fatah
which includes:
  • Yasser Arafat
  • Fedayeen (who Israel attacked in S Lebanon in 1982)
  • Black September (Munich Olympics killings).
Fatah used to be the Palestine Liberation Organisation (PLO).
Fatah also replaced the Popular Front for the Liberation of Palestine (PFLP), which was backed by China and Moscow.
	✓	

Syria	✓74%	
Mujahedeen (in Iran, they are the People's Mujahedeen of Iran) – fought Russia in Afghanistan and were backed by the USA.	✓	
Osama bin Laden	✓	
Iraq (ruling minority Sunni, but statistics disputed: when Kurds and Turkmen Sunnis are considered, becomes closer to 50/50).	30%	65%
Iran		✓90%
Saddam Hussein	✓	
Saudi Arabia	✓	
Pakistan	✓75%	20%
Lebanon	24%	33%
Afghanistan	✓75%	25%
Taliban	✓	
Kuwait	✓45%	30%
Egypt	✓	
Sudan	✓	
Turkey	✓	
Jordan	✓	
Kurds	✓90%	
Libya	✓	

15. Projection of possible speed of population growth and how the world's present population might have been reached from two parents within 67 generations or 1,675 years

Per generation or 25 years	No of years	parents	births	deaths	Net increase	Adjustment to roughly 1.5% growth a year*	population at end of generation
1		2	2	0	2	2	4
2		4	4	0	4	3	6
3		6	6	2	4	3	10
4	100	10	10	4	6	5	15
5		15	15	6	8	7	22
6		22	22	10	12	9	31
7		31	31	15	16	13	43
8	200	43	43	22	22	17	61
9		61	61	31	30	24	84
10		84	84	43	41	32	116
11		116	116	61	56	44	160
12	300	160	160	84	76	60	221
13		221	221	116	104	82	303
14		303	303	160	143	113	416
15		416	416	221	195	154	570
16	400	570	570	303	267	211	780
17		780	780	416	365	288	1,068
18		1,068	1,068	570	499	394	1,462
19		1,462	1,462	780	682	539	2,001
20	500	2,001	2,001	1,068	933	737	2,738
21		2,738	2,738	1,462	1,276	1,008	3,746
22		3,746	3,746	2,001	1,745	1,378	5,124
23		5,124	5,124	2,738	2,386	1,885	7,010
24	600	7,010	7,010	3,746	3,264	2,578	9,588
25		9,588	9,588	5,124	4,463	3,526	13,114
26		13,114	13,114	7,010	6,104	4,822	17,937
27		17,937	17,937	9,588	8,349	6,595	24,532
28	700	24,532	24,532	13,114	11,418	9,020	33,552
29		33,552	33,552	17,937	15,616	12,336	45,888
30		45,888	45,888	24,532	21,356	16,872	62,760
31		62,760	62,760	33,552	29,208	23,074	85,834
32	800	85,834	85,834	45,888	39,946	31,557	117,391
33		117,391	117,391	62,760	54,631	43,159	160,550
34		160,550	160,550	85,834	74,716	59,026	219,576
35		219,576	219,576	117,391	102,185	80,726	300,302
36	900	300,302	300,302	160,550	139,751	110,404	410,705
37		410,705	410,705	219,576	191,129	150,992	561,698
38		561,698	561,698	300,302	261,396	206,503	768,201
39		768,201	768,201	410,705	357,495	282,421	1,050,622

Appendix 15 continued

Per generation or 25 years	No of years	parents	births	deaths	Net increase	Adjustment to roughly 1.5% growth a year*	population at end of generation
40	1,000	1,050,622	1,050,622	561,698	488,924	386,250	1,436,872
41		1,436,872	1,436,872	768,201	668,671	528,250	1,965,122
42		1,965,122	1,965,122	1,050,622	914,500	722,455	2,687,577
43		2,687,577	2,687,577	1,436,872	1,250,705	988,057	3,675,634
44	1,100	3,675,634	3,675,634	1,965,122	1,710,512	1,351,304	5,026,938
45		5,026,938	5,026,938	2,687,577	2,339,361	1,848,096	6,875,034
46		6,875,034	6,875,034	3,675,634	3,199,400	2,527,526	9,402,560
47		9,402,560	9,402,560	5,026,938	4,375,622	3,456,741	12,859,301
48	1,200	12,859,301	12,859,301	6,875,034	5,984,267	4,727,571	17,586,872
49		17,586,872	17,586,872	9,402,560	8,184,312	6,465,607	24,052,478
50		24,052,478	24,052,478	12,859,301	11,193,178	8,842,610	32,895,089
51		32,895,089	32,895,089	17,586,872	15,308,217	12,093,491	44,988,580
52	1,400	44,988,580	44,988,580	24,052,478	20,936,102	16,539,520	61,528,100
53		61,528,100	61,528,100	32,895,089	28,633,012	22,620,079	84,148,179
54		84,148,179	84,148,179	44,988,580	39,159,599	30,936,084	115,084,263
55		115,084,263	115,084,263	61,528,100	53,556,163	42,309,369	157,393,632
56	1,600	157,393,632	157,393,632	84,148,179	73,245,452	57,863,907	215,257,539
57		215,257,539	215,257,539	115,084,263	100,173,276	79,136,888	294,394,427
58		294,394,427	294,394,427	157,393,632	137,000,795	108,230,628	402,625,055
59		402,625,055	402,625,055	215,257,539	187,367,516	148,020,338	550,645,392
60	1,500	550,645,392	550,645,392	294,394,427	256,250,966	202,438,263	753,083,655

Population figures below converted into millions

25 years	No of years	parents in millions	births in millions	deaths in millions	Net increase	Adjustment to roughly 1.5% growth a year*	population at end of generation in millions
61		753	753	331	422	333	1,086
62		1,086	1,086	535	551	436	1,522
63		1,522	1,522	753	769	607	2,129
64	1,600	2,129	2,129	1,086	1,043	824	2,953
65		2,953	2,953	1,522	1,432	1,131	4,084
66	1,650	4,084	4,084	2,129	1,955	1,544	5,629
67	1,675	5,629	5,629	2,953	2,675	2,113	7,742 **

*In 2007 it was announced that the world's population is growing by about 1.5% a year and with the unadjusted figures in this projection showing a growth at a higher percentage than this, these figures have been adjusted downwards.

**This is about 1 billion greater than the world's population in 2009.

The purpose of this appendix to show how it would not need millions of years for the world's population to reach its present level.

16. The many societies that possess a flood tradition

There are many in the developed world who dismiss Noah's Flood as being pure myth. However, when one considers that the following societies, from around the world, also have references to this cataclysmic event in their histories, it does make one wonder whether this great flood should not be investigated and considered more seriously.

Eastern Hemisphere:

Asia
Andamanese
Armenians
Assyrians
Babylonians
Chaldeans
Dravidians
Hebrews
Indo-Aryans
Japanese
Kurnai
Mongols
Persians
Phrygians
Syrians
Tatars
Toradjas

Africa
Barmegai
Carthaginians
Egyptians
Hottentots
Sudanese

Europe
Druids
Germans
Greeks
Gypsies
Icelanders
Laplanders
Lithuanians
Norse
Romans
Slavs
Voguls
Welch

Western Hemisphere and Oceania:

North America
Algonquins
Araphoes
Athabascans
Aztecs
Cherokees
Crees
Eskimos
Klamaths
Kolushes
Kwakuitis
Lenni Lanapes
Mayans
Michoacans
Papagos
Pimas
Snoqualmies
Texpi
Tlingits
Toltecs

Indonesia
Bataks
Dyaks
Fijians
Hawaiians
Melanesians
Menankabans
Micronesians
New Hebrides
South Polynesians

South America
Arawaks
Cauras
Incas
Maypures
Mechoachens
Tamanacs

Appendix 17A
Family Tree to show how the last pre-Norman kings were related:

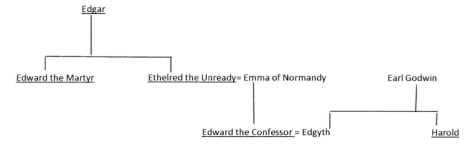

Underlined = kings of England

William the Conqueror was grand-nephew of Emma of Normandy

Appendix 17B
Family Tree to show how John of Gaunt was related to the kings of England between Edward III and Henry VI:

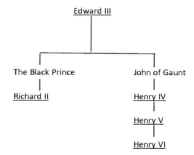

Appendix 17C
Family Tree to show how the Tudor monarchs were related:

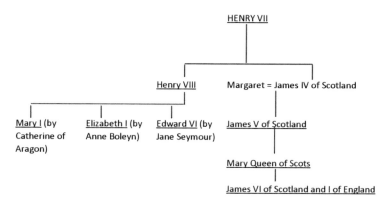

Underlined = kings

Appendices

Appendix 17D
Family Tree to show how the key figures involved in the Wars of The Roses were related:

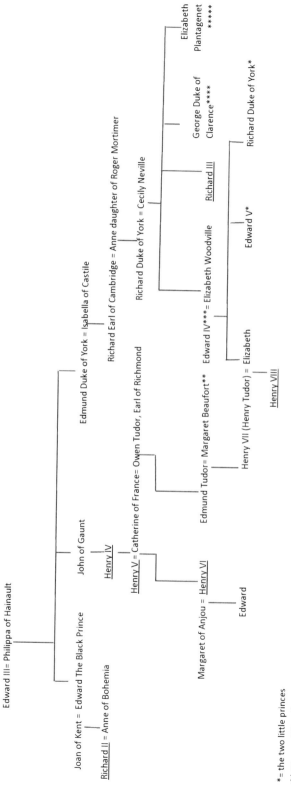

* = the two little princes

** Margaret Beaufort was a great grand-daughter of John of Gaunt

***Recent research (2012) seems to, not merely suggest but, prove that Edward IV was illegitimate (his father was away fighting when he was conceived), and so maybe, once Richard discovered this, and he realised that Edward IV's sons (the two little princes) had no right to inherit the crown, he had no option but to kill them to prevent either of them claiming the throne. He would have felt that this was his highly regrettable but necessary duty.

**** George Duke of Clarence was drowned in a butt of Malmsey wine on the orders of Edward IV. Clarence had declared Edward illegitimate, which we now know was true.

***** With all the claimants to the throne either dead or illegitimate, the rightful heirs to the throne should have descended from Elizabeth Plantagenet. However the heir, Michael Abney-Hastings, who died in Australia in 2012, was not interested in making a claim.

King's whose names are underlined have plays written about them by William Shakespeare

355